D0280597

766 AND ALL THAT

766 and All That

Over by Triumphant Over – How England Won the Ashes

Written by the Over by Over team

Edited by Paul Johnson and Matthew Hancock

ff

faber and faber

guardianbooks

First published in this edition in 2011
by Faber and Faber Limited
Bloomsbury House
74–77 Great Russell Street
London WC1B 3DA

Typeset by Faber and Faber Limited
Printed by CPI Bookmarque, Croydon

A CIP record for this book
is available from the British Library

ISBN 978-0-571-27781-0

10 9 8 7 6 5 4 3 2 1

Contents

List of Contributors   vii
Preamble   ix

First Test
The Gabba, Brisbane, 25–9 November 2010

First day   3
Second day   26
Third day   43
Fourth day   63
Fifth day   84

Second Test
Adelaide Oval, 3–7 December 2010

First day   103
Second day   125
Third day   144
Fourth day   156
Fifth day   173

Third Test
The Waca, Perth, 16–19 December 2010

First day   187
Second day   207
Third day   229

Fourth day   248

Fourth Test
Melbourne Cricket Ground, 26–9 December 2010

First day   257
Second day   279
Third day   297
Fourth day   319

Fifth Test
Sydney Cricket Ground, 3–7 January 2011

First day   341
Second day   357
Third day   376
Fourth day   395
Fifth day   417

Contributors

Rob Smyth has been writing for the *Guardian* since 2004, having previously worked at Wisden. His favourite cricketers are Martin McCague, Robin Smith, Graham Thorpe and Keith Miller.

Andy Bull joined the *Guardian* as a sports journalist in 2006 after spending several years scratching a living as a freelance. He has covered over 35 different sports for the newspaper and website, from archery through to yachting, but spends most of his time writing about cricket.

Sean Ingle is the Sports Editor of guardian.co.uk.

Rob Bagchi is a *Guardian* sports writer.

Simon Burnton is a *Guardian* sports writer.

Alan Gardner is a freelance sports writer.

Mike Selvey is the *Guardian*'s cricket correspondent and played Test cricket for England.

Vic Marks is the *Observer*'s cricket correspondent and played Test cricket for England.

David Hopps is specialist writer on cricket for the *Guardian* and the *Observer*.

Kevin Mitchell writes for the *Guardian* and the *Observer*.

Donald McRae is an author and writer for the *Guardian*, specialising in interviews. In 2010 he was named Sports Interviewer of the Year.

Duncan Fletcher was England's cricket coach. He now writes a regular column for the *Guardian*.

Malcolm Knox is a journalist and author who has written on cricket for many publications, including the *Sydney Morning Herald*.

Paul Johnson is Deputy Editor of Guardian News and Media and also Head of Sport for the *Guardian*, *Observer* and guardian.co.uk.

Matthew Hancock is Sports Features Editor for the *Guardian* and the *Observer*. He began his journalistic career at *Wisden*.

Preamble

It's late Boxing Day night. Freezing cold, an angry, icy wind and snow on the ground. The roads are empty. The *Guardian*'s London offices are deserted. Well, almost deserted. In one corner of the second floor two computer screens are alight and a couple of hunched, unshaven, bedraggled figures pore over the incoming messages. The debris of the night is all around them: beer bottles, coffee cups, discarded, half-eaten sandwiches, polystyrene-flavoured savoury snacks, bits of cake, piles of newspapers and notes. Every so often the motion-sensitive lights go off, plunging the room into darkness and forcing one of the figures to jerk into life, waving his arms above his head in mock celebration to get them back on again. Ten thousand five hundred miles away in Melbourne one of the most exciting Test matches in memory is under way; England are about to crush Australia in a manner we haven't seen in a generation. And yet, for tens of thousands of people, it is those two figures – usually Rob Smyth and Andy Bull, gentle, intelligent men far removed from the wild and wanton look of their newspaper picture bylines – who provide a window onto this epic, describing the game in their own unique way: vividly, with wit, repartee and more than a nod to the history and minutiae of the game. Welcome to the Over by Over.

Of course, there's another absolutely vital ingredient of the coverage: the audience. Many watch the games live on TV but follow the OBO to enjoy the mischievous entertainment. That's the difference with the OBO: you can join in. And join in they do. Readers let us know they were in Khartoum, Kazakhstan, Canada and the Cayman Islands. On a beach in Brazil drinking caipirinhas, at a party in Mexico City drinking tequilas, on the beach in Perth, knocking back the VBs. On a riding holiday in Patagonia, on a diving holiday in the Philippines. Climbing a volcano in Ecuador, climbing a volcano in Chile, on an archaeological dig on an island off Kuwait. In a traffic jam in Beijing trying to get a child to the Christmas play, stuck in a car in Tokyo, and caught in a snarl-up in Lagos. There was the fan who emailed from a strip club in Medellin, Colombia, saying he couldn't keep his eyes off the OBO; the diplomat writing budgets for the UN in New York who welcomed the distraction; the anxious England supporter messaging from Riyadh; and the lonely cricket lover living 30 miles from the North Korean border.

Thanks to all of you, and hundreds of others, who joined in to help make those winter nights so much fun via the OBO and Steve Busfield's Ashes blog. This is an edited version of those sessions – along with a sprinkling of wonderfully written pieces from Australia by the cricket writers of the *Guardian* and the *Observer* that capture the drama and joy of the series.

But let's go back to Boxing Day night. 'I'm a junior doctor halfway through my week of nights, and I wondered if you could give a shout out to all my glum patients stuck in hospital on orthopaedic wards 26 and 27,' says Dave Hogg. 'Each time we take a wicket I shout "Howzat!" and they give a little cheer, albeit somewhat diminished as we get into the early hours. They appreciate my providing top-class entertainment whilst meeting their medical needs, I'm sure.'

Paul Johnson
Deputy Editor GNM and Head of Sport

Preamble

It's late Boxing Day night. Freezing cold, an angry, icy wind and snow on the ground. The roads are empty. The *Guardian*'s London offices are deserted. Well, almost deserted. In one corner of the second floor two computer screens are alight and a couple of hunched, unshaven, bedraggled figures pore over the incoming messages. The debris of the night is all around them: beer bottles, coffee cups, discarded, half-eaten sandwiches, polystyrene-flavoured savoury snacks, bits of cake, piles of newspapers and notes. Every so often the motion-sensitive lights go off, plunging the room into darkness and forcing one of the figures to jerk into life, waving his arms above his head in mock celebration to get them back on again. Ten thousand five hundred miles away in Melbourne one of the most exciting Test matches in memory is under way; England are about to crush Australia in a manner we haven't seen in a generation. And yet, for tens of thousands of people, it is those two figures – usually Rob Smyth and Andy Bull, gentle, intelligent men far removed from the wild and wanton look of their newspaper picture bylines – who provide a window onto this epic, describing the game in their own unique way: vividly, with wit, repartee and more than a nod to the history and minutiae of the game. Welcome to the Over by Over.

Of course, there's another absolutely vital ingredient of the coverage: the audience. Many watch the games live on TV but follow the OBO to enjoy the mischievous entertainment. That's the difference with the OBO: you can join in. And join in they do. Readers let us know they were in Khartoum, Kazakhstan, Canada and the Cayman Islands. On a beach in Brazil drinking caipirinhas, at a party in Mexico City drinking tequilas, on the beach in Perth, knocking back the VBs. On a riding holiday in Patagonia, on a diving holiday in the Philippines. Climbing a volcano in Ecuador, climbing a volcano in Chile, on an archaeological dig on an island off Kuwait. In a traffic jam in Beijing trying to get a child to the Christmas play, stuck in a car in Tokyo, and caught in a snarl-up in Lagos. There was the fan who emailed from a strip club in Medellin, Colombia, saying he couldn't keep his eyes off the OBO; the diplomat writing budgets for the UN in New York who welcomed the distraction; the anxious England supporter messaging from Riyadh; and the lonely cricket lover living 30 miles from the North Korean border.

Thanks to all of you, and hundreds of others, who joined in to help make those winter nights so much fun via the OBO and Steve Busfield's Ashes blog. This is an edited version of those sessions – along with a sprinkling of wonderfully written pieces from Australia by the cricket writers of the *Guardian* and the *Observer* that capture the drama and joy of the series.

But let's go back to Boxing Day night. 'I'm a junior doctor halfway through my week of nights, and I wondered if you could give a shout out to all my glum patients stuck in hospital on orthopaedic wards 26 and 27,' says Dave Hogg. 'Each time we take a wicket I shout "Howzat!" and they give a little cheer, albeit somewhat diminished as we get into the early hours. They appreciate my providing top-class entertainment whilst meeting their medical needs, I'm sure.'

Paul Johnson
Deputy Editor GNM and Head of Sport

First Test

The Gabba, Brisbane
25–29 November 2010

First day

The morning session

BY ROB SMYTH

Preamble: Are you sitting uncomfortably? Then let's begin. Here we are again, queuing up to be put through the most moreish emotional wringer of them all: the Ashes. Between now and 7 January, you can forget Kate Middleton and Katie Waissel and student demonstrations and El Clásico and the inaugural UK *Twin Peaks* Festival and *Peep Show* and Christmas shopping and *Boardwalk Empire* and whatever's happening in *Emmerdale* these days. You can even forget – and I know this won't be easy – *The One Show*. The Ashes is all you'll need.

It's a huge relief that the series is finally starting. Not just for the obvious it's-Christmas-morning-wake-up-Mom feeling, but because we will finally get some certainties, some inscriptions into the tablet of Statsguru. It would seem there are only three things right with this England team: they can bat, they can bowl and they can field. Then again, given what happened to the 'can't bat, can't bowl, can't field' 1986–7 side, that is not necessarily a good thing. Whatever happens, we'll remember these next 43 days until we wince our last. Please, please, please let us get what we want.

Toss: England have won the toss and will bat first. No real surprise there. It's a decent toss to win. The moment Andrew Strauss said, 'We'll have a bat,' my heart started thumping violently; first-date violently. Now, finally, this feels real. Australia: Watson, Katich, Ponting (c), Clarke, Hussey, North, Haddin (wk), Johnson, Doherty, Siddle, Hilfenhaus. England: Strauss (c), Cook, Trott, Pietersen, Collingwood, Bell, Prior (wk), Broad, Swann, Anderson, Finn.

1st ball: England 0–0 (Strauss 0, Cook 0) The first ball deserves an entry of its own, given the importance it has assumed, but that's only when the ball is in the hands of clammy-palmed Englishman. This time, Ben Hilfenhaus does what Ben Hilfenhaus does: bowls a decent delivery outside off stump that Andrew Strauss leaves.

WICKET! 1st over: Strauss c Hussey b Hilfenhaus 0 (England 0–1) Andrew Strauss has gone third ball! He has gone to one of his favourite shots, the cut, slapping it straight to Hussey in the gully. I cannot believe that. I simply cannot believe that. There was a bit of bounce and maybe it was a touch too close for the shot – but even so, Strauss plays that stroke in his sleep. He puts his hand straight to his head in shock, and he is not the only one.

1st over: England 0–1 (Cook 0, Trott 0) If anyone can douse this atmosphere, it's Jonathan Trott. He takes guard, solves 74 complex mathematical problems and finally faces up to his first ball. He defends solidly, and Hilfenhaus has started the Ashes with a wicket maiden. Dear me. 'Goodnight, Rob,' says Luke Dealtry.

2nd over: England 0–1 (Cook 0, Trott 0) Peter Siddle, the mongrel of this Australian attack, shares the new ball. Alastair Cook almost slips over as he plays forward to his second delivery. Otherwise he is comfortable.

3rd over: England 8–1 (Cook 0, Trott 8) Hilfenhaus v. Trott should theoretically have all the excitement of a staring contest. Trott gets the first runs of the series when he squirts a low edge to third man for four. Every time an England player so much as moves his bat, I get a horrible feeling of impending doom. I'm too old for this. 'I'm sitting in an office in Sydney with two other Brits and a Swiss person,' says Tom Adams. 'Even without any Aussies here, the Swiss person has already had a good laugh about Strauss. I feel this could be a long summer.'

4th over: England 10–1 (Cook 1, Trott 8) Alastair Cook works Siddle into the leg side to get off the mark. Trott survives a referral to the third umpire! He played around his front pad at Siddle and was smacked just below the knee roll. Aleem Dar said not out, but Ricky Ponting went for the referral. It was shaving leg, which means the original decision stands – but to compound our not inconsiderable misery, the host broadcaster buggered it up and said that Trott was out! I can't take any more of this, and we're only four overs in!

5th over: England 11–1 (Cook 2, Trott 8) Trott is beaten by a snorting leg-cutter from Hilfenhaus. That was an absolute peach. Just one from the over. 'Don't panic,' says Paul Griffin. 'No team has won the Ashes when the bowler and catcher of their first wicket shared the first letter of their surnames with the first name of a member of S Club 7. The tide of history is already turning against Australia.'

6th over: England 12–1 (Cook 3, Trott 8) Trott in particular is only playing when he absolutely needs to do so. Just one from the over. 'Movember,' says my colleague Russell Cunningham. 'This is like the clone wars – every bugger looks like Lillee.' And, in my head at least, every bugger is bowling like him at the moment.

7th over: England 20–1 (Cook 6, Trott 12) That's a nice stroke from Cook, who works Hilfenhaus off his pads for a couple. Later in the over Trott dumps a filthy leg-stump half-tracker to fine leg for four.

8th over: England 23–1 (Cook 7, Trott 14) Drip by drip, ball by ball, it feels a little safer to emerge from behind the sofa. The moment I type that, Siddle turns Trott round and the edge falls just short of Ponting at second slip. Man, that was close.

9th over: England 27–1 (Cook 7, Trott 18) Hilfenhaus again goes full to Trott, but this time he is crunched nicely down the ground for a couple. Trott then plays a daft shot, trying to work a full delivery outside off stump through midwicket; instead he gets a leading edge that flies on the bounce to Hussey at gully. Trott isn't quite in his cat-on-a-hot-tin-roof mode from the South African tour a year ago, but he's a little manic.

10th over: England 28–1 (Cook 8, Trott 18) Trott blocks most of that Siddle over, and now there is a sense that both sides are waiting for probably the most important player in this series – Mitchell Johnson – to bowl. 'Is it wrong that I want to point out that H was in Steps (5th over), not S Club 7?' says Alastair Gerrard.

11th over: England 30–1 (Cook 9, Trott 19) Here is Mitchell Johnson. Nobody knows what we'll get from him. His first over is nothing to tweet home about, a range-finder that brings a couple of singles.

12th over: England 35–1 (Cook 9, Trott 24) Trott pulls a gentle, leg-stump short ball from Siddle to fine leg for four more. Trott then takes a tight single to mid-on, where Clarke fumbles. Our colleague and very good friend Tom Lutz has just brought over an illicit stash to keep us going tonight: Monster Energy Drink, Supermalt original and Barg's Olde Tyme Root Beer. He has also brought us a bag of Monster Munch each – but this wretched fool, this former friend, has chosen Pickled Onion rather than Flamin' Hot flavour. I'm not putting those in my mouth.

13th over: England 36–1 (Cook 9, Trott 25) You have to

love Johnson's run-up, full of snaking menace and sinister intent. That over was good, save from an attempted yorker that speared down the leg side. One run from it. 'The atmosphere in my household is so tense the cat's given up on the milk and has started getting stuck into the vodka,' says Phil Sawyer.

WICKET! 14th over: Trott b Watson 29 (England 41–2)
The golden arm of Shane Watson gets a wicket in his first over. It was a good delivery, a full-length off-cutter that roared through a big gate as Trott played a pretty loose drive, and England are in trouble. Already.

14th over: England 41–2 (Cook 9, Pietersen 0) Watson had actually started terribly: his first ball was on the pads and tucked away for four, and his second was a wide. I was just starting to congratulate myself for hexing Watson by making him my MVP in the Cricinfo Fantasy League when he took the wicket.

15th over: England 49–2 (Cook 14, Pietersen 3) Kevin Pietersen gets off the mark with a nice flick through midwicket for three. On Sky, Shane Warne is imploring Australia to pitch the ball up more.

16th over: England 50–2 (Cook 14, Pietersen 3) Pietersen takes a single and then Cook blocks/leaves the rest of the over. 'Those Australian 'taches look like they wouldn't get wet from a full pint of Guinness,' sniffs Adam Hirst. 'David Boon's 'tache used to come out from his helmet guard and irritate the batsman when he fielded at short leg. I guess Kevin Pietersen found a stray moustache hair up his nose earlier. He was digging around in there and definitely pulled something out.'

17th over: England 53–2 (Cook 15, Pietersen 6) Hilfenhaus replaces Johnson, a definite plan for Pietersen. He gets one to pop a little from a length and surprise Pietersen, but that's about all. England take three singles from the over.

18th over: England 56–2 (Cook 16, Pietersen 7) Watson is wided for a lolloping bouncer to Cook, who he then beats with a good one, full and a touch wider. 'Do we think,' begins Palfreyman, 'that despite the two wickets and Watson, that Australia's attack looks a bit thin?' We certainly don't. You may think what you like, but we are bloody terrified.

19th over: England 61–2 (Cook 21, Pietersen 6) Cook hasn't been fluent – far from it – but I can't really remember a false stroke, so he will be very happy. Saying which, he squirts Hilfenhaus low through the cordon for three.

20th over: England 66–2 (Cook 22, Pietersen 10) Watson floats up a full delivery on off stump and Pietersen thumps it back whence it came for his first boundary.

21st over: England 70–2 (Cook 23, Pietersen 13) Here comes the debutant left-arm spinner Xavier Doherty. He shambles up . . . and his first delivery is a beauty, turning pretty sharply from outside Cook's off stump. Cook then takes a single, which brings KP on strike. Pietersen starts positively, walking down the track to his second ball and whipping it through midwicket for three.

22nd over: England 70–2 (Cook 23, Pietersen 13) Apparently Pietersen and Watson aren't exactly Brylcreem buddies. As a consequence there's an extra frisson to this little spell – like we bloody need any more – and both play respectfully during a maiden over.

23rd over: England 73–2 (Cook 26, Pietersen 13) Cook works Doherty off his pads for a couple, and then a single. 'The Peckham posse comin' at ya straight from SE15 are liking Pietersen's street knowledge but think a few more instruction-manual forward defensives are in order, this is a Test match after all, y'know what I mean?' says Allan Crocker. 'Yours, Speed Queen, Preg-Nancy, Mr Blonde, Crox, Barboz, William, R-Money.' I bet Cardus didn't get correspondence like this.

24th over: England 75–2 (Cook 27, Pietersen 14) Alastair Cook is dropped by Doherty! He slapped a short one from Watson straight to point, but Doherty couldn't hang on to a relatively straightforward chance above his head. What a terrible thing to happen to a kid on his debut. Ponting runs up and gives him a pat on the hand.

25th over: England 79–2 (Cook 27, Pietersen 18) Pietersen is using his feet against Doherty and trying to dominate. He left his crease for four of the six deliveries in that over, which is a brave thing to do five minutes before lunch. Doherty saw him coming to the fourth ball and speared it in, but Pietersen got enough on it to tickle it fine for four.

26th over: England 86–2 (Cook 29, Pietersen 23) Johnson replaces Watson for the last over before lunch, and Cook, head falling over a long way to the off side, pings him not far short of North at short midwicket. A jittery morning has ended pretty even, although it would certainly have been Australia's session had Xavier Doherty caught Alastair Cook just before lunch.

England 86–2

The afternoon session

BY ANDY BULL

Preamble: What did we learn in that first session? It feels like this is going to be another dirty tussle of a series, with the advantage swinging to and fro. The office is empty now; the late staff have sent out the final edition of the newspaper and scurried off home. Now it is just Smyth, myself and whoever is out there reading. We've got half a can of Monster Energy Drink, a full packet of Pickled Onion Monster Munch, it's dark outside and we're sitting here under strip lights. 'Why don't you have a work-experience kid you can send out to the shops for supplies?' asks Andrew Mack. We used to have a work-experience guy. He got promoted above us.

27th over: England 91–2 (Cook 33, Pietersen 23) Hilfenhaus opens the attack after the break. His first ball is too short, and Cook slaps it away for four through midwicket with the self-confident air of a man sniffing his own expensive aftershave. A no-ball brings up the fifty partnership.

28th over: England 98–2 (Cook 38, Pietersen 25) And at the other end it is Mitchell Johnson. His line is wayward. He lands a ball on KP's pads, and it is another single to the score, and he ends the over with a half-volley on leg stump, which Cook glances to fine leg for four.

29th over: England 102–2 (Cook 39, Pietersen 28) KP whips three runs out towards leg. It is early in the session, I know, but England have made a good start after lunch.

30th over: England 102–2 (Cook 39, Pietersen 28) 'It is a great time to be a small-business owner in Beijing,' says Dominic Plastered (that's not your real surname, is it?). 'With the time difference I get to pretend to work at my PC and watch your live coverage all day.' Being self-employed, aren't you just diddling yourself? A maiden from Mitch.

31st over: England 103–2 (Cook 39, Pietersen 29) Hilfenhaus is bowling well wide of the off stump here. Whether that width is deliberate or not, he has just lured KP into reaching out for an ambitious drive, prompting all manner of oohs and ahhs from the fielders.

32nd over: England 107–2 (Cook 39, Pietersen 33) Pietersen creams four through cover.

33rd over: England 107–2 (Cook 39, Pietersen 33) A maiden from Hilfenhaus, Cook steadfastly refusing to play at a string of balls that pass by his off stump.

34th over: England 111–2 (Cook 39, Pietersen 37) Oh my! Pietersen has had enough of the waiting game and swings a wild haymaker of a hook away towards midwicket for four. A strange shot that. He made a bit of a mess of it. KP is trying just a bit too hard to bully Johnson here.

35th over: England 111–2 (Cook 39, Pietersen 37) 'I'm trying to inspire my four members of staff,' points out Dom Plastered (30th over), before revealing that his real surname is the distinctly less edgy Johnson-Hill. Another maiden.

36th over: England 117–2 (Cook 39, Pietersen 43) I'm loving the updates from the Walkabout in Shepherd's Bush, where, Richard Caulfield tells me, 'Three tramps have been thrown out so far but they haven't spotted the one in the corner yet. If I had to sum up the Australian banter in here in one word it would be: homophobic.' Johnson's last ball is overpitched, and Pietersen forces it away for four through cover.

37th over: England 117–2 (Cook 39, Pietersen 43) Xavier Doherty is back into the attack. His nickname is supposed to be X, but the close fielders seemed to have plumped for 'Doughy'. 'Aww yes, Doughy,' bellows Haddin as the bowler finishes a maiden over. 'Pietersen just passed Ian Chappell's career runs total,' says Chris Wright. 'Damn, I enjoyed writing that sentence.'

WICKET! 38th over: Pietersen c Ponting b Siddle 43 (England 117–3) Peter Siddle comes back into the attack. Oh, and he has done him! KP has gone, caught at second slip off the outside edge. The ball was just a little bit wide, it bit and broke off the pitch. The snick flew straight to Ponting. Australia go nuts. They wanted that wicket a lot.

39th over: England 121–3 (Cook 43, Collingwood 0)

Cook has four more here, flicking the ball fine to leg. A nice comeback from Doherty, drifting the ball across Cook's bat and pulling him across the crease.

WICKET! 40th over: Collingwood c North b Siddle 4 (England 125–4) Oh no! England are wobbling, toppling even. Collingwood has gone. Mere moments after he had hit a glorious on-drive down the ground for four, he edged the next ball straight to third slip.

41st over: England 125–4 (Cook 43, Bell 0) Doherty hustles through another quick maiden.

42nd over: England 129–4 (Cook 43, Bell 4) Bell narrowly avoided having his eyes pecked out by a rogue magpie yesterday morning. No, really. The Barmy Army trumpeter has just launched into 'The Great Escape'. Shot, sir! Bell cuts four pretty runs out square.

43rd over: England 129–4 (Cook 43, Bell 4) Sadly for English fans everywhere, 'Doughy' is really bowling quite well, with drift and variation in line and pace. 'On *TMS* Simon Hughes has perfected the pronunciation of Xavier Doherty,' or so Clare Davies tells me. 'He says, "Dirty." It's quite fun to hear, and already on Day One we England supporters are looking for things to enjoy.'

44th over: England 137–4 (Cook 43, Bell 12) Bell rocks back and cuts four runs over the head of the man at point. A bold and beautiful shot. At Shepherd's Bush Walkabout 'Three young lads have just been caught fortifying their drinks with illicit vodka. They've been moved on.' Just another day in paradise, eh? Thanks to Andrew Gates for that.

45th over: England 142–4 (Cook 46, Bell 14) Cook ends a run of 15 fruitless balls by turning two runs away to leg. Doherty's spell at the start of this over: 4–3–4–0. England have allowed him to settle into a groove.

46th over: England 146–4 (Cook 49, Bell 15) Siddle takes a bow, and Mitchell Johnson comes back into the attack. 'I'm watching the game on a fuzzy pirate web page in Vancouver,' grumbles Alfred Moore. 'I realise now that one of the great pleasures of following the Ashes in England is falling reluctantly asleep at 2 a.m. and dreaming that 83 for 2 will have turned into 326 for 2 by morning, Pietersen on 173 not out. My dreams would be crushed on waking. Now I haven't even had dinner and I can see England are neck deep in [stinky brown stuff]. The romance is gone.' Johnson is flirting with 90 mph now. Cook flicks three runs away to leg to move to 49, a single away from a truly painstaking half-century.

47th over: England 151–4 (Cook 51, Bell 18) A single puts Cook on strike, and he brings up his fifty.

REFERRAL! 48th over: Bell c Haddin b Johnson 18 (England 151–4) Has Bell gone? No, he is safe. Curious cricket from Australia. They have wasted their second appeal and all because Simon Katich was convinced that Bell got a feather of a touch. No one else seemed to share his conviction, and the review shows that Bell did not come close.

49th over: England 155–4 (Cook 54, Bell 18) 'There are a few clouds just building here in Brisbane,' says Nasser Hussain. 'We may be in for an afternoon shower here.'

50th over: England 158–4 (Cook 54, Bell 22) Australia have two men back for Bell, who can expect a few short snorters from Johnson some time soon. A good sharp single from Bell, pushing the ball out square and sprinting down the wicket.

51st over: England 159–4 (Cook 54, Bell 23) And here comes the rain, just like Nasser said. The umpires look up at the skies, and a few of the softer fans scurry for shelter.

52nd over: England 163–4 (Cook 54, Bell 23) Another three-over spell for Johnson, and he is hauled out of the attack again, this time to be replaced by Shane Watson. England have let

Doherty tie up his end – his current spell is 8–3–19–0 – and that is allowing Ponting to play around with his quicks at the other. By the end of the over the rain has gone again.

53rd over: England 167–4 (Cook 58, Bell 23) A great shot from Cook, who has waited and waited and waited some more for the bad ball. When it came, he thrashed it through midwicket for four. Stung by that, Dirty tightens his line, and Cook gets back to his blocking.

54th over: England 169–4 (Cook 58, Bell 25) The camera picks out Robbie Fowler in the crowd. Jeez, the Aussies really are short of celebrities, aren't they? Bell pulls two runs away to square leg.

55th over: England 170–4 (Cook 59, Bell 25) Ponting decides to give Marcus North a little bowl before tea, the sixth Australian bowler of the day. And Shane Warne has just called Graeme Swann 'the best bowler in the world, never mind spinner'.

56th over: England 172–4 (Cook 60, Bell 26) Two singles from the last two balls, and that means that England have scored 86 runs and lost two wickets in this session. Uncannily, that is identical to how they did in the first session. On that rather dry statistical note, I'm signing off.

England 172–4

The evening session

BY ROB SMYTH

Preamble: England will hope this Cook-and-Bell story runs throughout the evening session, although that would be quite some effort: we still have 34 overs to go. Coffee! Of course, the most remarkable performance of this Ashes is already complete: Olly Broom cycling through 23 countries, over 411 days, to make it to the Gabba. This is the Gooch 154 not out of charity efforts. An astonishing effort.

57th over: England 175–4 (Cook 60, Bell 28) Ben Hilfenhaus starts after tea, and an off-side wide brings up the fifty partnership.

58th over: England 176–4 (Cook 60, Bell 28) It's Shane Watson at the other end, and he also bowls a wide. Cook then squirts one along the floor to gully. A pretty quiet start to the session.

59th over: England 180–4 (Cook 60, Bell 31) Another over, another wide. Ricky Ponting isn't happy and shouts something at Billy Doctrove. Hilfenhaus is trying to lure Bell outside off stump, but when he digs one in Bell pulls it confidently through midwicket for three.

60th over: England 188–4 (Cook 64, Bell 34) Watson strays onto the pads and is worked through midwicket for three more by Bell, who is playing very nicely here.

61st over: England 188–4 (Cook 64, Bell 34) It's a battle of wills between Hilfenhaus and Bell. Hilfenhaus is bowling almost everything very full and wide of off stump, trying to draw Bell into the drive. Bell is having none of it, so that's a maiden.

62nd over: England 190–4 (Cook 66, Bell 34) England will really kick themselves if they lose a wicket before the second new ball, because batting is pretty easy right now. Cook works Watson through midwicket for two more, the only runs in that over. 'If only my eyes were as wide as Australia's bowling,' says Chris Faulkner.

63rd over: England 191–4 (Cook 66, Bell 35) Hilfenhaus beats Bell with a very good delivery, just straight enough to force Bell to feel for it nervously. This is a really interesting passage of play, with both sides straining not to blink.

64th over: England 196–4 (Cook 66, Bell 39) Here comes Peter Siddle, on for Shane Watson, and, like Hilfenhaus and Watson, he bowls a wide. Bell isn't interested in the fuller stuff, but when Siddle drops short Bell cuts him handsomely through the covers for four. He is so, so close to being an extremely good Test-match batsman.

65th over: England 197–4 (Cook 67, Bell 39) Hilfenhaus has been getting a bit of shape since tea, and there he curves a nice one past Bell's tentative grope. 'I hope Broad and Finn are watching, because this pitch requires a tight line and a fuller length than they bowl in England,' says Gary Naylor. 'Not rocket science, but it was beyond English bowlers for five Tests last time round.'

WICKET! 66th over: Cook c Watson b Siddle 67 (England 197–5) That is a huge wicket for Australia, and Peter Siddle has done it again. A good delivery, slanted across Cook and forcing him to play. Cook pushed forward firmly and the ball flew off the edge to Watson at first slip. Siddle has three for 33, deserved reward for pitching the ball up since lunch.

WICKET! 66th over: Prior b Siddle 0 (England 197–6) Matt Prior has gone first ball! This is marvellous stuff from Peter Siddle, who is on a hat-trick. That was a beauty to get first up: full, straight and angling in through the gate to smack into off stump as Prior waved all over it. That was a definite plan for Prior, and it worked perfectly.

WICKET! 66th over: Broad lbw b Siddle 0 (England 197–7) Peter Siddle has taken a hat-trick! This is astonishing stuff. He speared a superb swinging yorker onto the toe of

Broad, who was trapped in front of middle and leg. To add to the drama, Broad then decided to review the decision – but that was plumb and replays confirmed it. This is incredible: Peter Siddle, who many felt would not even play in this match, has taken an Ashes hat-trick.

66th over: England 197–7 (Bell 39, Swann 0) Swann stops Siddle from making it four wickets in four balls. So Siddle has to settle for a triple-wicket maiden. It's also his birthday. Can you believe that? What an amazing story. He now has figures of 12–3–33–5. And he didn't even bowl very well this morning. Until that over Australia were just sitting in this game, and now they are in the box seat.

67th over: England 205–7 (Bell 46, Swann 0) Bell carries on in his bubble, driving Hilfenhaus beautifully through the covers for four and then working him off the pads for three. 'Ian Bell wanted the opportunity to show Australia what he's made of,' says Alfred Moore. 'Well, this is it. I still say that pressure is to Bell as cold water is to testicles. PROVE ME WRONG, please.'

68th over: England 215–7 (Bell 53, Swann 3) Bell flicks Siddle confidently behind square leg for four to reach a supreme half-century, from 103 balls and with five fours. Two balls later he pings three more through midwicket, another excellent stroke. Swann completes an expensive over by leaning into a cover drive for three to get off the mark. 'Brilliant!' says Sarah Bacon. 'Never have I been so happy to rise at 3.45 a.m. to watch a first day's Test-cricket action. Happy birthday, Peter Siddle. You've done your country proud.'

69th over: England 226–7 (Bell 57, Swann 10) Mitchell Johnson has come on to replace Ben Hilfenhaus. I guess Australia want to rough Graeme Swann up. Johnson digs one in, and Swann employs the golden rule – if you're gonna flash, flash hard – to send the ball up and over the slips for four. He drives the next ball through the covers for three, and it's good to see that he is playing his natural game. As is Bell, who cover-drives imperiously for four more. Shot of the day, that.

WICKET! 70th over: Swann lbw b Siddle 10 (England 228–8) The greatest day of Peter Siddle's life continues. Swann whips around a straight one and is plumb, although he has decided to review it, just in case. 'This won't take long,' says Beefy, and he's right. That was bashing into middle stump, and Siddle has career-best figures of six for 43.

69.2 overs: England 228–8 (Bell 57) That was the last ball before rain stopped play, although it's only a shower so we should be back on in a couple of minutes. Sky show the pitch map of Siddle's wickets: five were from full-length deliveries, the other from a ball that was on the very full side of good.

70th over: England 229–8 (Bell 57, Anderson 0) The players return, and Brad Haddin puts James Anderson down. It was a very tricky chance, diving low in front of first slip when Anderson edged another good, full-length delivery. That would have been Siddle's seventh wicket. This is miserable. We've seen this storyline played out so many times before. 'Good effort, Siddle, you swine,' says Will Davies, generous to the last.

71st over: England 234–8 (Bell 62, Anderson 0) With just Anderson and Finn left, Bell moves into one-day mode. He gives Johnson the charge second ball and misses a massive yahoo, and then drives delightfully through mid-off for four. Then he swipes another windy woof on the bounce to third man.

72nd over: England 241–8 (Bell 65, Anderson 4) Bell steals two to fine leg and then takes a single from the fourth delivery. Anderson survives the last two balls, snicking one through the slips for four. If England could just repeat this for, say, the next four and a bit days, they should be OK.

73rd over: England 245–8 (Bell 69, Anderson 4) Bell pulls Johnson zestily through midwicket for two and then turns down a single, which brings some inexplicable boos from the crowd. 'Sitting in a traffic jam in Lagos while England collapse is not my idea of a fun Thursday,' says Richard Woods. 'Be that as it may, now he seems to have his mojo, is it time to move Bell to No. 5 and bring in Morgan for Colly?' The short answer, and indeed the long one, is no. If England lose this game they won't panic, and nor should they.

74th over: England 248–8 (Bell 70, Anderson 5) Anderson steals a single from Siddle's first ball, and then Bell works another through midwicket. 'Hello from Canada!' says Marcia Adair, with entirely inappropriate enthusiasm. 'Is it better to adopt a position of hope and do my best to weather the constant disappointment or should I rather spend the next five weeks fearing that nothing will happen to prove that fearing the worst was the wrong choice?'

75th over: England 249–8 (Bell 71, Anderson 5) This is a really interesting gamble from Ricky Ponting. He has brought on Xavier Doherty to replace Mitchell Johnson (whose figures of 15–2–66–0 reflect a mediocre day's work). That's a risk because Bell is such a clean, straight hitter and you would expect him to go for Doherty. He contents himself to a single for the time being.

76th over: England 254–8 (Bell 76, Anderson 5) Ben Hilfenhaus replaces Peter Siddle, and Ian Bell treats him like an off-spinner, running down the track and driving imperiously over extra cover for four. Man, he has played well.

WICKET! 77th over: Bell c Watson b Doherty 76 (England 254–9) A lovely moment for Xavier Doherty, who takes his first Test wicket. Bell came down the track and tried to lift Doherty over extra cover, but he didn't quite get hold of it and Shane Watson, running in from the cover boundary, took a straightforward catch. Bell played magnificently to make 76 from 131 balls.

WICKET! 77th over: Anderson b Doherty 11 (England

260 all out) Doherty makes it two wickets in five balls, hitting leg stump when Anderson misses a reverse yahoo. That's a wonderful performance from Australia, and particularly Peter Siddle, who ends with career-best figures of six for 54 on his 26th birthday. Shane Warne says England are 'only 40 short of par'. Hmm. We'll have a better idea after they bowl a few overs tonight.

Profound thought for the innings break: Eff. Eff. Ess.

Australia first innings

1st over: Australia 4–0 (Watson 4, Katich 0) It'll be Jimmy Anderson to start, and it's imperative he makes the batsmen play as much as possible. After three leaves, Watson blocks the fourth ball and cleaves the fifth through the covers for four. Cracking shot. He is going to get a lot of runs in this series. There was no real swing for Anderson in that over. 'I totally feel for Marcia Adair,' says Sara Torvalds. 'It's my first Ashes Down Under (since becoming a cricket fan) and I am absolutely not prepared for this emotionally.' Wait till Australia race to 974 for two by Saturday morning.

2nd over: Australia 6–0 (Watson 4, Katich 2) Here comes Stuart Broad from the Slaughtered Pom End. From the first ball Katich walks miles across his stumps, an incredible amount for a Test opener really. Broad concentrates on a shortish length, and Katich defends a little uncomfortably before working the last delivery through midwicket for two.

3rd over: Australia 8–0 (Watson 5, Katich 2) The first thing you check with Jimmy Anderson is: is it swinging? It's as fundamental as checking your flies before you go out for dinner. And it's not swinging. It's not bloody swinging. 'Go back to the OBO for the last Ashes tour in Australia,' says John Starbuck. 'I seem to recall quite a bit of suffering but we in OBOland gritted our teeth and stuck to it. It can't be as bad as that again. Can it?' Please no. That third day in Brisbane, when Australia batted on towards a lead of infinity in their second innings, was among the most miserable of my life.

4th over: Australia 11–0 (Watson 7, Katich 3) Broad has a huge shout for lbw against Watson turned down. There was a very late inside edge. That was an excellent decision from Billy Doctrove.

5th over: Australia 11–0 (Watson 7, Katich 3) Strauss might have been tempted to give Swann an over at this end before the close, but it's Anderson to continue. His length is good when it probably should be full, and Katich defends comfortably.

6th over: Australia 15–0 (Watson 8, Katich 6) Stuart Broad's length has been progressively fuller in this short spell, and Katich rifles him down the ground for three.

7th over: Australia 25–0 (Watson 9, Katich 15) Graeme Swann will bowl the last over of the day. His first ball is short and whapped through midwicket for four by Katich; his second is eased delightfully through the covers for another boundary. So that answers the question as to how Australia will play him. It's been an outstanding day for Australia, who trail by only 235 runs. England will have to bowl incredibly well to get a first-innings lead.

Australia 25–0; England 260

Slow-burner Cook shows value of old-fashioned virtues to the fancy dans

BY VIC MARKS IN BRISBANE

THURSDAY 25 NOVEMBER 2010

If only England could have displayed the neat footwork of the Australian selectors. Andrew Hilditch and his cohorts have been taking a fair amount of flak lately, but the Australian think tank got something spectacularly right when they chose Peter Siddle ahead of Dougie Bollinger for this match.

A bowler who takes a Test-match hat-trick is not guaranteed to finish on the winning side. Indeed, the last man to deliver an Ashes hat-trick was Darren Gough at Sydney in 1999, and he ended up on the losing side in that match. But Siddle, the one bowler capable of finding the right length for the Gabba pitch, upturned the balance of the game, and all of Australia rejoiced.

No doubt the jubilation was shared by Bollinger, even though the doughty left-armer may have spent the previous 24 hours tearing his hair out at his omission from the team – metaphorically, at least. Siddle was admirable; the selectors were vindicated, but the Australian birthday boy was assisted by some of the England batsmen.

My situation at the Gabba – square of the wicket – did not provide the perfect vantage point to witness the glimmer of away swing achieved by Siddle, but it gave an insight into the footwork of England's batsmen (admittedly some offered scanty evidence since three of them only lasted a total of five deliveries).

Those that prevailed adhered to the old mantra of using the crease decisively. They went right back or right forward, which soon seemed a necessity on a pitch that was not especially quick by Brisbane standards, but which offered just enough sideways movement for the bowler prepared to pitch the ball up.

The perils of minimalist foot movement were demonstrated by Paul Collingwood. He went deep into his crease against Siddle, the ball was propelled to a full length, and Collingwood could not reappear from the popping crease as he attempted a cover drive. On lower-bouncing, truer tracks like the one at Adelaide it is possible to survive and prosper without leaving the crease very far — as Collingwood did on the last tour. Not so at the Gabba.

The three England players able to cope were Kevin Pietersen and Ian Bell, who were in aggressive mode, and Alastair Cook, who wasn't. Watching from side on it becomes apparent that Pietersen is practically doing the splits in his stance, so wide apart are his legs. But until his dismissal he rocked into position decisively. He looked sharp and hungry; he always does when booed to the wicket.

Bell was equally positive, unveiling the best strokes of the day, rocking forward to drive the seamers, back in time to pull them. Against Xavier Doherty, who propels the ball at Panesar pace, he was up and down the pitch like a cat on a hot tin roof. Against the left-arm spinner he was skittish, almost to a fault; against the seamers he verged on the masterful with his twinkling toes. In this phase of his England career he declines to be subdued.

It is easier to be decisive with your feet when batting aggressively. But Cook managed this while compiling an important defensive innings. Out came that right foot, even when he was in survival mode.

Cook is a cricketer of contradictions. He has matinee-idol looks:

a gleaming smile, jet-black hair and eyebrows that supermodels might covet. Along with Jimmy Anderson he is an automatic choice for the moody posters now required by the marketing men. There is definitely a touch of glamour about him – until he picks up his bat.

At the crease he can conjure up memories of when Test cricket really could be a dour game. Think Geoff Pullar, stalwart opening batsman for Lancashire and for England (28 times) in the 1960s, rather than Marcus Trescothick.

Doggedness can be a virtue when the opposition is Australia and the venue Brisbane. While his colleagues flickered, Cook was the one player prepared to grind away with unrelenting self-denial. He was often ugly and crab-like in defence during an innings that was nearly all defence.

He allowed himself no liberties. Not a single cover drive was attempted. It is not his best shot; on this surface it was a risky one anyway. He left that one for the fancy Dans. Instead he displayed grim self-denial, which always seems faintly incongruous from a cricketer who still looks like the choirboy he once was.

Often Cook can give the impression of being a fragile cricketer. He may have a film-star face but he does not move easily in the field or when running between the wickets; he throws the ball delicately in a feminine sort of way (no letters, please) and with modest power; his catching is none too reliable. He rarely gives the impression of a battle-hardened Test cricketer, even though the statistics demand that he should be regarded as one.

After 61 Tests he has never been dropped from the Test team, though recently many have advocated that he should be. After his gritty innings on the first day it is not difficult to understand why they treasure him in the England dressing room.

Cook addressed the media of both countries two days before the Test. Even in this role, despite five years of experience, which

includes captaining the side in Bangladesh, he seemed remark-
ably nervous. That nervousness was betrayed by the constant
use of the word 'obviously'. One pedant counted 37 of them in
15 minutes. Not even Peter Beardsley in his pomp could match
that ratio, though Siddle did his best when reliving his hat-trick
for the press. However, a lack of verbal dexterity should not be
equated with a lack of resolution or clinical thinking about the
game.

It took Cook 15 overs to hit a boundary – a pull shot off Mitchell
Johnson – and it transpired that the pull shot was the only stroke
he played with true authority throughout his innings. Cook alone
was the glue to the England innings. When he departed, prodding at another demanding full-length delivery from Siddle, the
tourists became terribly unstuck.

Second day

The morning session

BY ANDY BULL

Preamble: Don't panic. Yet. Yes, it was a sorry start to the Ashes for England. But they are a resilient team. I'd say we owe them at least another 30 overs before we dissolve into angst, embarrassment and self-loathing. Anyone out there who is despairing already would do well to remember Boycott's third law: 'Never judge how good a score is until both sides have batted on the pitch.'

8th over: Australia 26–0 (Watson 9, Katich 15) Broad's first ball is a no-ball. Bah. Strauss has, Atherton points out, set a field with four men on the on side, which will encourage Broad to bowl straight and aim for the lbw. But there are only two slips in place.

9th over: Australia 34–0 (Watson 14, Katich 18) And at the other end it is Jimmy Anderson. England are thirsty for a first wicket here. We need some reassurance. Even a good appeal would do. Instead what we get is a meaty pull stroke from Watson, whacking the ball away for four through midwicket.

10th over: Australia 37–0 (Watson 17, Katich 18) Watson whips three runs through midwicket, and Broad then switches to bowl around the wicket at Katich.

11th over: Australia 42–0 (Watson 17, Katich 22) Anderson probes Watson's technique around his pads with a full, straight ball. It's just a little too far to leg, though, and the batsmen steal a leg bye. 'I'm spending a pleasant evening marking undergraduate essays on genocide,' chirrups Ed Packard, as Katich steers a dainty cut away for four. 'My mood has darkened now the cricket has started.'

12th over: Australia 42–0 (Watson 17, Katich 22) Good bowling from Broad here, peppering Watson's off stump. Strauss sticks a man back on the leg side, and Broad whistles down a bouncer. The batsman has sense enough to duck underneath it rather than take it on.

13th over: Australia 42–0 (Watson 17, Katich 22) That has to be out! But it's not. It could have been. The batsmen got into a terrible tangle. Katich was watching the ball as he ran and was halfway down the wicket when he realised Watson wasn't coming. Cook had time to line up a throw at the stumps, but his throw slid past them. Moments later Anderson beats Katich's outside edge with a jaffa, his best delivery of the day so far.

14th over: Australia 46–0 (Watson 21, Katich 22) That's another gem from Broad, ripping the ball past Watson's outside edge, but he forces the next ball for four through long-off. 'The Barmy Army's website proudly states that there are only "2 days" to go before the start of the Ashes,' chortles Phil White. 'Have the team taken the same approach?'

15th over: Australia 47–0 (Watson 21, Katich 23) Watson and Katich average 58 as an opening pair. That ranks them tenth among all the opening partnerships in the history of Test cricket to have scored more than 1,000 runs, well above the likes of Langer and Hayden (51) and Greenidge and Haynes (47). People still seem to think of them as a 'makeshift opening pair' (Atherton used that exact phrase earlier today), but Watson is now averaging 51 in 15 Tests as an opener.

16th over: Australia 48–0 (Watson 21, Katich 24) A brute of a ball from Broad that spat up at Watson. He flailed at the ball, which thumped into the inside of his upper left arm and deflected down towards his stumps. 'I have finally worked out what is so annoying/disturbing about Siddle,' says Ian Copestake. 'It's that he is the spit of Biff Tannen, the thug from *Back to the Future*. I knew I had other reasons to dislike him.'

17th over: Australia 55–0 (Watson 25, Katich 27) Strauss makes his first bowling change, bringing Steve Finn on for his first over in Ashes cricket. His first ball is a loosener down the leg side. His second is full, and Katich taps it away through the leg side for three runs. Oh dear. Watson crunches the next ball through long-on for four. That was the kind of shot that saps your spirits.

18th over: Australia 55–0 (Watson 25, Katich 27) Broad continues with his around-the-wicket attack to Katich. It's a maiden. 'I could do with Katich being got out soon,' writes PJ Atkinson. 'The way he staggers off his guard like a drunk on the deck of a ship in a gale is making me seasick.'

19th over: Australia 56–0 (Watson 26, Katich 27) The ball squirts off Watson's inside edge and away for a single. Finn whistles a sharp length ball past Katich's outside edge, and then tries a yorker. 'I am currently waiting to have left-knee arthroscopy in St Vincent's hospital in Sydney,' grumbles Matt O'Neill. 'I've got one of those ridiculous shower caps on and a pair of paper pants. This isn't a great day.'

20th over: Australia 59–0 (Watson 27, Katich 27) Anderson comes back into the attack at the other end. His first ball is a ripe half-volley which Watson clips away for two runs to long leg. 'Steven Finn from the Vulture Street End?' scoffs Ayal Nathan. 'It reads like a photo caption from the *NME*.'

21st over: Australia 63–0 (Watson 31, Katich 27) That's

a lovely ball from Finn, nipping back from outside off and sailing over the top of middle stump. All the confidence it inspires disappears when Watson whacks another straight drive down the ground for four.

22nd over: Australia 63–0 (Watson 31, Katich 27) Rob Smyth has spent the last hour building a cardboard thermometer a little like the ones they used for charity appeals on *Blue Peter*. Except ours measures Jimmy Anderson's bowling average in Australia. It is now up to 86.6.

23rd over: Australia 67–0 (Watson 36, Katich 27) 'Re. Matt O'Neill's shower caps and paper pants: in Australia, we feel that humiliation is an important part of the health-care system,' writes Nick Place. 'You English types could learn a lot from us.' Watson smears four with a cover drive. This is becoming pretty soul-destroying. I might even have to break open the emergency Pickled Onion Monster Munch.

REFERRAL! 24th over: Katich lbw b Anderson 27 (Australia 74–0) Hallelujah! Up goes the finger. Katich is given out lbw. But the batsmen consult and decide to refer it. Oh mercy me. What have we done to deserve this? The replays show the ball was going over the top and the decision is overturned. What a kick in the guts. I've opened the Monster Munch after all. They taste like defeat.

25th over: Australia 78–0 (Katich 34, Watson 36) Misery upon misery: Australia gain two runs in overthrows after a wild throw from Anderson at midwicket. I guess he's still fuming about that lbw decision.

REFERRAL! 26th over: Watson 36 lbw b Anderson (Australia 78–0) England decide to refer a not-out lbw decision by Doctrove. It does no good, the ball was missing leg stump. Doctrove's decision stands.

WICKET! 26th over: Watson c Strauss b Anderson 36

(Australia 78–1) They've got him this time. England have their wicket at last, and Watson can't refer this one. He edged it straight to slip. What sweet relief. That felt a very long time coming. English spirits soar. And then in walks Ricky Ponting.

27th over: Australia 79–1 (Katich 39, Ponting 0) England bring Broad into the attack, but he only gets to bowl one delivery to Ponting, the sixth of the over. Strauss does stick in a short leg, suggesting England – like everybody else in world cricket at the moment – fancy their chances of getting Ponting out with the short ball.

28th over: Australia 80–1 (Katich 40, Ponting 0) Anderson has two men back behind square on the leg side for Ponting, but then offers him a string of deliveries outside off. 'As a neutral Kiwi, I'd almost started feeling sorry for Australia pre-Ashes,' says Kathy Stodart. 'But now, after a day and a bit enduring Channel 9's oleaginous coverage, I am back in England's arms and fell off the sofa in delight when Jimmy did his stuff.'

29th over: Australia 81–1 (Katich 41, Ponting 0) 'Tell Matt not to worry about the paper pants – you'll be unconscious when anyone inspects,' writes Dave Lonsdale. 'It's wearing the surgical tights that will keep your mates entertained for the next week! Had my knee done on Monday.'

30th over: Australia 88–1 (Katich 44, Ponting 4) Anderson is coming around the wicket to Katich, trying to pull him across his stumps. Ponting gets his first runs with an ugly edge through third man for four.

31st over: Australia 90–1 (Katich 45, Ponting 5) Broad continues to bowl in the channel outside Ponting's off stump, then slips him the shorter ball to invite the pull. Ponting obliges. The fielders cry 'Catchit!', but the ball runs away into empty space for a single.

32nd over: Australia 91–1 (Katich 45, Ponting 6) That's

a beauty from Anderson, whistling the ball away from Ponting's outside edge. Oh, he's got Punter in all sorts of trouble in this over. The next ball is straighter, but still seams away. Ponting tries to play it to midwicket, but the ball flicks off the back of the bat and squirts to slip.

33rd over: Australia 96–1 (Katich 46, Ponting 10) Strauss has a quick thumb through his *MCC Big Book of Captaincy* and comes to page 47: 'Always give the spinner an over before lunch.' And so Graeme Swann comes on. Katich and Ponting swap singles from his first two balls. Three runs come from the final ball as Ponting chops a cut out to deep point.

Australia 96–1; England 260

The afternoon session

BY ROB SMYTH

Preamble: This session is a fascinating challenge for Swann, one that will set the tone for the rest of the match and the rest of the series. Australia's method for playing high-class spinners is to take them on from the get-go. It seems the better the spinner, the more they go after him. It's a tactic born of three things: logic, the desire to stay on top psychologically and machismo. Subservient to a slow bowler? On their own turf? No, no, no. It's an affront to their masculinity.

WICKET! Australia 96–2 (Ponting c Prior b Anderson 10) A mighty bonus from the second ball after lunch, with Ricky Ponting strangled down the leg side. He had started very slowly before the break, like a once-athletic octogenarian wincing his way out of bed in instalments, and now he has gone. It was a nothing delivery, drifting onto the pads; Ponting tried to work it away but got the thinnest of edges to Matt Prior.

34th over: Australia 96–2 (Katich 46, Clarke 0) Anderson's first ball to Clarke is an absolute jaffa, full and moving late past the edge. It's a wicket maiden. 'Pretty uncomfortable being labelled "the man in the paper pants",' says Matthew O'Neill. 'Sounds like a straight to DVD sequel of *The Girl with the Dragon Tattoo*.'

35th over: Australia 100–2 (Katich 50, Clarke 0) It'll be Steven Finn rather than Graeme Swann to begin at the other end. I guess that decision may have been influenced by the arrival of Clarke – back problems, immobility against the short ball and all. For now he is bowling to Katich, who tucks one very fine for four. That brings up a typically ugly, typically vital fifty.

36th over: Australia 100–2 (Katich 50, Clarke 0) Anderson is bowling beautifully here. He jags one back to bring a strangled shout for lbw against Clarke – inside edge – and then coaxes the next delivery past the edge.

WICKET! 37th over: Katich c and b Finn 50 (Australia 100–3) Another one gone! Katich chips a full delivery straight back to Finn, who shows the loose-limbed flexibility of a limbo dancer to get down quickly and claim a lovely low two-handed catch. It's his first Ashes wicket, and what a vital time to get it.

37th over: Australia 101–3 (Clarke 0, Hussey 1) Hussey so, so nearly goes first ball! It was a brilliant delivery from Finn, full, on off stump and demanding the stroke. The ball flew off the edge and bounced just short of Swann, diving to his right at second slip. Hussey then takes a very sharp single into the covers to get off the mark – if not quite a Red Bull single, then at least a Relentless one.

38th over: Australia 101–3 (Clarke 0, Hussey 1) Another

challenging over from Anderson, who is in a really good groove. It's a maiden to Hussey. Anderson's figures are outstanding: 17–7–36–2.

39th over: Australia 102–3 (Clarke 1, Hussey 1) England have used their second and final review. Clarke was cut in half by another very good lifter from Finn, and Matt Prior went up in celebration, thinking Clarke had inside-edged it through to him. Aleem Dar said not out, but England went straight for the review. Yet all the replays and all the technology showed the square root of eff all, so Clarke survived. Strauss shook his head in dismay.

40th over: Australia 102–3 (Clarke 1, Hussey 1) Another peach from Anderson snakes past Clarke's outside edge. That's yet another maiden from Anderson, who deserves high praise for his performance today after an underwhelming little mini-session last night.

41st over: Australia 106–3 (Clarke 1, Hussey 5) Now this is interesting: Snicko, which cannot be used by the third umpire, showed the thinnest of edges from Clarke in the 39th over. No wonder Strauss was so radged off. Finn bangs one in too short and is pulled easily for four by Hussey.

42nd over: Australia 110–3 (Clarke 5, Hussey 5) It's Broad for Anderson (18–8–36–2), and his length was fairly full in that over. That allows Clarke to get on the front foot and push nicely through extra cover for an all-run four. 'Two quick wickets and you have cheered me up, Rob,' says Neill Brown. 'It may be wrong to shoot the messenger but would it be so bad to man-hug him?'

43rd over: Australia 114–3 (Clarke 5, Hussey 9) Test cricket, will you marry me? This is true love. It's just a perfect thing, the most magnificent, nuanced sporting format, and still with (for the most part) an old-fangled integrity at odds with almost everything else in top-level sport. A classical, elegant beauty in an age of skinny jeans. I adore the thing. It's looking particularly good just now, because Australia are just starting to fight back after that traumatic half-hour. Finn is a bit too short again and Hussey swivel-pulls behind square for four. This is such good cricket.

44th over: Australia 115–3 (Clarke 6, Hussey 9) The first delivery of Broad's over is a beautiful short ball that smacks Clarke on the helmet. Clarke went nowhere really; he half tried to duck but couldn't get out of the way. Broad gives him a look that says, 'You are in trouble here, son, and by the way I am prettier than you.'

45th over: Australia 126–3 (Clarke 7, Hussey 19) Graeme Swann comes on for Steven Finn and goes straight around the wicket to Clarke. 'That's really interesting,' says Shane Warne, 'that he's doing that to Michael Clarke.' He says the words really slowly, so much so that you can almost hear that amazing cricket brain whirring to work out why Swann is employing such a tactic. Anyway, Clarke gets a single and then Hussey walks down the track and lifts Swann over long-on for six. Two balls later Hussey cuts a poor delivery for four, and now Swann is nursing figures of 3–0–26–0.

46th over: Australia 126–3 (Clarke 7, Hussey 19) Broad drives Clarke back with a series of short balls and then beats him with a good-length delivery outside off stump. A maiden.

47th over: Australia 134–3 (Clarke 8, Hussey 27) The calculated assault on Swann continues. His third ball is too short and Hussey rocks back to pull it for another four. Two balls later he does exactly the same again. This is extremely good cricket from Australia. Their plan could not have been more obvious had Tim Nielsen shoved it under Graeme Swann's hotel door two nights ago. But Swann gives them a reminder of that when his last delivery kicks nastily from outside Hussey's off stump. His figures are 4–0–34–0.

48th over: Australia 135–3 (Clarke 8, Hussey 27) Broad is bowling to Hussey rather than Clarke, which is not what he wants at all. Hussey, knowing this, is pretty happy to play out a maiden.

49th over: Australia 135–3 (Clarke 8, Hussey 27) I've had a recurring nightmare over the last couple of months. Not the usual one about being halfway into town only to realise I'm wearing odd trainers, but about Graeme Swann bottling the Ashes – or, rather, being bullied out of them. Australia's batsmen are so good at taking calculated risks, and they are really going for him here. Clarke dances down the track at least twice in that over, but he can't get Swann away, and so Swann gets the relief of a maiden.

50th over: Australia 139–3 (Clarke 8, Hussey 31) Hussey back-cuts Broad for four. He was lucky to survive his first ball, but thereafter he has played a gem of a counter-attacking innings. Thorpe-esque, in fact. 'Fascinating stuff to watch, and I'm in much more of a comfortable state of mind than the rest of your readership, as it's only 9.53 p.m. here in Iowa,' says David Naylor. 'Test cricket has beckoned me towards the back room, and I'm rather inclined to follow.'

51st over: Australia 140–3 (Clarke 9, Hussey 31) Graeme Swann has bowled a peculiar number of short balls. This is what the Ashes does to a man. But that was probably his best over yet – just one from it, despite more aggressive intent from Clarke in particular.

WICKET! 52nd over: Clarke c Prior b Finn 9 (Australia 140–4) Michael Clarke's grim, stodgy innings ends to the short ball. He tried to lap-pull one from Finn, in the first over of a new spell, but he top-edged it through to Matt Prior. And then he walked, which is not something you see every century from an Aussie batsman.

52nd over: Australia 141–4 (Hussey 31, North 1) The new batsman Marcus North is an all-or-nothing kinda guy – five hundreds and five ducks in 33 Test innings – but he gets off the mark from the last ball of Finn's excellent over. 'I've ended up in the Shepherd's Bush Walkabout, which I think might be the only public space in London with all-night coverage?' writes Lee Rodwell. 'The atmosphere is surprisingly serene and civilised. Or at least it was. Some guy just got thrown out by the weary-looking staff. As his friend said though: "Well, he's pissed himself in his sleep, ain't he? We can't really argue with that . . ." Amazing scenes.'

WICKET! 53rd over: North c Collingwood b Swann 1 (Australia 143–5) As that well-known cricket fan Simon Cowell would say, Graeme Swann is back in the game. That was a textbook off-spinner's dismissal: North pushed forward defensively, and the ball turned to take the edge and fly low to slip, where Paul Collingwood took a beautifully unobtrusive catch. This is turning into yet another fantastic Ashes Test.

53rd over: Australia 143–5 (Hussey 32, Haddin 0) In time, we might look back at that as the most important wicket of the series, because Swann's fragile ego (the fragile is tautologous, really) desperately needed it.

54th over: Australia 147–5 (Hussey 36, Haddin 0) Finn has been really good today with just two exceptions: a dodgy first two overs, and then a few short balls to Hussey that have been punished mercilessly. There's another, pulled vigorously for four.

55th over: Australia 148–5 (Hussey 36, Haddin 1) Swann spits a snorter past Hussey, who was groping forward defensively. He has a decent rhythm now. His first four overs cost 34; the next four have cost just three and brought the wicket of North. 'Thank goodness this is a cracker of a match,' says Jacob Geiger, 'because I'm in a turkey-induced food coma here after celebrating America's Thanksgiving holiday here in Virginia. Cricket is a salve after a long day with the in-laws.'

56th over: Australia 159–5 (Hussey 40, Haddin 8) That's a gorgeous stroke from Haddin, who rifles a full delivery from Finn almost perfectly straight for four. He then drives through mid-off for three. Hussey completes an expensive over – 11 from it – by yet again pulling Finn for four. That's at least the fourth time that's happened. Not there, Finny!

57th over: Australia 159–5 (Hussey 40, Haddin 8) A maiden from Swann to Haddin, including one big-spinning delivery that ripped back towards the breadbasket. So in his last five overs Swann has figures of 5–2–3–1. 'As I excitedly shimmied out of bed this morning at 5 a.m. my missus squeaked, "You're obsessed,"' says Stuart Wilson. 'She is, as always, correct, but she doesn't understand. Watching England play is an obsession, a roller-coaster ride and at the same time the most special and painful (clean) experience a man can have. I wouldn't have it any other way.'

58th over: Australia 159–5 (Hussey 40, Haddin 8) With ten minutes to go before tea, Paul Collingwood comes on. This is probably just to rest the quick bowlers on what is a fiercely hot day. It's a maiden to Hussey.

59th over: Australia 161–5 (Hussey 40, Haddin 9) The situation gets ever more precarious, but Hussey is still going for Swann. He comes down the track and is almost yorked as a result.

60th over: Australia 168–5 (Hussey 46, Haddin 9) In the last over before tea, Collingwood has a strangled shout for lbw against Hussey, the only real impediment being the tedious detail that it wasn't hitting the stumps. Hussey pings his ninth four off the pads from the penultimate ball of the session. He has played a gem of an innings, 46 not out from 81 balls, his positive attitude never wavering despite the chaos at the other end. This game is wonderfully poised, with Australia trailing by 92 runs. I'm off to shove my head under a tap before play resumes.

Australia 168–5; England 260

The evening session

BY ANDY BULL

Preamble: Honestly, a man slogs through two all but fruitless hours and then Smyth waltzes in and sees four wickets in a session. It's enough to make you sick. I've now caught a small dose of the fear. I'm being haunted by a premonition of Mitchell Johnson scoring a lot of runs.

61st over: Australia 172–5 (Hussey 49, Haddin 10) Swann starts the evening session. His first ball is a vicious off-break which turns two feet or so from outside off stump across the face of the bat. It turned so much that it beat batsman and 'keeper, flicked off the pad and dribbled away for a leg bye that puts Hussey on strike. He pulls three out to midwicket.

62nd over: Australia 175–5 (Hussey 50, Haddin 11) At the other end Stuart Broad looks irritated. He doesn't pause after delivering the ball, but turns and strops back to his mark. Hussey gets a single from the final ball of the over, bringing up his fifty from 85 balls. 'England are in good shape,' says Darren Paterson. 'As is the lass sitting opposite me who jumps and jiggles in all the right places every time the Aussies score a four. So I am in two

minds: I want to see wickets, but I love to "watch" the fours.'
Good grief.

63rd over: Australia 178–5 (Hussey 52, Haddin 12) All
that shaking and jiggling in the last over left me a little lost
for words. I couldn't even bring myself to crack a cheap joke
or make a snide remark. You'll just have to fill in the gap for
yourselves. A quiet over from Swann this, Haddin and Hussey
taking three singles off it.

64th over: Australia 181–5 (Hussey 53, Haddin 13) I just
know it. I'm going to get to describe Hussey and Haddin batting
for the next two hours with not even a sniff of a wicket. I can
feel it in my bones.

65th over: Australia 181–5 (Hussey 53, Haddin 13) Hussey takes two steps down the pitch and laces the ball to mid-
on, where KP picks up. He hurls in a return throw which passes
perilously close to Swann's head. He rocks back on his bottom
to get out of the way, and then shoots a mean glare back at
Pietersen.

66th over: Australia 187–5 (Hussey 58, Haddin 13) Hussey threads a fine drive through extra cover. 'Choose your own
adventure,' says Jay Buckley. 'You are at work in Sydney. A grip-
ping encounter is unfolding before your eyes. Your wife is waiting
downstairs for you to drive her into the city for a drinks function
where no one will be watching nor listening to the cricket. Do
you (a) be a good husband, go downstairs and talk to her about
her day; or (b) man-up and watch the rest of the session?'

67th over: Australia 187–5 (Hussey 58, Haddin 13) Haddin plays out a maiden from Swann, striding forward and blocking
each delivery back down the pitch. These two have put on 44 together now, and England's lead is down to 73. Pessimism is infectious: 'You're dead right,' sighs Jo Davis. 'This is a Steve Waugh/

Ian Healy set up, isn't it? 302–5 at the close, and a ten-wicket defeat by the close tomorrow.' That's the spirit.

68th over: Australia 188–5 (Hussey 59, Haddin 13) Broad takes a bow, and Anderson comes back into the attack. The speed gun is clocking him at 76 mph. The speed gun, Sir Iron Bottom suggests, is wrong. Just a single run from the over, patted through midwicket by Hussey.

69th over: Australia 189–5 (Hussey 60, Haddin 13) Swann pushes up a fuller ball, almost a yorker, in fact. Hussey turns that one through midwicket too. He is playing wonderfully well, Hussey. That hundred he scored for WA last week seems to have turned him into a new man.

70th over: Australia 192–5 (Hussey 61, Haddin 15) Anderson beats Haddin's outside edge, and the batsman smiles and shrugs as if to say, 'Not much I could do about that one.'

71st over: Australia 196–5 (Hussey 65, Haddin 15) 'It's odd,' reckons Burt Bosma. 'Even with an average team in poor form, we Aussies expect to win and are surprised when we don't. Meanwhile, you lot, with a decent team in good form, all expect to lose. Maybe that's why you do.' You can call it odd if you like, but I call it the natural effect of growing up watching English cricket in the 1980s and '90s. Hussey swats a pull through leg for four. Fifty of his 65 runs have come in boundaries.

72nd over: Australia 196–5 (Hussey 65, Haddin 15) Haddin wafts a loose drive at another wide delivery from Anderson, who rolls his eyes in frustration at how often he is beating the bat.

73rd over: Australia 197–5 (Hussey 66, Haddin 15) Just another solitary single from Swann's latest over, hustled to the off by that man Hussey.

74th over: Australia 202–5 (Hussey 66, Haddin 19) It is

Steve Finn's turn now. He allows Haddin j[...] width, and the predictable result is a four p[...] to go to the new ball, but it can't come quickl[y...] land. You'd have hoped Strauss could come up w[...] of trying to solve this problem than simply waiting [...] cherry to come around.

75th over: Australia 206–5 (Hussey 71, Hadd[in] 19) Another pull shot from Hussey. Four more to Mr Cricket. 'Lately Hussey has been undone by the well-pitched out-swinging ball that makes him come onto his front foot,' says Andrew Collins, 'and with the Gabba pitch proving batsmen will be undone by this, I don't understand why England aren't doing this.' 'Cause the ball ain't swinging all that much, I'd hazard.

76th over: Australia 213–5 (Hussey 76, Haddin 20) Hussey's umpteenth pull shot fetches him four more. Almost all his runs have come off Swann and Finn. 'Mr Cricket! Sigh! Swoon!' gushes Catherine Woods. Someone fetch the smelling salts. 'The few Englishmen in my Sydney office are now pleasingly silent for once today.'

77th over: Australia 215–5 (Hussey 78, Haddin 21) This over completely passed me by, I'm afraid. I was still catching up on what had gone before.

78th over: Australia 217–5 (Hussey 79, Haddin 22) Collingwood is on, filling the little gap before the new ball. So far as batsmen who trade in dibbly-dobbers go, Collingwood is distinctly inferior. He's not a patch on Mark Butcher.

79th over: Australia 217–5 (Hussey 79, Haddin 22) This new ball had better sing. Swann seems to have been on for an eternity now. This is the 18th over of his spell. 'I can't think of any reason other than cricket why I'd wake up at 5 a.m. and consider that not going back to sleep was perfectly sensible,' says Guy Hornsby, 'but 143–5 sure is a wonderful alarm call.'

Cruel game, cricket. Just as Anderson starts to mark out his run the umpires decide to take everyone off the field because the light is too poor to play in. Bah. That could be it for the day. Despite my best attempts to jinx Australia by banging on about the sheer bloody inevitability of the fact that I would have to watch the entire session without getting to describe a single wicket, I have had to watch the entire session without getting to describe a single wicket. Humbug.

Australia 220–5; England 260

Third day

The morning session

BY ROB SMYTH

Preamble: It's entirely conceivable that by 7 a.m. tomorrow morning we will know who is going to win the match; and it's entirely conceivable that whoever wins the match will win the series, given that no team has come from behind to even draw an Ashes series in Australia since the 1960s. Andy Flower is again absent from the Gabba today after the removal of a cancerous lesion. He should return tomorrow. Our very best wishes go to him.

81st over: Australia 220–5 (Hussey 81, Haddin 22) England take the new ball immediately, and here comes James Anderson. There are three slips and discernible swing, which will encourage England. Haddin defends solidly, one drive excepted, and it's a maiden. 'Right,' says Stuart Bulloch, 'Ms Optimism has sat provocatively on my lap, I have Peroni and I've got my cat addicted to Pickled Onion Monster Munch. Let's roll. Wickets please, Rob. P.S. The cat said no to Flamin' Hot.'

82nd over: Australia 221–5 (Hussey 81, Haddin 22) It's Stuart Broad at the other end, as you'd expect. Haddin is beaten by a good delivery early on, and then slams a drive to mid-off when Broad pitches one up. 'I'm DJing in a bar in Manchester till

2 a.m.,' says James Pole. 'Couldn't find a stream on my laptop that I'm pretending to DJ off, so I'll be following the *Guardian*'s OBO like I did through my days at uni. Yes, I've got a degree. And the best job I can get? Shit bar DJ. Brilliant.'

83rd over: Australia 222–5 (Hussey 82, Haddin 23) Hussey survives on review, having originally been given out. BAH. What a big moment. He was pinned in front of leg stump by a good delivery from Anderson that moved back into him, but he called for the review instantly and there was always a doubt as to whether it pitched outside leg. Replays showed it did, but only just. That was so tight.

84th over: Australia 225–5 (Hussey 83, Haddin 23) A rare piece of shoddy glovework from Prior, who fails to claim a short one from Broad and thus concedes two byes. 'I am currently in Oslo (for work),' says Caroline Cowan. 'It is freezing and I have been chatted up by two of the tallest guys I've ever seen. Do I stay up for a while to put myself through the emotional wringer that is the Ashes or do I do the sensible thing and go to bed so I can go sightseeing tomorrow?' Stay up. This is the only emotional wringer in town!

85th over: Australia 227–5 (Hussey 83, Haddin 23) Hussey has been very busy this morning, stealing a couple of sharp singles and generally looking like a man who won't be dictated to. He almost gets in trouble then, trying to leave outside off but then steering it to slip on the bounce via the face of the bat. Anderson is bowling well, Hussey is playing well. Who will blink first?

86th over: Australia 227–5 (Hussey 83, Haddin 23) Broad hasn't quite been on it thus far, but then he produces a superb delivery, full and jagging past the outside edge of Haddin's bat. And then he so nearly gets Haddin with another full delivery that induced a sliced drive low towards Pietersen at backward point.

87th over: Australia 229–5 (Hussey 85, Haddin 23) Anderson has huge shouts for lbw against Hussey turned down from consecutive deliveries, but England have no reviews left. The second was a great shout. It came back sharply to Hussey, who was only saved by two noises and the perception of an inside edge. Except replays suggested the two noises were the sound of pad on pad, and showed nothing to suggest an inside edge. That was out, basically, and England are really unlucky. Brilliant over from Anderson.

88th over: Australia 229–5 (Hussey 85, Haddin 23) This is great stuff, and I can hardly keep up with it. A maiden from Broad to Haddin.

89th over: Australia 230–5 (Hussey 86, Haddin 24) This is a fantastic spell from Anderson, and the last ball of his over cuts Haddin completely in half. It moved back a long way but bounced over the stumps as Haddin went for a big yahoo.

90th over: Australia 233–5 (Hussey 88, Haddin 24) Finn replaces Broad, whose figures are a Walshesque 24–5–44–0. As a child of the 1980s, I could read economical bowling figures all day. I think I know who's winning. Finn has a very big shout for lbw against Haddin with his third delivery. Instinct was that it was going over, and replays confirmed it. A good decision from Billy Doctrove.

91st over: Australia 237–5 (Hussey 88, Haddin 25) Anderson beats Hussey with a regal lifting leg-cutter. What an utterly preposterous jaffa that was. You'd have struggled to CGI a delivery so good. Even Don Bradman wouldn't have nicked that.

92nd over: Australia 241–5 (Hussey 88, Haddin 29) The Sky chaps are talking about the cracks, which are getting wider and wider. That's great news for England, especially with two tall fast bowlers. Haddin is beaten by a good one from Finn and then scorches a cover drive that is brilliantly fielded by Collingwood.

Haddin can't go through the covers, so instead he goes down the ground, driving handsomely for four. This is wonderful, cerebral cricket.

93rd over: Australia 242–5 (Hussey 89, Haddin 30) A misfield from Broad at mid-off gives Haddin a single, and that brings up the century partnership. They have ridden their luck this morning, Hussey in particular, but both have played very well.

94th over: Australia 250–5 (Hussey 89, Haddin 37) Finn goes wider on the crease, and Haddin leans into a nice cover drive that brings three runs and the 250. 'My housemate just nipped in to ask why, on a Friday night, I am on my own in my room with a dodgy *TMS* link and half a bottle of a dubiously sweet liqueur called Amarguinha,' says Terri Loska. 'My reply that 'This is wonderful, cerebral cricket' did not, apparently, answer his question.' Maybe if you'd belched as well?

95th over: Australia 257–5 (Hussey 90, Haddin 42) Haddin is now starting to enjoy himself and drives Anderson's first ball thrillingly over mid-off for four. That will probably be Anderson's lot for now. It's been a wonderful spell of bowling: 8–2–14–0.

96th over: Australia 258–5 (Hussey 91, Haddin 42) Haddin misses a big cut shot off Finn, who has probably been the loosest of the England bowlers this morning. (These things are relative.)

97th over: Australia 260–5 (Hussey 92, Haddin 43) Anderson does come off and is replaced by Broad. A couple of quick singles bring Australia level with England. 'Feeding off the crack in the pitch is one thing,' says Ian Copestake, 'but the bowlers look like they're already on speed.'

98th over: Australia 269–5 (Hussey 92, Haddin 52) Haddin belabours a cut stroke off Finn for four to take the Aussies into the lead. The next ball is driven for four to bring up an extremely good fifty: mature and two-paced. The first 25 runs took 111 balls, the second 25 just 23. 'Caroline (84th over) should go with both the characters who are chatting her up,' says John Starbuck, 'on condition that they sort out her Ashes feed for the night.' Who says romance is dead? How does the Pulp song go? *I know you won't believe it's true, I went with him because I wanted to watch some wonderful, cerebral cricket.*

99th over: Australia 269–5 (Hussey 92, Haddin 52) Haddin drives Broad right back into the stumps at the bowler's end. He is hitting it beautifully now. 'I've now seen Australia score 116 without seeing a wicket, which is disappointing,' says Jo Davis, with interesting use of the word 'disappointing'.

100th over: Australia 274–5 (Hussey 97, Haddin 52) Graeme Swann comes on, and you know what that means: a calculated assault from Mike Hussey. He charges the second ball and dumps it over mid-off for four, an outstanding piece of batting.

101st over: Australia 280–5 (Hussey 102, Haddin 52) Michael Hussey cover drives Broad delightfully for four to reach a fantastic century, fluent yesterday and dogged today. This means so much to him: he crouches, clenching his fist furiously, then raises both hands before letting rip a simple 'WOOOO!' and embracing Brad Haddin. What a lovely moment this is for one of cricket's good guys. He was under huge pressure before the match.

102nd over: Australia 286–5 (Hussey 104, Haddin 56) It hasn't happened for Swann yet.

103rd over: Australia 293–5 (Hussey 105, Haddin 62) Haddin hooks Broad emphatically for four, and for the first time England look just a little ragged. There is a horrible history of Australian lower-order batsmen slugging a tiring England side all over the place: Fleming, Reiffel and Geoff Lawson.

104th over: Australia 299–5 (Hussey 110, Haddin 62)
Hopelessly short from Swann, and Hussey pulls him handsomely
for four. The runs are coming very quickly now. Swann is really
struggling – three overs for 17 so far, more Richard Dawson than
Jim Laker.

105th over: Australia 306–5 (Hussey 110, Haddin 70)
Brad Haddin has been dropped by Alastair Cook! It was the
very first ball from the new bowler, Paul Collingwood, and Haddin drove it very high back whence it came. Cook charged after
it from mid-off, but couldn't hold onto a difficult, diving, two-
handed chance.

106th over: Australia 307–5 (Hussey 110, Haddin 71) 'I
have told a number of people tonight that I won't sleep until
we've bowled Australia out,' says Kat Petersen. 'I am a little worried that I will run out of caffeine/sugar/electricity before that
happens.' At this rate I'd be worried about running out of breath
before it happens.

107th over: Australia 308–5 (Hussey 110, Haddin 72)
Collingwood continues. One from the over, so at least England
have quietened things down a bit in these last two overs.

108th over: Australia 311–5 (Hussey 111, Haddin 74)
Hussey is dropped by Prior. Well, sort of. He chopped a ball
from Swann that was too close for the shot, and it flew off the
edge and straight onto Prior's pad before he had chance to react,
never mind say, 'Oh, good ball, Swanny, darn tough luck there.'

109th over: Australia 312–5 (Hussey 111, Haddin 75)
After that little spell of hitting, Australia seem fairly happy to
play for lunch now. England certainly are, so Collingwood hurries
through another over for just a single.

110th over: Australia 313–5 (Hussey 111, Haddin 76) The
milking of Graeme Swann continues. One from the over. At least
England have control, because boy did they need it. 'Typical,'

says Ben Jackson. 'I've been working in Oslo for the last month and the one weekend I decide to have a break in Stockholm a seemingly eligible OBO-reading female advertises her availability. At 6'6" I reckon I'd rival them for height as well. Tonight really couldn't get more depressing.'

111th over: Australia 315–5 (Hussey 111, Haddin 78) The 974th near miss of the session, with Haddin driving Collingwood this far short of Anderson in that daft mid-on position just off the cut strip at the bowler's end. England have been desperately unlucky this morning.

112th over: Australia 328–5 (Hussey 123, Haddin 78) Anderson returns for a two-over spell before lunch. Hussey takes a couple off each of his first two deliveries and then top-edges a whirling pull stroke miles over the slips for four. For heaven's sake.

113th over: Australia 329–5 (Hussey 124, Haddin 79) Two singles from Collingwood's over. 'I'm so beyond pain I feel quite optimistic,' weeps Ian Copestake. 'We are, as Boycott's optimistic brother (the one he keeps locked in a cellar) would say, only a hat-trick away from being on top.'

114th over: Australia 329–5 (Hussey 124, Haddin 79) Anderson charges in, but Hussey is solid. 'This is ridiculous – which of the team do you reckon smashed a mirror, walked under a ladder and ran over a black cat this morning?' says Lizzy Ammon. 'I suspect the latter was probably Swanny.' Australia lead by 69 after an extended session that was thrilling, dispiriting and heart-warming. England aren't out of this – a deficit of 99 is just about manageable – but they need five wickets quick smart.

Australia 329–5; England 260

The afternoon session

BY ANDY BULL

Preamble: For English folk it is all looking a little bleak right now.

115th over: Australia 330–5 (Hussey 124, Haddin 80)
Swann will take the first over after lunch, with Haddin on strike. He only bowls one ball before he turns to Aleem Dar to grumble about the state of the ball. Dar is having none of it. Swann starts with a tight line, hugging off stump.

116th over: Australia 330–5 (Hussey 124, Haddin 80)
James Anderson starts at the other end, pushing the ball out wide of off. England are going to play a patient game this afternoon, forcing the batsmen to stretch for the ball if they want to score runs. Their bowling coach, David Saker, is an advocate of attritional cricket in these situations.

117th over: Australia 332–5 (Hussey 125, Haddin 81)
'Gah!' scoffs Andy Buckley as Hussey pushes a single out to the off side. 'An extremely unlucky England attack against an under-fire Aussie batsman, who then goes on to make a century in the First Test? I'm horribly reminded of Mark Taylor in the late '90s. Still, the team that won that match lost the series. That counts for something, right?'

118th over: Australia 340–5 (Hussey 125, Haddin 89)
Anderson tries a yorker but gets it all wrong. Two runs to fine leg it is. This stand is exposing a lot of those latent concerns about England's attack. Are four bowlers enough? And what will they do if Swann can't tie up his end? The answer to that second one seems to be this: suffer. Haddin hammers four through long-

on, then forces two more out to midwicket. Anderson looks spent, deflated by his lack of luck in the morning session.

119th over: Australia 341–5 (Hussey 126, Haddin 89)
Hussey glances a single away to leg. Swann musters a desultory lbw appeal at the end of the over as Haddin pads away an off-break, but there's no conviction in it. Umpire Doctrove dismisses it with a quick shake of the head.

120th over: Australia 351–5 (Hussey 136, Haddin 89)
Anderson is being taken apart by Hussey here. He threads three glorious drives through the covers, the first off the back foot and the second two off the front. Four, four and two make it ten from the over.

121st over: Australia 357–5 (Hussey 137, Haddin 94)
Haddin drops to one knee and drags a delivery from outside off and away through midwicket for four with a slog-sweep. Swann is all over the place. He suffered terribly with nerves during the first Ashes Test in 2009. Surely the cocksure little so-and-so isn't suffering a similar bout of the heebie-jeebies on his first Test Down Under?

122nd over: Australia 357–5 (Hussey 137, Haddin 94) 'Is there anything better than lying on the beach listening to the Ashes?' asks Jon Nolan. 'It's a scorcher on Bondi Beach today.' Hussey swings and misses with a cut shot, then realises that is exactly what England want him to do and decides to watch the rest of the over sail harmlessly by.

123rd over: Australia 364–5 (Hussey 137, Haddin 100)
There's Haddin's hundred, raised with a lofted on-drive for six. That's a hell of an innings by him. He's outplayed Hussey today. 'At what point in the current proceedings does it cease to become cowardly to pray for rain?' asks Grant Cartledge.

124th over: Australia 370–5 (Hussey 142, Haddin 102)
Unless you've got a really strong masochistic streak I'd suggest

this is a good time to go to bed. Hussey has just slaughtered a short ball from Finn, walloping a pull through midwicket for four.

125th over: Australia 376–5 (Hussey 143, Haddin 107)
Haddin carts a half-volley from Swann back past the bowler's head for four. Botham has started talking about 'the third new ball'. Man, that makes me nostalgic for Ashes series of the past. 'Yeah, the third new ball. That's what we need. That's what will turn this match around for us.'

126th over: Australia 380–5 (Hussey 143, Haddin 111)
Haddin cuts four more through second slip, prompting more moaning from old Iron Bottom.

127th over: Australia 384–5 (Hussey 147, Haddin 111)
'Catch it' shouts Swann as the ball whistles away to the pickets. Maybe he was talking to the punter in the front row at long-off.

128th over: Australia 385–5 (Hussey 147, Haddin 111)
Another 20 runs and these two will have outscored the entire England team. Paul Bourdin says he is 'Sitting here in the bar of a dive resort in the Philippines. I'd chosen this spot for the family weekend away as I knew they had a big-screen TV, and the place is owned by an Aussie, so I assumed, you know, that there might be a chance of seeing some of the Ashes. They've got Crawley v. Swindon Town on.'

129th over: Australia 388–5 (Hussey 149, Haddin 113) In desperation rather than expectation, Strauss brings Collingwood into the attack. 'Bor-ing, bor-ing, bor-ing' comes the cry from the crowd. Ingrates. 'I remember when the Barmy Army used to entertain with amusing and well-thought-out singing,' reminisces Moz. I think he's being a little too generous in his recollections, but still. 'Now it's just "Barmy Army . . . Barmy Army . . . Barmy Army . . ." all bloody day long.'

130th over: Australia 389–5 (Hussey 149, Haddin 114)
Have you seen hope lately? She's not been around our way for a

while. Stuart Broad is back into the attack. There's hope! There she is! Just coming over the horizon! Oh no. It's a mirage. That's a drop. A bad one. Haddin hoicks a pull out to midwicket. James Anderson is underneath it, running backwards, but he makes a terrible mess of it and the ball drops to the turf. Strauss buries his head in his hands and Broad turns crimson.

131st over: Australia 391–5 (Hussey 150, Haddin 115) 'In the drinks break, did anyone ask for hemlock?' asks Gary Naylor. Funny you should ask. Smyth has just gone over the road to see if they sell it at the BP garage. As I type this he will be having a conversation through the security window with the guy at the check-out. 'All right, mate, two packets of Skittles, a bag of Flamin' Hot and, oh yes, do you have any hemlock?' Hussey hits a single straight through midwicket and gets a raucous cheer in recognition of his 150.

132nd over: Australia 396–5 (Hussey 155, Haddin 116) Broad continues from around the wicket. Rob has just got back from the garage. Either he's made some bold decisions about taking a new direction in aftershave or he's been tucking into an illicit bag of Flamin' Hot.

133rd over: Australia 409–5 (Hussey 156, Haddin 127) All England's moaning has finally paid off – the umpires are changing the ball. Much good it has done too – Haddin thrashes four through long-on, crashes four through cover, and then steers three to fine leg.

134th over: Australia 410–5 (Hussey 157, Haddin 127) What does a man have to do? Broad has just delivered an absolute snorter. Of course, Hussey got nowhere near it. His average against England in Australia is now up to 122 in seven innings. He cuts a single away square past cover.

135th over: Australia 421–5 (Hussey 164, Haddin 131) Anderson is back into the attack. Hussey flicks his first ball fine for four, and pushes his next out to midwicket for three. Haddin then plays an immaculate Chinese cut down to fine leg for four. Anderson grins. There's not much else he can do at that point. These two have put on 278 now, the highest partnership in the history of Test cricket at the Gabba.

136th over: Australia 421–5 (Hussey 164, Haddin 131)
Hussey plays out a maiden from Broad, who is bowling with a lot of heart right now.

137th over: Australia 424–5 (Hussey 164, Haddin 131)
'Ah! What sweet nostalgia,' sighs Kevin McMahon, 'reading the pessimism and the abandonment of all hope. Just like the last time, and the time before that.'

138th over: Australia 430–5 (Hussey 171, Haddin 133)
Ten minutes till tea. Goodness knows what kind of mood England will be in in the dressing room. Hussey drives four more through the covers. It's another fantastic shot.

139th over: Australia 431–5 (Hussey 172, Haddin 133) In my last three sessions of Ashes cricket I've reported on a single wicket.

140th over: Australia 436–5 (Hussey 174, Haddin 134)
Swann will get a single over before the break. Crikey, he must be sick of the sight of these two. He is going to bowl over the wicket to Hussey, and then around the wicket to Haddin. It makes no difference. And here, at last, is tea.

Australia 436–5; England 260

The evening session

BY ROB SMYTH

Preamble: 'Is this the greatest-ever partnership btwn 2 Hs?' asks Ian Kennedy, who did so well by typing full words only to realise towards the end of the marathon that he didn't have the strength to type three more Es. Anyway, yup it is: the next best is 264 between Len Hutton and Wally Hammond at the Oval in 1939. Did I have to look that up? A gentleman never tells.

141st over: Australia 437–5 (Hussey 177, Haddin 134)
When you get to do something you love – behave – you just want to keep on doing it. And we all know what Mr Cricket loves. He is within six of his Test-best score. Here comes Steven Finn, and Hussey taps him into the leg side to move to 177.

142nd over: Australia 440–5 (Hussey 179, Haddin 135)
Swann is bowling around the wicket to Haddin, but he isn't doing much more than going through the motions.

143rd over: Australia 446–5 (Hussey 184, Haddin 135)
Hussey survives a very big appeal for caught behind off Finn. He went for the pull but missed it and the ball flew through to Prior. There was a noise and a deviation, but that was ball on trousers rather than bat. Yet another excellent decision from Aleem Dar. Hussey then tucks Finn to fine leg for four; that brings up the 300 partnership and also takes him past his highest Test score. What a wonderful performance.

144th over: Australia 448–5 (Hussey 185, Haddin 136)
Strauss and Haddin are exchanging a few words out in the middle. Strauss has seemed a bit grumpier than usual in this game. 'We were always going to lose at the Gabba,' says Nick

Stone. 'Better to get record-breaking partnerships and hat-tricks by the opposition in this game. They've been wasted!'

145th over: Australia 449–5 (Hussey 186, Haddin 136) Finn has decided to pepper Haddin with short stuff. One run from the over, and just 13 in five overs since tea.

WICKET! 146th over: Haddin c Collingwood b Swann 136 (Australia 450–6) I've seen it all now. England have taken a wicket. Haddin pushed forward at a decent delivery from Swann, bowled from around the wicket, and when it flew off the edge to the right of slip Collingwood took a fantastic low catch. That's the end of the innings of Brad Haddin's life – 136 from 287 balls – and an extraordinary partnership of 307.

146th over: Australia 450–6 (Hussey 187, Johnson 0) Be careful what you wish for: that wicket has brought the slugger to the crease. England could be entering a whole new world of pain.

147th over: Australia 451–6 (Hussey 188, Johnson 0) Australia are still in no hurry. Johnson is having a few sighters, playing himself in carefully before he flogs 664646204661636, so there's just one from Finn's over.

148th over: Australia 452–6 (Hussey 189, Johnson 0) Hussey drives Swann for a single. That makes it 66 from 101 balls off Swann, which is outstanding. Johnson blocks the rest of the over. Sixteen from eight overs since tea. That's far too slow, although it almost certainly won't matter. 'See, I am not drunk,' says Som Bandyopadhyay. 'I can't be. I am sitting in my office and the clock shows it is 10.56 a.m. I hope my friend Jon Walgate is reading this. He belongs to those famous Walgates who once fielded 11 Walgates in a cricket match. That's on record on Cricinfo!'

WICKET! 149th over: Hussey c Cook b Finn 195 (Australia 458–7) Hussey is out at last. Having pulled Finn for four earlier in the over, he went for the shot again but holed out to

Cook at deep midwicket. In a way that's a fitting end, because the pull stroke defined his innings. He walks off to a standing ovation, and you can pretty much choose any praise you like for that performance. It was immense.

149th over: Australia 458–7 (Johnson 0, Doherty 0) 'I went to the cinema back at over 112 (I live in Toronto), confident that when I returned, England would be batting,' says Marcia Adair. 'Instead, I find the boys mired in the quicksand of failure, the sinking lead weight of which is now resident in the pit of my stomach.' You could have gone to watch *Das Boot* on loop and you still wouldn't have returned to England batting.

150th over: Australia 461–7 (Johnson 0, Doherty 3) Xavier Doherty is very lucky to avoid a golden duck on debut. He got his bat stuck as he played around a straight one from Swann, but Billy Doctrove rejected England's massive lbw appeal. Later in the over he gets three to get off the mark. The camera cuts to his dad in the crowd, sporting a huge grin and proudly giving the thumbs up.

151st over: Australia 462–7 (Johnson 0, Doherty 4) The Barmy Army are singing, 'Swann, Swann will tear you apart, again.' He has figures of two for 122. Johnson, meanwhile, has 0 from 15 balls. Weird.

152nd over: Australia 462–7 (Johnson 0, Doherty 4) A maiden from Swann to Doherty. Australia are still in no hurry. Sometimes the box seat is so comfortable that you can't help but doze off. 'I just got in from a night out and I honestly don't know which is worse: over-by-over or the kebab I'm eating whilst reading it,' says Rachel Fort. 'I'm thinking the cricket, no matter how bad I'll feel in a few hours.'

WICKET! 153rd over: Johnson b Finn 0 (Australia 462–8) Mitchell Johnson's bizarrely passive innings ends when he is bowled off the pads by Steven Finn, who is now one away from

a five-for on his Ashes debut. Johnson made 0 from 19 balls, and
that means the rest of Australia's team have scored 110 for six.
Apart from a hat-trick and a Gabba-record partnership, what exactly have these clowns achieved in this game?

153rd over: Australia 467–8 (Doherty 8, Siddle 1) Siddle
works Finn just in the air but past Cook at short leg. Doherty
then steers Finn smartly to third man for his first boundary.
'Hoping you can clarify something for a newbie to the game,' says
Craig Anderson. 'What are the numbers on the left breast of the
England players? It seems to me each player has a different number.' It's basically what number Test player they are for England.
So Andrew Strauss is the 624th man to play Test cricket for England, and so on.

154th over: Australia 468–8 (Doherty 8, Siddle 2) 'Admittedly it is easier to retain one's optimism on a pleasant late au-
tumn day in Japan than a bleak cold November night in the UK,
but England can save this,' says Robert Elsam. 'We are not looking at facing an attack of Warne and McGrath, but a debut spinner with a first-class average of 48, Johnson, who often finds it a
challenge to hit the cut strip, Hilfenhaus, a far from devastating
prospect, and the admittedly in-form Siddle.'

**WICKET! 155th over: Siddle c Swann b Finn 6 (Australia
472–9)** Steven Finn takes a five-for in his first Ashes Test. He dug
in a bouncer from wide on the crease; Siddle was far too early
on the hook shot and the ball looped off the glove to Swann,
running round from second slip.

155th over: Australia 472–9 (Doherty 8, Hilfenhaus 0)
After a quick fiddle with Statsguru, I'm pretty sure Finn is the
youngest Englishman to take an Ashes five-for since Jack Craw-
ford in 1908. Even if a five-for flatters him a touch, that's a seriously impressive achievement. It's also his third five-for in his
fledgling nine-Test career.

156th over: Australia 475–9 (Doherty 11, Hilfenhaus 0)
'I was weak last night, and went to bed before play started – to be fair I am two hours ahead of the U.K. so no 11.30 p.m. start for me,' says Nicola Kelly in Istanbul. 'However, that meant getting up early this morning to catch the end of the day's play. So my score is now 53 for three. Does this mean I'm not allowed to sleep for the rest of the Aussie-batting Ashes?' It's far too late for superstitions.

157th over: Australia 479–9 (Doherty 15, Hilfenhaus 0)
A preposterous appeal from England for caught behind after Doherty misses – by some distance – an attempted uppercut at Finn. Doherty then whaps a cut through the covers for four.

158th over: Australia 481–9 (Doherty 16, Hilfenhaus 1)
Hilfenhaus slog-sweeps Swann a fraction short of Anderson, diving forward at deep midwicket.

WICKET! 159th over: Doherty c Cook b Finn 16 (Australia 481 all out) Doherty hooks Finn straight to deep midwicket, where Cook takes a good tumbling catch and then runs straight off the field. His real work is about to begin. Steven Finn leads England off after taking career-best figures of six for 125, and Australia lead by 221. England have just under an hour's play to negotiate. I am going to hand over to Andy for the England innings, as my head is a bit heavy and I need to reset the caffeine drip.

England second innings

BY ANDY BULL

1st over: England 1–0 (Strauss 1, Cook 0) Hilfenhaus paces out his run. Strauss is on strike, on a pair, and oh my word that's close. So close Australia have referred it! Strauss shouldered arms to a ball that pitched in line and swung back in, hitting him on the knee flush in front of off stump. Strauss's heart almost burst up his throat and out of his mouth. Aleem Dar shook his head, but Ponting reckoned it was worth a punt. The replays show the ball was just, just passing over the top of the wicket. What a start. He knocks the third ball away to leg to get off his pair.

2nd over: England 3–0 (Strauss 2, Cook 1) Siddle will start at the Vulture Street end. Vicious Sid's first two balls sail by off stump, and Strauss eases his third away square for another single. Later in the over Cook gets off the mark as well, also with a flick to leg.

3rd over: England 3–0 (Strauss 2, Cook 1) 'My stomach has contracted and relaxed so many times today that I should have a six-pack by the end of the Test,' says Celes, '(not to mention buns of steel, but maybe don't dwell on that image).' Right, yeah, a lifetime spent on the sofa watching cricket really can do wonders for a man's physique. A maiden over from Hilfenhaus.

4th over: England 8–0 (Strauss 6, Cook 1) A lovely shot from Strauss. He pats a no-ball back down the ground, and times it so well that he gets four through long-off.

5th over: England 9–0 (Strauss 6, Cook 2) Cook pushes a single out to mid-off. Hilfenhaus's next five balls all hug off stump.

6th over: England 9–0 (Strauss 6, Cook 2) Cook plays out a maiden from Siddle. 'This game actually reminds me quite a bit of the Melbourne Test I went to on the last Ashes tour,' says Jake Groves. 'England won the toss and batted and made a below-par total. Australia slumped to 80-odd for five. But Symonds and Hayden then proceeded to put on about 300 together and England lost by an innings inside three days. What a great way to spend Christmas that was.'

7th over: England 13–0 (Strauss 10, Cook 2) Strauss swings a pull shot at a straight delivery from Hilfenhaus and chops the ball into his own hip and away for four through third man.

8th over: England 13–0 (Strauss 10, Cook 2) Siddle comes around the wicket to Cook. He steers the ball away to point, and turns his head just in time to see Mike Hussey dive down to the turf and cut the ball off. That was a fine piece of fielding.

9th over: England 13–0 (Strauss 10, Cook 2) Most of the pitch is in shadow now. The day's play is coming to a close. Strauss plays out another maiden.

10th over: England 17–0 (Strauss 10, Cook 6) Intriguing. Ponting has brought Marcus North on as first change, the idea being that he will turn the ball away from the outside edges of the two left-handers. And they say Ponting is an unimaginative captain. Nice theory. Shame about the practice. North's first ball is dismissed for four through point by Cook.

11th over: England 18–0 (Strauss 10, Cook 6) Just a solitary leg bye from this over. I'd say more but truth is my brain's not working too well at this point in the proceedings.

12th over: England 19–0 (Strauss 11, Cook 6) North continues. Very strange piece of captaincy this. Who do you think Strauss would rather be facing at this point? North, the club off-spinner, or Johnson, the 90 mph quick with a knack for delivering occasionally unplayable deliveries? A single from the over.

13th over: England 19–0 (Strauss 11, Cook 6) No sooner said than . . . Johnson comes into the attack with ten minutes of the day left. 'North at first change? More idiotic captaincy by Ponting,' grumbles David Siddall. It's a scrappy first over from Johnson, though in typical style he follows five filthy short and wide deliveries with an awkward full, straight ball that Strauss does well to drop his bat on.

14th over: England 19–0 (Strauss 11, Cook 6) North takes a spell on the sidelines, and Xavier Doherty will get a turn. A maiden.

15th over: England 19–0 (Strauss 11, Cook 6) This should be the last over. By the time it's over Johnson is finally starting to find the right line and Strauss is forced to play at his two final deliveries, whereas most of the rest had whizzed untouched past his stumps. Ponting brings in the field for the final ball, just to distract Strauss as much as anything else. He'll need to do better than that. Strauss blocks the last ball, and England have reached the safety of stumps.

England 260 and 19–0; Australia 481

Fourth day

The morning session

BY ANDY BULL

Preamble: This is going to be the most revealing day of the series so far. We're going to learn a lot about the two teams and their respective strengths. Is the Australian attack good enough to force through their advantage? Do England have the strength of will they need to resist? Andy Flower is out on the ground after missing three days of play while he had a cancerous lump removed from his cheek.

16th over: England 20–0 (Strauss 11, Cook 7) Andrew Jolly is at the Gabba. And he still wants sympathy: 'At the Gabba after about three hours' sleep. What kind of special madness has driven me to sit in the sun in a concrete bowl whilst watching my team be punished horribly? Urgh.' First run of the day is scored by Cook. Siddle shaves splinters from Strauss's outside edge with a pair of perfect deliveries that slide across the face of the bat.

17th over: England 21–0 (Strauss 11, Cook 8) Hilfenhaus starts at the other end, and there's a lovely ball, sliding across the face of Strauss's bat.

18th over: England 28–0 (Strauss 11, Cook 14) Siddle comes around the wicket to Cook. He tries to slap away a loose drive, but the ball screws off the outside edge and away through third man. It draws 'ohhh's and 'ahhh's from the Australians. 'Today was my wife's due date for our third child and no sign of the arrival any time soon,' writes Ben Powell. 'So I'm taking the chance to watch the cricket while I can. When it does arrive, do you think I should suggest that night feeds are by bottle and could be done by me in front of the TV?'

19th over: England 31–0 (Strauss 13, Cook 16) Cook picks off a leg glance. Again it was the kind of shot that makes you sweat to watch. Cook has been positive so far this morning. Later in the over Strauss knocks a couple out to the deep. Doherty fields, and his throw is rewarded with a patronising cry of 'Good boy, Doughy' from Haddin.

20th over: England 39–0 (Strauss 14, Cook 21) Shot, sir! Cook cuts four runs through cover, the crack of bat and ball ringing out around the ground. There are quite a few empty seats at the Gabba this morning. Warne reckons the locals will filter in after lunch once they've shrugged off their hangovers.

21st over: England 41–0 (Strauss 15, Cook 23) Whisper it: England are on top of the bowlers.

22nd over: England 45–0 (Strauss 19, Cook 23) Shane Watson comes on as first change for the day. Ponting snubbed Johnson for North last night, and has done so again for Watson today. He doesn't seem to have much faith in the man. Strauss leaves his first three balls alone, watching them whizz by his off stump. By the fourth he has had enough of letting them go by and swings a vicious cut, cracking the ball past point for four.

23rd over: England 47–0 (Strauss 20, Cook 24) I'm running behind myself. Sara Torvalds can have this over: 'I feel calm and full of trust as I watch Cook and Straussy. I didn't know that was even a theoretical option during an Ashes Down Under.'

24th over: England 48–0 (Strauss 21, Cook 24) Strauss clumps a drive to cover.

25th over: England 54–0 (Strauss 27, Cook 24) Hilfenhaus is coming around the wicket to Strauss now, with a man in at silly mid-on. The last ball of the over is dispatched to the cover boundary with ease and even a little contempt.

26th over: England 58–0 (Strauss 27, Cook 28) The first cries of 'Four more to the En-ger-land, four more to the En-ger-land' accompany a cut shot for four from Cook.

27th over: England 61–0 (Strauss 29, Cook 29) Mitchell Johnson gets his first bowl of the day. He starts with a bouncer, which Strauss sways away from. This is the 16th fifty partnership Cook and Strauss have put on together. Surprisingly enough, they are the most prolific partnership England have ever had, and the ninth-most prolific in the history of Test cricket.

28th over: England 70–0 (Strauss 37, Cook 29) 'I've just enjoyed a rather overpoured dose of grappa in the local Italian,' says Stuart Bulloch. 'Is there a more potent drink than grappa for throwing you south pillowards?' Well, until recently I would have put the home-brewed basil liqueur I was plied with in a restaurant in the Apennines quite high up the list. But since then I've been to Tokyo and tried Denki Bran Fix. Anyway. Strauss is playing wonderfully well. He has just uppercut four over cover, and followed it up with a firm drive for another boundary down the ground.

29th over: England 74–0 (Strauss 37, Cook 32) Cook leans back and larrups a pull away to midwicket and scurries two runs, then comes onto the front foot to glance a single away square.

30th over: England 78–0 (Strauss 42, Cook 32) Watson is bowling to a seven–two field, which is enough to make Botham furious. 'There is a crazy old Japanese lady who lives at the bottom of my garden in a granny flat,' says Toby Ebbs, sounding more than a little frantic about it. 'She texted me today asking: "Have you got balls?" What does she mean?' She means, 'Be scared. Be very scared.'

31st over: England 81–0 (Strauss 43, Cook 34) 'Strauss & Cook's prolific production – in a way, ninth in runs scored is not such a good return, given that they have had the fifth most innings as an opening partnership,' points out Matthew Harries. 'Amazing that they've batted together so often – testament to the England selectors' admirable new belief in stability.' Strauss and Cook swap singles.

32nd over: England 83–0 (Strauss 44, Cook 35) Doherty comes on for a fiddle. England really let him get away with far too much in the first innings. It will be interesting to see how they play him now. Cook steps out to his first ball and pushes a single to mid-on. Strauss also takes a single. Australia appeal for a catch down the leg side, trying to burgle Cook of his wicket. Problem was he didn't touch the ball. Johnson stops and shoots the batsman a mean glare, but his ludicrous moustache means he looks less menacing than the policeman from the Village People.

33rd over: England 92–0 (Strauss 50, Cook 38) Strauss forces four through long-off with a clipped drive, and then drops to one knee to sweep a single fine. That raises his 22nd Test fifty, but he hardly stops to celebrate. Cook lofts a risky slog sweep away to leg, and for a moment it looks as though he might be caught out. But the fielders can't quite get there and the ball lands safely.

34th over: England 96–0 (Strauss 53, Cook 39) 'Johnson's action must be deteriorating over time,' suggests Richard Marsden. 'Come the 2013 Ashes he'll be slithering up to the crease on his belly and flipping it down the other end like an epi-leptic salmon.' Strauss leans back and forces a drive away through extra cover. 'Yeah, come on,' he cries to Cook as the ball races away past the fielder. They run three.

35th over: England 104–0 (Strauss 61, Cook 39) Ponting decides to bring Peter Siddle back into the attack. And Strauss welcomes him to the wicket with a sweet drive through extra cover that brings up the 100 partnership. Smyth is on top form today. He's just pointed out that this is England's first 100-run partnership for the first wicket in Australia since Atherton and Gooch did it in January 1991.

36th over: England 108–0 (Strauss 62, Cook 42) Johnson decides to come around the wicket to Cook, which is interesting. Otherwise his only tactic has been to bang it in short, which is clearly not the way to bowl on this pitch.

37th over: England 116–0 (Strauss 69, Cook 43) That's just a glorious shot from Strauss. He caresses the ball away for four through extra cover as Siddle offers him just a little too much width. 'Pls advise Ben Powell that the deal with night feeds is to put up with it for one month,' suggests Pete Gay. 'After one month, feed the little bleeder at midnight with milk and give it water at 4 a.m. He will have three nights of screaming and then the kid will realise it's not worth making a fuss about and sleep through the night. Worked for us – the child we ran this exercise on now runs a very tasty pub just off Bond Street.'

38th over: England 120–0 (Strauss 70, Cook 46) Johnson is taken off and Doherty comes back on, and that's a drop! Johnson has spilled a simple catch at mid-off, reaching up above his head with both hands. He was just snoozing after finishing his spell. Strauss had hit the ball straight to him. We just had a lovely piece of commentary from Goldenhair Gower: 'So far so good then for Englan . . . aaaarrrrrgggghhhh!' His words choked off in a scream. Apparently Nasser put a chair on his foot.

39th over: England 126–0 (Strauss 73, Cook 49) So Strauss bats on, pulling two runs around the corner. Thomas Jenkins's verdict on that Gower moment: 'Vindication. Three and a half days of Sky coverage instantly made worthwhile.'

41st over: England 126–0 (Strauss 73, Cook 49) Doherty races through another over. The wonders of the internet. Less than ten minutes after it happened, that Gower incident is now up on YouTube.

42nd over: England 127–0 (Strauss 74, Cook 49) 'Rather amusingly,' chortles Ben Hendy, 'some poor lass in America has the twitter name @theashes and is getting rather annoyed by the amount of people using her name in reference to the cricket.' Yes, Douglas Green was telling me about her earlier on: '@theashes : I AM NOT A FREAKING CRICKET MATCH!!! That means you @matywilson @zandertrego @thesummats @ atonyboffey and MORE.'

43rd over: England 130–0 (Strauss 77, Cook 49) We're coasting in towards lunch now. What a wonderful session it has been for England.

44th over: England 131–0 (Strauss 78, Cook 49) Marcus North will just get a little spell before the break. Cook has been on 49 for ten balls now, searching for the single that will bring him his second half-century of the match.

45th over: England 134–0 (Strauss 78, Cook 51) And there is Cook's fifty, at last. He has played wonderfully well in this match. At the same time, as Rob says, it is difficult to remember a single shot he has played. He's just been very patient and unobtrusive.

46th over: England 135–0 (Strauss 79, Cook 51) One more over from North then, Strauss taking just a single off it. 'Woah woah woah!' shouts Lorna Batty. 'Sky commentators just said that Anderson is buggering off home at some point in the tour to be with his wife for the birth of his child. Is this true?' It is indeed, Lorna. He's going to pop back in the break between the second and third Tests. 'What the hell was he doing having sex nine months prior to an Ashes series, with all the "happy" consequences this could bring? Totally unprofessional in my book.'

England 260 and 135–0; Australia 481

The afternoon session

BY ROB SMYTH

Preamble: With the possible exception of David Gower, that was such a good session for every cricket-loving Englishman. But of the ten sessions so far in this match, five have been OBOed by Bull and five by Smyth. The wicket count? Smyth 17–3 Bull. For those who are intractable in their belief that sporting events are frequently determined by the arbitrary selection of text commentators thousands of miles away, it's a bitter blow.

47th over: England 136–0 (Strauss 80, Cook 51) Xavier Doherty will start after lunch. He has a short leg and a slip, and Strauss walks down the track to work the fifth ball to leg and move into the 80s. He once made 177 when he was on a pair (and, indeed, the end of his England career). Just saying.

48th over: England 140–0 (Strauss 84, Cook 51) Strauss plays yet another sumptuous extra-cover drive, this time off Hilfenhaus. It split the field perfectly and raced away for four. He hasn't made a century since Lord's 2009, 14 Tests ago, and he may not have batted as well since then either.

49th over: England 145–0 (Strauss 88, Cook 52) Strauss charges down the track to clout Doherty back over his head for four. Beautiful shot. 'Any chance of inducing Cook and Strauss to take over from Osborne and Alexander at the Treasury?' says Gary Naylor. 'They seem to be rather good at painlessly reducing deficits (though equally keen on cuts).'

50th over: England 146–0 (Strauss 88, Cook 53) There isn't much going on for Australia. Hilfenhaus is accurate, but Cook defends carefully.

51st over: England 148–0 (Strauss 88, Cook 55) Docherty grrrrs in frustration as Cook squeezes a couple wide of slip. He has been pretty accurate, but there doesn't seem to be too much from him for England to worry about at this juncture.

52nd over: England 156–0 (Strauss 96, Cook 55) A very streaky shot from Strauss, who tries to whap Hilfenhaus to leg and top-edges it over point. The two runs he gets as a consequence move him into the 90s and England into the 150s. To compound Hilfenhaus's agitation, Strauss edges low through the slips for four. That was an excellent over from Hilfenhaus, yet it costs him eight.

53rd over: England 157–0 (Strauss 96, Cook 56) Doherty has a huge lbw shout against Strauss with a quicker, very full delivery. It looked close, but Aleem Dar said not out. Ricky Ponting thought about a review for a long time, but he only has one left and decided against it. Replays showed Strauss was outside the line.

54th over: England 160–0 (Strauss 96, Cook 59) Cook cuts Hilfenhaus very nicely for three. They are close to overtaking Slater and Taylor on the Test partnerships list.

55th over: England 165–0 (Strauss 100, Cook 60) Andrew Strauss has made his first Test century in Australia! There's just a little tingle down the spine, because this has been a marvellous performance. He back-cut Doherty for four and then punched the air with real feeling. 'OK – clearly I am drunk now but can I just say how much I love Strauss?' says Rachel Clifton.

56th over: England 171–0 (Strauss 101, Cook 65) Cook rifles Hilfenhaus through extra cover for four. It was in the air for a while but right off the middle and nowhere near any of the fielders. England trail by just 50 now. There have been so many momentum shifts in this fantastic Test, and there will be a few more.

57th over: England 171–0 (Strauss 101, Cook 65) A maiden from Doherty to Strauss.

58th over: England 173–0 (Strauss 101, Cook 67) Australia look very flat, wondering where the next false stroke is coming from, never mind the next wicket. Welcome to our world.

59th over: England 174–0 (Strauss 102, Cook 67) Marcus North has replaced Xavier Doherty, and Strauss sweeps a single in another quiet over. 'My good lady wife is away on business, my fridge is well stocked with beer and snacks, and England are batting superbly, so I'm all set up for a great afternoon's viewing,' says Neill Brown. 'Why can't I enjoy this? Honestly, every delivery that passes is like watching the Russian roulette scene in *The Deer Hunter*.'

60th over: England 175–0 (Strauss 103, Cook 71) Nothing is really happening. 'Can I just second Rachel Clifton, on both fronts?' says Richard Marsden. 'Yes, it may be late; yes, I may be drunk; yes, there may be security measures; but right now I'd happily dig straight through the planet to emerge in Brisbane and give that England captain a big wet dose of man love, straight from my glistening cricket glands.'

61st over: England 182–0 (Strauss 106, Cook 71) The best thing about this partnership is how eminently mature and sensible it has been. If you took this partnership home to meet your folks, they'd be imploring you to get hitched to it as soon as possible. 'Yet Another Emaul About Strauss,' says Chris Milner, who may or may not have been down the Slug & Manic Depression quaffing pints of Temporary Happiness Facilitator. 'Just got back to the flat from a night out, when I contrived not to pull, which only adds to the anguish of being dumped two weeks ago by text. But Strauss just hit three figures, so it's fine.'

62nd over: England 183–0 (Strauss 107, Cook 71) Siddle replaces Hilfenhaus, who got no reward for some hard yakka after lunch.

63rd over: England 183–0 (Strauss 107, Cook 71) A maiden from North to Strauss. Australia are sitting on the game, and England are rightly in no hurry. 'It's my 28th (I think) wedding anniversary today,' says Pete Gay. 'Do you think it's right that I am up at 3 a.m. reading the OBO? What would Mariella Frostrup make of that?'

64th over: England 185–0 (Strauss 108, Cook 72) Siddle tries a slower ball. Strauss defends. Then he carts a wide full toss to deep point for a single. That's drinks. 'Just woken up,' says Alex Netherton. 'Bloody hell.'

65th over: England 186–0 (Strauss 109, Cook 72) Cook, pushing forward at North, edges just short of the diving Clarke at slip.

66th over: England 188–0 (Strauss 110, Cook 72) 'Morning,' says George Winder. 'I'm currently in Pucon, Chile. Nice town. Cheap wine and steak. I should be sleeping as I'm climbing up a nearby active volcano in a few hours. Instead I'm hitting "refresh" a lot and hoping not to wake my girlfriend, who is quietly snoring next to me. Should the inevitable collapse happen, I am concerned I may well not be able to resist sacrificing myself in the lava.'

WICKET! 67th over: Strauss st Haddin b North 110

(England 188–1) Ricky Ponting's apparently inexplicable faith in Marcus North is rewarded with a huge wicket. Strauss came flying down the wicket, but North bowled it a lot wider and the ball turned past the outside edge for Brad Haddin to complete the stumping. Strauss walks off slowly, knowing the job is not done yet. But by heaven he played well, and he leaves England just 33 runs adrift.

67th over: England 189–1 (Cook 72, Trott 1) Strauss actually hesitated for a split second before desperately shoving his bat back into the crease. Had he not done so, he might just have survived. Anyway.

68th over: England 195–1 (Cook 72, Trott 6) Siddle digs one into the ribs of Trott, who tickles it in the air and not too far wide of Haddin on its way to the fence. 'Just think,' challenges Alex Netherton. 'There are thousands of socially awkward male cricket fans operating on about four hours of sleep a night for the next two months. Women who are prepared to talk to people like us, watch out. LOL?!' They'd be laughing out loud all right.

69th over: England 195–1 (Cook 72, Trott 6) Absolutely nothing of note happens, with Trott playing out a maiden from North. That's a waste of an over for Australia really, giving Trott six free balls of the 30 or so he needs to get his eye in.

70th over: England 198–1 (Cook 74, Trott 7) Now Mitchell Johnson comes into the attack, replacing Siddle. Cook steals a sharp single to mid-off, with Siddle growling after the ball and then missing with a shy at the stumps. Cook was home anyway. Johnson's first over doesn't really have much going for it, and England's deficit is down to 23.

71st over: England 203–1 (Cook 78, Trott 7) North continues, a ridiculous tactic that will doubtless be vindicated with a triple hat-trick now that I've typed that. England milk him for five runs, in ones and twos.

72nd over: England 210–1 (Cook 79, Trott 14) A couple of very close shaves for Trott in that Johnson over. First he was beaten by a jaffa, full and zipping off a crack past the outside edge as Trott went for an expansive drive. Then he chopped a wide delivery just past the left hand of the leaping Clarke at backward point and away for four.

73rd over: England 214–1 (Cook 83, Trott 14) Cook cuts North for a couple and then sweeps fine for two more. He really deserves a century here. Meanwhile, a lesson in the value of punctuation comes to you from Simon Pettigrew. 'Strauss has been out 136 times in Test matches,' says Simon, 'and that is the first time he has been out stumped interestingly.'

74th over: England 225–1 (Cook 86, Trott 22) England go into the lead during a very expensive over from Johnson that costs 11. Trott drove three, Cook cut three, and then Trott feathered a delightful boundary through extra cover.

75th over: England 230–1 (Cook 90, Trott 23) Xavier Doherty replaces Marcus North, and Cook cuts him for four to move into the 90s.

76th over: England 230–1 (Cook 90, Trott 23) A nothing over from Johnson, who looks as lost as his spiritual sibling Steve Harmison did at this ground four years ago.

77th over: England 237–1 (Cook 97, Trott 23) Cook pumps Doherty over midwicket for four. Doherty goes round the wicket as a result and skids a good delivery through the gate as Cook shaped to cut. He gets hold of the shot next ball, which brings three more runs.

78th over: England 238–1 (Cook 98, Trott 23) Another anodyne over from Johnson takes us to tea. That was another fantastic session for England, who have gone a long way to saving this match.

England 260 and 238–1; Australia 481

The evening session

BY ANDY BULL

Preamble: Well, England have played wonderfully well, and Australia have been powerless to counter them. That said, there are two overs to go till the new ball, and England are prone to collapsing. They need to get through this final session before the match is anything like safe yet.

79th over: England 244–1 (Cook 99, Trott 27) Hilfenhaus is marking out his run from the Stanley Street End. Cook pats the first ball of the session to square leg and sprints a single. He's on 99.

80th over: England 248–1 (Cook 103, Trott 27) And Siddle starts at the other end. Cook edges down the wicket looking for a single to bring up his hundred, but retreats back to the crease before he has gone three yards. He gets it with his next ball, though, steering four through third man. He punches the air, then rips off his helmet and grins up at the heavens. Sky flash up a stat on the screen – this is the first time both English openers have scored a century in the same Ashes innings since 1938.

81st over: England 255–1 (Cook 109, Trott 28) So, could this be the next twist in the tale? Australia have taken the new ball. Hilfenhaus banged in a short ball that was too close to pull, but that didn't stop Cook from trying. He screwed the shot high into the air towards fine leg. Siddle ran around the boundary and just got his hands to the ball, but it spilled from his grasp. 'I'm awake,' says Sarah Cox, 'on an archaeological dig on Failaka Island just off the coast of Kuwait and have rattled through my site work this morning so I can get on with some *vital* office work instead, which looks suspiciously like OBO.'

82nd over: England 261–1 (Cook 110, Trott 32) A lovely shot by Trott, who hops across his stumps and bunts the ball away through square leg for four. 'It's been a long night, and I'm down to my last Carlsberg,' says Pete Baxter. 'Torn between moving onto my housemate's vodka or my own port. Does this innings qualify as a special occasion?' Port on top of Carlsberg? That sounds like one of the worst conceivable combinations of intoxicants.

83rd over: England 261–1 (Cook 110, Trott 32) Hilfenhaus fires in an inswinging yorker which slides past both Cook's bat and the stumps. Haddin leaps to his left to make a great take. 'I was under orders from my wife to go to bed hours ago,' says Paul Shields. 'But obviously as I had the fate of England resting on me staying up, I couldn't. I'm wondering whether if I go to bed now for ten minutes and then come back downstairs to resume watching she'll be any wiser. Hopefully she'll recall me coming to bed, but won't know what time that was or how long for. I'm hoping she'll think I just got up early to carry on watching. Any flaws in the plan, anyone?' It's not a bad plan, but if I were you I'd think about rigging up some kind of dummy out of the spare pillows and a mop to leave in bed alongside her when you sneak out. At least that way if she rolls over she'll have something to hug.

84th over: England 261–1 (Cook 110, Trott 32) Trott hammers a straight drive down the wicket, and Siddle leaps across to bat it out of the air with his right hand. Otherwise it is an uneventful over, and another maiden. 'I'm still up,' says Jack

Howden. 'Fourth day in a row. I'd love to write something witty here, but I'm just too tired.' Trust me, the feeling is mutual.

85th over: England 262–1 (Cook 110, Trott 32) Hilfenhaus slings down a wide. This new ball is doing nothing for the bowlers, and Hilfenhaus is already staring at it resentfully.

86th over: England 265–1 (Cook 110, Trott 34) Umpire Doctrove calls wide for a bouncer that flew high over Trott's head. And then . . . another drop. This time Trott was the lucky man. He cut the ball to Michael Clarke at point. Again the chance was a hard one – he had to leap across one-handed to his left – but again, on another day he would have taken it. 'Hello from Buenos Aires,' chirps Guy Mavor. 'Where it's only just 2 a.m. This is usually about my time for a "poke, prod and feeble collapse", but luckily for her my wife is in England, so can I just say hello to her via OBO?'

87th over: England 267–1 (Cook 112, Trott 34) William Kay is another man who is still awake. Only he's in Tijuana, where it is only 9 p.m., so it's not much of a feat. 'The wife has just stepped out to go to a bachelorette party (hen night to you and me) and left me alone with a computer,' he says. 'And here I am, Tecate beer in one hand, taco in the other, and Over by Over on the laptop. Why, what else would I do left alone with a computer and internet access?' Oh I don't know, check up on what's been happening with the FTSE?

88th over: England 267–1 (Cook 112, Trott 34) Mitchell Johnson is on. And so is Sarah Cox (81st over): 'Failaka Island is 20 km off the coast of Kuwait City. Forcibly evacuated during the Gulf War, then used as a military training ground – pretty much abandoned now. I'm assured all the mines have been cleared, which is good news considering why I'm here.' A maiden over from Johnson, economical but utterly unthreatening.

89th over: England 268–1 (Cook 112, Trott 34) Another

no-ball from Australia. They look spent, devoid of inspiration. At the moment Cook and Trott are doing well just to see off the new ball, but you just feel that England could really twist the knife later in this final session by being more attacking.

90th over: England 272–1 (Cook 112, Trott 38) Trott taps two runs away through midwicket off his pads.

91st over: England 277–1 (Cook 112, Trott 42) A four! The first in what feels like a long time. And then – Referral! Trott 42 lbw b Hilfenhaus. Aleem Dar gave it not out with a shake of his head, but Australia are desperate so they ask for the review. A poor decision – the ball was passing by the off stump and the decision stands. Trott bats on and Australia are out of reviews.

92nd over: England 280–1 (Cook 115, Trott 43) The lead is up to 57. 'I'm in Astana in Kazakhstan,' says Steve Larcombe, 'overlooking the frozen river that runs (when it's not frozen) through the centre of the city. The city is going to be closed down from tomorrow because of the large number of politicians flying in for the OSCE summit. The radio is advising people not to go onto their balconies for a smoke or risk being shot by snipers.' Sounds charming, Steve.

93rd over: England 281–1 (Cook 115, Trott 43) This may be the email of the day, from our man in Tijuana, William Kay: 'Ha! Just texted my luvverly wife to tell her that my email was mentioned in OBO. She replied that it was all well and interesting, but if I was going to interrupt her conversation with a locksmith I could at least also tell her if any more wickets had fallen. Don't know whether to be happy that my Mexican wife wants an Ashes update or worried that there is a locksmith at the hen party?' Johnson has now bowled 31 overs in the match and taken no wickets for 114 runs.

94th over: England 284–1 (Cook 116, Trott 43) Another quiet over. At the risk of jinxing this, it may be a good time then to throw in Smyth's latest statistical gem: the last time any Test team reached 300 for the loss of just one wicket against Australia was 1991.

95th over: England 289–1 (Cook 122, Trott 45) Johnson slings down a filthy short ball, Cook disdainfully pulls it away for four. He might as well have cried 'Next!' as he played the shot. Here's Paul Bacon: 'Given what you said in over 89 – "but you just feel that England could really twist the knife later in this final session by being more attacking" – I will hold you personally responsible if we lose.'

96th over: England 290–1 (Cook 122, Trott 45) Shane Watson is coming into the attack. If you need an idea about how shoddy Australia look at the moment, this next email from Greg Wilkinson should tell you all you need to know: 'Ian Healy on Channel 9 is just now starting to bitch and moan about the Aussies. "Siddle . . . flat in the field" . . . "Hilfenhaus a little disappointing" . . . "Strange tactic to give Cook a single." It's music to my ears!' Healy, if you didn't know, is as one-eyed as commentators come. When he turns against the team, then you know Australia are in trouble.

97th over: England 301–1 (Cook 124, Trott 54) Trott gloves four down the leg side, and then raises his fifty with a single to mid-off. 'It is nearly 11 p.m. here in Alberta, outside the temperature is −15°C,' says Matt O'Driscoll. 'It is a 50 km drive along snow-covered tracks to the nearest civilisation. I am doing a night shift on a drilling rig and will still be awake long after play is over for the day. I don't think there is anyone else within several hundred miles who even knows, much less cares, that there is a cricket match taking place.'

98th over: England 302–1 (Cook 125, Trott 54) 302–1? What the hell is going on?

99th over: England 305–1 (Cook 128, Trott 54) Johnson is taken out of the attack and, quite possibly, out of the team too.

100th over: England 305–1 (Cook 128, Trott 54) Ponting brings himself in to field at a very short mid-on to Trott. He stands there chewing gum and scowling as Trott plays out a maiden over.

101st over: England 309–1 (Cook 132, Trott 54) Doherty is into his third over now. His first 17 balls only cost a single run. But Cook takes four from the last of the over. Oh! That's a surprise. The umpires have taken everyone off the field because the light is too poor to play in. As Cook walks off a couple of the Aussies run up to shake his hand. He gets an ovation from the crowd. I imagine that will be the end of play for the day, so Cook has batted right through from start to finish. A wonderful innings from him.

Right. That's stumps. This must rank as one of the finest days of Test cricket in England's recent history. They have been absolutely marvellous. And, after watching them bat all night long, I'm absolutely shattered. So I'm off. I really enjoyed that last session. Australia may yet fight back tomorrow morning – it will be their last chance to force a result. We'll see. Cheerio.

England 260 and 309–1; Australia 481

Odd couple join the greats as they pass Hobbs and Sutcliffe

England's openers may not be an institution but they have carved their names in history

BY DAVID HOPPS IN BRISBANE

MONDAY 29 NOVEMBER 2010

Andrew Strauss's impromptu media acceptance speech on behalf of himself and Alastair Cook on the day that they became the most prolific opening pair in England's Test history was not that of a batsman who imagined that he had suddenly been touched with greatness. And in Australia especially it was all the more impressive for that.

The day when Jack Hobbs and Herbert Sutcliffe are surpassed, for longevity at any rate, is not a day for egotism, it is a day for humility, and Strauss's sense of perspective on one of the finest days of his career provided further proof that English cricket is in good hands.

If Strauss and Cook, with 3,415 runs, now surpass Hobbs and Sutcliffe (3,249), a careless suggestion that they had 'beaten' them brought a snort in the media centre from one of cricket's most eminent historians. Hobbs and Sutcliffe averaged 87 runs per stand, more than double the 42 of Strauss and Cook, but then they should not feel too shaken by that; the record of Hobbs and Sutcliffe dwarfs all-comers.

'People have been talking about this record for about six months, and since then we have been averaging about ten as an opening partnership,' Strauss joked. 'It is good. I suppose those sort of records come because the two of you stay in the side, and you need quite a lot of resilience to be able to do that.'

Hobbs and Sutcliffe were an institution. Hobbs, The Master, was genial and unassuming; Sutcliffe's brilliantined hair came with an equally orderly, flattened-down temperament. They stole singles telepathically. Strauss and Cook are a long way from being an institution, but they, too, have developed a character. Strauss is the more assertive, more eager to carry the fight; Cook is the fighter, a batsman for whom first impressions are entirely misleading. They also stole singles yesterday, although that was primarily because Ricky Ponting allowed them.

Resilience might be Cook's middle name. He was called 'elegant' on Australian radio as he dutifully assembled his first Ashes hundred in Australia, but he was leaning on his bat at the non-striker's end at the time. It probably had a lot to do with his film-star looks. When Cook gets to the business end, the overriding message is not one of elegance but that he is tougher than he looks.

'Cookie is a very resilient character,' Strauss emphasised. 'He is able to do the hard yards, as he has demonstrated in this game.' He could have added that he had argued passionately for Cook's survival when there was pressure to drop him before the final Test at the Oval last summer. His faith has been vindicated.

Cook returned the favour, verbally rotating the strike as the best openers do. 'Straussy set the tone yesterday,' he said. 'We are very similar minded and we suit each other. We don't get too flustered about a lot of things and we keep things in perspective. If someone bowls a really good ball, we laugh it off and move on to the next one.'

Australia know better than any cricketing nation that modern-day achievement must go hand in hand with an awareness of what has gone before. Strauss began his second innings with Australian cricketing historians comparing his batting record in Australia to Mike Brearley's (not necessarily a good thing); he ended it being mentioned in the same breath as Hobbs. That is not a bad day's work.

You always know Australia are dominating an Ashes when Don Bradman gets a mention. 'Best since Bradman' is the invariable cry as another Aussie tyro seeks to make his own dent on cricket history. In Australia even Don Corleone would have to bow the knee to Don Bradman.

English cricket has never quite agreed on its champion; a sense of history is often disappointingly lacking — no surprise considering secondary-school curriculums. But this was a day when Strauss and Cook stood next to not only Hobbs and Sutcliffe but also Len Hutton and Charlie Barnett, the last England openers both to make hundreds in an Ashes Test — at Trent Bridge 72 years ago. If the Gabba was flat, Trent Bridge on that day was reputedly flatter; England declared at 658 for eight.

Hutton was Yorkshire's finest, and a bit of a social climber to boot. Barnett sounds like a bit of a snob. After he retired, one journalist suggested he was running a fish shop. He wrote back indignantly, saying he was not a fishmonger but a purveyor of high-class fish and game to the Duke of Beaufort.

It was accurate to observe this is not a great Australian attack and that the pitch at the Gabba was playing quietly. But it is more accurate simply to reflect that England began their second innings 221 behind, with more than two days remaining; that after only three days their reputation was on the line, and by the end of the day they had responded so magnificently that they had summoned memories of giants from the past. History will tell you that this was one of England's great Ashes days.

So Australia beware. Yesterday, four of England's finest lined up against Bradman. Six, if you include Strauss and Cook. Eight, if you include Michael Atherton and Graham Gooch, who racked up England's last Ashes century opening stand against Australia in Adelaide in 1991. Eight v. Bradman? That'll be right, mate.

Fifth day

The morning session

BY ROB BAGCHI

Preamble: Ay up. How excited are we all this chilly November evening? I'm on tenterhooks here, time-honoured pessimism giving way to a strange sense of pride that started taking hold midway through yesterday's afternoon session. I know we've all been here before with England, but the way both openers and then Jonathan Trott went about their business yesterday made me feel this is a genuinely tough side.

Daddy hundreds: Goochie is being interviewed by Nasser Hussain on Sky and he says he wants a 'daddy hundred' from Alastair Cook. Is this a Keith Fletcher Essexism? It surely sounds like it. Gooch reckons in the best of worlds they'll bat for three hours and take it from there. Sounds like a plan.

102nd over: England 310–1 (Cook 132, Trott 54) Siddle to Cook and he immediately hits Sir Geoff's corridor, and Trott watches them pass, then steers the third ball to gully's feet. Will Sinclair, a Sydneysider, has this to say of the Gabba: 'It occurred to me this morning that the Gabba pitch is a metaphor for Queensland itself. Exciting and interesting for a couple of days – hot, dry and boring thereafter.' Glad you said that, Will, not me.

103rd over: England 310–1 (Cook 132, Trott 54) The

majestic Hilfenhaus resumes and, understandably, looks a bit tired. He sticks to an off-stump line. Maiden. It's pretty empty in the stands out there.

104th over: England 312–1 (Cook 134, Trott 54) Danny Clayton has had ITV4 rage: 'I took a decision to watch ITV4+1 and watch *MOTD2* at 10 p.m. Imagine my horror when I came across this message at 11 p.m.: "Sorry, for legal reasons we cannot broadcast the programme that was shown earlier on ITV4." Can you imagine my rage? Furious.'

105th over: England 316–1 (Cook 135, Trott 57) Sky have just put up the Adelaide scoreboard from 2006 to make sure we're not too optimistic. Hilfenhaus is sticking to his plan and an off-stump line.

106th over: England 320–1 (Cook 139, Trott 57) Cook gets a thickish edge that flies through the empty third-slip place for four. And on 139 Cook now has England's highest Test score in Brisbane.

107th over: England 320–1 (Cook 139, Trott 57) There seems to be some problem with the Gabba members and their usual privileges not being honoured. That may have something to do with the lack of numbers. The prices, though, are still cheaper than they are here. Maiden from Hilfenhaus.

108th over: England 327–1 (Cook 146, Trott 57) Cook pulls Siddle for four off the bottom edge, streakily down to the finest of fine legs. Then a glorious cover drive from Cook and they run three.

109th over: England 327–1 (Cook 146, Trott 57) Here's Sarah Bacon, among many: 'Crowd figures over the past few days have been healthy from a "home" perspective. They should both be reminded that (a) it's a Monday, and (b) unlike the English, strangled as they're being by the worldwide recession, most

Aussies still have jobs to go to.' Maiden from Hilfenhaus – I'm going to get a macro of that.

110th over: England 337–1 (Cook 147, Trott 66) A ripsnorter from Siddle is dealt with very well by Trott. It bounced slightly higher than expected, but he rode the bounce and turned it to midwicket and strolled a single. Siddle then overpitches, and Trott squirts it with an open face behind point for four. And he follows it with another slightly streaky four.

111th over: England 340–1 (Cook 150, Trott 66) Huge delay while Ponting tinkers with the field before the start of Hilfenhaus's over. Here's Gary Naylor! 'All these Aussies with jobs to go to – none of them seem to be working as "Test Match Bowler"'. Very good. Cook punches the ball through the covers and runs three to get to 150 and the 150 partnership. The Barmies sing 'Ali Cook' to the tune of 'Baby Give It Up'.

112th over: England 343–1 (Cook 152, Trott 67) Here comes Johnson. His arm really is as low as Lasith Malinga's at the moment. Here's Dom O'Reilly: 'Listening to *TMS* while following OBO. Michael Vaughan has just told CMJ that he's a "great advert for the Barmy Army". And then repeated it. I feel he meant "advocate" but I like the sound of Vaughan walking around Brisbane with "Barmy Army" emblazoned on his clothing.'

113th over: England 343–1 (Cook 152, Trott 67) Hilfenhaus went unmolested.

114th over: England 343–1 (Cook 152, Trott 67) Thomas Bowtell has this insight on Cook: 'Cook's a month shy of his 26th birthday and has scored 4,583 Test runs. At the same age, his mentor Graham Gooch (who ended up with 8,900) had a grand total of 547 runs. Not sure what point I'm trying to make, but there you go.' Maiden from Johnson.

115th over: England 347–1 (Cook 156, Trott 67) Watson comes on for Hilfenhaus, and he's targeting the cracks with more accuracy than the other three quicks. Cook thick-edges four off his last ball through the underpopulated slip area. Watson has what you would call a classic Yorkshire fast bowler's backside. I'll leave that observation there.

116th over: England 355–1 (Cook 156, Trott 75) Trott breaks the shackles and smashes Johnson through cover for four. Fine shot, and he then opens the face to smear the next wide of gully for four more. He's still gardening. Has there been a batsman more in his own concentration zone?

117th over: England 360–1 (Cook 161, Trott 75) Another edge from Cook reaps four through the slips. Then huge roars as Michael Clarke drops a sitter in the slips. Straight into his hands from Trott's low cut and straight out again. Wheels are coming off. Pretty ordinary, as they say in Oz.

118th over: England 370–1 (Cook 166, Trott 75) My God, Johnson has just bowled a huge wide for four. From round the wicket it flew to long leg. That was as bad as Harmison's from four years ago. He looks as if he doesn't have any confidence in his method at all and is just, as he said, whanging it down.

119th over: England 371–1 (Cook 167, Trott 75) Here's the man Shane Warne calls Ex-Avier Doherty. And his first ball turns, but Cook turns it into the leg side. Marie Meyer has a query: 'I've only ever seen Mitchell Johnson bowl against England. What did he used to do that he doesn't do now?' Against South Africa he got bounce and movement at decent pace. He looks slow by comparison now.

120th over: England 379–1 (Cook 175, Trott 75) Someone moves behind the sightscreen and makes Cook stop Watson in his tracks. Brad Haddin shouts, 'Sit down, you muppet.' And Mitchell Johnson sits down. Another fine cut shot from Cook takes him to 171, followed by a glorious cover drive for four to register his highest Test score.

121st over: England 387–1 (Cook 175, Trott 83) 'Ex' is round the wicket to Trott, who rocks onto his back foot and creams four to third man. Then more of an edge gets him four more.

122nd over: England 388–1 (Cook 176, Trott 83) A single posts the 200 partnership. Watson responds with a bouncer to Trott, who was caught on the front foot and hooked down in front of midwicket. Good improvisation but it looked ugly.

123rd over: England 402–1 (Cook 182, Trott 83) Cook climbs into Doherty, dancing down the wicket and lofting him for four. Doherty gets big turn from the rough and the ball skittles down the leg side for four byes. Then Cook gets half down to sweep, but it fizzes off a crack and that's four more byes. We have the Holy Grail of 400-plus for one. Amazing.

124th over: England 409–1 (Cook 182, Trott 89) Clare Davies: 'Always good fun to read the Aussie press, but I found Peter Roebuck's comment quite hard to swallow – while being critical of the Aussies, he just had to say this: "Now England, or at any rate a team bearing that name . . ." Where does that man get off? I don't remember the Aussies ever calling Andrew Symonds a Brummie!' Trott gets four more through the vacant wide slips.

125th over: England 409–1 (Cook 182, Trott 89) Shall I make the mother of all hostages to fortune? There has been some shambolic stuff from the Australians this morning, fielding and bowling. Ah . . . here's Warnie. And he says it's been pretty poor.

126th over: England 414–1 (Cook 184, Trott 92) This is the first time a side has ever got to four hundred for the loss of one wicket in the second innings of a match. Remarkable. Marcus North on now. Why doesn't Ponting have a bowl himself, or Katich, or Clarke? Captaincy by numbers?

127th over: England 419–1 (Cook 188, Trott 93) James Duffy captures the odd sensation of being in this position for all England fans with longish memories: 'What I'm loving about this is just how un-English it is. We're never as unrelenting in piling on the runs; in snatching away what appeared a good winning position from the other side and making that side look foolish for ever being so confident. It's what other teams do to us.' Lovely cover drive off Doherty from Cook, against the spin.

128th over: England 419–1 (Cook 188, Trott 93) They seem to be calling Marcus North 'Snorts' when he bowls a good one. He's bowling at Emburey pace here, but it's not turning as much for him this innings. Maiden nonetheless.

129th over: England 420–1 (Cook 189, Trott 93) 'Doh' resumes, and Cook takes a single.

130th over: England 430–1 (Cook 199, Trott 93) Great, expansive batting from Cook, with a pair of scintillating boundaries and a two that takes him to 199. They're milking old Snorts now.

131st over: England 432–1 (Cook 200, Trott 94) Paddle sweep from Trott puts Cook on strike, and with a chance to become the fifth Englishman to score a Test double hundred in Australia. And he does it thanks to a misfield after Australia had a Hussain/Richard Dawson moment and tried to keep him waiting. It's his highest-ever score – 200 off 361 balls.

132nd over: England 434–1 (Cook 201, Trott 95) Snorts comes in, and Cook straight-bats his first two balls. William Sinclair points out, not unreasonably: 'I wouldn't get too carried away with this record-breaking England performance, Rob. Remember, we've seen two top-order wickets (three if you include Haddin, which is a stretch) in two and a half days.'

133rd over: England 439–1 (Cook 201, Trott 100) Matthew Hardy writes: 'I'm an Australian comedian working/living in London who has endured disrupted shows all weekend due to "our" (Australian cricket team) haphazard, rapid unravelling. Crowds hear my accent and it's apparently "game on". All in good spirits and nothing I can't handle but relentless for the whole half-hour nonetheless.' Trott picks off two, then sort of flat-bats it to mid-off before taking an easy three to midwicket, turned off his pads. Two Ashes Tests for Trott and two second-innings centuries. What resilience. That's lunch.

England 260 and 439–1; Australia 481

The afternoon session

BY ROB SMYTH

Preamble: Hello again. Everyone remembers Trent Bridge 1989. Geoff Marsh and Mark Taylor batting throughout the first day. The nadir's nadir. Yet it's often forgotten that the second day was hardly a laugh riot either. At various stages Australia were 329–0, then 430–1, then 502–3. I remember lying on my bed, idling away the summer holidays like any other working-class kid who didn't know any better, flicking back and forth between that on BBC1 and *Scooby Doo* on ITV (seriously, watching *Scooby Doo* at the age of 13. Psychoanalysis please!), wondering if I'd ever see England pose such absurd high-rise scores. And today I did. I've been like a pig in Statsguru all morning. Four hundred and thirty-nine for one. David Lynch wouldn't script this in his wildest dreams. David Lloyd wouldn't script this in his wildest dreams.

134th over: England 441–1 (Cook 201, Trott 102) Mitchell Johnson, who appears hell-bent on proving that 2009 wasn't –

as we previously thought – his Ashes *horribilis*, starts after lunch. Trott drives him nicely through extra cover for a couple.

135th over: England 442–1 (Cook 202, Trott 102) Xavier Doherty bowls a tidy over that brings one run. 'Your views on strategy please, Rob?' says Chris Wright. The best thing to do is to land psychological blows by batting on and on and on.

136th over: England 443–1 (Cook 203, Trott 102) Johnson's radar is more Jackson Pollock than Shaun Pollock. It's shocking stuff, all over the show. Cook pings one off the pads, but Watson at short midwicket fields well.

137th over: England 444–1 (Cook 204, Trott 102) The game is drifting, with just one coming from that Doherty over. England's sedate start after lunch suggests they have no thoughts of victory. That might not be very exciting, but it's entirely realistic and also sensible given the fact that we are at the start of a five-Test series squeezed into seven weeks. 'The call to prayer echoes across the Diplomatic Quarter of Riyadh before every dawn,' says Peter Hall, 'but this morning it was a very welcome early-morning call: "Get up and watch the cricket." What a nice morning it is!'

138th over: England 449–1 (Cook 205, Trott 106) That's a fine, trademark shot from Trott, working Johnson off the hip and through midwicket for four. He plays that shot remorselessly. Right here, right now, Jonathan Trott has a Test average of 58.45.

139th over: England 452–1 (Cook 208, Trott 106) 'It's a stats fest!' says Bumble on Sky as Alastair Cook drives Doherty for three, moving past Nasser Hussain's 207 as the highest score by an Essex batsman in an Ashes Test.

140th over: England 457–1 (Cook 209, Trott 106) Johnson snakes in to bowl to Cook and Harmisons a shocking delivery miles down the leg side for four byes. Haddin does well to stop a repeat next ball. This is a full-scale meltdown, and pretty sad to see really. Nobody deserves this.

141st over: England 457–1 (Cook 209, Trott 106) Doherty so nearly gets a wicket when Cook chips one low to Ponting, diving forward at short midwicket. Ponting did not celebrate, and the umpires went to the TV replay. Cook survives. As so often in these cases, instinct suggests it was probably a clean catch, but the third umpire could not have given that with a clear conscience. Ponting is very unhappy. He has a few words with Aleem Dar and then storms off, shouting, 'Piss-weak umpiring.' Part of the confusion was Ponting's non-celebration: at first you thought that was an admission that he did not know whether it carried, but in fact it was just because of the score. He was certain he had caught it.

142nd over: England 466–1 (Cook 214, Trott 110) 'That is filth from Mitchell Johnson,' says Nasser Hussain when Cook blazes a short, wide delivery up and over backward point for four. 'Earlier on, someone defended the presence of wall-to-wall South Africans in the England team by claiming that Andrew Symonds was a Pom,' says Burt Bosma. 'Say that to his face and you'd have no face three seconds later. He came to Australia when he was five months old and learnt all his cricket here. You can't compare that to Trott and Pietersen.'

143rd over: England 476–1 (Cook 218, Trott 115) Cook survives a big lbw shout when he misses a sweep. That looked a pretty decent shout. The only thing that could have saved Cook was getting outside the line – and replays show that he was, indeed, fractionally outside the line. That is yet another exceptional decision from Aleem Dar. Gee, he is good.

144th over: England 485–1 (Cook 223, Trott 119) Cook hooks Watson contemptuously for four, and then he is dropped by Ponting. Unreal. Cook went for a big drive and it flew off the edge to Ponting in a wide slip position. He dived to his right but couldn't hold on. It is the first time in Test history that a team has passed 450 for the loss of only one wicket against Australia. This is astonishing, and Trott adds to the mood by lifting Watson disdainfully back over his head for four. Ridiculous.

145th over: England 487–1 (Cook 224, Trott 120) On Sky, Warne and Atherton reckon England should declare. They know a wee bit about cricket between them, so I'm now hastily rewriting earlier entries to the contrary on this subject.

146th over: England 494–1 (Cook 225, Trott 126) Trott drives Watson for a single to bring up – and you'll like this – the 300 partnership. The 300 partnership. The 300 partnership. The 300 partnership. Trott is now batting like a dream, and he waves Watson gorgeously wide of extra cover for four.

147th over: England 502–1 (Cook 229, Trott 127) Yet another statgasm: England have, for the first time in Test history, gone past 500 for the loss of only one wicket. Nurse, the *Wisdens*! First Cook clouted Doherty sexily over mid-on for four, and then there were four byes when Doherty speared a yorker down leg. Ricky Ponting can only smile wryly as another piece of his empire goes into the river. I wonder what odds you'd have got on England being 500–1? 500–1 maybe? I bet Dennis Lillee never thought he'd see that in an Ashes Test again.

148th over: England 505–1 (Cook 230, Trott 128) Marcus North is on for Mitchell Johnson (27–5–1,004–0). Nothing happens.

149th over: England 509–1 (Cook 231, Trott 131) Alastair Cook's 230 is the highest Test score at the Gabba, ahead of Don Bradman's 226 against some poor helpless suckers back in the day. There's a statgasm per over at the moment. Trott works Doherty to leg for a couple.

150th over: England 513–1 (Cook 233, Trott 133) Trott takes a sharp single to mid-off. Watson hits the stumps, but Trott was home. A few more singles take the score up to 512 for one. It's 512 for one. Someone should make an emoticon for this, although I don't know if one graphic can simultaneously portray confusion, joy, incredulity, delirium, delirium tremens, confusion, joy and multiple statgasms.

151st over: England 515–1 (Cook 234, Trott 134) 'There is now a Twitter campaign (#gettheashestotheashes) to persuade Qantas to get @theashes on a plane to Australia,' says Scott Collier. 'Which rather makes me wish I had thought of that username.'

152nd over: England 517–1 declared (Cook 235, Trott 135) Here comes the declaration from Andrew Strauss. This has been an extraordinary innings, one that nobody on the planet could have imagined. Cook ends on 235, Trott on 135, their partnership an unbeaten 329 and England's lead 296. It hurts just trying to comprehend those statistics. I'm off for a 182-second power nap.

Australia second innings

1st over: Australia 0–0 (Watson 0, Katich 0) A good, straight first over from Anderson is defended well by Watson. England certainly fancy him for lbw early on.

2nd over: Australia 2–0 (Watson 0, Katich 2) Broad is steaming in with purpose to three slips, but while this is not a 517–1 pitch, nor is it a 51–7 pitch. I'd be amazed if we had any drama.

3rd over: Australia 2–0 (Watson 0, Katich 2) The ball isn't swinging much, but Anderson is extremely accurate, and again Watson is restricted to defence. Another maiden.

4th over: Australia 4–0 (Watson 0, Katich 3) Broad is wided on height for a bouncer to Katich. 'So everyone else has gone to bed at this hostel in Patagonia – one month into four months travelling in South America, where lack of Ashes coverage is the only sour note,' says Charlie Talbot.

5th over: Australia 5–0 (Watson 0, Katich 4) Anderson beats Watson with a beautiful delivery that cut away just enough to beat the edge. The match is winding down really. I like this period of a drawn Test, where we all have our last drink before the lights go on and try to make sense of what has happened before moving on to the next match. It'll take a helluva long time to make sense of this game.

WICKET! 6th over: Katich c Strauss b Broad 4 (Australia 5–1) England's day just gets better. Katich fiddled unnecessarily at a shortish delivery outside off stump, bowled from around the wicket, and Strauss took a straightforward catch at first slip.

6th over: Australia 6–1 (Watson 0, Ponting 1) Ricky Ponting is booed to the wicket by a phalanx of morons. One of the all-time greats, treated like something out of a pantomime. That crap disgusts me. He is greeted by a bouncer from Broad that he completely ignores, and then awkwardly shovels one into the leg side to get off the mark.

7th over: Australia 11–1 (Watson 0, Ponting 6) Anderson turns Ponting round with a good delivery. The ball squirts into the off side, and Ponting sets off for a quick single. There is no chance of a run-out, but Pietersen throws the ball anyway, miles wide of the stumps and away for four. Anderson is justifiably radged off and has a few words with Pietersen. He takes his frustration out on Watson with a storming leg-cutter that beats the defensive grope. Watson has 0 from 20 balls, and that's tea. I'm off to shake my head repeatedly and mumble '517 for one.'

Australia 481 and 11–1; England 260 and 517–1 dec

The evening session

BY ROB BAGCHI

Preamble: Aussie Seamus Byrne has Cardiff revenge on his mind: 'I'm annoyed because I was prepared for THIS before day one. Then Siddle, Hussey and Haddin had to go and build my hopes up again! What will save this Test for me is if we get to nine down and Strauss just can't take the last one . . . fast forward to Sydney and a series still in the balance and the screams of "If only" will ring in your ears like Cardiff '09 still does for us.'

8th over: Australia 17–1 (Watson 5, Ponting 7) Mikey Holding reckons they'll try to play some big shots to show they're not at all cowed. Broad begins with another short ball that Ponting rides around the corner. Andrew Goulden feels a T-shirt coming on: 'I'm not sure if it's already been mentioned but a T-shirt with "517–1, it doesn't get any better" would look pretty natty, I feel. Maybe having a picture of a downcast Ponting underneath would really set it off.'

9th over: Australia 26–1 (Watson 14, Ponting 7) Anderson's been pretty much on the money from the start: off-stump line, fullish length and he's getting good carry. James Hudson is taking pleasure where he can: 'I'm living in the comforts of a possible war zone in Seoul, South Korea – just 30 miles from the border with the North. I've got an emergency survival bag ready in case we have to do one but not even the threat of a nuclear winter can tear me away from how much I'm loving the shelling of the Ozzies.'

10th over: Australia 30–1 (Watson 17, Ponting 8) Jimmy Anderson and Ricky Ponting exchanged a few words, and the umpires had to get involved. The stump mic was turned down as it started, so not sure what was said. Here comes Broad, and he gives Ponting the hurry-up with one that lifts and jags back into him, and he under-edges it into his box. Broad is diplomatically carrying on where Anderson left off with a few pithy phrases.

11th over: Australia 36–1 (Watson 18, Ponting 13) Graeme Swann comes into the attack with a silly point, short leg, slip and short midwicket. Good flight and dip with the first ball, then Ponting hits a beautiful on-drive for four. Oh, and Collingwood drops Watson, an easyish chance, at first slip.

12th over: Australia 36–1 (Watson 18, Ponting 13) Paul Connelly writes: 'You know if every match turns out this way, the Aussies will retain the Ashes, don't you? I'm not trying to rain on your parade, but not getting hammered isn't the same as winning.' If they held them, they would, Paul. But they don't. James Elroy puts the call out in Argentina: 'In Buenos Aires, here working on a film, and my American colleagues are at a loss as to why I'm so oddly tired these past few days. I told them I had met a girl. Didn't want to confuse them by mentioning the word "cricket", let alone the Ashes.' Maiden from Broad.

13th over: Australia 37–1 (Watson 18, Ponting 14) Swann returns with the swagger still in his stride and tempts Watson to swish outside leg, and Prior whips the bails off. Good flight and not as short as he was in the first innings.

14th over: Australia 40–1 (Watson 20, Ponting 15) Watson gets the maker's name out a couple of times and plays the ball back to Broad.

15th over: Australia 43–1 (Watson 22, Ponting 16) Brief hesitation almost gets Ponting into run-out trouble, but Watson sprints through to make his ground.

16th over: Australia 54–1 (Watson 22, Ponting 26) Here comes the Finn. And he tries an inswinging yorker first up but overpitches, and Ponting launches into it with a lovely straight drive for four and then a trademark swivel pull for four. Kat

Petersen is thinking of doing a gloating wake-up call: 'I have just woken up from migraine-induced hallucinations to see the genuine score (though it took much blinking to convince me), but the only person to share it with was my sister, who is German – shouting "517–1! 517!!!" doesn't quite have the same effect if you then have to spend ten minutes trying to explain the basic concepts of cricket. I am waiting for my Aussie housemate to wake up so I can share the news with her instead.'

17th over: Australia 62–1 (Watson 23, Ponting 33) We have a lot of correspondents in Seoul this morning, keeping calm and carrying on. 'I'm sat here in north-east Seoul, about 20 miles from the DMZ, just waiting for Kim Jong-Il to rain down fire on me,' writes John Allen. 'Still, when he does at least I'll have the memory of 517–1 to go out with. Thanks, boys!' Ponting finishes the over by going down on one knee and thwacking Swann for six over mid-on.

18th over: Australia 68–1 (Watson 24, Ponting 38) This has been a fine, positive partnership from Ponting and Watson, a bit like Strauss and Cook at the beginning of yesterday's play. Finn keeps feeding Ponting's pull, but he hasn't got the pace, and neither has this pitch, to be effective unless Ponting misjudges the length. He doesn't, and spanks him for four just in front of square.

19th over: Australia 71–1 (Watson 24, Ponting 41) Time for the Monty Panesar song as Swann keeps it tight and Ponting opens the face of his bat to steer it past slip for three, and Watson gets very far forward and over the ball in two identical forward defensives.

20th over: Australia 77–1 (Watson 29, Ponting 41) Ponting gets over another short ball from Finn and toes a pull for a single. Watson unveils his hook now and blasts it through mid-wicket for four. Not good from Finn this innings so far. And another leg-side ball is pushed for a single. His last is better, forcing Ponting onto the back foot with an assured backward defensive.

21st over: Australia 83–1 (Watson 31, Ponting 41) Swann spins his first ball, and the second rips past the bat and goes for four byes down the leg side. Big talk of Mitchell Johnson getting dropped, apparently gleaned from someone overhearing Greg Chappell saying he was on borrowed time. Good morning, Neil Gouldson: 'I'm currently working as a kindergarten teacher in Guangzhou, China. I've been sat in the computer room on my lunch break surrounded by the entirely female staff, following OBO. They are wondering why I am looking so delighted at the moment, but the language barrier alone deters me from any attempted explanation.' Finn's going to get a lengthy spell, though he doesn't look at his best, in the low 80 mphs and more than a tad too much variation in length. When he pitches it up, as he does twice to Watson, he looks impressive and keeps Watson on the front foot, looking assured for now but not too threatening.

22nd over: Australia 90–1 (Watson 33, Ponting 47) Swann bowling to Watson and being turned to the deep fielders with the spin. Ponting follows suit with a pair of shorter balls. 'We're going to win 4–0,' sing the gleeful Barmies. Hmm.

23rd over: Australia 99–1 (Watson 35, Ponting 49) Kevin Pietersen is having a bowl now and drops the first ball horribly short and gets a taste of his own medicine with overthrows from Finn that hit the helmet and cost him an extra five. His last ball grips and rips but he's been very short this over. Two overs left if they agree to call it a day.

24th over: Australia 105–1 (Watson 40, Ponting 50) Ponting takes a single to get to 50, and then Watson creams an on-drive for four. Useful stuff from the Australians, no psychological scars and refusing to let Swann settle. Here's Kat Petersen: 'Suggestion for Neil Gouldson (21st over): I've found an easy way to explain cricket-related happiness/despair with as little language as possible is to pretend the score works as in football. Point to the 517 and say "England" (*ying guo*), point to the 1 and say "Australia". They will understand.'

25th over: Australia 107–1 (Watson 41, Ponting 51)
Pietersen again, better length this over. Perhaps having spent 11 hours padded up he needed to get the lethargy out of his legs. And both captains shake hands and that's it. England have drawn the first Test at the Gabba for the first time since 1998, and this time they didn't need the rain. A fine, absorbing Test. No, it was better than that. It was a simply gobsmacking fightback from England. It was a counter-attack of real character and courage.

England 260 and 517–1 dec; Australia 481 and 107–1. Match drawn

Second Test

Adelaide Oval
3–7 December 2010

First day

The morning session

BY ANDY BULL

Preamble: Evening everyone. Night time in the city. And it's *cold* out there. So cold it makes your head hurt and your feet ache. Out on the street in London the snow has been ground down into a thick paste of slush and grit, so slippery a man can hardly move in a straight line. 10,257 miles away England are going back to the scene of the crime. Adelaide. Three years and 360 days ago the headlines on the back pages read like this: 'Dad's Army 2 Dud's Army 0' (the *Herald Sun*); 'Wombats 2 Wombles 0' (the *Sun*); 'Night of the Living Dead' (*Daily Mail*). Today six of that team are still standing: Strauss, Cook, Bell, Pietersen, Collingwood, Anderson. Older, wiser and better. They've a few ghosts to exorcise in the next five days.

Toss: Australia have won the toss and will bat. That's advantage Ricky. Strauss called 'heads' but lucked out. Australia look like this: Watson, Katich, Ponting, Clarke, Hussey, North, Haddin, Harris, Doherty, Siddle, Bollinger. England line-up: Strauss, Cook, Trott, Pietersen, Collingwood, Bell, Prior, Broad, Swann, Anderson, Finn.

WICKET! 1st over: Katich run out 0 (Australia 0–1) James Anderson has the new ball, and his first delivery is a good one – full, on a length and a little away swing. 'I wouldn't mind bowling on this pitch,' says Mikey Holding, 'a lot of grass on the surface.' Got him! What a start! And what a shambles from Australia! Katich is run out without facing! Watson pushed the ball to midwicket and hared off for a quick single, but Katich didn't respond. Trott picked up and threw down the stumps with an insouciant but excellent throw from midwicket. I'd say more BUT . . .

WICKET! 1st over: Ponting c Swann b Anderson 0 (Australia 0–2) Ponting has gone first ball! I don't believe it! An unbelievable start for England! Ponting has gone for a golden duck in his 150th Test, and England have gone wild. Stop the clocks! Hold the front pages! Shout it from the rooftops! Australia are in utter disarray! It was a lovely ball from Anderson, full and swinging away. Ponting prodded at it and the ball moved just enough to take the edge and shot straight to second slip, where Swann took the catch.

2nd over: Australia 2–2 (Watson 0, Clarke 2) Clarke swings and misses a wild cut shot at Stuart Broad's first ball. Oh my word. Excuse me while I pick my jaw up off the floor and push my heart back down my throat into my chest. Smyth has been quick with his stats – this is only the third time in history that Australia have been 0–2, and the first time since 1950. Clarke edges a short ball away down the leg side for a single. 'I'm so excited I'm screaming loudly like an idiot in the *X Factor* audience,' bellows Dean Butler, who at least had enough self-restraint not to type out that email in full caps.

WICKET! 3rd over: Clarke c Swann b Anderson 2 (Australia 11–3) I'm delirious. I can hardly type. What did I say? 'Win the toss and bat?' I should resign right now. At least then I could leave my computer and run screaming down the street. Anderson has another one! Anderson has bowled seven balls and taken two wickets for one run. It was a bad shot by Michael Clarke, trying to cream a straight drive down the ground. The ball was too good for him, swinging in and then seaming away. It was another edge, straight to second slip. England's fielders are running around screaming like little girls. Who can blame them? Australia are disintegrating. 'This is bloody inconvenient,' says Ally Fogg. 'I have a crucial meeting first thing in the morning. Thought I would just check the score on the way to bed. There goes my career.'

4th over: Australia 11–3 (Watson 7, Hussey 2) Broad hammers down a bouncer at Hussey, who ducks underneath the ball. The next delivery whips by the outside edge. Here's Ant Pease: 'Does it necessarily make me a bad father that I'm holding my three-week-old daughter in my arms, and on the Clarke dismissal jumped up in the air, shouting, "Get the f**k in!" and nearly dropped her?' A maiden over from Broad.

5th over: Australia 11–3 (Watson 7, Hussey 2) Hold on, they might have another one here – referral! Watson 7 lbw b Anderson. The ball swung in, hitting the pad on the knee roll in front of middle stump. Umpire Hill shakes his head, but England opt to refer it anyway. Decision upheld, Watson bats on.

6th over: Australia 12–3 (Watson 7, Hussey 3) Hussey leans over to off and clips a single away square.

7th over: Australia 14–3 (Watson 7, Hussey 5) Anderson fires in a brilliant yorker, which Hussey pats back down the wicket. In fact, that's a drop from Anderson. He got his fingers to it, but no more. My word, there's almost a wicket every other ball at the moment. Hussey has chopped Anderson's latest delivery back onto his feet, the ball ricocheting just past the stumps.

8th over: Australia 24–3 (Watson 12, Hussey 10) And now Broad is at it too. He jags one back in at Watson and watches it snick off the inside edge past the stumps.

9th over: Australia 25–3 (Watson 12, Hussey 11) And

that's oh so close to another wicket for England, Hussey edging the ball just shy of second slip. 'I'm taking screen shots of this page so I can explain my absence from my daughter's Christmas play this morning,' admits Dominic in Beijing. 'Scorelines like this come but once in a lifetime.'

10th over: Australia 31–3 (Watson 17, Hussey 12) Strauss makes his first bowling change, bringing Steve Finn into the attack. I like that move. Don't let the batsmen settle, even for an instant. I love this email from Kat Petersen. After five years I think she may finally have come up with a new catchphrase for the over-by-over: 'Is it cowardly to pray for snow? Ideally enough to snow me in. But just enough to stop the District Line from running would be plenty.'

11th over: Australia 36–3 (Watson 17, Hussey 16) OK, my breathing is just settling down now. And so are Australia. Hussey forces a fine straight drive down the ground for four.

12th over: Australia 40–3 (Watson 23, Hussey 16) That's Watson's fourth four, and for the first time the Aussies in the ground have plucked up enough heart to start a chant of 'Ozzie! Ozzie! Ozzie! Oi! Oi! Oi!' It was another meaty extra-cover drive. Finn squeezes a yorker underneath Watson's bat, and the ball loops up over Prior's head and runs away for two.

13th over: Australia 43–3 (Watson 23, Hussey 17) Anderson starts his seventh over. He has figures of 6–1–17–2 so far. He has Hussey groping for an away-swinger outside off stump. The next delivery is flicked away square for one, and Watson leaves the rest alone.

14th over: Australia 48–3 (Watson 25, Hussey 20) These two have been scoring at almost four an over. They're playing aggressively, trying to accelerate away out of the skid. It's not a bad tactic, though they've had a little luck along the way.

15th over: Australia 52–3 (Watson 25, Hussey 24) Broad

comes back into the attack for his second spell, Anderson taking a break after a stint of 7–1–18–2. 'To cope with this scoreline I've had to drink some home-made Romanian twika,' says Dom O'Reilly. 'Think tractor fuel but with more of a kick.' Hussey flicks a full ball down to fine leg for two, a shot he repeats for the same result later in the over. That brings up the fifty partnership from 74 balls.

16th over: Australia 61–3 (Watson 30, Hussey 28) Watson clubs a straight drive back down the ground for four. The next delivery squirts off Hussey's outside edge and shoots away to the boundary at third man.

17th over: Australia 61–3 (Watson 30, Hussey 28) At the risk of being greedy, it's at times like this I'd really like to see a decent fourth seamer in the England team. Even Watson would be useful as a second change on this surface, nibbling the ball about off a full length.

18th over: Australia 62–3 (Watson 30, Hussey 31) The first throw of the dice from Andrew Strauss. He brings Graeme Swann into the attack. This is going to be fascinating. Will Hussey look to attack him again? He definitely had the better of the duel at the Gabba. Can Watson resist the temptation to try and wallop him out of the ground? And can Swann improve on his mediocre performance at Brisbane? Hussey knocks a single out to cover. Watson prods at the final five balls.

19th over: Australia 64–3 (Watson 30, Hussey 31) Broad is steaming in around the wicket now. He's already red in the face. Which is understandable – it is over 30°C in Adelaide.

20th over: Australia 66–3 (Watson 32, Hussey 31) Swann pins Watson down with five good balls, all of them hugging off stump. But his sixth is too short, and Watson taps it away to deep square for two runs.

21st over: Australia 67–3 (Watson 32, Hussey 32) Broad

continues from around the wicket. I've had two emails in complaining that Swann did not do badly at the Gabba. Not bad, no, but mediocre by his own standards. His length was too short.

22nd over: Australia 67–3 (Watson 32, Hussey 32) A good start by Swann here, he's settled quickly into his groove. He bowls a maiden to Hussey, who skips down the pitch to a couple but only succeeds in cracking his shots straight to the fielders.

23rd over: Australia 76–3 (Watson 37, Hussey 32) Broad hangs the ball out wide of off stump, trying to lure the batsman into a loose drive. Watson duly obliges. That's four, and the next ball shoots away off the pads for four more.

24th over: Australia 82–3 (Watson 43, Hussey 32) After playing five dot balls from Graeme Swann, Watson gets sick of pussyfooting and lofts a majestic six away over midwicket. My word, that's gone a long way. 'Worrying shots of Katich sitting and scowling outside the Australian team box, Nigel No-Friends-like, while his teammates dish the dirt on the upper level,' says Sarah Bacon.

25th over: Australia 87–3 (Watson 43, Hussey 36) Finn comes back into the attack for a final burst before lunch. His first four overs cost 26 runs. He's bowling from around the wicket now. Hussey has a huge yahoo pull at his fourth ball and connects with nothing but fresh air. He cuts the next away for four.

26th over: Australia 90–3 (Watson 46, Hussey 36) Again Watson plays out the first five balls of Swann's over before taking runs off the sixth, this time with a push for three to the off side. What a small world it is: Jason Smith writes: 'I'm sat in Beijing traffic on the way to my daughter's Christmas play. Staying up to date with the OBO as I drive.'

27th over: Australia 94–3 (Watson 50, Hussey 36) Watson brings up his fifty with a hefty pull for four. Finn has now bowled 32 balls for 35 runs. That's his 11th Test fifty. It seems amazing that he has been able to do so well since moving up to open the innings. And that, ladies and gents, is lunch.

Australia 94–3

The afternoon session

BY ROB SMYTH

28th over: Australia 96–3 (Watson 51, Hussey 37) Swann starts after lunch, and Hussey comes confidently down the track to drive his second ball through the covers for a single. Watson then pushes a single into the covers to end the over. I'd imagine Swann will bowl straight through for the rest of this session.

WICKET! 29th over: Watson c Pietersen b Anderson 51 (Australia 96–4) This is a huge wicket for England and a text-book dismissal on this Adelaide pitch. Anderson lured Watson into a big drive with a slightly wider delivery, and the ball flew off the edge to deep gully, where Pietersen took a fine low catch to his left. Jimmy Anderson now has figures of 8–2–18–3.

30th over: Australia 97–4 (Hussey 38, North 0) Does Hussey dare attack Swann now? He does, and he almost loses his wicket as a result. Hussey came down the track but could only crunch the ball into his pads; it plopped towards short leg, where Cook had turned his back on the ball as Hussey lined up the shot. Had he stood still it would have been a straightforward low catch. Do you criticise Cook for that? From this seat, maybe; but we all know what would have happened had either of us been at short leg.

31st over: Australia 101–4 (Hussey 42, North 0) Hussey times Anderson nicely through the covers to bring up the hundred. The other batsman, Marcus North, is an all-or-nothing batsman. If he goes early, and England can keep Hussey and Haddin to just 150 this time, they will be well on top.

32nd over: Australia 102–4 (Hussey 42, North 1) A few clouds are converging, and not just around Marcus North. He crunches a drive off Swann into the ground to get off the mark, but England clearly fancy Swann against him. 'As a chastened but still relatively unbowed Australian, it is a bit unfair for No-Mates Katich to be singled out for scowling,' says Gervase Greene. 'That's just how he looks.'

33rd over: Australia 106–4 (Hussey 42, North 5) That's a lovely stroke from North, a really pleasant drive through mid-off for four. Then he is beaten on the inside by a good one. Don't be fooled by the score. These are very good batting conditions.

34th over: Australia 107–4 (Hussey 43, North 5) Hussey continues to walk down the track to Swann as and when the mood takes him. He has played Swann masterfully in this series thus far. Swann then has a decent shout for lbw against North, who went a fair way across his stumps. 'I went to log onto the OBO at work this morning, only to find it had been blocked,' says Will Sinclair. 'Apparently our internet boffins had deemed it a "dating and matrimonial" site.'

35th over: Australia 108–4 (Hussey 44, North 5) Just one from Anderson's over. He has bowled delightfully in both spells today.

36th over: Australia 112–4 (Hussey 48, North 5) A sumptuous stroke from Hussey, who dances down the track to Swann and crunches him wide of mid-on for four.

37th over: Australia 116–4 (Hussey 48, North 9) North defends watchfully against Anderson until he gets a wider delivery, which he laces classily through extra cover for four. He is such a beautiful driver, this bloke.

38th over: Australia 120–4 (Hussey 51, North 10) Hussey sweeps Swann fine for three to bring up an extremely good half-century. He was finished two weeks ago, and now he's Australia's banker. This game, eh?

39th over: Australia 122–4 (Hussey 52, North 11) Anderson is replaced by Stuart Broad, who has the seriously unjust series average of 116. Given that his batting average for the series is 0, that all-rounder quotient could do with a nice massage. Two from the over.

40th over: Australia 124–4 (Hussey 53, North 12) Oof. North leaves a delivery from Swann that turns a touch and just misses off stump. North is taking no attacking risks and that has helped Swann, though still not at his best, to gain a degree of control. His figures are 12–1–27–0.

41st over: Australia 124–4 (Hussey 53, North 12) A fine over from Broad, mixing his length up in an attempt to jolt the becalmed North. A maiden.

42nd over: Australia 129–4 (Hussey 54, North 16) Swann tries to dupe North with a quicker, wider delivery, but North doesn't move his feet and simply screams it through point for four. He has done the hard part now and will be utterly furious if he slogs one straight up in the air in the next over. In fact, there's absolutely no way that will happen. Not a chance. Nup.

43rd over: Australia 129–4 (Hussey 54, North 16) Broad has gone into experimental mode – as he often does on the subcontinental wickets you get in places like, er, Adelaide and the West Indies – and is bowling very well. It's another maiden, this time to Hussey. 'In the wake of the World Cup this summer, I cannot for the life of me understand why the vuvuzela has not become the instrument of choice for the Barmy Army,' says Toby.

'Seriously, if they wanted to annoy Australians (and a fair few English viewers as well, I might add) the vuvuzela would be perfect.' The thought makes me want to prise out my eyeballs with a cotton bud.

44th over: Australia 130–4 (Hussey 54, North 17) Swann continues to wheel away with a slip and a short leg. Nothing happens. 'Given the trigger-happy nature of Cricket Australia – and after vuvuzelas were banned for the T20 Champions League – I feel sure they wouldn't find a home at an Ashes cricket match,' says Sarah Bacon. 'England's lucky that even their fabled trumpeter had his banning overturned, and even then I think he's on "mute".'

45th over: Australia 134–4 (Hussey 54, North 21) North times Broad nicely off the pads for four. 'A politico-wagering update from cloudy Melbourne,' says Tom Cameron. 'As my Federal Minister boss said over coffee yesterday, sometimes you've got to buy when everyone is selling and run in when the crowd's heading in the opposite direction. Walked down the road shortly after the Clarke wicket to a local betting shop in Moonee Ponds (suburban home of Dame Edna) and whacked $50 down on an Australian win.'

46th over: Australia 135–4 (Hussey 55, North 21) Sky have just shown Swann's Hawk-Eye graphic for today and at Brisbane, and his length has been noticeably fuller. He has control, partly as a result, although he hasn't really threatened to take a wicket.

47th over: Australia 138–4 (Hussey 58, North 21) Paul Collingwood replaces Stuart Broad. He will doubtless bowl cutters on this slowish pitch. I wonder how Collingwood, in particular, feels about returning to Adelaide. Everywhere he looks he must see bits of his soul that he left behind on that final day in 2006–7. Four from the over. 'There is something gloriously surreal about sitting in your PJs in front of a roaring fire (OK, fake-effect gas fire) with the snow outside the window, watching blazing sunshine and tumbling Aussie wickets,' says Lizzy Ammon. 'Is this what it's like being on LSD?'

48th over: Australia 139–4 (Hussey 59, North 21) Just the single to Hussey.

49th over: Australia 143–4 (Hussey 62, North 22) Collingwood continues to bustle in, and Hussey works him behind point for three. England are sitting in, giving their seamers a rest, while Australia cannot afford to lose another wicket before tea and are thus accumulating with as few risks as possible.

50th over: Australia 146–4 (Hussey 62, North 25) Three from Swann's over, the last of which brings up a serene fifty partnership.

51st over: Australia 147–4 (Hussey 62, North 26) Collingwood has figures of 3–0–8–0, which will do nicely.

52nd over: Australia 147–4 (Hussey 62, North 26) A maiden from Swann to North. Swann definitely looks better today, both in terms of his length and his demeanour, although he still isn't at his best. That said, figures of 18–2–38–0 on a first-day pitch are perfectly reasonable.

53rd over: Australia 154–4 (Hussey 69, North 26) Steven Finn replaces Paul Collingwood. He wasn't at his best this morning, and when he overpitches the penultimate delivery of that over he is timed through the covers for four by Hussey. The next ball is also too full, and this time Hussey works it off the pads for three.

54th over: Australia 155–4 (Hussey 70, North 26) Swann continues to shove pennies in the slot, but he is not getting anything back. He almost beats the charging Hussey in the flight, but Hussey reacts well to stretch and work the ball into the covers for a single. 'Lord Richie is currently advertising the "Vodafone iPhone cricket A. P. P." on the Channel 9 coverage,' says John Leavey. 'Is this an Aussieism or just an old geezer not quite up with the new-technology terminology?'

WICKET! 55th over: North c Prior b Finn 26 (Australia 156–5) Having topped the session with a bonus wicket, England tail it with one too. Marcus North, having done all the hard work, fiddled unnecessarily outside off stump and thin-edged it through to Prior. That was a horrible and ungainly shot from such a frequently graceful player. 'I'm in the Qantas lounge in Sydney,' says John Davis. 'My flight's been cancelled along with the usual crowd of partisan semi-sober Aussie cricket fans, I couldn't be deeper behind the lines if I was wearing a huge false moustache and discreetly dispensing tunnel soil out of my trousers. BUT there is a definite chink in the armour. The world has shifted, just a little bit, on its axis.' Repeat after me: it's still 0–0, it's still 0–0, it's still 0–0, it's still 0–0, it's still 0–0, it's still 0–0, it's still 0–0.

56th over: Australia 159–5 (Hussey 71, Haddin 2) Lord Beefy's on one about England not having a silly point for Haddin against Swann, with tea so close, but it's curmudgeoning by numbers and you can tell his heart's not really in it.

57th over: Australia 159–5 (Hussey 71, Haddin 2) A maiden from Finn to Hussey, and that's tea. It was attritional stuff this afternoon – 65 for two from 30 overs – but the dismissal of North just before the break made it incontrovertibly England's session.

Australia 159–5

The evening session

BY ANDY BULL

Preamble: Right. Where were we? The players are back out on the field, Hussey is marking his guard and Swann will take the first over.

58th over: Australia 161–5 (Hussey 72, Haddin 3) Hussey picks off a quick single from the fifth ball of the over, and Haddin adds another from the sixth.

59th over: Australia 165–5 (Hussey 72, Haddin 7) 'How many wickets can you promise me after tea?' demands Mark Herrington. 'Three and I stay up. Less and I go to bed. Your choice.' Right now I'd settle for one – Mike Hussey. Anderson whistles down an inswinger which Haddin clips away to midwicket for four.

60th over: Australia 174–5 (Hussey 78, Haddin 10) A wonderful shot from Mike Hussey, coming down the pitch and glancing the ball through midwicket for four. 'Still on Failaka Island,' says Sarah Cox. 'Still unable to watch any of the cricket, and Ponting goes for a golden duck. It's possible I should sacrifice my own pleasure for the sake of wider joy as every time I'm not hanging on every word of the OBO, we seem to do something impressive. Bribes happily accepted.'

61st over: Australia 174–5 (Hussey 78, Haddin 10) Anderson is bowling around the wicket to Hussey. He gets just a touch of away-swing. If only England could solve this Hussey conundrum they'd be running away with this series. He plays out a maiden over. Here's Austin Hill: 'Do you think another early-morning appearance in my newsagents reeking of liquid mood enhancer might finally push Abdul, my local *Grauniad* purveyor, to break from his till-now routine of cheerful but tactful bonhomie and finally force him into asking me why it is that I no longer appear to be in full-time employment?'

62nd over: Australia 181–5 (Hussey 82, Haddin 13) Haddin clumps away a cut shot past point, a clunky sort of stroke but it gets him three runs. Swann's next ball is a stinker, a full toss. Hussey creams it for four through midwicket.

63rd over: Australia 182–5 (Hussey 82, Haddin 14) Haddin squeezes a single away to leg. Anderson is bowling wonderfully well here. 'Maybe Austin Hill should tell Abdul he's considering a move to academia,' suggests Sarah Cox.

64th over: Australia 182–5 (Hussey 82, Haddin 14) Swann is yanked from the attack, replaced by Stuart Broad. Haddin picks out the fielder at short extra cover with a cracking drive, then prods and pokes his way through the rest of the over. It's a maiden.

65th over: Australia 184–5 (Hussey 84, Haddin 14) Anderson switches back to bowling over the wicket at Hussey. It's another maiden. I've just been explaining in an email to Lord Selvey that the BBC archive genuinely didn't contain any clips of his Test wickets (Richards, Fredericks, Kallicharran . . .) and he has sent this back: 'Story of my life. I played in a Lord's final and got a neighbour to video the highlights (he was well-off so had a video recorder). They showed one delivery only, which Alan Butcher hit for six. The other 71 they didn't show produced two for 11.'

66th over: Australia 187–5 (Hussey 85, Haddin 16) A rather half-hearted lbw appeal from England for a ball that was passing down the leg side. Umpire Erasmus wasn't impressed. England are beginning to look like they're flagging. Which is understandable – hard yakka, this.

67th over: Australia 189–5 (Hussey 85, Haddin 17) Steve

Finn has come back on for his fourth spell of the day. A leg bye, a single and that's your lot.

68th over: Australia 190–5 (Hussey 86, Haddin 17) It's as hot as it has been all day in Adelaide, and the torpor seems to have spread all the way to our office. My eyelids are heavy. Just as they are about to fall shut, the crack of the bat rouses me awake. Hussey has cut a single to deep point. It was hardly worth waking for.

69th over: Australia 191–5 (Hussey 87, Haddin 17) Another over, another solitary single. 'Is it wrong that I am sat in a strip club in Medellin, Colombia,' Nicholas Ross-Gower (some relation, I presume?) asks (after reading those first few words I'm surprised you even need to ask in the first place, let alone continue), 'surrounded by the most artificially enhanced women in the world, squinting at a 2' by 5' screen hoping that Mr Cricket treads on his wicket?' Ah, I see. 'I can't decide if it makes me superior or inferior. I'm sure my wife will be able to inform me in no uncertain terms when I return home. The question is, which version of the truth will appeal more?'

70th over: Australia 196–5 (Hussey 90, Haddin 19) Swann is back on, bowling around the wicket. Australia have scored nine runs in the last eight overs, so it is almost something of a relief when Hussey clips three out to midwicket.

71st over: Australia 201–5 (Hussey 91, Haddin 22) Up comes Australia's 200. England are coasting towards the new ball here. Thing is, they all look so knackered that it's difficult to imagine them mustering much strength to make an impression with it.

72nd over: Australia 203–5 (Hussey 92, Haddin 22) Haddin drops to one knee and launches a huge slog sweep at Swann's first ball. He's utterly misjudged it though, and the ball slips past the bat.

73rd over: Australia 206–5 (Hussey 93, Haddin 26) 'Thought you might be interested to know that the word "yakka" comes from the Irish word "*deachar*",' says Fergal Collins. And indeed I am. Though for all I know Fergal could be talking utter bunkum. Either way, it takes us a little closer to that new ball. 'Pronounced "dak-er", which means hard (as in difficult).'

WICKET! 74th over: Hussey c Collingwood b Swann 93 (Australia 207–6) Well, never mind the new ball. England may yet want to keep the old one. Swann has struck. Lovely bowling from him.

WICKET! 74th over: Harris lbw b Swann 0 (Australia 207–7) Swann's got him for a golden duck! Hasn't he? That looks stone dead. Or 'salmon trout', as Warney has it. Umpire Erasmus's finger is up, but Harris has decided to review it. Oh, this is a tough one. Has he got a faint inside edge on it? Looks like it. There is certainly a tiny deflection. But it's not enough evidence for the decision to be overturned. What's worse, Virtual Eye shows that the ball was barely hitting leg stump. But that's all irrelevant now, because the decision stands. So Swann is on a hat-trick. Doherty leans forward and plays an unsteady defensive shot to the hat-trick ball, blocking it back down the wicket. It looks like Harris has been wrongly given out. Hussey's dismissal was a real gem. Swann was bowling around the wicket, and flighted the ball up on off stump. Hussey stretched out to meet it, then watched it turn away and snick off the outside edge of his bat. The catch flew to Collingwood. That was the best ball Swann has bowled all series.

75th over: Australia 212–7 (Haddin 32, Doherty 0) Haddin slashes four through third man.

76th over: Australia 215–7 (Haddin 33, Doherty 2) Swann's got his mojo working. I confess – I haven't.

77th over: Australia 224–7 (Haddin 38, Doherty 6) Haddin has decided to start hitting out before he runs out of partners. 'Perhaps I'm a little delirious after what's just happened, this far into a long night,' says Thomas Jenkins, 'but didn't Bumble just inform us that "Ryan Harris has got a stiffy there"? Surely it's enough that he got that decision, there's no need to ridicule the poor man as well.'

REFERRAL! 78th over: Haddin lbw b Swann 38 (Australia 225–7) Haddin misses another slog sweep, and after seeing the ball thump into his front pad, England decide to use a referral. The replays show the ball was just hitting outside the line of off stump. Umpire Erasmus got it right the first time. Haddin is not out.

79th over: Australia 226–7 (Haddin 40, Doherty 6) Will England take the new ball? Probably not quite yet – Swann is bowling as well as he has done since he arrived in Australia at the moment. Haddin takes a single from the first ball, and Doherty plays out the rest of the over.

WICKET! 80th over: Doherty run out 6 (Australia 227–8) This mob are a shambles. An utter shambles. Another farcical run-out, as Doherty refuses to run for a quick single. He soon comes to regret that when the return throw comes in from Strauss and he's only halfway down the wicket. Actually, watching the replay of that it is a really smart piece of fielding by England. Strauss dived across to his right at mid-on, then, still flat on his back, underarmed a throw in to Alastair Cook at short leg. He tossed the ball on to Matt Prior, who completed the run-out. Smart stuff.

81st over: Australia 227–8 (Haddin 40, Siddle 1) Strauss has decided to take the new ball and has given it to Anderson. England will think they can finish this innings off tonight. My word, what a start to this Test match it has been. 'Please stop referring to OZ as a shambles and an utter shambles,' says Peter

Morris. 'You're tempting fete too much with that type of carry on.' I like tempting fetes. I'm a big fan of the Frome cheese show.

82nd over: Australia 230–8 (Haddin 41, Siddle 3) And Stuart Broad has the new ball at the other end. 'My girlfriend has now got up and is saying stupid things about cricket and non-cricketing matters,' gripes Dean Butler. 'She's spoiling it and I want her to go away. To work.' That's the typically sociopathic attitude of a man who has been up all night, Dean. I know it well.

83rd over: Australia 242–8 (Haddin 53, Siddle 3) Anderson bangs in a short ball that catches Haddin on the wrist. He hooks two more down to third man. Sky may want to turn their stump mic down. The fielder was just a little slow coming in off the rope, which was enough to prompt a loud cry of 'For f@ck's sake!' from Matt Prior. Oh my. That's a great shot by Haddin, scooping the ball over deep square leg for six. That brings up his fifty.

84th over: Australia 242–8 (Haddin 53, Siddle 3) A maiden over from Broad.

WICKET! 85th over: Siddle c Cook b Anderson 3 (Australia 243–9) It's so easy England are hardly bothering to celebrate the wickets any more. Siddle clips a catch straight to short midwicket, where Cook takes a simple catch. Doug the Rug is in.

86th over: Australia 243–9 (Haddin 54, Bollinger 0) 'Just two questions, if you please,' says Finbar Anslow. 'Why was England's 260 at the Gabba a defendable total but Australia's 256 today a shambles?' Ah. Ahhh. Well. That really has sucked the wind from my sails. Actually, it's not the total that stinks so much as the performance – Australia have been very, very sloppy: two golden ducks, two run-outs, and now . . .

WICKET! 86th over: Haddin c Finn b Broad 56 (Australia 245 all out) Haddin has a huge hoick of a hook, and the ball sails high up into the air. Finn is underneath it at long leg, and takes a decent catch. The innings is over, and Australia have been routed.

England first innings

1st over: England 1–0 (Strauss 1 Cook 0) Harris's speed is touching 90 mph now, and his fourth is up at over 91 mph. Shame it was down the leg side. The last ball is a yorker, and that, ladies and gents, is stumps. Ponting has a mouthful of words for Strauss as the players walk off. Strauss sticks up his palm and turns the other way. Well, what a brilliant day for England. For weeks now we've been saying that this is the weakest Australian team we've seen.

England 1–0; Australia 245

England were flawless here. A perfect day. And for Australia, only the grimmest of inquests

BY MIKE SELVEY IN ADELAIDE

FRIDAY 3 DECEMBER 2010

For English cricket there are, for all the dog days, times when things go right, and they are good, there to be savoured. But then occasionally, very occasionally in Australia these past two decades, there are days when nothing goes wrong.

At Adelaide yesterday, in the still-beautiful rafter-packed Oval, Jimmy Anderson bent down to his left in his follow-through and just failed to grasp a return catch offered by Mike Hussey. The Australian had three runs at the time and went on to fall seven runs short of a third Ashes century in successive matches. That apart – and the fact that the England openers had to face, albeit successfully, a single over before stumps – from the moment the sun rose in a cloudless azure sky to when Alastair Cook calmly knocked a Ryan Harris yorker to midwicket and marched off to the dressing room, England had produced a flawless performance. A perfect day. Lou Reed wrote a song about it.

To bowl Australia out for 245 in such conditions, having lost a toss they were anxious to win, would have required the most vivid imagination beforehand: an incisive start with the new ball, and patience and skill thereafter to execute the plans they had so carefully put in place.

By the time Anderson was two deliveries into his second over of the match, three batsmen were back in the dressing room, two runs had been scored, and the statisticians were trawling the records to find a worse beginning to any Australian innings against anyone. Eventually, 60 years back, in their second innings against England at Brisbane, where they lost three wickets before scoring a run, they found one. Thereafter England nagged away until the edifice came tumbling down. As in Brisbane, Anderson was outstanding, but this time, with four for 51, he got some reward, putting to bed for ever the idea that he cannot bowl in Australia.

Ricky Ponting, who has scored five of his 39 Test hundreds here, marked his 150th Test by edging his first ball to second slip, which is one more delivery than Simon Katich had the opportunity to face before he was run out to the previous delivery, the fourth ball of the innings. Thus, in the space of two balls of the opening over, England had taken twice as many wickets as Australia managed in 152 overs in Brisbane. Michael Clarke then fared little better, gone to second slip in a stiff-backed, six-ball trice. Later, as Shane Watson and Hussey began to dig Australia out, England simply sat back and waited, so that Watson succumbed immediately after his half-century and lunch, and the beleaguered Marcus North suffered strangulation before prodding abjectly, the pressure cooker doing for him during an afternoon session in which England conceded only 65 runs from 32 overs. That was brilliant cricket.

For a while thereafter, the spectre of Hussey and Brad Haddin, triple-century partners at the Gabba, loomed as they laid the brickwork for another rescue operation. All the while, though, Graeme Swann had been toiling to no reward, save knowing that his containing role was crucial to England's four-man attack. If off the pace in Brisbane, he was excellent here: the virtue of persistence finally saw him strike twice in successive deliveries as Hussey, who had batted superbly, edged to slip and Harris, promoted beyond his station to eight, was lbw first ball, the inevitable referral failing to convince the third umpire Billy Doctrove that he had made faint contact with his inside edge.

It was timely. The new ball was due and it hastened the finish, with a second comedy run-out, a further wicket for Anderson and a single deserving one for Stuart Broad.

These then are torrid times for Australia. To be bowled out in such conditions can happen, but to do so in such a catastrophic fashion demands recrimination whatever the final outcome. This is a ground on which they have posted in excess of 400 in the first innings of each Test since 1999, while it is six years before that since they made fewer than 350, batting second, and a year before that since India put them in to bat and dismissed them for 145. Consolation comes only in the knowledge that they went on to win the latter game and lost the first by a single run.

When a performance is so complete, it is tempting to forget the preparation that goes in. But Simon Rattle and the Berlin Philharmonic do not just wing it. Much, rightly, has already been made of the smooth nature of England's warm-up matches, played competitively to a high standard. Andy Flower has overseen the most complete build-up in memory and surely is the outstanding coach in English sport. But the results from yesterday can be passed down the chain. In Brisbane, the hard work and words of Graham Gooch finally instilled into Cook the need to play the percentages, and not be satisfied with the glory of a hundred but develop an appetite for more.

Next consider the contribution made by the bowling coach, David Saker, a man whose knowledge of Australian conditions is second to none. Saker has drilled into his pace-bowling charges the absolute necessity of the correct lengths and lines for the conditions and the value of discipline. In Adelaide, he has stressed, you bowl full, you attack the stumps. Yesterday, all the England bowlers were driven, which is as it should be, for then, as Ponting and Clarke showed, there is the chance of the edge. No width was offered for the cut, no length to be pulled, as Hussey in particular managed in Brisbane.

And when England saw the need to sit back and wait in the afternoon heat, the bowlers scarcely deviated from bowling to Andrew Strauss's carefully constructed fields. Strauss, proactive and thoughtful, had perhaps his best day in the field as England captain.

Then finally consider all the work put in by the fielding coach, Richard Halsall. England were magnificent yesterday, the bowlers backed to the hilt, and it began in the first over when Watson clipped gently to midwicket and galloped off in search of the first run. Katich did not respond immediately, but running round to midwicket Jonathan Trott was able to field, take aim and hit the single stump available to him. It was no fluke but the product of hours of technical practice for just such an occasion. Australia should complain: there were 16 players on the field yesterday.

Second day

The morning session

BY ROB SMYTH

Preamble: Expectation is everywhere after England enjoyed a stunning first day in Adelaide. England will resume on 1 for 0 in reply to Australia's 245. But England don't tend to win Ashes Tests in the modern era when they bat second. Since 1989, England have won only two Tests batting second. The first 20 overs will give us a great idea. If England get through the new ball unscathed, they will be in an outrageously good position. But they will have to do so against a triumvirate of mongrels in Ryan Harris, Doug Bollinger and Peter Siddle. These men share one thing, and it's not a feminine side.

WICKET! 1st over: Strauss b Bollinger 1 (England 3–1)
Here we go. Andrew Strauss has gone in shocking circumstances: he left a straight one that simply went on to hit the off bail. That was an appalling leave from Strauss – I presume he left it on length, which you can do at Brisbane (as he found out) but not at Adelaide. That was a weird dismissal.

2nd over: England 7–1 (Cook 1, Trott 4) Trott squeezes his first ball behind point but is then beaten by a good one. Bollinger ends an excellent over with a sharp bouncer and a few words for Trott. He can bowl: that's his 50th wicket in only his 12th Test.

'I'm doing Speed Drinking,' says Dean Butler. 'Preparing for the inevitable nemesis that follows our hubris.'

3rd over: England 10–1 (Cook 2, Trott 6) Harris's second delivery goes through the top of the pitch, which widens eyes on the field and in the stands. Cook takes a single into the off side, and then Trott pushes two behind square on the leg side. This is going to be a lively hour. 'If Strauss had referred that,' says Lord Selvey, 'Virtual Eye would have shown it to be going six inches over the top.'

4th over: England 16–1 (Cook 4, Trott 6) Cook tries to swat a high bouncer from Bollinger, but misses completely and the ball flies over Haddin for four byes. Bollinger gives Cook a stare of sheer hate. He beats the groping Cook with the final delivery of another dangerous over.

5th over: England 16–1 (Cook 4, Trott 6) Trott, driving loosely outside off, is beaten by Harris. Then he is very lucky to survive a run-out chance. He set off for a ludicrous single, was sent back by Cook, and would have been out had Doherty hit from square leg. He missed, and by a distance too. These are nervous times.

6th over: England 21–1 (Cook 5, Trott 10) Bollinger over-pitches and Trott drives him authoritatively through the covers for four. That was a fine stroke. In other news, James Mullion's life is going well. 'Step 1 – Wake up to the news and yell at my girlfriend to shut up whilst I listen to the Ashes score. Scream out of bed and hightail it out of the flat. Step 2 – Spend all day at work firstly reading your esteemed OBO and then proceeding to listen to the repeat of *TMS* on iPlayer (I estimate at least five hours of work wasted trying to find Boycott's first thoughts on the Aussies' opening). Step 3 – Trudge my way home through the snow and sign my soul away to the Murdoch empire in order to watch Bumble and co. make complete fools of themselves. Step

4 – Tell the girlfriend there's no snuggles tonight as I'm watching the Ashes. I am cool, I am sad, I shall not be broken.'

7th over: England 21–1 (Cook 5, Trott 10) England need an old-fashioned approach this morning – block the good ones, hit the bad ones – and they have two very old-fashioned players at the crease. Cook defends well in an accurate over from Harris, which is a maiden.

8th over: England 23–1 (Cook 5, Trott 12) On Sky, Mike Atherton points out that Trott is the only player on either side in the top ten of the ICC batting rankings. Bollinger fields a defensive shot and then stares at Trott as if he's a paediatrician who has just moved into a small English town. And then Trott is dropped. He sliced a drive low to gully, where Mike Hussey put down a very presentable chance.

9th over: England 24–1 (Cook 6, Trott 12) Cook thinks about hooking a sharp, high bouncer from Harris and then pulls out very late. These two have bowled well this morning.

10th over: England 28–1 (Cook 10, Trott 12) Peter Siddle replaces Doug Bollinger, who bowled a sharp spell of 4–0–15–1. His second ball is a really full toss at which Cook misses a drive. The next is a perfect length and beats Cook as he pushes forward, bat slightly hidden in the Jimmy Adams style. Then Cook pushes pleasantly through mid-off for his first boundary of the day. He looks very solid, with no sign yet of mental or physical fatigue after Brisbane.

11th over: England 38–1 (Cook 11, Trott 21) 'Buzzers!' chuckles Bumble as Siddle's throw from the deep hits the stumps and flies away for two extra runs. So Trott, having already run two, gets four for that – and four more from the final delivery of Harris's over with a beautiful ping through midwicket. 'Will James Mullion (6th over) still have a girlfriend by the end of play?' says Mark Taylor. 'May I suggest Step 5 – Flowers from the local

Texaco.' Now that's what I call romance. Why not go the whole way and arrange a candlelit microwaved dinner from Aldi?

12th over: England 41–1 (Cook 13, Trott 22) Three singles in that Siddle over, which ends with Trott being beaten outside off stump. England are doing OK, but there is still plenty of work to do this morning.

13th over: England 45–1 (Cook 14, Trott 22) Bollinger replaces Harris, who bowled well for figures of 6–3–14–0. A quiet over brings four runs.

14th over: England 55–1 (Cook 14, Trott 32) Consecutive boundaries for Trott off Siddle. The first was edged low through the cordon, the second crunched splendidly through midwicket. That brings up a surprisingly quick fifty partnership. 'Couldn't get home tonight because of the snow,' says Ian Davies. 'Appeared on my parents' doorstep, bedraggled, pleading for a couch to crash on and lugging a bag full of cheap booze. My old man asked what the beer was for. I explained it was Friday night and I was going to get quietly drunk on my own, into the early hours listening to the cricket. I could almost see him mentally totting up the cost of my further education.'

15th over: England 64–1 (Cook 18, Trott 32) More extras, as Bollinger's errant bouncer escapes Haddin's desperate leap and flies away for five wides. Cook then half-steers a thick edge to third man for four. England are going at more than four an over. 'As a child of the 70s/80s, I'm still in mourning for the Aussie cartoon ducks of my youth that used to accompany the likes of Norman Cowans/David Capel heading back to the pavilion,' says Jim Clear. 'Is that wrong?' No, but what is wrong was the fact that my first thought upon reading this was, 'But David Capel didn't play any Ashes Tests.'

16th over: England 72–1 (Cook 20, Trott 37) Shane Watson comes into the attack, and Trott greets him with another princely ping through midwicket. 'State of this team . . .' chuckles Bull to my left. This is a weird thing to write, and a scary one too, but Australia are not far away from being a complete rabble here. They have bowled fairly well, but their fielding is so scruffy it's untrue.

17th over: England 72–1 (Cook 20, Trott 37) 'I popped into Caos Café in Hindley Street before start of play for the compuls-ory *Guardian* pre-match latte, fruit and muesli, only to lose my place in the queue to a very large Australian supporter,' says our own David Hopps. '"Bacon and eggs and four VBs," he said. "Jeez it's hot. I need another beer. The Poms are gonna bat for two days. I think I'll just sit on this sofa and watch it here for a while." First Australian supporter to give up: timed at about 9.40 a.m.'

18th over: England 72–1 (Cook 20, Trott 37) Australia's two seamers have gone into Kallis mode: bowling miles wide of off stump and challenging Cook and Trott to chase the ball. This could be a very long staring contest, because Cook and Trott are the least likely of England's top six to go chasing the ball.

19th over: England 73–1 (Cook 21, Trott 37) Trott is temp-ted to chase one outside off stump and misses a drive at Siddle. 'This is like finally smashing your dad for six over his head,' says Stu. 'It was going to happen one day, you feel a tiny bit guilty, but ultimately you just try to hide the snigger and embrace the warm feeling of superiority. God, we're scoring with abandon. Hope Guardian Towers is rocking.'

20th over: England 74–1 (Cook 22, Trott 37) Watson is bowling to Cook with five men in the ring on the off side. It's a game of patience, and thankfully Cook has more than most. 'Agree with your rabble comment,' firsts Emma John. 'I hugely enjoyed hearing Nasser say that the Australians needed to learn how to bowl a consistent line and length: something so twilight zone about hearing this, as if the world's been sucked through a black hole.'

21st over: England 78–1 (Cook 26, Trott 37) After a number of leaves, Cook reaches for a wide one from Siddle and scorches it past point for four. The response is excellent, a perfect line and length with just enough seam movement to beat Cook's defensive stroke.

22nd over: England 78–1 (Cook 26, Trott 37) More off theory from Watson. Trott ignores most of it. A maiden. 'On *TMS* we have just learned from Justin Langer that the Aussie fielding coach is an American, tobacco-chewing, "very passionate" former baseball player – who is a real "character",' says Neil Hargreaves. 'Is anyone else imagining disturbing scenes redolent of the first half of *Full Metal Jacket*?'

23rd over: England 81–1 (Cook 29, Trott 37) Siddle errs onto Cook's pads and is worked through midwicket for three. 'KP has now been waiting for 445 minutes and 410 runs in order to get a knock,' says Lord Selvey. 'It's got nought written all over it.'

24th over: England 85–1 (Cook 33, Trott 37) Now Watson strays onto Cook's pads, and he is timed through midwicket for four. That's poor bowling. 'I have to confess I deliberately put the gas fire on at 11.15 knowing it would induce an almost immediate drowsy stupor on my girlfriend's part, allowing me to indulge in unopposed Ashes viewing. It worked a treat but I feel Strauss was my karmic retribution. I'm pretty sure carbon monoxide is an urban myth though, right?'

25th over: England 87–1 (Cook 34, Trott 38) With 12 minutes to lunch, here comes Ryan Harris. Bumble compares him to Darren Gough, whom he then describes as 'jaunty'. I think 'jaunty' might be the best word in the entire English language.

26th over: England 89–1 (Cook 35, Trott 39) Here comes Xavier Doherty for the token over before lunch. Shane Warne will love that. No real turn. All the England players to have scored over 150 runs in an innings have an average for their next innings that is below their career averages. On average they average 12 runs below their career average.

27th over: England 90–1 (Cook 35, Trott 39) Trott plays out a quiet over from Harris, and that's lunch. England have had a fine morning and are in control of this match.

England 90–1; Australia 245

The afternoon session

BY ANDY BULL

Preamble: Remind me, which team is which again? Australia are the guys who keep dropping catches, making misfields and bowling wide outside off stump because they can't think of anything else to do? Yes? They're the ones frumping around with their hands on their hips and disconsolate scowls on their faces, and moaning about how they are being sledged too much, is that right? And England are the team who are quietly, ruthlessly, remorselessly grinding the opposition down? Yes? Just checking. Thought I might have got a little confused.

28th over: England 102–1 (Cook 47, Trott 39) The batsmen stroll out after lunch. They've been batting together for eight hours over England's last two Test innings now, and have put on 416 runs together. Whatever plan Australia came up with in the dressing room during the break, I don't suppose it looked much like this. Cook insouciantly steers four more through backward point. Just the 12 runs from the over then.

29th over: England 107–1 (Cook 47, Trott 44) Harris creaks up to the crease like a tea lady in a retirement home. His second delivery is decent enough, but Trott is having none of it. He dispatches it through midwicket for four with undue contempt.

30th over: England 109–1 (Cook 48, Trott 45) A sniff of a wicket! But the ball lands short of the fielder. Bollinger banged in a short ball which was too quick for Trott's clipped pull shot. The ball looped up towards midwicket, but no one got close to claiming the catch. Ricky Ponting spits on his hands and stares into the middle distance.

31st over: England 112–1 (Cook 48, Trott 47) Doherty seems to have been talked into daubing zinc sun cream all over his face by Bollinger. Feels a little like the nervous new guy will do anything to fit in. Cook pops a catch up to short leg, but no one is there to take it. This next email from Jim Clear has made Smyth sick with fury: 'In the interests of the excellent *Guardian* standards that you set, I must inform you that David Capel apparently did indeed play two Ashes Tests in '88–9 (according to Cricinfo), so I was actually half correct with my earlier assertion, although no duck, but Rob was wrong with his statement that he hadn't played in the Ashes.

32nd over: England 119–1 (Cook 52, Trott 51) That's Cook's fifty, and Trott follows him to that same landmark moments later with a stylish flick through the leg side.

33rd over: England 119–1 (Cook 52, Trott 51) Ponting just does not know how to captain spinners, which is unsurprising given that for so long he didn't have to because he had Warne in the team. Look at the mess he made of handling Nathan Hauritz in India.

34th over: England 125–1 (Cook 52, Trott 57) Smyth has gleefully discovered that Jim Clear has got his dates wrong –

Capel played in 1989, not 1988–9. That seems to have made up for some of the disappointment of being caught out on a stat. '"Watching" the game here in Bali I can confirm that David Capel was at least in an England squad for one Ashes series,' says Richard Lofthouse. 'How do I know? Because Texaco produced player cards which were cartoons of the players with outsized heads. I remember having a few David Capel cards I couldn't get rid of. With his bleached mullet/perm and caddish moustache, he was, in every respect, the poor man's Botham.'

35th over: England 132–1 (Cook 59, Trott 57) Shot, sir! A short, wide and ugly delivery from Harris is marmalised for four through backward point by Cook.

36th over: England 136–1 (Cook 63, Trott 57) Doherty is into the attack. His first ball is driven for four through cover. Ouch.

37th over: England 138–1 (Cook 63, Trott 57) I seem to have blundered into the middle of the annual meeting of the David Capel reappreciation society. 'Capel didn't play in 1990,' grumbles Ian Callendar – I know, my mistake. 'The '88–9 reference did not refer to the winter season. He played in the one-off Sydney Test in January 1988 and one Test in the 1989 series, the last at the Oval.' England have scored 48 runs in ten overs since lunch.

38th over: England 140–1 (Cook 64, Trott 60) Cook takes two quick steps down the wicket and wallops a drive to mid-on.

39th over: England 145–1 (Cook 64, Trott 65) Siddle is on for his first spell of the afternoon session, and Trott welcomes him to the fray by threading four more through midwicket. Remember when England first picked Trott for their Twenty20 team back in 2007? He made 9 and 2, and it was 18 months before we heard from him again. I remember thinking, 'Where did they call this chancer up from?'

40th over: England 145–1 (Cook 64, Trott 65) Doherty hurries through a maiden to Trott.

41st over: England 145–1 (Cook 64, Trott 65) Siddle continues with the short-ball barrage, to no effect. It's a maiden, and that's drinks.

42nd over: England 145–1 (Cook 64, Trott 65) Another maiden, the third in a row. Thing is, these two will happily bat like this all day and not break. 'I'm in Dallas enjoying the show,' says Ben Mimmack. 'When I lived in Australia a while back, a constant refrain from the Aussies was that they wished we could at least get a competitive team together so they could enjoy some decent competition for the Ashes at home. Now that we're making a decent showing in this series, I assume your inbox is full of relieved emails from excited Antipodeans. Am I right?'

REFERRAL! 43rd over: Cook c Haddin b Siddle 64 (England 146–1) Australia think they have Cook here, caught behind off the glove down the leg side. Umpire Hill's finger goes up, but Cook is having none of it and the decision is overturned. He was nowhere near hitting the ball.

44th over: England 155–1 (Cook 65, Trott 74) 'That's a poor delivery from Doherty,' says Nasser. 'Filth,' utters Smyth. Whichever way you want to put it, it is four more for Trott, thumped away through cover.

45th over: England 156–1 (Cook 66, Trott 75) Siddle is flagging now. But aren't we all? The batsmen excepted, that is.

46th over: England 170–1 (Cook 78, Trott 76) Four! Four! Four! Cook takes 12 runs from three deliveries by Doherty, all three of them laced through the off side. Imperious batting.

47th over: England 172–1 (Cook 78, Trott 76) Harris replaces Siddle, and you imagine that Ponting may be thinking of bringing someone else on at Doherty's end as well. Haddin leaps high to his right to take a brilliant catch. Unfortunately for him, Trott didn't hit it. He did snick the next though. Only this time Haddin didn't catch it. You couldn't make this up. Absolutely nothing is working for Australia.

48th over: England 176–1 (Cook 82, Trott 78) North is on now. He serves up a juicy full toss here. It should have come with a silver dome and a sprig of parsley. Cook thumps it through long-off for four.

WICKET! 49th over: Trott c Clarke b Harris 78 (England 176–2) And there, at last, Australia have their wicket. After all the drops, this was a good catch by Michael Clarke at mid-on, diving one-handed to his left. Trott is furious with himself. And it was a slightly soft way to get out, clipping the ball lazily through the air. Pietersen steals a single off the first ball. That will be a relief seeing as he has been waiting six days to get to the middle.

50th over: England 185–2 (Cook 82, Pietersen 9) England still trail by 68. Doherty comes back into the attack, Ponting remembering KP's dismal record against slow-left-arm bowlers. But KP thrashes a four through extra cover. He does make a mess of the next ball though, edging it away in the air square of the wicket.

51st over: England 186–2 (Cook 83, Pietersen 9) KP has fairly raced to nine. He's a little more sedate against Harris, swaying away from one short ball and patting the rest down towards his feet.

52nd over: England 189–2 (Cook 86, Pietersen 10) Cook comes forward to play Doherty and is almost undone as the ball turns across the face of his bat. KP comes on strike, and Ponting moves himself into an intimidatingly close mid-on. Pietersen pats a drive past him for a single.

53rd over: England 193–2 (Cook 89, Pietersen 10) Marcus North comes back into the attack, bowling his off-breaks from around the wicket. Cook slots a drive out to deep extra cover for two. Here's David Mooney: 'And by getting himself out, Trott drops back to fourth place in the all-time batting standings. It's a real shame . . . he only needed another 802 not out and he would have overtaken Bradman.'

54th over: England 197–2 (Cook 89, Pietersen 14) Pietersen plays that characteristic flick away to midwicket, dragging the ball across from outside off and cocking his back leg as he does so. The batsmen take an all-run four, and given that it is well over 35°C, three minutes from tea and Alastair Cook has been out there all day, the fact they came back for four really tells you a lot about England's fitness levels.

55th over: England 198–2 (Cook 90, Pietersen 14) This may be the last over of the session. Cook pats a single out to deep cover, and that is the last run of the session. England have scored 108 runs off the 28 overs they faced in the afternoon, just for the loss of Trott.

England 198–2; Australia 245

The evening session

BY ROB SMYTH

Preamble: The Cook/Trott axis finally ended at 502 runs. England are still on course for a decisive lead. If they don't get a lead of at least 150, they will kick themselves for ever more. An essentially meaningless but very pretty stat: England are averaging 75 runs per wicket in this series. 75 runs per wicket. That's an

Ashes record, although that will drop significantly by the time the series is over.

56th over: England 199–2 (Cook 91, Pietersen 14) This will probably be a two-and-a-half-hour session, such has been Australia's negligent over rate. Bollinger hustles in, and Cook works the first ball for a single. That's the lot.

57th over: England 204–2 (Cook 92, Pietersen 18) Here comes Xavier Doherty. Cook cuts a single, and then Pietersen plays a stunning stroke, walking down the track and whipping delightfully through midwicket for four. The placement was supreme.

58th over: England 212–2 (Cook 97, Pietersen 21) Pietersen crunches Bollinger through midwicket for three. He looks pretty chipper for a man who has been padded up for about 19 hours. Cook then times the next ball off his pads for four, an effortless stroke. Apparently Sir Beefy has predicted no play at all for the last two days because of rain.

59th over: England 212–2 (Cook 97, Pietersen 21) A maiden from Doherty to Pietersen, who may or may not have a voice in his head telling him to lift every single ball from Doherty back whence it came for six.

60th over: England 220–2 (Cook 99, Pietersen 27) Cook cuts Bollinger for a single, which takes his SERIES AVERAGE to 400, and then pings some leg-stump filth off his pads to move to 99. Pietersen then hooks witheringly for four. England are in complete control of this game.

61st over: England 229–2 (Cook 103, Pietersen 32) There goes Pietersen, charging Doherty and dumping him over mid-off for four. Contempt. Pietersen drives a single down the ground to put Cook back on strike, on 99. And Cook cuts the next ball for four to reach his second century of the week! What a staggering feat of physical and mental strength this is. I think he is the first Englishman to make consecutive Ashes centuries since David Gower in 1985, and the first English opener to do so since Herbert Sutcliffe in 1925. Eighty-five years.

62nd over: England 229–2 (Cook 103, Pietersen 32) Siddle returns in place of Bollinger, whose figures are a grim 13–0–69–1. Pietersen defends carefully and it's a maiden.

63rd over: England 235–2 (Cook 104, Pietersen 37) Pietersen is starting to manhandle Doherty now, and he drives him inside out through extra cover for another boundary.

64th over: England 238–2 (Cook 104, Pietersen 40) A bizarre shot from Pietersen, who flaps a short one from Siddle just back over the bowler's head and down the ground for three. 'You'd have to make up a new word for that shot,' says David Gower in the Sky box. Cook's form just shows that, like William Goldman said, nobody knows anything. In his previous Ashes series he made 276 runs at 27.60 and 222 runs at 24.66. Now he has 406 runs at 406.00. Utterly preposterous.

65th over: England 242–2 (Cook 104, Pietersen 44) Doherty is having a nightmare against Pietersen. His second ball is a hopeless full toss on the pads that Pietersen flicks almost absent-mindedly through midwicket for four. You have to feel for Doherty, whose figures are 15–3–70–0.

66th over: England 243–2 (Cook 105, Pietersen 44) 'I'm here,' announces Lord Selvey. 'For all those Cook naysayers, can I point out that only Sachin had more hundreds than he has at his age.' And, indeed, more runs.

67th over: England 244–2 (Cook 106, Pietersen 44) Xavier Doherty is put out of his misery, with Shane Watson replacing him. That's not the worst move because Watson might just trigger some misplaced machismo from Pietersen. Meanwhile, Gower and Atherton are in the Sky box, talking about the time – at Trent Bridge in 1989 – when Australia were 500 for two and

Gower sent the 12th man, Greg Thomas, to the press box to ask them if they had any ideas. Gower and Atherton's historical digressions are lovely, informative and full of mischief.

68th over: England 253–2 (Cook 108, Pietersen 51) Pietersen completes a profitable over with a gorgeous whip wide of mid-on that takes him to a pretty majestic half-century.

69th over: England 262–2 (Cook 109, Pietersen 59) Another regal stroke from Pietersen, this time a lazy cover drive for four off Watson. He is playing with such authority, and nails another one for four later in the over – this time with marvellous placement.

70th over: England 265–2 (Cook 111, Pietersen 60) I put it to you, ladies and gentlemen, that England are 265 for bloody two?!?!?!?!?!?!?!?!?! 'Still here in dark and cold Tijuana,' says William Kay. 'We are huddled around the gas fire, sipping Vat 69 – can you still get Vat 69 in England? – eating toast with Marmite! Yes, a pupil found Marmite across the border in the USofA and brought me a jar. Marmite and Vat 69, can it get much better? Well, apart from passing the Aussie score with eight wickets still in hand. Do you reckon the rain is a real threat?' I like the fact that with every email he sends, William Kay asks whether we can still get Vat 69 in England. I have absolutely no idea what Vat 69 is, but Bull tells me it's whisky.

71st over: England 269–2 (Cook 115, Pietersen 60) Watson overpitches, and Cook cover-drives beautifully for four. In the Sky box, Beefy and Bumble think Australia might not take the new ball because they are completely shattered. It's available in nine overs' time.

72nd over: England 274–2 (Cook 118, Pietersen 62) Marcus North comes on to replace Siddle, who has been game throughout the day and has figures of 16–3–50–0. Cook drives classily through extra cover for three. Australia look desperately tired. 'I am here in Sydney, watching on TV and following OBO,' says Kate. 'I am nursing a catastrophic hangover from a work party last night. I have only left the couch for painkillers and two hours' sleep at the lunch break. Cook is a handsome devil!' Wait till you see our fast bowlers, lady. You'll go all light-headed faster than you can say, 'Jimmy Anderson, Attack Leader.'

73rd over: England 274–2 (Cook 118, Pietersen 62) A maiden from Watson to Pietersen, who is walking down the track whenever he feels like it.

74th over: England 279–2 (Cook 119, Pietersen 66) Pietersen slams North through the covers for four, a brilliant shot that brings up the century partnership from just 153 balls. England's run rate has been excellent today: they have scored 279 from 73 overs at 3.82 runs per over.

75th over: England 280–2 (Cook 120, Pietersen 66) 'Vat 69?' sniffs Lord Selvey. 'We used to say it was tax on *soixante-neuf*.' Arf.

76th over: England 281–2 (Cook 121, Pietersen 66) North spits a delivery past Cook's defensive push, which will interest Graeme Swann. The game is drifting towards the second new ball, which it seems Australia are going to take straight away.

77th over: England 281–2 (Cook 121, Pietersen 66) I'm not sure whether it's by accident or design, but Watson has given Ponting a bit of control here. That's a maiden to Cook, which makes it one run from Watson's last three overs.

78th over: England 285–2 (Cook 121, Pietersen 70) Pietersen blocks a few deliveries from North and then slog-sweeps almost impatiently for four. Get that filth out of my face. We haven't seen that shot for a while. 'How old are you that you don't know what Vat 69 is?' says Amanda Gaines-Cooke. 'I assumed sage old souls wrote the OBO. This is sobering news.' 'Sage old souls'? Well, one out of three ain't etc.

79th over: England 288–2 (Cook 122, Pietersen 72) Cook turns Watson to square leg and goes through for a very tight single. Doherty missed the stumps at the striker's end, but Pietersen would have been home. 'It's my department's Christmas party in the midst of the not snowy end-of-term shenanigans in Riverside, in Southern California,' says Gareth Funning. 'A number of times I have stumbled into the room where we have been displaying a somewhat dubious stream of the cricket and had to scratch my eyes and make sure that what I was seeing wasn't part of some gin-fuelled dream.'

80th over: England 289–2 (Cook 123, Pietersen 72) North hurries through another over, but it looks like Australia are going to continue with the old ball for now.

81st over: England 291–2 (Cook 125, Pietersen 72) Cook cuts Watson up and over the top for a couple. England's lead is 46. Yikes. 'Trying to explain to my cat the rules of cricket as I near the end of a fine bottle of Australian red (ouch),' says Hannah Slosarski. 'I think I'm hallucinating for the first time since my university days . . . say it ain't so.'

82nd over: England 294–2 (Cook 127, Pietersen 73) Pietersen drives North just short of the diving Ponting at short midwicket. England have slowed up in the last few overs, which is understandable from Cook in particular at the end of a long day. He has now been batting for more than 14 hours since his last dismissal. In an Ashes series. In Australia. That's mind-blowing. 'Good morning from Khartoum. Looks like being a warmish day here,' says Tony Brennan. 'Every Ashes, we get the same Aussie propaganda about targeting the England captain, especially if he's an opener. Theory seems to be that if the captain struggles so will the team. Leaving aside the plain absurdity of this boast (as Lord Selvey wrote – who else would the opening bowler target? Kylie Minogue?), and the word 'Brearley', do Strauss's 0 and 1 from three innings explain England's current struggles?'

83rd over: England 294–2 (Cook 127, Pietersen 73) Watson is doing a decent containing job here, bowling very straight to Pietersen. That's a maiden, and Watson's figures are 14–5–31–0.

84th over: England 295–2 (Cook 128, Pietersen 73) North continues, around the wicket to the relatively becalmed Pietersen. Just one from the over. Everyone looks pretty tired out there.

85th over: England 297–2 (Cook 129, Pietersen 74) Ryan Harris is back into the attack, with seven overs (or 24 minutes) remaining, but he starts with the old ball. Pietersen pings a couple of drives straight to the fielders and then gets one to the left of mid-on for a single.

86th over: England 298–2 (Cook 129, Pietersen 75) Bollinger replaces North (10–0–28–0). Still no sign of the new ball – presumably Ponting is giving them one over each to get loose – and Pietersen takes a very sharp single into the covers. He was just home, although Clarke's throw was wide anyway.

87th over: England 302–2 (Cook 129, Pietersen 79) Australia have taken the new ball. Ryan Harris has a couple of slips, but his third ball is leg-stump garbage that Pietersen flicks imperiously through square leg for four. Just before that you could hear Shane Warne say, off mic, 'It could be over by Melbourne.'

88th over: England 310–2 (Cook 130, Pietersen 86) Four more to Pietersen, swivel-pulled very fine off Bollinger. After all those brilliantly made runs in a losing cause over here four years ago he will be loving every minute of this. He is also homing in on his first Test century since March 2009.

89th over: England 317–2 (Cook 136, Pietersen 86) Cook works Harris fine for a couple, and in doing so breaks Wally Hammond's record for the most runs between dismissals by an English batsman: 367. The next ball is full and wide and square-driven splendidly for four, and the next produces a big lbw shout. There were two doubts – height and whether it pitched outside leg – so Australia decide not to review. Replays show that it was indeed too high. And that's the end of a staggeringly good day for England, and particularly Alastair Cook. He has 136, and England lead by 72.

England 317–2; Australia 245

Third day

The morning session

BY ANDY BULL

Preamble: I know I should really have a lengthy preamble ready for you all, but the truth is I don't. For the English fans out there I think this email from Ross Moulden should suffice: 'Ha-hahahahahahahahahahahaha. That is all.' Strange, isn't it? Surreal even. Alastair Cook needs another 52 runs and he'll already have scored more runs in this series than any single Englishman managed in 2006–7. Kevin Pietersen needs another 15 for his first Test century in 18 matches. For England it's all going swimmingly well. Ricky Ponting sprints out onto the field, spits on his hands and rubs them together, then calls a team huddle. Doug Bollinger and Simon Katich have exchanged friendly gropes of each other's behinds. Really. I'm not making this up.

90th over: England 321–2 (Cook 136, Pietersen 89) Bollinger opens with a rank loosener. His second two are straighter, and Pietersen pats them both away. Ponting has put two slips and a gully in place. By the end of the over Pietersen has adjusted his sights and found his range, and he carts a drive through extra cover for four.

91st over: England 323–2 (Cook 137, Pietersen 90) And at the other end it is Ryan Harris. Cook clips his first ball around the corner for a single, rather as though night had never fallen at all and he was simply carrying on from where he was last evening. Pietersen squirts an inside edge away to fine leg and his score moves on to 90.

92nd over: England 324–2 (Cook 137, Pietersen 91) Another inside edge and another single for Pietersen.

REFERRAL! 93rd over: Pietersen lbw b Harris 91 (England 329–2) Australia think they have Pietersen here, but no one else does. Least of all the umpire. Harris darted the ball back in towards the stumps from outside off and it hit Pietersen's front pad, but it was at least three inches outside the line of off stump. That's a waste of a review by Ponting. Cook ends the over by flicking four through midwicket.

94th over: England 335–2 (Cook 144, Pietersen 94) KP threads a drive through cover and the batsmen run three. 'Could someone tell me if any batsman has ever scored back-to-back Test double centuries?' asks Ben Hendy. 'I know it's presumptuous and will probably jinx Cook, but equally I feel I have to know.' Walter Hammond has done it in consecutive Test innings, Ben, in the 1928–9 Ashes, and again against New Zealand in 1932–3. And so have Don Bradman and, more surprisingly, Vinod Kambli.

95th over: England 343–2 (Cook 146, Pietersen 100) And there's Pietersen's hundred, raised with a dab to the leg side off a short ball from Harris. Earlier in the over he had thumped a glorious four through midwicket to move to 99. He's delighted and punches the air, hugs Cook and then takes off his helmet to acknowledge the ovation he is getting from his teammates in the dressing room. Now he's reached that landmark this could get really entertaining.

96th over: England 347–2 (Cook 146, Pietersen 104) Bollinger baffles Pietersen with a slower ball, but then serves up an inviting short delivery which disappears to the square-leg boundary. Alan Gardner points out that Kumar Sangakkara has done the back-to-back double tons too, against Bangladesh in 2007. This from Jeffrey Chapman: 'My friend Dan, inspired by England's heroics, has proposed to his girlfriend of 20 years and mother of his two children. Liz said yes and the Oompah band is playing "Bohemian Rhapsody" in their front room to celebrate. Strange but true – the things cricket does to people.'

WICKET! 97th over: Cook c Haddin b Harris 148 (England 351–3) Harris clatters a vicious bouncer into Pietersen's elbow. Good ball that. Pietersen is incensed, and even a little agitated. Harris follows it up with another bouncer, and Pietersen swings a wild hook at this one, screwing the ball up in the air. There's no one underneath it though, so he gets away with it. Cook comes on strike and . . . well, I'll be. They've got him. Cook falls at last, caught behind by Haddin off the inside edge. It was a strange dismissal – Australia hardly seemed to appeal, and after what seemed a very long time umpire Erasmus finally put his finger up. The decision was the right one though – there was the slightest of nicks as the ball slid through the gate.

98th over: England 357–3 (Pietersen 112, Collingwood 0) Pietersen steps across well outside his off stump and wallops a full delivery from Bollinger away through midwicket for four. That was utterly contemptuous. A word for all the England fans from Richard Finch: 'All this hubris is absurd. Without wanting to sound like Mr Pessimistic or Lord Miserable/Low Self-Esteem, England have bowled Australia out cheaply on a batting track, but that is all. There is still the second innings to come and there is enough talent in the Australian batting and/or enough naivety in the English bowling to see an outcome not dissimilar to the first Test.'

99th over: England 357–3 (Pietersen 112, Collingwood 0) Harris has had to call out the physio for a little boundary-side treatment on his right shoulder. He still gets through a maiden over though, as Collingwood reacquaints himself with what it is like to be out in the middle. 'I think "the Oompah band is playing 'Bohemian Rhapsody'" might be the best euphemism I've ever heard,' chuckles Joe Meredith. 'Well, they are celebrating.'

100th over: England 366–3 (Pietersen 121, Collingwood 0) Peter Siddle has come into the attack now. Ponting puts three men back on the boundary. Much good it does him. KP crashes and then bashes two fours to square leg, picking out the gap between the fielders on both occasions. 'Maybe think again, Ricky,' says Bumble. 'Not very smart cricket this,' agrees old Iron Bottom. 'The batsman's got a hundred and he's bowling pies halfway down the wicket.' That was one of the most demoralising pieces of cricket I can recall seeing (demoralising if you're an Australian that is; if you're English you can substitute in the word 'hilarious').

101st over: England 372–3 (Pietersen 122, Collingwood 4) Collingwood's first runs come with a push to long-off which allows the batsmen to run four.

102nd over: England 378–3 (Pietersen 122, Collingwood 7) That's an intriguing delivery from Siddle. The ball swung a country mile after pitching, whistling past batsman and 'keeper and running away for four byes.

103rd over: England 387–3 (Pietersen 126, Collingwood 11) Xavier Doherty is given the ball for the first time. This might just be the final chance he gets for the foreseeable future to try and blow the flickering embers of his fledgling Test career back into life.

104th over: England 389–3 (Pietersen 128, Collingwood 12) Siddle looks a shadow of the bowler he was in the first Test, and Colly and KP work him this way and that in their own distinct styles.

105th over: England 393–3 (Pietersen 128, Collingwood

16) Collingwood clumps the ball onto Katich's helmet at short leg, and then sneaks two runs as the ball ricochets off into the outfield.

106th over: England 402–3 (Pietersen 129, Collingwood 24) Collingwood is batting to the manner born at the moment. He pulls Siddle for four through midwicket, and then drives another boundary down past mid-off too. Up comes the 400, and England's lead is now 157. These two have put on over fifty now, at five and a half runs an over. It all looks insultingly easy.

107th over: England 409–3 (Pietersen 136, Collingwood 24) Going, going, gone. Pietersen steps down the pitch and lofts an enormous six over long-off. What a glorious shot. 'I actually feel aroused,' says Dean Butler. He may regret being so frank in the morning. Never mind, that's six hours away yet.

108th over: England 410–3 (Pietersen 136, Collingwood 24) Siddle delivers an ugly wide, then has a grumble at the umpire about the fact that Pietersen had come so close to hitting it. Courtesy of Simon Israel: 'Speaking of the Ashes, I am following OBO from Baños, a town at the foot of a giant volcano currently in the news: "The Tungurahua volcano in Ecuador is billowing ash into the sky and sending super-hot pyroclastic flows surging down its slopes, causing authorities to evacuate nearby villages." There is plenty of ash but no lava flows nor fleeing, screaming villagers . . . at least not yet. They are all partying in town like it's the end of the world . . . The guy running the guest house is an Aussie. Nothing finer than to greet him in the morning with "We've just whipped your butt . . . again."'

109th over: England 412–3 (Pietersen 136, Collingwood 26) Just two runs from Doherty's latest over, allowing Charlie Talbot a little room to prove that actually, whatever those of us with smutty minds may have thought, 'the Oompah band is playing "Bohemian Rhapsody"' wasn't a euphemism at all.

110th over: England 416–3 (Pietersen 140, Collingwood 26) Doug Bollinger replaces Siddle. Nasser points out that Ponting has set a 7–2 off-side field. And also that two of Bollinger's first three deliveries have disappeared down to fine leg for two runs apiece. Oops. Ponting screws up his face and stares at the turf.

111th over: England 424–3 (Pietersen 140, Collingwood 34) Collingwood clips four through midwicket, and Australia have their second centurion of the innings – Doherty has now gone for 100 off his 20 overs.

112th over: England 428–3 (Pietersen 144, Collingwood 34) Pietersen skims a drive over the head of cover. The shot was accompanied by a cry of 'Catchit!' which preceded the sound of the ball thumping into the boundary hoarding by a fraction of a second.

113th over: England 432–3 (Pietersen 144, Collingwood 38) Marcus North comes on for a couple of overs before lunch. He finds more turn than Doherty did at any point in this session.

114th over: England 439–3 (Pietersen 149, Collingwood 39) Bumble and Nasser are discussing what constitutes a wide. 'If you can't reach it with a proper cricket shot it's a wide,' says Bumble. 'It's not supposed to be something you can only reach with a yard brush or a washing prop.' 'A what?' says Nasser. 'A washing prop. You probably don't have them in Essex.'

115th over: England 449–3 (Pietersen 158, Collingwood 40) Last over of the session, and Pietersen raises his 150 with a murderous slog sweep off North. His last 50 runs have come off just 52 deliveries. Pietersen finishes the session on 158. He's been quite brilliant so far today, back to his imperious best. That, of course, is the exact score he made at Adelaide four years ago. Lunch.

England 449–3; Australia 245

The afternoon session

BY ALAN GARDNER

Preamble: Yes, this is my Ashes bow. 'Morning, Alan. What a great time to make your debut. Here's hoping it's more Steve Finn than Alan Mullally. I'm sure you're well versed in the Ashes OBO Down Under now. Half-cut Brits, delirious ex-pats, but this time all in a positive situation. Totally unreal, and utterly fantastic to watch Australia fall to bits. Hope is standing in the wings, toying with us, but right now I think we're all in there.' Aye, Guy Hornsby is not wrong. I contemplated likening myself to Colly in 2005, but I think I may plump for the mercurial Alex Tudor, who made his debut, appropriately, in the second Test of the 1998–9 series. If I manage to rack up ten caps, I'll probably die happy.

116th over: England 449–3 (Pietersen 158, Collingwood 40) Pietersen launches himself at Watson's first delivery but finds the man at mid-on. Then mid-off, followed by extra cover. That's a maiden.

117th over: England 451–3 (Pietersen 158, Collingwood 40) Marcus North runs through a quick six balls of right-arm over, Collingwood scampering a couple. Here's Andrew Mullinder with an email entitled 'The Doyen': 'I'm sitting here in Moscow watching the Australian coverage. Just thought I'd share Richie Benaud's opening comments this morning: "Morning, everybody. Down the barrel, I think, is the phrase."'

WICKET! 118th over: Collingwood lbw b Watson 42 (England 452–4) Collingwood plays back to the man with the golden arm/chief pie thrower, Watson, and is plumb leg before. Collingwood was so deep in the crease there, practically cosying up to his stumps, and that ends a quicksmart partnership of 101 between him and his old batting buddy Pietersen.

119th over: England 458–4 (Pietersen 158, Bell 5) 'Hi, Alan, it's good to have a new name on the OBO on a night when it's actually quite good for England,' begins Clare A. Davies cheerfully enough. 'Obviously it will be all your fault if it goes wrong!' Oh. 'However, the signs are good. Not only did I fail to get an email on with Bull – we usually win when that happens – but my small black cat is doing all the running-around-mad-cat things that she did in 2005 on the last day at the Oval.'

120th over: England 458–4 (Pietersen 158, Bell 5) Bell inside-edges a forward defence onto his pads, his back foot then deflecting the ball off its stumpward path. Watson lets out a cry of anguish – but it wasn't really all that close.

121st over: England 459–4 (Pietersen 161, Bell 5) After a rollicking little morning session, England have gone postprandially quiet.

122nd over: England 464–4 (Pietersen 166, Bell 5) Brad Haddin tries standing up to the stumps to curb Pietersen's attacking instincts. There are then shouts of 'Catchit!' and 'Howzat!', but although the ball struck Pietersen on the pads he got some bat on it and the ball ballooned away to safety.

123rd over: England 465–4 (Pietersen 167, Bell 5) As North runs through another innocuous over, Johnny Hodgetts has a cunning plan: 'I think I've found a cure for all Australia's selection woes. The Australian front-line bowling attack for the next Test should be all part-timers: North, Watson, Katich and Steve Smith. That way they can bat further down the order and not have to worry about their quicks getting embarrassed!'

124th over: England 472–4 (Pietersen 171, Bell 8) Pietersen and Bell run well between the wickets to take seven from the over.

125th over: England 477–4 (Pietersen 172, Bell 12) Bell skips forward and then back to slash the ball backward of square for a boundary. He's looking very active at the crease so far, Bell, obviously keen to get on and neutralise that threat of precipitation.

126th over: England 486–4 (Pietersen 181, Bell 12) Shane Warne calls Hussain a 'muppet' and tells him to 'shut it' in the commentary box after Hussain began the over by baiting Warne on what he would do were he Australia captain. Warne then suggests Australia 'start practising their rain dance'.

127th over: England 491–4 (Pietersen 182, Bell 16) In pictures that sum up Australia's performance in Adelaide, Simon Katich is limping around in the field. Not sure why, but he's going off. There are some faint 'oohs' as Bell deflects the ball near to one of the close catchers. Nothing doing.

128th over: England 492–4 (Pietersen 183, Bell 16) Pietersen, who already has a 'daddy hundred' and must be looking at the next level up (a 'granddaddy' doesn't have quite the same ring to it), clips a single. 'England are all over Australia like a cheap suit . . . but it's still 0–0,' opines Warne.

129th over: England 493–4 (Pietersen 184, Bell 16) Ryan Harris is thrown the cherry and immediately beats Pietersen with one that nibbles away. Bell is then left groping at another good delivery outside off that keeps a touch low.

130th over: England 494–4 (Pietersen 185, Bell 16) For all his jive talk, Warne speaks great cricket sense. Push on, declare and have a go at Australia is essentially his argument. As the lead approaches 250, England are somewhat becalmed: just one off the over.

131st over: England 499–4 (Pietersen 186, Bell 16) 'The advertising hoarding behind the batsmen is for MAC – the Major

Accident Commission,' notes Bull to my right. 'I wonder if any photographer has lined up a picture of Ponting in front of it yet.'

132nd over: England 504–4 (Pietersen 187, Bell 20) Pietersen brings up the 500 with a single before Bell punches four through midwicket.

133rd over: England 509–4 (Pietersen 192, Bell 20) England continue serenely on, smoother than the thousands of freshly de-Movembered top lips around the world.

134th over: England 520–4 (Pietersen 193, Bell 30) The collective voice of the Barmy Army is booming out around the Oval. 'Mighty, mighty England . . .' they croon. Bell is now motoring, driving the last ball of Siddle's over sweetly for four down the ground. That's ton up for Peter.

135th over: England 524–4 (Pietersen 197, Bell 30) Pietersen whips an overpitched Harris delivery for four to edge closer to what Nicholas Cocks has helpfully classified as a 'Sugar-Daddy Hundred'.

136th over: England 524–4 (Pietersen 197, Bell 30) Ricky's trying to gee up his men in the field. There are plenty of grim-faced, hands-on-hips types out there today. The Rug is back on and he bowls his first maiden at the 24th attempt. That'll make his figures look much better. Bull points out that 'This is now the largest first-innings deficit Australia have conceded at home since they were bowled out for 76 by the West Indies in 1984 . . .'

137th over: England 525–4 (Pietersen 198, Bell 30) Xavier Doherty is given another opportunity to improve his Test obituary, conceding just a single. Surely this is the last we'll hear of the not-so-young Tasmanian?

138th over: England 526–4 (Pietersen 199, Bell 30) Pietersen edges ever closer to the second double century of his

Test career. He's taken 73 balls for his fourth fifty, by my rough calculation. 'Dude,' begins Matthew Sackman, 'it's 4.11 a.m. Tomorrow, I'm playing Verdi's *Requiem*, for which I've not been to a single rehearsal. Can KP just get his something-double-ton-thingy please, and then I'll stop drinking this awful whisky and go to bed?'

139th over: England 530–4 (Pietersen 200, Bell 33) There it is – Pietersen's double hundred. He lets out a cry as he dashes a quick single into the covers, partly out of excitement but also partly because he seems to be nursing a slight leg problem. That hasn't held him up though. This has been quite an innings, full of controlled aggression, barely a chance given that I can recall. Matthew Sackman, you can go to bed and dream about KP playing Verdi, which he could probably pull off right now.

140th over: England 534–4 (Pietersen 200, Bell 37) That's a corking stroke from Bell, rocking back and guiding a pull off Bollinger straight to the fence.

141st over: England 535–4 (Pietersen 201, Bell 37) As we tick towards tea, there are plenty of people in my inbox enjoying England's day in the Aussie sun. Tom Adams: 'I'm sitting on the edge of a beach two hours south of Sydney in glorious sunshine, catching up on the OBO, and just overheard an Australian man who was walking past explaining what a "diamond duck" is to his daughter. Today is a good day.'

142nd over: England 537–4 (Pietersen 202, Bell 38) England are still biding their time, stalking their prey. Just two singles off Bollinger. Michael Holding pronounces on Sky's commentary that if the Pietersen–Bell partnership reaches triple figures, it will be the first time since 1938 that England have had four century partnerships in a match.

143rd over: England 551–4 (Pietersen 213, Bell 41) Now that's more like it! Bell takes two and one off the first of Doughy's deliveries, then Pietersen launches the left-armer twice over the top, clearing the field and finding the boundary on both occasions. Another two and a single from the final two balls means that England have taken 14 off the over. Tea.

England 551–4; Australia 245

The evening session

BY ANDY BULL

Preamble: The bad news is that the rain has arrived and the covers are on. That's all, folks. Play has been called off for the day.

England 551–5; Australia 245

Fourth day

The morning session

BY ROB SMYTH

Preamble: Australia will delighted with a weather forecast which suggests they will have significant competition for the title of 'Adelaide's Biggest Shower' over the next 48 hours. An email from Anton Lawrence: 'Dear Ricky. Please find book enclosed titled *Is It Cowardly to Pray for Rain?* Hope you enjoy. Love and kisses, England cricket supporters. PS The answer is yes.' England are batting on.

144th over: England 558–4 (Pietersen 220, Bell 41) One of the reasons for batting on is that England have their two best strokeplayers at the crease, so there's not much danger of them propping and cocking. Pietersen proves the point by flaying Bollinger's second delivery gloriously through extra cover for four. Meanwhile, Lord Selvey tells us that England will bat for half an hour and then declare.

145th over: England 561–4 (Pietersen 222, Bell 42) Peter Siddle, whose hat-trick seems a long, long time ago, starts at the other end. There is an urgency to the batting, with both batsmen dancing down the pitch to the quicks.

146th over: England 564–4 (Pietersen 223, Bell 43) A preposterous incident at the start of the over. Just as Bollinger was about to bowl, the sightscreen behind him suddenly changed to a picture of Shane Warne advertising a McDonald's Chicken Legend! Pietersen backed away in shock.

WICKET! 147th over: Pietersen c Katich b Doherty 227 (England 568–5) This is an odd move: Ricky Ponting has decided to feed Xavier Doherty to the lions. With cruel predictability, Pietersen dismisses his first ball through midwicket for four to go to 227, his highest Test score. But he falls next ball, toe-ending a violent hoick to Katich at slip.

147th over: England 577–5 (Bell 49, Prior 3) Bell is such a beautiful straight hitter against slow bowling, and he dances down the track to lift Doherty over mid-on for six. Thirteen from the over.

148th over: England 578–5 (Bell 49, Prior 4) Matt Prior is trapped in front by a fine yorker from Siddle that hits him flush on the toe. He decides to review it, just because he can, but that's surely a waste of 90 seconds. No, it isn't – he's not out!

149th over: England 589–5 (Bell 54, Prior 10) Bell drives a single to move to another seriously classy fifty, and then Australia have another shocker in the field. Prior skied a slog sweep, and both Ponting and North left it to each other. The look on Ponting's face is a picture.

150th over: England 596–5 (Bell 58, Prior 13) Prior sweeps Siddle for two. England are doing as they please now. Later in the over Bell gives Siddle the charge and flaps a short one over cover for four. 'Would you swap England winning the Ashes (as we know they will) for England winning the World Cup?' asks Jonah Gadsby. Lord, no. Is there anyone who would?

151st over: England 610–5 (Bell 63, Prior 22) Bell lifts Doherty over extra cover for two to take England past 600. It's the first time they have scored 600 against Australia since 1964. England are treating Doherty with total contempt: fourteen from it.

152nd over: England 620–5 declared (Bell 68, Prior 27)
Prior skims a cover drive for four off Siddle to bring up the
fifty partnership in only 33 balls. Ten more from that over, and
there's the declaration. England lead by 375 – that's the biggest
first-innings lead a touring team has taken in Australia since
1974–5. 'I'm struggling with this new topsy-turvy world,' says
Dan Smith. 'Do I now need to bleach my hair/drink VB/list bar-
becuing as a hobby/get a bar job in London?'

Australia second innings

1st over: Australia 10–0 (Watson 9, Katich 1) James
Anderson starts with three slips, and his third ball is a good one
that Watson thick-edges into the ground and wide of third slip
for four. Watson plays a princely cover drive for four to end an
expensive over.

2nd over: Australia 17–0 (Watson 15, Katich 2) Australia
have started aggressively, which England won't mind as it will obviously increase their chances of taking wickets. And there's the
proof: Watson leans into a booming drive that slices off the edge
and into the air between slip and gully.

3rd over: Australia 17–0 (Watson 15, Katich 2) Katich
leaves a delivery from Anderson that curves back appreciably
and doesn't miss the stumps by too much. A maiden.

4th over: Australia 17–0 (Watson 15, Katich 2) Broad has
bowled with impressive discipline in this series. He is trying to
draw Watson into the corridor, but Watson isn't tempted so
that's another maiden.

5th over: Australia 29–0 (Watson 15, Katich 14) Katich
pulls Anderson decisively behind square for four and then pushes

consecutive boundaries through mid-off to make it 12 from the over.

6th over: Australia 30–0 (Watson 16, Katich 14) Broad has only taken two wickets in this series, and as such has been England's unsung hero, because he has bowled really well for the most part and has certainly helped to build pressure.

7th over: Australia 34–0 (Watson 20, Katich 14) Watson looks in fine touch and times Anderson wide of mid-on for his fourth four. 'I'm having trouble understanding the satisfied purring of some comments on your site,' says Adam Levy in New Zealand, as thrown as the rest of us by the oxymoron of the positive Englishman. 'As I understand it, the first Test was drawn and the second Test is not yet over.'

8th over: Australia 35–0 (Watson 20, Katich 15) Katich hooks Broad in the air but well short of the man at deep backward square. Testing the immobile Katich with the short ball is a good tactic. On Sky, Beefy reckons Swann should come on first change, and you can see why. Even though England marmalised Doherty this morning, he got a fair bit of turn.

9th over: Australia 44–0 (Watson 24, Katich 20) Katich chases a wide, full delivery from Anderson and slices it over point for four. Later in the over Watson slaps a cut over the top for four more. Anderson has figures of 5–0–35–0. This has been an excellent, purposeful start from Australia.

10th over: Australia 45–0 (Watson 24, Katich 20) Graeme Swann is coming into the attack, which is surely a good move from Andrew Strauss. Will Australia still attack him with a deficit of nearly 350? Not for the time being. Watson defends carefully in a decent first over that included enough turn to keep us all happy and expectant.

11th over: Australia 46–0 (Watson 24, Katich 21) Stuart Broad has switched ends to replace James Anderson. Another tight over brings just a single to Katich. If we take the rain as a given, the destiny of this game probably lies in the right hand of Graeme Swann. 'The Aussie commentators seem a little obsessed with Katich,' says David Harding, 'and claim he is a real man/tough guy because he doesn't wax.' I wonder if Brian Close ever waxed. I'd pay a lot of money to see somebody suggest the concept of waxing to a thirty-something Brian Close.

12th over: Australia 50–0 (Watson 25, Katich 24) Watson flicks Swann just wide of the diving Strauss at short midwicket. Or was it short mid-on? Show a replay, darn it. Either way, that was very close, and now it's time for drinks.

13th over: Australia 50–0 (Watson 25, Katich 24) Broad has a ludicrously optimistic shout for lbw against Watson, who was well outside the line and also a long way forward. Not even Competitive Dad would have reviewed that. Another maiden from Broad.

14th over: Australia 51–0 (Watson 25, Katich 25) Swann has a slip, short leg and silly point, but Australia have played him comfortably thus far. That's a maiden to Watson. 'What with living over there for four years and having a British wife, I've always felt an affinity for you lot,' says Nick Watts. 'It's not been until these last few days, watching our batsmen crumble on a flat deck and yours score at will, that I've truly understood what it means to be English.'

15th over: Australia 52–0 (Watson 25, Katich 26) This is excellent bowling from Broad, who drags Katich across the crease and beats him with a beautiful full leg-cutter. Then he beats Watson outside off stump.

16th over: Australia 55–0 (Watson 26, Katich 28) Three near misses in that Swann over. First Katich pushes him right between the legs of Cook at short leg, and then he gets a leading edge just past the diving Strauss at short extra cover. Finally

Watson inside-edges onto the pad and just in front of the diving Ian Bell, running back from silly point. An excellent over from Swann.

17th over: Australia 55–0 (Watson 26, Katich 28) That's another excellent maiden from Broad, and England are building pressure very well: the last five overs have produced just five runs. Broad's figures are 8–4–11–0.

18th over: Australia 56–0 (Watson 27, Katich 28) Swann is getting into a nice groove now and has a big shout for lbw against Watson. It was too high and he was outside the line, so they don't review, but Swann is starting to look pretty threatening.

19th over: Australia 60–0 (Watson 31, Katich 28) Steven Finn on to replace Broad. His first few balls are a good length, but when he drags one down just a touch it is pulled witheringly for four by Watson. If he didn't do a big rubbery one upon reaching 50, Watson would be one of the best openers in the world.

20th over: Australia 60–0 (Watson 31, Katich 28) Swann has a shout for lbw, this time against Katich. Well, I say Swann; it was actually only Prior who went up. It was sliding down leg. Another maiden from Swann, who is bowling nicely and has figures of 6–2–9–0.

21st over: Australia 64–0 (Watson 35, Katich 28) In a reversal of traditional roles, the seamers aren't doing much more than keeping an end dry while Swann chips away in pursuit of wickets.

22nd over: Australia 66–0 (Watson 35, Katich 30) Katich works Swann through midwicket and winces up and down the pitch for a couple. Swann probably fancies a bowl at Watson, who was starting to look twitchy against him, but it's been just Katich for his last two overs.

23rd over: Australia 66–0 (Watson 35, Katich 30) Finn beats Watson with a nice delivery outside off stump, and then Watson toe-ends a vigorous pull stroke straight to midwicket. A maiden.

24th over: Australia 69–0 (Watson 35, Katich 33) Swann beats Katich with a fine delivery, slower and flighted. Katich responds with a very fine sweep for three.

25th over: Australia 78–0 (Watson 36, Katich 41) Katich reaches away from his body and snicks Finn right through the vacant fourth-slip area for four, the second boundary of the over after he worked one off the pads two balls earlier. And that's lunch. Australia have done extremely well, showing both moral and – particularly in Katich's case – physical courage. Andy Bull has seen a picture of the two of us in today's *Guardian*. 'We look', he says, 'like a pair of clowns . . .' Yep. Whatever street cred the OBO had has just been obliterated. Can you obliterate something that doesn't exist?

Australia 245 and 78–0; England 620–5 dec

The afternoon session

BY ANDY BULL

Preamble: Evening, everyone. No one said it was going to be easy. Did they? [Disclaimer: we may have said it was going to be easy.]

'Re: Rob's question "Can you obliterate non-existent things?"' writes Jay Buckley. 'The answer is, of course, erm, well, of course. For example, the photo also managed to obliterate your and Smyth's dignity.' Those photos actually seem to get worse each time they reappear. They seem to be deteriorating as the series goes on. Just like us, I suppose.

26th over: Australia 78–0 (Katich 42, Watson 35) Swann starts the afternoon session, bowling around the wicket to Katich. Each and every ball is accompanied by a grunt of appreciation from Matt Prior.

27th over: Australia 82–0 (Katich 42, Watson 39) Anderson starts at the other end. For the first five balls he gives Watson nothing to hit: each is tight on off stump. His sixth is full and straight though, and Watson whips it away to fine leg for four.

28th over: Australia 84–0 (Katich 43, Watson 40) Katich shovels the first ball away through the leg side and hobbles a run.

29th over: Australia 84–0 (Katich 43, Watson 40) Anderson hangs the ball outside Watson's off stump, trying to lure him into losing his patience. But the batsman doesn't succumb – he watches the wide ones pass by and blocks the rest.

WICKET! 30th over: Katich c Prior b Swann 43 (Australia 84–1) There's the breakthrough. Swann gets his man, caught behind off the outside edge. Katich turned and walked off the field, stopping only when Watson called out to him to ask if he had definitely hit the ball. The answer must have been yes. And here's Ricky Ponting, arriving at the crease on a king pair. Collingwood seems to have plenty to say for himself at slip – no doubt he's just reminding Ricky of the various pressures weighing down on his shoulders. Ponting strides out to meet all five balls. It's a wicket maiden though, and he is still on a pair.

31st over: Australia 84–1 (Watson 40, Ponting 0) Anderson persists with this plan to try and bore Watson into an indiscretion. He still won't bite though, and it is another maiden.

32nd over: Australia 84–1 (Watson 40, Ponting 0) Swann

is bowling a lovely spell to Ponting here, suckering him into lunging forward at a ball that drifted on and beat his outside edge. It's another maiden, the fourth in a row. Ponting is playing a cagey game. Swann's figures so far are almost as handsome as that photo of Smyth in the paper: 12–5–15–1.

33rd over: Australia 85–1 (Watson 41, Ponting 0) The run of dot balls finally ends as Anderson opens the over with that full, straight delivery again, and Watson glances it away for a single out to deep square.

34th over: Australia 90–1 (Watson 41, Ponting 4) Ponting is off and running. He clips a short, wide delivery from Swann away to the cover boundary.

35th over: Australia 94–1 (Watson 45, Ponting 4) Watson glances three away through the leg side. 'Whisper it,' says Magnus Blair, 'but is the weather forecast improving?'

WICKET! 36th over: Ponting c Collingwood b Swann 9 (Australia 98–2) Got him! Swann strikes. Collingwood should get just as much of the credit – he took a fantastic catch at slip, low down to his left. He plucked the ball out of the air just before it touched the turf. And it was wonderfully canny bowling by Swann. Ponting had swept the previous delivery viciously away from outside off stump for four through square leg. So Swann sent the next one straight on, and it slipped off the outside edge as Ponting was playing down the wrong line. What a huge wicket for England that is.

37th over: Australia 106–2 (Watson 45, Clarke 8) Strauss immediately brings Broad into the attack. 'Good move,' mutters Smyth, 'bomb him.'

38th over: Australia 106–2 (Watson 45, Clarke 8) Clarke is using his feet well to get to the pitch of the ball, but is still managing to look out of sorts when it comes to playing the shots. It's a maiden over. 'I wonder if any other ex-pats could answer this question,' says Raymond Coffey. 'I'm an Englishman living in Australia with two young Australian sons aged 3.5 and 1.5. When can I expect them to start calling me a Pommie b@st@rd?' I'd say just as soon as we've won this series, Raymond.

39th over: Australia 111–2 (Watson 46, Clarke 12) Clarke latches onto a short ball, collaring it with a pull that brings him four through midwicket. So Broad bangs the ball in harder, shorter and faster, and has Clarke ducking underneath the next one. And the one after as well. '"Collingwood should get the credit" but, Andy – we simply EXPECT St Paul of Collingwood to catch those,' points out Clare Davies. "Cos not only can he leap like a salmon, but he can dive like a, like a – well, a diving thing! Perhaps we should liken him to a dolphin. Both leaping and diving.'

40th over: Australia 111–2 (Watson 46, Clarke 12) Watson has been quietly going about his work at the other end, unobtrusively occupying the crease. He's looked the part today, Watson, though he has been all but strokeless since lunch. The man only seems to have two gears to his batting.

41st over: Australia 121–2 (Watson 50, Clarke 18) Clarke chops Broad's first ball through gully, where Pietersen dives full stretch to his left to try and cut it off. It passes by his fingertips and skips away across the grass for four. Watson thrashes the final ball of the over down the ground for four. That brings up his fifty.

42nd over: Australia 122–2 (Watson 51, Clarke 18) Just a single from this over. 'I've been taking morphine (prescribed!) with extra morphine for extra pain,' says Chris Drew. 'Pink elephants to go . . . Tell me this is not just part of my delirium, please.'

43rd over: Australia 123–2 (Watson 52, Clarke 18) Steve Finn replaces Broad and beats Clarke with a cracking delivery that nips away off the seam and beats the outside edge.

44th over: Australia 127–2 (Watson 56, Clarke 18) Watson swings a loose cut at an arm ball from Swann and nearly gets himself out as he does so. A little like a bear who has had his paw burnt, he reacts by lashing out at a short ball, which he wallops away for four over square leg.

45th over: Australia 129–2 (Watson 56, Clarke 20) Two off the over. But the focus is off the pitch rather than on it.

46th over: Australia 134–2 (Watson 57, Clarke 24) Bad news from the England dressing room: Stuart Broad has strained a stomach muscle and gone off the pitch. If this is a serious injury, England's four-man attack is going to be horribly exposed. Clarke steers four through cover.

WICKET! 47th over: Watson c Strauss b Finn 57 (Australia 134–3) Finn conjures a wicket from nowhere almost, nipping the ball away from the bat off the pitch. Watson leant forward to block it, and the ball slipped off his outside edge and flew to first slip, where Strauss took another good catch. Watson has come up short again then. Smyth tells me that Watson has the worst conversion rate of fifties into hundreds of any regular Australian opener in history. Hussey is in then, and this is the key wicket between England and the match.

48th over: Australia 139–3 (Clarke 24, Hussey 5) Swann switches to bowling around the wicket. Hussey steps down the pitch and flicks four through square leg. That's a great shot for a man who has just come to the crease.

49th over: Australia 141–3 (Clarke 26, Hussey 5) The rain clouds are gathering on the horizon behind the old scoreboard, or so Athers tells us. Clarke pulls two runs to midwicket. He's played well so far, Clarke. His early jitters have disappeared. 'A message to Raymond Coffey about his *ahem*, "Australian sons",' writes Ian Berrisford. 'As an exiled Pom in a similar position (living in Melbourne, both boys 3.5 and 1.5, spookily), it may help him to start regarding them instead as "My English sons". A little psychological trick that's worked for millions, though I couldn't vouch for KP's mother with 100 per cent certainty, of course.'

50th over: Australia 144–3 (Clarke 28, Hussey 5) Watching Clarke play well here it is becoming increasingly clear that we're looking at a man who is – assuming Australia do not end up winning this series – going to be captaining the Test team sooner rather than later.

51st over: Australia 144–3 (Clarke 28, Hussey 6) All of a sudden Steve Finn is starting to get the ball to reverse swing. He's bowling from around the wicket and is causing Hussey all sorts of problems. This is wonderful stuff from the young 'un in England's attack.

52nd over: Australia 144–3 (Clarke 28, Hussey 6) Another maiden, and another telegram from Mike Selvey Down Under: 'Thought you might be interested in this from the Australian Bureau of Meteorology: "SEVERE THUNDERSTORM WARNING for FLASH FLOODING, DAMAGING WIND and LARGE HAILSTONES."'

53rd over: Australia 148–3 (Clarke 28, Hussey 10) Well, on the one hand that storm may ruin England's chances of winning this match. But on the other it will stop all the commentators Down Under making smug references to the fact that it is snowing 'back home in Britain'.

54th over: Australia 150–3 (Clarke 30, Hussey 10) Stuart Broad is back out on the field, so his injury can't be as serious as all that. We're closing in on the end of the session now.

55th over: Australia 157–3 (Clarke 35, Hussey 12) Botham and Atherton are discussing the effects the heavy rain will have on the international wheat trade. Really, they are. Finn swears to himself through gritted teeth after giving Clarke a full delivery which was dispatched to fine leg for four.

56th over: Australia 160–3 (Clarke 36, Hussey 14) One more over then. Matt Prior jokingly blocks Marais Erasmus's path towards the dressing room to force the umpires to allow six more balls before tea. England will know the forecast. Tea.

Australia 245 and 166–3; England 620–5 dec

The evening session

BY ROB SMYTH

Preamble: Weather watch – 'As I look to the north out of my 14th-floor office window in the city it is looking pretty black in that direction,' says Marcus Howard. 'A mate who is a brickie is working about 50 km north of Adelaide and has just messaged me to say it is currently bucketing down.'

57th over: Australia 166–3 (Clarke 36, Hussey 20) James Anderson starts what could be a pretty short evening session. He goes around the wicket to Hussey, who drives through the covers on two occasions, first for two and then for four. The second delivery disturbed the surface of the pitch though, so that's a dangerous shot to play.

58th over: Australia 168–3 (Clarke 37, Hussey 21) Clarke has used his feet quite beautifully against Swann – almost exclusively as a defensive tactic, to smother the spin – and he does so on four occasions in that over, which also includes a flash of lightning behind the scoreboard. 'A couple of days ago there was a chap wanting to know if the Ashes were on in Beijing,' says

Jonathan White. 'He's in luck – The Den and Paddy O'Shea's are both definitely showing the series.'

59th over: Australia 169–3 (Clarke 37, Hussey 22) There is a bit of reverse swing for Anderson, as there was for Finn in his excellent pre-tea spell, and he beats Hussey with consecutive deliveries that draw him into Geoff Boycott's beloved corridor.

60th over: Australia 170–3 (Clarke 37, Hussey 23) If England can just get one more tonight, however much play we get, they will sleep pretty happily. With a long tail and a struggling Marcus North to come, this is – with the exception of the first partnership involving Brad Haddin – the most important of the innings by some distance. One from Swann's over.

61st over: Australia 175–3 (Clarke 41, Hussey 24) Anderson sends down some rare filth: short, wide and slapped for four by Clarke. The over ends with a reverse inswinger that Clarke just manages to defend. Anyone out there?

62nd over: Australia 175–3 (Clarke 41, Hussey 24) That's the last over we'll see for a while, because it has started raining. It appears the players have actually gone off for bad light, with the rain very light. Andrew Strauss is still on the pitch, asking the umpires why the artificial lights were not turned on in preparation for this.

63rd over: Australia 181–3 (Clarke 47, Hussey 24) These overs are a big bonus for England, who probably thought that was it when they went off an hour ago. There are potentially another 17 overs to be bowled tonight.

64th over: Australia 183–3 (Clarke 48, Hussey 25) The other good thing about these overs is that if we get them all, England will have a new ball first thing tomorrow morning. Swann spits a peach past Hussey's forward defensive stroke.

65th over: Australia 192–3 (Clarke 56, Hussey 26) Clarke steers Anderson to third man for four to bring up a cathartic half-century, his first of the winter. He celebrates by pulling the next ball disdainfully for four. He has played extremely well, as he usually does in Adelaide.

66th over: Australia 199–3 (Clarke 63, Hussey 26) Clarke has played delightfully since the break, and now he comes down the track to take seven from consecutive Swann deliveries, the first driven through the covers for four and the second fizzed through midwicket for three – although it looked as if Broad was touching the rope when he fielded the ball. 'During this Test I've been struck by one thing,' says Tom Van der Gucht. 'Ryan Harris! Now that's what a real man looks like. I bet he wears Old Spice and not Le Male by Jean Paul Gaultier. Watching him vainly chug up and down the pitch glistening with sweat I felt ashamed that my last haircut cost £17 and that I use Tresemmé conditioner.'

67th over: Australia 203–3 (Clarke 67, Hussey 26) This is an interesting move. Paul Collingwood is coming on to bowl. The first ball is too short and cuffed contemptuously through square leg for four by Clarke. He has scored 24 runs from 25 balls since play resumed.

68th over: Australia 204–3 (Clarke 67, Hussey 27) Michael Clarke is given out caught at slip off Graeme Swann, but the decision is overturned on review. From the next ball, Clarke slog-sweeps right onto the rump of Cook at short leg. Ian Bell pats Cook on the bum, which should make all the difference.

69th over: Australia 208–3 (Clarke 67, Hussey 31) Hussey snicks Collingwood just past the stretching Anderson at slip and away for four. That was so close.

70th over: Australia 208–3 (Clarke 67, Hussey 31) This excellent contest between Clarke and Swann continues. Swann mixes up his flight, line and spin in that over, and Clarke defends expertly. A maiden. Swann's figures are now 31–10–63–2.

71st over: Australia 212–3 (Clarke 69, Hussey 33) A much less threatening over from Collingwood brings four singles.

72nd over: Australia 217–3 (Clarke 70, Hussey 33) A viciously spinning delivery from Swann gets away for four byes, and then Clarke gets away with a hideous stroke. He came flying down the pitch and inside-edged a big mow to the left of Cook at short leg. England just need one more wicket before the close. They have 28 minutes in which to get it.

73rd over: Australia 218–3 (Clarke 71, Hussey 33) Collingwood continues, and Hussey only plays when absolutely necessary. Which isn't very often.

74th over: Australia 220–3 (Clarke 72, Hussey 34) Clarke gloves a brute from Swann right through the vacant leg-gully area. As soon as it happens, Strauss puts a man there. This is excellent stuff from Swann, who has a muted lbw appeal when Clarke misses a slog sweep. He was outside the line.

75th over: Australia 221–3 (Clarke 72, Hussey 35) Steve Finn replaces Paul Collingwood. One more wicket, please. Just one more wicket. Clarke thinks about pulling and then pulls out of the shot. One from the over, and there are five more overs left today.

76th over: Australia 227–3 (Clarke 72, Hussey 41) Swann starts with a disgusting, breast-high full toss that Hussey carts for six. But he so nearly falls next ball. He got in a tangle trying to sweep, and the ball went off his gloves before dribbling just wide of the off stump.

77th over: Australia 230–3 (Clarke 75, Hussey 41) Clarke jabs a short one from Finn through midwicket for a couple and then top-edges a pull well short of deep backward square.

78th over: Australia 235–3 (Clarke 77, Hussey 44) Pietersen replaces Graeme Swann after a marathon spell of

34–10–72–2. Hussey tickles one off the pads for three to bring up a high-class century partnership. 'Stuart Broad's injury could work out pretty well for England,' says Alfred Moore. 'I feel I should whisper it, but he's been a pretty ineffective (though far from bad) bowler for a long time now.'

79th over: Australia 238–3 (Clarke 80, Hussey 44) Finn's last over of the day passes quietly, with Clarke tucking two and then a single off his pads.

WICKET! 80th over: Clarke c Cook b Pietersen 80 (Australia 238–4) Kevin Pietersen strikes with the last ball of the day! What a bonus for England. Clarke touched a delivery that turned and bounced onto his thigh, and it looped up for Alastair Cook to take a diving catch as he ran back from short leg. Clarke started walking – but then stopped, and Tony Hill did not give him out because he thought Clarke was walking. England reviewed it, knowing it was out, and replays showed it came right off the face of the bat before deflecting onto Clarke's leg. What a moment for Pietersen, who got his highest Test score this morning and has now taken only his fifth Test wicket. It was the second ball of the over, but because the wicket fell that meant it was the close of play.

Australia 245 and 238–4; England 620–5 dec

Fifth day

The morning session

BY ROB SMYTH

Preamble: P16 W0 D4 L12. That's England's record in live Ashes Tests in Australia in the last 24 years. It puts the 'dire' in 'diabolical'. And while some of the statgasms we've experienced in this series have been so good as to be almost epiphany-inducing, they will count for nowt unless England record that pesky first win since the days when 'The Final Countdown' and 'Take My Breath Away' were near the top of the hit parade. Whether they will do so is largely dependent on the Adelaide weather. As any competent journalist, or me, could tell you, being on deadline can be a serious pain at the best of times. But England don't even know when their deadline is. They have to take six wickets as quickly as possible, because when the clock stops and the hooter goes and the heavens open, that's probably it. That's such a headpuck that they could turn it into a Phillip Schofield game show. Stuart Broad is out of the series. He is flying home and will be out for the entire tour – including the one-day games – with an abdominal tear. You have to feel for him. His series stats are appalling – no runs at nought with the bat and two wickets at 80.50 – but he has actually bowled extremely well, building pressure through his accuracy.

80th over: Australia 239–4 (Hussey 44, North 1) Kevin

Pietersen has four balls remaining of the over that he started last night. 'Is it insecure to pray for sunshine?' sniffs Niall Taylor.

81st over: Australia 239–4 (Hussey 44, North 1) It is Swann to North with the old ball. He has a slip, silly point and short leg, and starts with a very full length to North. The first ball was a yorker, the fourth a full toss. It's a maiden.

82nd over: Australia 243–4 (Hussey 46, North 3) Pietersen continues, but it's a fairly harmless over and Australia take four singles.

83rd over: Australia 248–4 (Hussey 50, North 3) Swann's second over of the day is a dramatic one. The first ball brought an extended shout for lbw against North, but England went for the review. The replay showed that North was just outside the line, so the decision stood. Later in the over Hussey used his feet to flick one through midwicket for four, which took him to his third 50-plus score of the series. He's been superb. And then, off the final delivery, he was dropped by Prior.

84th over: Australia 254–4 (Hussey 51, North 8) England have taken the new ball. That's not a surprise, but the fact Steven Finn is bowling with it is slightly unexpected. His first ball is a touch wide and slapped behind point for four by North.

85th over: Australia 261–4 (Hussey 52, North 14) James Anderson shares the new ball, and North sends one of those delicious extra-cover drives to the boundary. I'm surprised England have taken Swann off here. 'What exactly do you do during the middle session?' says Phill Wainwright. 'I hope it's exciting and glamorous, but I'm guessing you do exactly as you are now, *sans* the typing?'

WICKET! 86th over: Hussey c Anderson b Finn 52 (Australia 261–5) I told you it was a mistake to give Steven Finn the new ball! The second ball of his second over is a shortish, straight delivery that Hussey, cramped for room, mispulls straight up in the air. After an age – a bloody eternity, enough time for you to do about seven *Countdown* conundrums – it drops towards Anderson at mid-on, and he holds onto a routine catch before celebrating with a frenzied abandon I don't think we've ever seen from him before. What a vital wicket this is – not just one step closer to the tail, but bloody Hussey as well. 'Finn's bowled well in this match,' says Shane Warne, a split second before he spears a vile delivery miles down the leg side for five wides.

87th over: Australia 276–5 (North 15, Haddin 9) Anderson steams in to bowl at his old mate Haddin, and beats him twice in three balls. Haddin comes back with consecutive boundaries, a lovely push through extra cover and a flick through midwicket when Anderson strays onto the pads. Excellent stuff.

88th over: Australia 279–5 (North 16, Haddin 11) Haddin has started positively and with the time/runs equation starting to come into play – Australia's deficit is into two figures now – I'm sure he will play his natural game.

89th over: Australia 280–5 (North 17, Haddin 11) A quiet over from Anderson. During it, Nasser Hussain went through the possible replacements for Broad in the Performance Squad and uttered two chilling words: Liam Plunkett. 'Did you hear Nasser, just now, saying that there is history between Anderson and Haddin?' says Marie Meyer. '"They don't like each other." The relish with which he pronounced those five words. Nasser, it seems, is very much in favour of cricketers not liking each other.'

90th over: Australia 286–5 (North 22, Haddin 12) Graeme Swann is coming back on, a good move surely. He will get plenty of bounce with this new ball, and has four men in close for North. But the first ball is far too short and cut easily for four. After that he finds his length, but North and then Haddin are comfortable.

WICKET! 91st over: Haddin c Prior b Anderson 12 (Australia 286–6) James Anderson, I heart you. I love you with every particle of my being. He has picked up the huge wicket of Brad Haddin with a wonderful delivery, full of length and moving away just enough to take the edge as Haddin pushed outside off stump. England are into the tail, and even those who are stricken with a mighty dose of man flu can sniff victory.

WICKET! 91st over: Harris lbw b Anderson 0 (Australia 286–7) Ryan Harris has got a king pair! He panicked completely and padded up to his first delivery from Anderson, a sharp in-ducker which rapped him on the pad in front of off stump. That was a diabolical leave. Tony Hill gave him out straight away, but, after a word from North, Harris decided to review. The replays showed it was just clipping the bails – and because he was given out on the field, that's enough for the decision to stand. England are three wickets away from their first victory in a live Ashes Test in Australia since 1986.

WICKET! 92nd over: North lbw b Swann 22 (Australia 286–8) Another one gone! Three wickets in four balls! This is sensational stuff from England. North pushed defensively at a straight one from Swann that hit bat and pad almost simultaneously. It was definitely hitting the stumps, but what came first: the baldness or the midlife crisis? The bat or the pad? North was given not out by Marais Erasmus, but England were very confident and went for the review. To wild cheers, the replays showed that it was indeed pad first. Swann hits the stumps – and the bails stay on! Unreal. Siddle pushed the ball defensively into the ground, from where it spun back onto the stumps. But the bails, like the lady, were not for turning and stayed in their groove.

93rd over: Australia 287–8 (Doherty 1, Siddle 0) Anderson's over passes peacefully. I was so excited by that last wicket that I completely forgot about his hat-trick ball. He didn't get it, anyway. That's the kind of detail and insight you come here for.

94th over: Australia 291–8 (Doherty 5, Siddle 0) Swann beats Doherty with yet another vicious delivery. This is what a last-day pitch should be like. Doherty responds with a nice stroke through point for four. 'For once the OBO is ahead of my dodgy internet feed,' says Ben Mimmack. 'I feel like an omnipotent entity, looking down on the players knowing exactly what they're about to do.'

95th over: Australia 295–8 (Doherty 5, Siddle 4) Imagine if it rained now. All day. I'd never trust anything ever again. Anderson doesn't make Siddle play quite enough in that over. 'I was five years old in 1986,' says Georgie Lewis. 'Five years old! I'll be thirty in a matter of weeks. And this is the first night I've been able to stay for the cricket this series. Tory government? Recession? Ignore all that. There's no better time to be alive than now.'

WICKET! 96th over: Doherty b Swann 5 (Australia 295–9) Lovely bowling from Graeme Swann, who skids a quicker one through Doherty and into the top of middle stump via the pad. England are one wicket away. One wicket. 24 years. One wicket. Swann needs one for his five-for. Australia have not lost by an innings on home soil since January 1993. Curtly's game. 'Pinch me' doesn't even come close. 'Cattle-prod my netherlands until I can feel something, anything, that will tell me this is real' is more like it.

97th over: Australia 298–9 (Siddle 5, Bollinger 2) Bollinger edges Anderson on the bounce to second slip.

98th over: Australia 300–9 (Siddle 6, Bollinger 3) 'It's raining in Adelaide!!!' says Jay Buckley. 'No, it isn't. But just for a second you panicked. Didn't you, Smyth?' I know where you live, Buckley. Remember that. OK, I don't, but I have your email address and from there it's just joining the dots and shattering the kneecaps.

99th over: Australia 304–9 (Siddle 6, Bollinger 7) I don't know about you, but my head's all over the place. I can hardly feel my fingers, such is the excitement. Bollinger flashes the new bowler Finn just wide of the diving Pietersen at gully and is then beaten by a smart, fuller delivery.

WICKET! 100th over: Siddle b Swann 6 (Australia 304 all out) ENGLAND WIN BY AN INNINGS AND 71 RUNS! It's all over! Swann rips a beauty through the gate to bowl Peter Siddle, and England have battered Australia. Absolutely thrashed them. This is the first time since January 1993 that Australia have lost by an innings at home, and the first time since December 1986 that England have (a) beaten Australia by an innings anywhere, and (b) won a live Ashes Test in Australia. Swann gets his five-for, and he has showed a lot of mental strength to come back from a bit of a mauling in Brisbane. It's the third time in 18 months that he has taken the final wicket in a Test win over Australia. He grabs a stump, as do Kevin Pietersen and James Anderson. These are beautiful scenes. England are just one victory away from retaining the Ashes. Already.

Australia 245 and 304; England 620–5 dec. England win by an innings and 71 runs

'Jeez, you've got 200 in a Test in Australia'

Alastair Cook has batted for 22 hr 32 min and averages 225. As far as he is concerned, he has only just begun

BY DONALD MCRAE

TUESDAY 14 DECEMBER 2010

On a quiet night in another Australian hotel room, with the hours dragging until battle resumes in the Ashes on Thursday, Alastair Cook tells a vivid story. But the England opener does not linger over his epic innings in Brisbane, when he helped save the first Test and broke Don Bradman's record for the highest score at the Gabba by batting for ten and a half hours for his undefeated 235.

He also skips across his seven-hour knock in Adelaide, when his 148 set up a crushing innings victory.

Cook focuses instead on an amusing anecdote. His wry account is framed by distant hurt as he remembers an English summer day, earlier this year, when he went shopping in his local supermarket. Midway through a difficult series against Pakistan, after a dismal season in which he had failed to score more than 29 in eight successive Test innings, Cook drifted through Morrisons. He noticed then that he was being trailed.

'This little kid followed me around,' Cook says as, in his memory, he slips past the ready meals and heads towards the fruit and vegetables. 'Eventually, he said, "You're Alastair Cook, aren't you?"

When I nodded, he looked me up and down and said, "You're not batting very well, are you?"'

Was he tempted to give the mouthy squirt a clip? 'I don't think I was too rude to him. But I didn't hang around either. He was about 14 and so we didn't have a conversation. It sent my blood pressure rocketing because you think, "Aw, what a little shit – what right has he got to say that?"'

That same kid could be swanning around Morrisons now – telling everyone how his mate, Cookie, has spread awed dejection across Australia, batting for more than a thousand minutes between dismissals. 'Yeah, probably,' Cook chuckles. 'I can see him right now.'

Cook might restrict himself to a narrow range of emotions stretching from the wooden to the mechanical in a typical press conference, where he talks with the same lack of flourish with which he bats, but here he is open and involving as he discusses his strangely turbulent year. 'I try not to read the papers but, naturally, it gets back to you. So in the summer I felt under huge pressure. It was, without doubt, the lowest time in my Test career. I've never been under the microscope like that – with people calling for my head.'

Cook responded to his Morrisons mauling by scoring a century in his very next Test, at the Oval. Yet even that innings did not prevent various experts suggesting that England's Ashes campaign should begin with the axeing of Cook – whose average against Australia after ten Tests was 26. 'There was talk, quite rightly, because I hadn't had the greatest summer or the best record against Australia,' Cook says. 'But I felt I deserved my place. We measure our annual stats from September 2009 to this September, and even before the Oval I was averaging over 40 with three Test hundreds – one in Durban and two against Bangladesh. But it's amazing how quickly the game bites you in the arse.'

He captained England in Bangladesh, but Cook refuses to believe a return to the ranks affected his batting – which was let down more by sluggish foot movement. 'I'm not one of those blokes who's crying for the limelight and desperately wants to be captain. I was very happy when Andrew Strauss came back.'

Strauss was his most passionate defender – even when he failed twice in the tour's first warm-up match. Cook regained his rhythm, hitting a century against South Australia, but on the morning of the first Test he was more nervous than he'd ever been. 'I'd begun to find a bit of form and I was desperate to have an impact on the series – because I'd failed in my two previous Ashes. That's why I was so nervous.'

He endured a lonely moment in the first over at the Gabba when, at the non-striker's end, he watched Strauss offer a simple catch off the third ball of the series. 'I just stood there and the noise was incredible. I looked down and thought, "Right, we really need to get something going here." It was hard. But Trotty [Jonathan Trott] came out and he's a very simple bloke when it comes to batting. He's got all his mannerisms but he likes us to have a little target – which might be scoring the next five or ten runs. We used that to get through the first few overs that morning, especially when the noise was so intense. Trotty showed no fear.'

Cook was angry with himself when he finally lost his wicket. His 67 had not been a thing of beauty, but he'd created the right platform. 'I was so disappointed after doing all the hard work. The first two hours of a Test, facing the new ball, is tough anywhere. But it's especially true in Australia with the Kookaburra. I was thinking, "Get past tea and it will be a lot easier." But I didn't cash in. Sixties are all well and good, but they're not match-winners. Worst of all I got out playing a defensive push to [Peter] Siddle. My whole game plan was based on leaving those balls.'

That wicket was the first in Siddle's hat-trick, as England collapsed. 'Yeah,' Cook says ruefully, 'it's one of those dismissals you'll see a lot of over the years – unfortunately.'

Disappointment fuelled his desire. 'We came out for our second innings 221 runs behind and we had to face 15 overs at the end of the third day. Straussy was on a pair and the first ball was close [after a huge lbw appeal]. Very close. But that was a crucial session. They bowled well, the conditions were helpful and they had momentum. But Straussy had that look which said, "Right, we're getting through these 15 overs." We only put on 19 runs but it was vital. The next morning Straussy batted with such freedom [scoring 110] that it was not only me who grew in confidence. In three and a half hours we put on 180, and he got out just before tea. We were almost level and I could see a way out if we continued to play well.'

As 300 for one became 400 and then 517 for one, did Cook, batting with Trott, savour the history whenever he glanced at the scoreboard? 'To be honest, I didn't. There was only one moment when I looked up and said to myself: "Jeez, you've got 200 in an Ashes Test in Australia." I half smiled to myself because the game was safe. But, as a batsman, you get greedy and you want more. I only got a big surge of pleasure back in the dressing room. Graham Gooch [England's batting coach] said: "I'm taking a picture of that scoreboard because it's just perfect." That's when we started to laugh. Like most things in life, it seems sweeter looking back.'

Gooch loves to talk about 'daddy' hundreds. It must have been especially gratifying that Cook followed his grand-daddy in Brisbane with another daddy in Adelaide? 'In Goochie's harshest moments 148 is still not a daddy. It has to be 150. Maybe if has a glass of red he might give it to you. But we've been through a lot together – what with everything in the summer and trying to change my technique a bit. We worked through our problems and the most pleasing thing about Adelaide was backing up what I did in Brisbane.

'That took a huge mental effort. Brisbane was almost the perfect innings and to start again on nought in Adelaide, so soon after such a high, and score the runs I did was very satisfying.'

Did he sense Australia unravelling? 'Yeah, when a 250 partnership becomes 350 then, naturally, their heads drop. But people are saying how easy it was. You should've been in our dressing room after Adelaide. It was a very tired place after back-to-back Tests in hot conditions. It took a lot out of us.'

Only Cook, even at his most obdurate, looked cool. He batted on and on in the same gloves, while Kevin Pietersen called for new pairs repeatedly while racking up a double century. 'I tell people it's my fitness,' Cook jokes, 'but it's not quite true. I was born this way. I'm just not very sweaty.'

Hard graft, despite the meagre sweat, will again be evident as Cook and England try to secure the Ashes with victory in the third Test at the broiling Waca in Perth. He is bolstered further by the memory of his 116 on this ground four years ago. 'To do that against Warne, McGrath, Lee and Clark, as a 21-year-old, was important – even if the rest of that series went horribly.'

Australia now appear confused and in disarray as they call up rookies or players they discarded two weeks ago. 'It's not our position to worry about Australia,' Cook says. 'We can only focus on ourselves and there's no way we'll get complacent. At the moment we're nowhere near where we want to be. There's still a lot more to get out of this side and we can become more consistent.'

Cook is level with Bradman, and behind only Sachin Tendulkar, after scoring 15 centuries by the age of 25. He turns 26 on Christmas Day and laughs shyly when reminded of this latest statistic and the chance to edge past The Don if he scores another century in Perth.

Cook murmurs appreciatively when I tell him that while recently interviewing Tendulkar he spoke admiringly to me of the England opener and revealed that they'd just seen each other. 'Yeah, I was in Nobu [the Japanese restaurant], and Sachin was there. I didn't want to badger him for long. It's surprising he spoke about me because, with Ricky Ponting, he's the greatest batsman I've ever seen. He probably had 30 Test centuries when he was 25.'

That self-effacing pragmatism, allied to intense ambition, means Cook will not marvel at the fact that in three Test innings he has amassed 450 runs at an average of 225. There should be many more runs to come before the series ends on 7 January. Cook will return home soon afterwards, his frustration at not playing one-day cricket tempered by the simple pleasure of working on the Bedfordshire farm owned by the family of his girlfriend, Alice Hunt. 'It's the lambing season, around mid-February, and we'll be getting ready for it soon after I'm back. I really enjoy it.'

'Small hands' are his best asset when lambing but, in the Ashes, a giant heart and searing concentration are far more important. Cook has them both – and he and England will be sustained by a hunger that lasts far beyond this series. 'We know the task ahead of us,' he says intently. 'We're in a very good position but let's not get carried away. Our goal is not only to win the Ashes but to become the No. 1 side in the world. We're heading in the right direction but there's still a huge amount to do.'

Third Test

The Waca, Perth
16–19 December 2010

First day

The morning session

BY ANDY BULL

Preamble: Morning, everyone. It's 1.33 a.m. If you're still up, congratulations. You've made the right choice. I've just realised how extremely excited I am about this Test. My foot is thumping upanddownandupanddown on the floor in anticipation. I can't stop it. And I can't recall feeling quite like this about a cricket match since 2005. Whatever happens in the next five days, this is going to be one fascinating match. Two questions: are England really that good? And are Australia really that bad?

News from the toss: England have won it and decided to bowl. Australia look like this: Hughes, Watson, Ponting, Clarke, Hussey, Haddin, Smith, Johnson, Harris, Siddle, Hilfenhaus. England have picked Chris Tremlett: Strauss, Cook, Trott, Pietersen, Collingwood, Bell, Prior, Swann, Anderson, Finn, Tremlett.

1st over: Australia 0–0 (Watson 0, Hughes 0) Anderson swings his arms around his head and nods his head from side to side. Is there any jet lag left in those limbs? 'I wasn't going to be here at this point,' says Austin Hill. 'Thought I'd get an early night and just check how it was going in the morning. And yet I just happened to hear the result of the toss. It would be rude not to have a quick look, wouldn't it? Then I'm off to bed. Definitely.

But if we get Hughes flashing wildly early on, I might be found still drooling on the couch when my lovely wife gets up. And she always looks so proud when that happens.'

REFERRAL! 1st over: Watson c Prior b Anderson 0 (Australia 0–0) Is that it? England think so, but Watson is very quick to refer it after being given out caught behind down the leg side. He's survived, just. The ball passed by the bat and clipped his pocket. It was a great take by Prior, leaping across to leg.

WICKET! 2nd over: Hughes b Tremlett 2 (Australia 2–1) And here is the gangling Chris Tremlett, bowling his first ball in Test cricket in over three years. Hughes pats his first delivery down to the off, and then ducks underneath a pounding bouncer. This is a good start from Tremlett. The next ball squeezes off the outside edge for two down to third man then . . . he's gone! Bowled him. Oh my, what a start. Hughes has been clean bowled swiping across the line of a fullish, inswinging delivery.

3rd over: Australia 4–1 (Watson 2, Ponting 0) Hello, Ricky. Back again so soon? That was a great first over from Tremlett. He made Hughes look a chump. Anderson doesn't make Watson play the first five balls in this over, they are all too wide. The sixth, though, squirts off the edge and shoots away for two.

4th over: Australia 12–1 (Watson 2, Ponting 4) That's a chance! But the ball flies through a hole in the slip cordon and shoots away for four. Atherton is agonised by the missed opportunity. He has so much relish in his voice it sounds as if he'd like to be out there himself. Ponting wallops the next delivery away off his hip for four through midwicket.

5th over: Australia 17–1 (Watson 3, Ponting 12) And another chance. Strauss was so close to taking that, but he couldn't quite hold on. Watson tried to thrash the ball away to cover but made a mess of it, toe-ending the ball up and over slip. Strauss tried to hang in the air like a basketballer making a jump shot, but he couldn't quite defy gravity long enough to complete the catch. Instead, they scurry a single, and Ponting then flicks four runs away through square leg.

WICKET! 5th over: Ponting c Collingwood b Anderson 12 (Australia 17–2) He's gone. Ponting has gone, caught at third slip. Brilliantly caught at third slip. And I mean brilliantly caught. By Paul Collingwood. Of course. He didn't leap to his right so much as explode as though he had trodden on a pin. He shot off the ground and plucked the ball from the air as it whistled past his head. Australia are 17–2 and I'm too giddy to type. It was a poor shot by Ponting, playing away from his body and misjudging the bounce of the ball, but had it not been for that superb piece of fielding he would have got away with it.

6th over: Australia 18–2 (Watson 4, Clarke 0) A quieter over this, thank goodness. 'How prescient does this Phil Hughes quote from earlier in the week now sound? "Being a short opening batsman, [the bowlers] like it up around your ears and face as much as they can. Often it's not the short balls that get you out, it's the follow-up balls,"' writes Nick Hughes.

7th over: Australia 23–2 (Watson 5, Clarke 4) Clarke slices a drive through the two gullies, and Anderson allows himself a wry grin as he watches the ball run away for four. 'Got to love that,' grins David Adams. 'That's just the sort of start we grew used to in the '90s. Early wickets, captain gone to unbelievable piece of fielding. That sinking feeling of knowing you're in desperate trouble inside the first hour of a game that will struggle to last four days. And the flimsy selectorial logic shredded by first contact with the enemy. All the more delicious for the knowledge that they'll have years of this before they get their shit together. Just like we did.'

8th over: Australia 28–2 (Watson 9, Clarke 4) 'I'm in Adelaide in an open-plan office and all I can see are the tops of the Aussie heads shaking slowly from side to side,' guffaws Michael Owen. 'It doesn't get any better than this.' Well. You say that . . .

WICKET! 8th over: Clarke c Prior b Tremlett 4 (Australia 28–3) This is like watching a man shoot salmon in a barrel with a blunderbuss. Clarke goes, caught behind playing a shot that was no kind of shot at all outside off stump on the back foot. What a disgusting shot. 'That's what pace and bounce will do to a batsman,' Mike Holding tells us. He would know.

9th over: Australia 28–3 (Watson 10, Hussey 0) Anderson is not really troubling Watson: he blocks three of these and leaves the rest.

10th over: Australia 29–3 (Watson 10, Hussey 1) 'I just screamed and giggled (again),' says Danny Whitehead, 'which may have given my colleagues an inkling that I'm not wholly focused on our meeting discussing massive budget cuts and staff lay-offs.'

11th over: Australia 29–3 (Watson 10, Hussey 1) Steve Finn is into the attack, Anderson having bowled 5–2–12–1. Really though he should only claim a half for that wicket and let Colly have the rest. A little like RAF fighter pilots splitting kills in a war movie. Finn's first over is a good maiden, watchfully played by Hussey.

12th over: Australia 29–3 (Watson 10, Hussey 1) It's another maiden from Tremlett, 'Oh for goodness sake,' cries Austin Hill. 'Do England ever run out of ways to punish you? That bed nonsense was just some wishful thinking of mine earlier.'

13th over: Australia 33–3 (Watson 10, Hussey 5) Runs, for the first time in what feels like a long time. 'I'm a teacher working at a boys' school in Sydney,' writes Annette Emms. 'The staff room has just gone from a skipping and frolicking PE dept playing cricket down the centre of all of our desks with the recycling bin as stumps to "We're going outside to play ultimate frisbee." Mass exodus.'

14th over: Australia 34–3 (Watson 11, Hussey 5) I was all over the place in that first hour. Sorry about that. I've settled down a bit now. As have Australia. These two have only faced 26 balls, but in the context of Australia's batting so far in this match that feels like a decent length of time. The pressure got to Ponting and no mistake.

15th over: Australia 35–3 (Watson 12, Hussey 5) Have England worked out how they are going to get that man Hussey? You kind of wonder if they have a big question mark under his name on the suggestions sheet they have pinned up on a noticeboard in the dressing room.

16th over: Australia 35–3 (Watson 12, Hussey 5) Anderson is back into the attack. Warne is explaining how he used to bowl with his back to the wind at this ground. 'Brett Lee and people would say to me, "I'm a bit faster than you, I think I should bowl with the wind," and I'd reply, "Listen, mate, I've got 500 Test wickets. Get down there."'

REFERRAL! 17th over: Watson lbw b Finn 13 (Australia 36–3) Finn thumps an inswinging yorker onto Watson's big toe. It looks plumb straight in front of off stump and the finger is up, but Watson refers it.

WICKET! 17th over: Watson lbw b Finn 13 (Australia 36–4) Much good it does him. The decision stands and he is out. This is a turkey shoot. He referred it out of hope, not expectation. He was just a little late to pick the length and brought his bat down into his boot as he tried to dig out the ball. Here's the boy Steve Smith. Warne is appalled that they have promoted him above Haddin.

17th over: Australia 45–4 (Hussey 13, Smith 1) Warne is insisting that the ball hit Watson outside the line. The camera closes in on the disgusted reactions of the Aussie support team in the dressing room. Hussey takes successive fours from the two final balls of the over, one whipped through fine leg and the other steered through the slips.

18th over: Australia 45–4 (Hussey 13, Smith 1) Smith can be quite a difficult man to bowl to. He's an awkward but aggressive sort of player. For the moment though Anderson is tying him up in knots outside off stump.

19th over: Australia 45–4 (Hussey 13, Smith 1) 'Do we think that the Andrex puppy "Pup" Clarke is still Australia's captain-in-waiting?' asks Clare Davies. 'They don't have that expression FEC down there, do they? They just have the JWFPTG – just waiting for Ponting to go. I think it's a matter of when not if now, don't you?' Greg Chappell was very clear that he saw him as the next captain in an interview he gave last weekend. And Chappell seems to be the man with his hand on the tiller at the moment.

20th over: Australia 48–4 (Hussey 13, Smith 4) Smith pats a single away square in an otherwise barren over. 'Funny how Shane Warne immediately said that Watson shouldn't have called for the referral because "that's not what the system's for",' points out Tim Muller. 'Suddenly he's changed his tune now he thinks an injustice has been done.'

21st over: Australia 49–4 (Hussey 13, Smith 5) Hussey swings a wild pull at a short ball from Finn, who is now bowling from around the wicket. He fails to hit it, and so Finn stands and stares and whistles through his teeth. 'In replacing Stuart Broad with Chris (grandson of Maurice) Tremlett, England have replaced the son of Test cricketer Chris Broad with the grandson of Test cricketer Maurice Tremlett,' points out Alex Holland. 'Given our population of 50 million-odd, this would suggest that the cricketing world is a little incestuous.'

22nd over: Australia 49–4 (Hussey 13, Smith 5) Another maiden from Anderson, bowled to Smith. Holding and Atherton are slating Anderson's bowling, but his nine overs have cost only 15 runs, so he is at least doing something close to the holding job that Broad was doing for the team.

23rd over: Australia 62–4 (Hussey 25, Smith 5) Hussey smears one here, the ball flying over Prior's head and away over the boundary behind him. Finn makes a mess of the next ball and serves up a full toss which is dispatched disdainfully through extra cover. An expensive over, that.

24th over: Australia 63–4 (Hussey 26, Smith 5) The knee Trembler is back into the attack for a final short spell before lunch. Tremlett finds Smith's outside edge, but the ball drops well short of slip.

25th over: Australia 65–4 (Hussey 28, Smith 5) A quirky piece of captaincy from Strauss. At least, quirky is one word for it. He brings Paul Collingwood into the attack ahead of Graeme Swann for an over or two before the break. He starts with a pair of full balls and the rest of the over is rubbish.

26th over: Australia 65–4 (Hussey 28, Smith 5) And Tremlett finishes with a maiden, the second of a superb session. Well. What a start to the Test. Those two questions I had back at the start of the match? I think they've been answered now.

Australia 65–4

The afternoon session

BY ROB SMYTH

Preamble: In many ways the hard part starts now, as the lower-middle order has been Australia's strongest suit in this series. Michael Hussey looked good again, leaving the ball on length as expertly as a Waca vet should, while Steven Smith showed his usual hyperactive fearlessness. Still, 65 for four is 65 for four is 65 for four, and it vindicated the decision of the England captain to bowl first. We're all doomed department: in the Ashes Test here four years ago, Australia were 69 for three at lunch. They won by 206 runs. Just saying.

27th over: Australia 67–4 (Hussey 29, Smith 5) Jimmy Anderson starts after lunch. His morning figures of 9–3–15–1 flattered him in a way that Alan Mullally's often did, because he didn't make the batsmen play nearly enough. Hussey and Smith scamper a couple of singles.

WICKET! 28th over: Smith c Strauss b Tremlett 7 (Australia 69–5) This is extremely good cricket from England. Smith had just pulled unconvincingly for two, so Tremlett pitched one up, found the edge of Smith's leaden-footed poke with a smidgin of seam movement, and Strauss at first slip took an accomplished low catch to his right. Tremlett has been outstanding today, and not just for his frankly terrifying Popeye forearms.

28th over: Australia 69–5 (Hussey 29, Haddin 0) Haddin is beaten by each of his first two deliveries. Tremlett's figures are 10–2–21–3. In an unrelated development, you'll notice that we have a fixed advert at the top of the OBO page. For Cricinfo. And their ball-by-ball coverage. Of the Ashes.

29th over: Australia 71–5 (Hussey 31, Haddin 0) A quiet

over from Anderson to Hussey. Let's not get carried away with this scoreline. Anything over 200 is potentially playable. We don't know how England's batsmen will react to this pitch.

30th over: Australia 75–5 (Hussey 32, Haddin 3) Haddin gets off the mark with a nice push through the leg side for three, and then Hussey pushes a single off his hip.

31st over: Australia 77–5 (Hussey 33, Haddin 4) Missed that over as I had to attend to some business. No, no euphemism. 'Astounding revelation: Stuart Broad on *TMS* has just revealed that the England bowlers mostly lunch on milkshakes,' says John Starbuck. 'Batsmen, though, eat meat and two veg. What about all-rounders?' Pints?

32nd over: Australia 79–5 (Hussey 34, Haddin 5) Another dangerous over from Tremlett. First Haddin pushes one in the air and not far wide of short leg. Then Hussey rightly survives a fairly big lbw appeal.

33rd over: Australia 86–5 (Hussey 35, Haddin 11) Anderson beats Hussey with a jaffa, perfect length and just swerving away enough. Haddin leans into a lovely, on-the-up cover drive for four. Anderson gives him a look that says, 'Sure, keep playing that shot on this pitch, lad.'

34th over: Australia 89–5 (Hussey 36, Haddin 13) England miss a very good run-out chance. There was a mix-up between Haddin and Hussey, but Trott's throw from square leg was high and wide of the stumps. Prior did well to pick up and hit the stumps with an underarm throw, but by then Haddin was just home.

35th over: Australia 95–5 (Hussey 42, Haddin 13) Lovely stroke from Hussey, who pushes a full delivery from Anderson back whence it came for four. His scores in this series are 195, 93, 52 and now 42 not out. England will have to think about introducing Graeme Swann soon.

36th over: Australia 99–5 (Hussey 42, Haddin 17) Tremlett pitches one up on off stump and Haddin plays a princely drive through mid-off for four. Tremlett comes back well, first with a heavy ball that Haddin fences on the bounce to gully, and then with a fuller delivery that beats a windy woof outside off stump.

37th over: Australia 107–5 (Hussey 47, Haddin 20) Hussey pulls Anderson vigorously for four. He got Australia to a workable score here against England last time round and he's threatening to do so again. Anderson ends the over with an optimistic shout for lbw.

38th over: Australia 112–5 (Hussey 47, Haddin 25) Steven Finn (7–1–28–1) replaces Chris Tremlett (14–2–34–3), and Haddin steers a very full delivery into the ground and over point for four. It's a completely different game when these two are together, as it has been throughout the series. 'Has the Doctor called yet?' asks John Starbuck. Hard to say from an airless bunker on the other side of the world, but he must be due.

39th over: Australia 122–5 (Hussey 47, Haddin 35) Here, finally, comes Graeme Swann. Australia continue their policy of calculated risk against him: Haddin comes down the track to the third ball and slices a drive over mid-off for four. And you have to admire the intent and execution of the next shot, a delicious, lazy drive over long-on for six. It brings up a very rapid fifty partnership.

40th over: Australia 134–5 (Hussey 59, Haddin 35) Michael Hussey makes it four 50-plus scores out of four in this series, uppercutting a disgusting delivery from Finn to the boundary. Man, he has played well. He pulls the next delivery through midwicket for four more, and then swivel-pulls a third boundary from the final delivery. The last four overs have disappeared for 35.

WICKET! 41st over: Hussey c Prior b Swann 61 (Australia 137–6) This is a huge breakthrough for England, and it's a wonderful piece of bowling from Graeme Swann. From around the wicket he got one to drift in, turn and bounce away from the bat, and maybe just kiss the edge of Hussey's defensive stroke on its way through to Prior. He went up straight away, signalling for the review. Hotspot showed a thin edge, and Hussey was on his way.

41st over: Australia 139–6 (Haddin 37, Johnson 1) Johnson gets off the mark. Incredibly, that's the first run a No. 8 has scored in this series. 'Tell John Starbuck (38th over) that the sea breeze (as the Doctor is actually called here) has not kicked in, and it's filthy hot still,' says Gervase Greene. 'Set to get hotter all week, too.'

42nd over: Australia 147–6 (Haddin 45, Johnson 1) Haddin waits for a short ball from Finn and steers it deliberately over third man for four. Finn is bowling far too short here. He has been out of sorts today, and Michael Holding suggests it might be a fitness issue.

43rd over: Australia 148–6 (Haddin 45, Johnson 2) 'It's 1 p.m. on the beautiful island of Samed in the Gulf of Thailand,' says Kevin Bowman. 'Does anyone know of an appropriate alcohol to mix with watermelon juice? Any help greatly appreciated.'

44th over: Australia 156–6 (Haddin 45, Johnson 10) Finn is struggling. He's stretching between deliveries and looks pretty uncomfortable, but England don't have many options because Tremlett is recovering and Anderson is off the field. Johnson larrups a wide delivery through the covers for four and then slices a cut over the cordon for another boundary.

45th over: Australia 158–6 (Haddin 46, Johnson 11) Swann has a biggish shout for lbw against Johnson, but he was a long way forward and it was probably going down leg side as well. Johnson responds with a filthy mow, absolutely disgusting. He slices it off the edge to fine leg for a single. 'May I volunteer that the problem with Steven Finn is not his fitness but his new hairstyle?' writes Nick Hughes. 'The radical move from fringe to quiff has clearly upset his equilibrium.'

46th over: Australia 159–6 (Haddin 46, Johnson 12) Warne tells us that Tremlett can put his whole fist in his mouth. Cheers, Shane! Of more interest is Warne's repeated observation that when the two played at Hampshire, Tremlett was frequently unplayable in the nets but struggled to take that into the match.

47th over: Australia 163–6 (Haddin 46, Johnson 16) Johnson leaves a quicker arm ball from Swann that doesn't miss off stump by too much, but then he connects with a trademark slog sweep, pinging it viciously for four. 'I tried explaining cricket to a Spaniard at our work Christmas party out here in Mexico City today,' says Ben Leather. 'Even after an hour and four tequilas he was still unimpressed.'

48th over: Australia 168–6 (Haddin 47, Johnson 20) Johnson cuts a short, wide delivery from Tremlett for four. He is playing pretty well, you know. This might not be another Ashes *horribilis* after all.

49th over: Australia 169–6 (Haddin 48, Johnson 20) Haddin has reined himself in against Swann since the loss of Hussey, probably a sensible tactic given how well Johnson is playing. Then if Johnson falls he can go again. For now he is content with a gentle push to leg for one. 'Tremlett can put his fist in his mouth?' says Gervase Greene. 'Until he can put his foot in there too, Warnie will still have one over him.'

50th over: Australia 170–6 (Haddin 49, Johnson 20) This third spell, and the fourth later on, will be a good test for Tremlett. 'Three times I woke up in the night and I was greeted with

2–1, 65–4 and 95–5,' says Guy Hornsby. 'I was so overcome I thought each previous occasion was some sort of utopian dream, but the alarm at 6.30 a.m. and 156–6 showed it was the real McCoy. I almost opened a beer, then realised that'd be a bit over the top considering I've got a full day in the office.'

51st over: Australia 173–6 (Haddin 51, Johnson 21) Haddin pushes Swann for a single to reach a superb fifty: counter-attacking early on and responsible from the moment he became the senior partner. We used to think of him as a stroke-maker with only one gear, but he has shown that to be nonsense.

52nd over: Australia 173–6 (Haddin 51, Johnson 21) Tremlett beats Haddin with a snorter, a good-length leg-cutter that may have swung a touch as well. He gives you such control, does Tremlett. 'I agree with Nick Hughes, Finn's new cut is a disaster,' says Tom Van der Gucht. 'He looked much better when modelling himself on Shaggy from *Scooby Doo*.'

53rd over: Australia 177–6 (Haddin 51, Johnson 25) Johnson pings another slog sweep over the man at deep midwicket for a one-bounce four. He loves that shot against the spinner. This is a very decent recovery from 69 for five.

54th over: Australia 179–6 (Haddin 52, Johnson 25) It'll be Paul Collingwood to bowl the last over of the session. Johnson leaves one that doesn't miss off stump by much, and that's tea.

Australia 179–6

The evening session

BY ANDY BULL

Preamble: Morning, everyone. Where have you been? Sleeping? And you call yourself a cricket fan?

55th over: Australia 185–6 (Haddin 52, Johnson 31) Johnson drops to one knee and larrups a six over long-on off Swann's sixth delivery. They've played Swann well today, refusing him the chance to settle into a groove by hitting him over the top back down the ground.

56th over: Australia 187–6 (Haddin 53, Johnson 32) Anderson takes the other end. We're told that Steve Finn has a tight calf and is struggling a bit. This could yet turn into a tricky situation for England. The fifty partnership comes up – off 92 balls – with a scampered single.

57th over: Australia 188–6 (Haddin 53, Johnson 33) One-shot Johnson tries that hoick to the leg side again but doesn't quite connect.

WICKET! 58th over: Haddin c Swann b Anderson 53 (Australia 188–7) Got him! And it is the one they wanted too. A soft dismissal that, given that Haddin had been so scrupulously tight in his innings so far. He wafted the bat as though it were a magic wand, he expected the ball to disappear to the boundary – poof! – he succeeded only in slicing the ball straight to slip. Harris survives his first ball, and so avoids extending his king pair into another match.

59th over: Australia 192–7 (Johnson 37, Harris 0) 'Any sign of video of Collingwood's take appearing online?' pleads Tim Maitland. 'Sharing a link would be nice for those of us stuck in cold, miserable Hong Kong offices.'

60th over: Australia 199–7 (Johnson 42, Harris 0) OK, I take it back about Johnson only having the one shot. He's played a sweetly struck glance through midwicket here.

WICKET! 60th over: Harris b Anderson 3 (Australia 201–8) That's how you do it. Jimmy Anderson splashes Ryan Harris's stumps all over the ground with a devilish yorker. He raises his finger to his lips and tells the Aussie batsmen to button it as Harris walks off the pitch.

61st over: Australia 202–8 (Johnson 44, Siddle 0) Johnson threads a single through cover, and that's that.

62nd over: Australia 208–8 (Johnson 49, Siddle 1) Johnson squeezes the ball through third man, a horrid shot but it gets him a flukey four.

63rd over: Australia 213–8 (Johnson 51, Siddle 4) Siddle steps across and chops three runs to third man. Then Johnson brings up his fifty by forcing two runs out through extra cover, a feat rewarded with bows of supplication from the yellow-clad Aussie posse on the hill.

64th over: Australia 215–8 (Johnson 51, Siddle 6) Anderson wings down a trio of gentle inswingers, bending the ball back in towards Siddle's leg stump. He clumps two runs away square.

65th over: Australia 216–8 (Johnson 52, Siddle 6) Another quiet over from Swann. He is baiting Johnson with some loop and flight, but the batsman isn't biting.

66th over: Australia 218–8 (Johnson 53, Siddle 7) Tremlett comes back into the attack. He hammers a short ball down at Johnson's head, to Sir Iron Bottom's immense gratification. Tremlett whistles up a pair of lovely deliveries to Siddle, shaving splinters from the outside edge of the bat with a ball that nipped away after pitching.

67th over: Australia 222–8 (Johnson 54, Siddle 10) The

two batsmen scratch around for another over against Swann, finding runs here and there.

68th over: Australia 225–8 (Johnson 55, Siddle 12) Siddle picked the delivery was just a little fuller and carted it over mid-wicket for two. He has to pull out of the next delivery just as Tremlett is about to release the ball because a seagull flew low across the wicket.

69th over: Australia 228–8 (Johnson 57, Siddle 13) These two have put on 27 together now, and as Gower says, 'This is just getting a little irritating now.' He sounds rather like a man who has just heard that the restaurant's cheese trolley has run out of both of his favourites.

REFERRAL! 70th over: Siddle lbw b Tremlett 13 (Australia 229–8) Has Tremlett got his man? England think so, but the umpire doesn't. So Strauss refers the lbw. Siddle was throwing the bat across the line, and the ball crept in between the bat and pad and hit the back pad in front of middle stump. Virtual Eye shows that the ball would have clipped the bails, but that's not conclusive enough to overturn the on-field decision. So Siddle bats on.

71st over: Australia 233–8 (Johnson 58, Siddle 13) That's an ugly shot. Johnson is really cutting loose now. He screws a top-edge away over long stop for four, and then jumps across to the leg side and smears an awkward drive to mid-on. England need to get him quickly or this partnership could run right away from them. No sooner said than . . .

WICKET! 71st over: Johnson c Anderson b Finn 62 (Australia 233–9) Johnson goes. That was actually the best shot he had played in the over so far. He middled a pull shot, but only picked out Jimmy Anderson at square leg. As he took the catch Anderson cramped up and collapsed onto the turf as he was halfway through his celebration. Prior grabs Anderson's leg and forces his foot back towards his shin.

72nd over: Australia 235–9 (Siddle 16, Hilfenhaus 0) 'Andy, the alcohol is not deadening the pain,' mopes Michel Quin. 'Any advice from the northern hemisphere for a poor Aussie?' Umm, Nembutal?

73rd over: Australia 243–9 (Siddle 18, Hilfenhaus 5) Hilfenhaus cuts four past backward point, then pokes the next ball down towards slip and scurries a single.

74th over: Australia 256–9 (Siddle 23, Hilfenhaus 13) Siddle gets four, but it is by accident rather than design. Tremlett's bouncer hit the bat so hard that the ball looped up over slip and went away to third man. This is starting to get stupid. The over ends up costing 13. 'Nembutal?' asks Michel Quin. 'Is he Australian? Does he bat or bowl?'

75th over: Australia 267–9 (Siddle 34, Hilfenhaus 13) Another vicious attacking shot from Siddle, and that's four. Oh. It's enough to make you weep, this. He fetches the next delivery from outside off and pulls it through long-on for another boundary. These two have put on 31 runs together now. Make that 33, as Siddle slaps a lousy pull to mid-off. Finn's 15 overs have cost 86.

76th over: Australia 268–9 (Siddle 34, Hilfenhaus 13) Bumble points out that Swann has not bowled a maiden yet today, which is a sign of just how well Australia have played him. Not that they've come close to mastering the man, just that they haven't let him dictate the match.

WICKET! 76th over: Hilfenhaus c Cook b Swann 13 (Australia 268 all out) And there, at last, is the wicket England needed. Hilfenhaus edged the ball straight to short leg. England will settle for that, having won the toss. But given that Australia were 69–5, that's a great recovery. Hilfenhaus and Siddle sprint off, and England will have 12 overs to face, starting any moment now.

England first innings

1st over: England 0–0 (Strauss 0, Cook 0) Hilfenhaus starts with two full balls, both of them swinging back in towards off stump after pitching just outside the line. Strauss pats them away square. The next two are both a little wider, and Strauss plays them away to the off side. 'England going in at the end of day, after a wagging tail,' trembles Nick Donovan. 'The fear has returned.'

2nd over: England 3–0 (Strauss 1, Cook 2) And the man with the luxury of having the breeze at his back is Ryan Harris. Here's Dan Smith: 'Given the disarray in the Australian bowling selections, can we now say, with hindsight, that picking Darren Pattinson for England was a masterstroke to prevent him bailing out this Australia attack two years later?'

3rd over: England 4–0 (Strauss 1, Cook 3) Cook knocks a single away fine. And Strauss provokes a few groans and gasps from the fielders, fans and commentators alike by playing inside the line of an inswinger.

4th over: England 11–0 (Strauss 1, Cook 10) Sound batting this. Startling batting even. Cook has just hit the fifth six of his Test career. He saw that the ball was short and wide and reasoned he could throw the bat at it and the ball would fly away with the breeze to the boundary.

5th over: England 15–0 (Strauss 1, Cook 14) 'There he goes again,' mutters Bumble as Cook lashes another cut away for four. Hilfenhaus comes back at him with a tidy inswinger that Cook leaves alone. It passed perilously close to his off stump.

6th over: England 21–0 (Strauss 7, Cook 14) Harris already seems to be huffing and puffing like the big bad wolf, trudging back to his mark like a man pulling a laden shopping trolley up a hill. His next delivery is a little rank, and Strauss gratefully glances it away for four to fine leg.

7th over: England 21–0 (Strauss 7, Cook 14) My computer is running treacle-slow, but thankfully there wasn't a great deal to describe in this over as it was a maiden.

8th over: England 21–0 (Strauss 7, Cook 14) Here's Robin Hazlehurst: 'Given that Strauss almost inevitably gets out in the morning when he bats overnight, shouldn't England have sent a nightwatchman in for him now?'

9th over: England 21–0 (Strauss 7, Cook 14) Siddle comes into the fray. His first delivery swings way down the leg side, allowing Haddin to leap across and make a brilliant take. Australia go through a half-hearted appeal for a catch behind two balls later, trying to con the umpire into deciding that Cook edged the ball behind. No such luck. It's another maiden over though, the third in a row.

10th over: England 25–0 (Strauss 11, Cook 14) And here is Mitchell Johnson, trotting up to the wicket with a crease of concentration across his brow. He's getting the ball to move away from Strauss, which is interesting because it suggests he may just have rediscovered that long-lost inswinger that made him such a potent bowler back in 2007–8.

11th over: England 29–0 (Strauss 12, Cook 17) This is the penultimate over of the day, and Cook begins it by knocking two runs away to leg. 'I think it's very unfair of the Australians to give the new ball to their batsmen,' quips Tom Adam. 'When they must be so very tired.'

12th over: England 29–0 (Strauss 12, Cook 17) Six more balls then, and we can all go to bed. Johnson wastes most of them, spraying the ball over Strauss's head and past his off stump. The fifth ball is in the right place, but Strauss's block is equal to it. That was a superb final little session for England. They trail by just 239 runs now.

England 29–0; Australia 268

Second day

The morning session

BY ROB SMYTH

Preamble: Hello. There are two scenarios for today's play, and both are utterly thrilling in very different ways.

Scenario one: England's top order play with the detached authority they have shown in their last two innings, calmly batting Australia right out of the game. When they close on 312 for four, the Ashes have effectively if not actually been retained.

Scenario two: Australia rage, rage against the dying of the light, their quintet of quicks (we'll upgrade Shane Watson in the name of some cheap alliteration) hustling through an England batting line-up that struggles to adapt to life on the back foot. After a day of the highest-octane cricket, England are all out for 271 and Ricky Ponting spends the night visualising the innings of his life.

13th over: England 29–0 (Strauss 12, Cook 17) The first over will be bowled by Ryan Harris. In the first innings of the first two Tests, Andrew Strauss fell to the third ball of the day. So it's probably a good thing that Alastair Cook takes strike here, although he is beaten by that pesky third delivery, a good leg-cutter to the left-hander. A maiden. 'We should prepare ourselves for Strauss's early (perhaps immediate) departure this morning,' says Ian Copestake. 'But, if you will excuse me poking fate in the eye, we just don't collapse like we used to. England are actually ace.'

14th over: England 33–0 (Strauss 16, Cook 17) As you'd expect, it's Ben Hilfenhaus from the other end. His first ball lifts a bit nastily and almost takes Strauss by surprise. He manages to pop it down in front of him though, and then tucks a pair of twos off the pad from the next two deliveries. The fourth delivery curves back beautifully and doesn't miss off stump by very much as Strauss shoulders arms. Another interesting over.

15th over: England 40–0 (Strauss 20, Cook 20) A huge let-off for Strauss! He drove at a full-length delivery from Harris, and the ball flew off the edge at catchable height between the 'keeper Haddin and Watson at first slip – but they both left it to each other and it went away for four. 'What is going on?' says Bumble. 'Gracious me!'

16th over: England 40–0 (Strauss 20, Cook 20) Hilfenhaus is getting some nice shape into the left-handers, but Cook is in wonderful touch and he simply blocks the straight ones and leaves the wide ones. A maiden.

17th over: England 52–0 (Strauss 32, Cook 20) Twelve from the over? Yes please. Harris tries a surprise short ball and Strauss pings it classily round the corner for four. Strauss dumps the fifth delivery in front of square for four. The next is much fuller but too straight, and Strauss times it through midwicket for his third boundary of the over. It brings up the fifty partnership.

18th over: England 54–0 (Strauss 33, Cook 21) Two from Hilfenhaus's over. That Strauss reprieve has done something unpleasant all over Australia's bonfire; they've been pretty flat since. 'I just had my glasses pinched (I'm virtually blind without them) on the Tube and have had to grope my way back into work after the Xmas do rather than going home,' says Alec Gregory. 'It seemed like the best idea at the time, but now I have to stay the night at work, like you. But without the legitimacy. It's a grim state of affairs, but OBO might just get me through. Yep, I appear to still be drunk.'

19th over: England 59–0 (Strauss 38, Cook 21) Mitchell Johnson replaces Ryan Harris, who rather worryingly looked tired at the end of a three-over spell. It's one more than Shaun Tait can bowl, I suppose. Anyway, here's Johnson. You can't see Australia winning this game without him making a significant contribution. He's the one who can run through a side, as he did in that amazing Test against South Africa on this ground two years ago.

20th over: England 65–0 (Strauss 39, Cook 26) Cook is beaten by a good leg-cutter from Hilfenhaus, but the next ball is a touch too wide and is cut viciously for four. This is all going worryingly well for England.

21st over: England 69–0 (Strauss 42, Cook 27) Strauss pushes Johnson into the covers, calls for a single and then sends Cook back. He would have been home even if Clarke's throw had hit the stumps. That's 40 runs from nine overs this morning. Australia need a wicket very soon or they face some seriously hard yakka. 'Re: Alec Gregory (over 18),' says Alex Gaywood. 'If he is virtually blind without his glasses, how is he reading OBO?'

22nd over: England 71–0 (Strauss 43, Cook 28) Hilfenhaus has bowled pretty well this morning and beats Strauss outside off stump. This is now looking a very good pitch though, and having almost seen off the new ball England are in a fantastic position. Australia are right on the brink here. 'In reference to Alec Gregory claiming to have had his glasses "stolen" on the Tube,' says Alex Haslam. 'I have to admire the lengths Alec has gone to in order to contrive a reason to "grope his way back into the office after the Christmas party". My old boss used to do something similar. Until they fired him.'

23rd over: England 75–0 (Strauss 43, Cook 32) Johnson digs one in, and Cook uppercuts him superbly for four. He has played that shot expertly in this innings. 'I wouldn't put that past me,' says Alec Gregory, who is unravelling quite gloriously. 'Now going to sleep under my coat. My coat smells of wine. Night! PS I keep a spare pair at work, obviously. Who doesn't?'

24th over: England 78–0 (Strauss 45, Cook 32) Hilfenhaus now has a 7–2 field, which has amused Sir Ian Botham in the Sky box. Strauss drives through the covers for two. 'The voice of OBO?' says Mark Webb. 'Terry Christian.' Oof.

WICKET! 25th over: Cook c Hussey b Johnson 32 (England 78–1) This is such an important wicket for Australia on three counts: it's a wicket, it's the wicket of the run-machine Cook, and it's the first wicket of the series for their potential match-winner Mitchell Johnson. Cook drove loosely at a wide delivery and sliced it low to gully, where Michael Hussey took a smart two-handed catch. Cook asked if it carried, Hussey said yes, and Cook walked.

25th over: England 78–1 (Strauss 45, Trott 0) This is a uniquely difficult wicket on which to play yourself in, so there is scope for a collapse, and how Australia need one. So does this series, if we're two-eyed about it. Trott pops a short one down in front of his body, and that's a very good wicket maiden from Johnson. Cook's series average, meanwhile, is down to 160.66. 'Why the hell doesn't Alec Gregory go home now that he's got his spare pair of glasses?' says Jo Staniforth. 'Does he work for MI6? Is there a time lock on the door?' It's a not unreasonable question.

26th over: England 78–1 (Strauss 45, Trott 0) A maiden from Hilfenhaus to Strauss. It must nearly be time to get that vicious mongrel Siddle on and try to rough England up from both ends. 'Voice talent for the OBO transcript CD highlights . . .'

says Sean Boiling. 'Ray Winstone. Has to be.' Arf. 'WICKET! you c@!$,' and so on.

WICKET! 27th over: Trott lbw b Johnson 4 (England 82–2) It's happening. Mitchell Johnson, having worked Trott over with a couple of short balls, traps him in front with a beautiful inswinger. Trott planted his front leg and had nowhere to go as the ball snaked back at the last minute. It would have hit off stump halfway up. That's Johnson's magic ball, the inswinger to the right-hander. It was brilliant bowling, and these are extremely good signs for Australia.

WICKET! 27th over: Pietersen lbw b Johnson 0 (England 82–3) This is sensational cricket! Johnson has nailed Pietersen with another full inswinger. Pietersen referred it, but that was plumb. Like Trott, he wafted around his front pad and was stone dead. It would have hit leg stump. Johnson may well have got his inswinger back, a ball that has hardly been seen for two years. If he has, that is a serious plot twist.

27th over: England 82–3 (Strauss 45, Collingwood 0) Against South Africa, on this ground two years ago, Johnson took five wickets for two runs in 20 balls. Now he has three for four in 12, and you'd fancy him for some more.

28th over: England 88–3 (Strauss 51, Collingwood 0) Strauss carries on as if nothing had happened, pinging Hilfenhaus off the pads for four. Then he tucks two more off the pad to reach his second 50-plus score of the series. 'Do you realise you are in a sledge war with Australian radio?' says Andrew Jolly. 'The last wicket was greeted with a shout of "What do you have to say about that *Guardian* over by over?!"' Haha, this is brilliant. Bull is now looking for their commentary online. It's one thing being sledged in the comments section on the *Guardian* blog, but on the radio?

29th over: England 89–3 (Strauss 51, Collingwood 1) England could have done with Strauss taking strike against Johnson. Anyway, the right-handed Collingwood is comfortable in a mercifully inswinger-free over.

30th over: England 92–3 (Strauss 51, Collingwood 4) Collingwood works Hilfenhaus through midwicket for two. Fetch that, Jim Maxwell!

31st over: England 94–3 (Strauss 52, Collingwood 5) Strauss does well to dig out a nasty swinging yorker from Johnson, who has got the battle fever on and no mistake. This is great cricket, and Ricky Ponting has the beaming smile of a man who has just found his lucky pants after 18 months without them.

WICKET! 32nd over: Strauss c Haddin b Harris 52 (England 94–4) Ryan Harris returned to the attack and struck with his third delivery, a good one in the corridor that swung in a touch and found the edge as Strauss fished outside off. The line was excellent. England have lost four for spit, and the whole series has been blown open in a crazy, bewildering and magnificent half-hour.

32nd over: England 98–4 (Collingwood 5, Bell 4) Bell starts brilliantly, timing his second delivery through mid-off for four. What a glorious shot that is. Harris responds with a cracker that beats Bell on the inside. 'This is the first time on the tour we've seen Collingwood put into the sort of situation you have a Collingwood in the team for in the first place,' says Chris Wright. '88–3, under pressure, while still far behind your opponent's score is what Colly was invented for.'

WICKET! 33rd over: Collingwood lbw b Johnson 5 (England 98–5) England are suffering death by inswing. Paul Collingwood jabbed around another big in-ducker and, although he was given not out by Marais Erasmus, it looked very close and Australia went for the review. Virtual Eye showed it was straight and hitting a good portion of the stumps. England have lost five wickets for 20 in 8.3 overs; if that wasn't bad enough, Australia's match-winner Mitchell Johnson has got everything back: his groove, his mojo, his dignity and most of all his inswinger.

33rd over: England 98–5 (Bell 4, Prior 0) 'In the words of Ron Burgundy, that all escalated pretty quickly,' says John Allen. 'Any sign of rain? I'll just take the draw right now, thank you very much.'

34th over: England 101–5 (Bell 7, Prior 0) Bell plays another very confident stroke, easing Harris through extra cover for three. It's a bit daft to judge an innings after four balls, so that's exactly what we'll do. Bell looks great. 'You guys are toast!' says Johan Mostert. 'Goodnight, Poms!' That didn't take long.

35th over: England 101–5 (Bell 7, Prior 0) Johnson gets to bowl to Bell for the first time. A maiden. 'Mitchell Johnson likes bowling to South Africans in Perth,' chuckles Denis Heath.

36th over: England 107–5 (Bell 7, Prior 2) Prior pulls the ball high to leg, and the ball drops into the wide-open spaces for a couple. 'No offence,' says David Harding, and that's always a promising way to begin an email, 'but personally I blame this on whoever made the decision at *Guardian* HQ yesterday to start an online poll asking if this is the worst Australian team ever. From that moment we were finished. So now we have lost the series 3–1, who should replace Cook?' Did we do that? Really?

37th over: England 114–5 (Bell 10, Prior 2) Peter Siddle replaces Mitchell Johnson, who bowled a marvellous spell of 9–3–20–4. Bell is beaten but responds with a classy back-foot force through the covers for three. Siddle then spears some filth down the leg side for four byes.

38th over: England 119–5 (Bell 13, Prior 3) Bell squirts a drive behind square for three off Harris, and then Prior loops an unconvincing pull for two. That's lunch. What an exhilarating session that was. England, having made 1,215 for six – 1,215 for six! – in two and a bit innings, then lost five for 20 as Mitchell Johnson found his inswinger to devastating effect.

England 119–5; Australia 268

The afternoon session

BY ANDY BULL

Preamble: Two hours ago I was walking down the Regent's Canal on my way to Guardian Towers and, after days of self-denial, allowed myself to sip in the satisfaction of thinking that yes, Australia were that bad. And yes, England really are that good. And yes, the Ashes really will be over for Christmas. Well, Australia could hardly have left it any later to prove that they can actually play the game after all. And at last we've a contest to watch rather than a turkey shoot.

39th over: England 123–5 (Bell 16, Prior 4) Siddle starts the bowling after the break. He's got to have his best bowler on, surely? Johnson may have bowled a long spell in the morning session, but he has just had a 40-minute break. And one more wicket and Australia are into the tail.

40th over: England 126–5 (Bell 19, Prior 4) Hilfenhaus starts at the other end. His first delivery is short, so short that it sails over Bell's bat and his head. When Hilfenhaus does pitch the ball up, Bell strides out to meet it and essays a sweet cover drive. It gets him three.

41st over: England 127–5 (Bell 20, Prior 4) Bell pats a single off his hip.

42nd over: England 130–5 (Bell 21, Prior 6) Bell flicks another run down to long leg, and Prior then swings a rusty-gate pull shot away to mid-on for two more.

43rd over: England 134–5 (Bell 25, Prior 6) That's a glorious shot from Bell, a pull that kicks like a mule for four through midwicket. It was a poor ball from Siddle mind, dragged down.

44th over: England 140–5 (Bell 25, Prior 12) Prior thumps the ball back into the pitch with a straight drive. The ground is so hard that the ball loops up over the leaping bowler and runs away for four. Later in the over he pushes two more past point.

45th over: England 141–5 (Bell 26, Prior 12) After an interminable delay while he dilly-dallies over his field, Ponting sets Siddle to bowl bouncers from around the wicket at Prior's head. His first two deliveries are so filthy you'd struggle to clean them with bleach.

46th over: England 141–5 (Bell 26, Prior 12) Now we're getting heat from Peter Roebuck, or so I'm told by Denis Heath. Apparently he is quoting 'an esteemed English newspaper and your premature call of the demise of the Aussies'. I can see we're going to have to have some kind of enquiry into this poll. No doubt it will end up with the office boy being taken outside to the bike shed and shot. A maiden from Hilfenhaus, by the way.

WICKET! 47th over: Prior b Siddle 12 (England 145–6) Siddle whangs down a wide bouncer that whistles away over Haddin's head for four byes. Oh. What a way to get out. Prior has played on in the most unfortunate manner. It was a half-tracker that hit Prior's thigh pad, then took a double ricochet back onto his bat and onto the stumps. Siddle welcomes Swann to the crease with a 91 mph short ball.

48th over: England 149–6 (Bell 30, Swann 0) So England are all out of batsmen now, Bell aside. How will Bell play it? Beautifully, is the answer. He clips two runs to leg, and then pulls away a couple more.

49th over: England 156–6 (Bell 35, Swann 1) 'Swann does have four first-class centuries,' says Oliver Pattenden. 'He can bat. Occasionally. Right? Please?' Mick Newell, his coach at Notts, once said: 'Swanny doesn't bat, he hits.' Well, he gets a single off the first ball here, which is all he needs to do. That allows Bell to swat away another imperious four.

50th over: England 159–6 (Bell 35, Swann 4) Hilfenhaus readjusts his sights now Swann is on strike, dropping the ball a lot shorter than he normally would. Australia still remember the pounding they gave Swann at Cardiff last year.

51st over: England 159–6 (Bell 35, Swann 4) Mitch is back in the attack, to the delight of the Australians in the crowd. His third ball is a beauty, full and swinging back in towards Bell's boots. He drops his bat down on it just in time to save himself a cracked toenail or two.

52nd over: England 163–6 (Bell 35, Swann 8) Swann sees that there'll be just enough width on Hilfenhaus's second ball for him to unfurl his drive, and he duly laces it through extra cover for four.

53rd over: England 165–6 (Bell 37, Swann 8) Johnson's jaffas, available by the crate. This was an absolute snorter, swinging back in past Bell's off stump, cutting him in two and leaving him dangling over his bat, face down and staring at the turf. Here's Carl Pilcher: 'Listening to the Aussie TV commentators as Swann swatted a four through cover, to which they said, "He has an eye like a dead fish." Is this a good thing?'

54th over: England 165–6 (Bell 37, Swann 8) Hilfenhaus is still on, and Swann plays out a maiden over.

55th over: England 170–6 (Bell 42, Swann 8) Bell glances the ball away for a glorious four through midwicket with all the ease of a man skimming the cream off the top of the milk with a knife. That takes the deficit underneath a hundred.

56th over: England 178–6 (Bell 50, Swann 8) Hilfenhaus is off, replaced by Harris. Carl Pilcher wanted to know whether or not the fact Swann had 'an eye like a dead fish' was a good thing. Well, his answer could hardly have come from a better source. 'Just seen Chappelli,' says Mike Selvey, 'and he says "eye like a dead fish" means he has a good eye. "But how can it be if it is dead?" I wondered. "You know," he said, "it sticks out like a dog's bollock." So basically Swanny has an eye like a dead fishy dog's bollock.' As does Ian Bell, who is playing superbly well here. He slashes four through point and then cuts away another to the same part of the ground. That's his fifty.

57th over: England 178–6 (Bell 50, Swann 8) Bell has batted so beautifully. He will surely move up the order soon enough – he is wasted at No. 6. England may just have erred here though – Swann has kept the strike. 'Stand back, Belly, I'll handle this.'

WICKET! 58th over: Swann c Haddin b Harris 11 (England 182–7) Swann's gone. He edged that straight through to Haddin. He leant tentatively forward, poking at a ball which moved away from him just enough to snick straight off the outside edge. Tremlett is in, hauling his huge frame down underneath a cheery welcome of a fast ball from Harris.

59th over: England 182–7 (Bell 51, Tremlett 0) If only someone can stay out there with Bell this deficit of 86 will shrink like that nice sweater granny gave you in a hot wash.

60th over: England 184–7 (Bell 52, Tremlett 1) 'I say this with an unblemished record of heterosexuality . . .' Shankar Kalyanaraman assures us as Tremlett takes his first run. 'But Tremlett's massive Greek body recommends itself to deposing Anderson off the covers of *Attitude*.'

61st over: England 185–7 (Bell 53, Tremlett 2) Tremlett gets stranded on strike to Johnson, but survives.

WICKET! 62nd over: Bell c Ponting b Harris 53 (England 186–8) This innings is all over now, bar the final rites. Bell stretches out to reach a wide ball and slices it to slip. It was a simple enough catch for Punter at second slip, flying towards him at head height. Australia's lead is 82.

WICKET! 63rd over: Tremlett b Johnson 1 (England 186–9) That's too good for Tremlett. It was a near-perfect in-swinger, slipping through the gate and shattering the stumps. Johnson has 5–37 now, and he raises the ball up above his head to acknowledge the applause of the crowd.

WICKET! 63rd over: Anderson c Watson b Johnson 0 (England 187 all out) Ding ding ding! Mitch v. Jimmy round two. Oh. That's a win by knockout. So long, Jimmy Anderson. England are 187 all out and trail by 81. In other words, they're in it. Deep in it. So from 78–0 they have lost all ten wickets for 109. Mitchell Johnson has figures of 12.3–4–21–6. Tea will be taken. This is going to be a fascinating final session.

England 187; Australia 268

The evening session

BY ROB SMYTH

Preamble: In 1990–1, the Ashes were decided in 13 days. In 1994–5, the series was over after 15 days. In 1998–9, it was 13. In 2002–3, 11. In 2006–7, 15. But in 2010–11, the Ashes series began on the 12th day, with Mitchell Johnson dragging Australia into the contest in stunning style. England are in trouble here, 81 runs behind, but it's crucial that they keep their nerve. Perth is a wicket that ages as beautifully as Sophia Loren.

1st over: Australia 0–0 (Watson 0, Hughes 0) This is a vital spell for Jimmy Anderson, who wasn't at his best yesterday. He starts with a reasonable maiden to Watson.

2nd over: Australia 4–0 (Watson 0, Hughes 4) Hughes leaves a couple and then drags the last delivery through mid-on for four. 'Rob,' says Daniel Sheehan, 'I think the readers need an early-morning update from the office of Alec Gregory.' I'd forgotten about the exploits of Dignity's Alec Gregory! That seems ages ago. A more innocent time; when England were a couple of days away from retaining the Ashes; when I could feel my eyes.

3rd over: Australia 4–0 (Watson 0, Hughes 4) Australia have started very carefully – particularly Watson, who plays (or rather leaves) another maiden from Anderson.

4th over: Australia 6–0 (Watson 1, Hughes 5) This will be a mammoth session: two hours 40 minutes, with a maximum of 39 overs. Not quite Melbourne 1998, but still a beast. Tremlett galumphs in to Hughes, whom he has dismissed thrice on tour already, and Hughes squirts one through point for a single. Watson then gets off the mark.

5th over: Australia 6–0 (Watson 1, Hughes 5) This is interesting. England half appeal and half celebrate when Watson pushes at a booming delivery from Anderson that flies through to Prior. Marais Erasmus said not out, but England decided not to review it. So why did they appeal quite so vociferously? Replays show it just hit the trousers on the way through.

6th over: Australia 11–0 (Watson 2, Hughes 9) With every ball Hughes survives, the danger of him punishing England increases. Obviously. You know what I mean. He has looked OK so far, and drills Tremlett down the ground for three.

7th over: Australia 16–0 (Watson 5, Hughes 11) 'I've just woken up to read this filth,' says Martin Quinn, which just about sums it up. 'If there is an upside I suppose it's that Hussey and Haddin apart, our bowling attack has the hoodoo on this lot and we remain a very tough team to beat; our second-innings batting has a track record of saving and winning games.' Is this the best England team ever?

8th over: Australia 16–0 (Watson 5, Hughes 11) Tremlett gets one to pop a little, and Hughes fends it on the bounce to gully.

9th over: Australia 30–0 (Watson 19, Hughes 11) Steven Finn replaces James Anderson. He goes for 14! Watson goes for him straight away, hitting three boundaries. That sound you can hear in your head is the theme from *Jaws*. England are in serious trouble here.

10th over: Australia 30–0 (Watson 19, Hughes 11) 'Thank you, Mitch,' says Eamonn Maloney. 'Just the tonic I need to wake up to the morning after the all-singing, all-dancing office Christmas party. No wait . . . the tonic I need is "gin and".'

11th over: Australia 30–0 (Watson 19, Hughes 11) Finn's second over is a maiden. That's a very good comeback actually, with a really tight line that dared Watson to risk the cut stroke. He didn't. In other news, Alec Gregory is answering questions from six hours ago. 'Why didn't I go home? Flat's being painted, sister's flat's in Chiswick and Tubes have finished. Or they had by the time I got to work.' So hang on, you were always planning to sleep at work? Or are you offering three part-excuses in the hope they add up to a whole?

12th over: Australia 31–0 (Watson 19, Hughes 12) Anderson has switched ends. He's still getting nice shape but he simply isn't making the batsmen play enough. One from the over.

WICKET! 13th over: Hughes c Collingwood b Finn 12

(Australia 31–1) Boy, did England need that. Finn angles a good one across Hughes that bounces enough to take the edge of a crabby defensive push before flying to Collingwood at third slip. Hundreds of young bowlers would have crumbled after disappearing for 14 in their first over, but Finn followed up with an excellent maiden to Watson and now he has the wicket of Hughes. It makes him the top wicket-taker in the series.

13th over: Australia 32–1 (Watson 19, Ponting 1) What a moment for Ricky Ponting. If he fails and Australia lose, it could be his last innings in Test cricket. If he gets a century and Australia win, it could be his greatest innings in Test cricket. He gets off the mark from his first ball, scuffing a hook to fine leg from a very good bouncer.

14th over: Australia 32–1 (Watson 19, Ponting 1) Anderson immediately pitches it fuller than he has to the openers, trying to get Ponting driving. After a series of outswingers, Anderson slips an inswinger back into the pad, but it was far too high. Excellent bowling though.

15th over: Australia 34–1 (Watson 19, Ponting 1) Another good over from Finn, save for a no-ball – only England's third of the series. Their discipline is superb.

16th over: Australia 34–1 (Watson 19, Ponting 1) This is fascinating stuff. Watson defends really solidly against Anderson, and it's a maiden. 'Given Ponting's wonderful grumpiness,' begins John Starbuck, 'what's the next in the instalment of most likely ways to get him out and really make him mad?' What's Gary Pratt doing these days?

WICKET! 17th over: Ponting c Prior b Finn 1 (Australia 34–2) Unbelievable. England have strangled Ricky Ponting down the leg side for the second time in the series. He tried to flick a short one from Finn off the hip as he jumped across the crease, and England went up very confidently for the caught behind. Marais Erasmus gave it not out, but England reviewed it – Andrew Strauss looked a little reluctant, actually – and Hotspot showed that it kissed the glove on the way through. Ponting looked unhappy with the decision but there's no doubt he was out.

17th over: Australia 40–2 (Watson 19, Clarke 6) Oof! That's quite a start from Clarke, who dumps a pull stroke through midwicket for four from his first delivery. This is wonderful Test cricket. Every single run could be decisive.

18th over: Australia 43–2 (Watson 21, Clarke 8) Anderson, who has the battle fever on, whistles a good bouncer past Clarke's nose. 'What do you reckon we could successfully chase in the fourth innings?' says Chris Wright. I think England won't be fazed by anything under 300.

19th over: Australia 56–2 (Watson 26, Clarke 16) Watson tickles an errant delivery from Finn to fine leg for four. Maybe Finn is tiring, because he angles another one onto the pads, and Clarke does the necessary. Four more, and then four more when Clarke pulls through square. Finn has figures of 6–1–36–2. I would have described his spell as a curate's egg had I not received 50 of the crispest lashes for misusing that phrase in another OBO earlier this year.

20th over: Australia 63–2 (Watson 29, Clarke 20) Clarke forces Anderson through the covers for four. He has 20 from 17 balls and looks like a completely different batsman to the one we have seen in the series to date. One with a cob on, basically.

WICKET! 21st over: Clarke b Tremlett 20 (Australia 64–3) Tremlett has struck in his first over back! Clarke, having started so well, tries a forcing shot with an angled bat and the ball cannons back into the stumps. What a Test match!

21st over: Australia 64–3 (Watson 30, Hussey 0) So Australia lead by 145. This game is so intoxicating. 'You want emails?'

says Yemon Choi. 'You can't handle the emails! It's coming up to 3 a.m. in Saskatoon, it's probably about −25°C outside and I'm having to fight toothache with Scotch. Oh, and England went from 70+ for none to under 190 all out. Talk about swinging from high to deep extremes of sweet and sour.'

22nd over: Australia 65–3 (Watson 31, Hussey 0) 'Absurd innings from Clarke,' says Gary Naylor. 'Disgraceful from a senior batsman and vice-captain.' That's harsh. It's easy to say he was too skittish, but disgraceful? Disgraceful is what 94 per cent of our readership did at their Christmas party last night. (What's 94 per cent of two, etc. and so honk.)

23rd over: Australia 69–3 (Watson 35, Hussey 0) Watson is playing so well, and back-cuts Tremlett for four. This is an important partnership because England will fancy their chances against the next batsman, Steve Smith. 'Waking up this morning and turning on *TMS* I had a Pamela Ewing moment,' says Jason Deans. 'The last eight days of Ashes play with England rampant was but a dream, and Bobby's stepping out of the shower.'

24th over: Australia 76–3 (Watson 39, Hussey 3) When he is in form, Michael Hussey is a remorseless bugger. He gets off the mark by working Anderson through square leg for three; Watson then larrups a couple of pulls for two runs each.

25th over: Australia 79–3 (Watson 41, Hussey 4) 'Looks like we've got a result wicket for a change,' says Pete Gay. 'Don't fancy batting last on it.' Nah, it's a decent pitch. The main factor today has been swing. England have nothing to worry about on this pitch – not least because they will almost certainly be chasing on day four rather than day five.

26th over: Australia 81–3 (Watson 41, Hussey 5) Graeme Swann is on. Apparently the Fremantle Doctor is on as well, which will help him with the drift. Hussey comes down the track to the first ball here, driving for a single. A quiet first over.

27th over: Australia 83–3 (Watson 43, Hussey 5) Tremlett has a strangled shout for lbw against Watson, who was miles forward and almost certainly outside the line. That was a good, accurate over from Tremlett, and Watson had little option but to defend.

28th over: Australia 91–3 (Watson 44, Hussey 12) Hussey will not allow Swann to bowl, and rocks back to pull his first ball meatily for four, works two to fine leg and then comes down the track. Finally Swann fires it a bit wider, and Hussey reaches to drive for a single. Lovely cricket.

29th over: Australia 95–3 (Watson 46, Hussey 15) With just over 20 minutes to the close, Finn replaces Tremlett (9–2–20–1). England could really use one more wicket today. Nothing doing in that over. 'Any chance you can pretend this is not the greatest Test match ever?' says David Thompson. 'I am in Sweden where they moan cricket is the most boring sport while they happily watch hours of cross-country skiing. No TV or radio coverage to be had here.'

30th over: Australia 105–3 (Watson 50, Hussey 21) Hussey cuts Swann's first ball through Trott at backward point and away for four. That was poor fielding, and he puts his hand up in apology. A flurry of ones and twos make it ten from the over. The last of them brings Watson to yet another fifty. He has to convert one of these into a century – or even a sixty – soon.

31st over: Australia 109–3 (Watson 54, Hussey 21) Finn looks tired, and a poor short delivery is swivel-pulled round the corner for four by Watson. The last four overs have yielded 26 runs. The game was precariously poised when Hussey came in, and he has played with marvellous certainty.

32nd over: Australia 115–3 (Watson 57, Hussey 24) Even with eight minutes to the close Hussey is coming down the track to Swann, and he drives charmingly through extra cover for three. This has been a gem of a cameo from Hussey. Watson has played beautifully too, and cuts three more to bring up the fifty partnership. It has the whiff of a match-winner. 'Rob, where would you place the Fremantle Doctor on a list of great Australian doctors?' says Dan Smith. 'I have it below the flying doctors but ahead of Dr Karl Kennedy.'

33rd over: Australia 119–3 (Watson 61, Hussey 24) Finn chugs in for his last over of the day, and Watson nails a superb extra-cover drive for four. That takes the lead up to 200 and is the end of a brilliant day's play. It should be another superb day's play tomorrow.

Australia 268 and 119–3; England 187

Rebooted destroyer Johnson swings where he had only sledged

Australia's troubled strike bowler has changed the dynamic of this series

BY DAVID HOPPS IN PERTH

FRIDAY 17 DECEMBER 2010

How do you solve a problem like Mitchell Johnson? Australia are probably still no wiser, but yesterday they had no need to ask. In Brisbane, he had more error messages than a virus-ridden laptop. Then he was rebooted for Perth, he swung the ball at pace, and yesterday England disintegrated in his presence.

Johnson likes his cricket simple: run in, feel strong, bowl fast.

When he plays at the Waca it is as if he undergoes an immediate virus check. His registry is fixed, the Trojans lurking in his mind are quarantined, if not entirely removed. Midway through his fourth Test on his home ground, after demolishing England with six for 38, his Waca record stood at 27 wickets at 18.51 apiece.

A few Australian observers had sensed this coming. They watched Johnson make runs on the first evening, witnessed his verbal aggression and sensed a fast bowler back in a positive frame of mind. This expectation had not entirely reached England. When they were 78 without loss this morning, the *Mitchell Johnson Joke Book* had the makings of a Christmas stocking filler.

Johnson's sledging of Jimmy Anderson, in particular, had seemed the last resort of a desperate man. Historians may reflect that this is the first Ashes series where two relatively shy fast bowlers have goaded each other about their respective glamour shoots. Johnson has done macho stuff, with muscles and tattoos on show; Anderson was confident enough in his sexuality earlier this year to become a gay icon by posing for *Attitude* magazine. You can imagine the sledging potential in all that.

Keep your mouth shut until you have taken some wickets was the gist of the advice Johnson received. He seemed to misinterpret it. The intended message was that he should, indeed, keep his mouth shut, but he took wickets instead. He started bowling booming left-arm inswingers at around 85 mph and suddenly it was England's batsmen who despaired. Alastair Cook, Jonathan Trott and Kevin Pietersen fell in the space of 12 balls in an explosive spell of four for 20 in nine overs. An England side that had lost six wickets for 1,215 runs had suddenly lost four for 16. In an Ashes series that some had deemed all over, a switch had clicked.

Perhaps Johnson's in-your-face cherry-blossom tattoos carry some power after all. During the Second World War, the Japanese government created the image that the souls of downed warriors were reincarnated in cherry blossom. Johnson, Australia's downed warrior, fighting a seemingly hopeless cause, had become a lone resistance unit.

The Johnson cherry blossom is timed to fall upon Western Australia around the end of the year. In December two years ago, he destroyed South Africa with his Test-best figures of eight for 61. Yesterday was his second-best return. Cook poked a catch to gully – an outswinger to the left-hander – three right-handers were lbw to inswingers, and he cleaned up a couple of tail-enders. Put it like that and Test cricket sounds easy.

It looked easy as he roared in. But who knows how ephemeral this may prove to be. Ian Chappell, the former Australia captain, reckons that you don't need to overanalyse at the Waca. The dumber the better, he suggests. Just set basic fields, and if you have a rip-roaring fast bowler with a point to prove, let him loose.

What made this all the more remarkable was that this was the bowler who before the first Test in Brisbane had proclaimed that he was not interested in swinging the ball any more, he was just going to bowl fast.

It felt like a statement of breathtaking naivety, a rejection of a natural gift. But in essence it was a reflection of a fast bowler who was short of confidence and suspicious of technical coaching. He wanted the possibility of inswing to prey on a batsman's mind; he did not want the absence of inswing to play on his own. He wanted the days when it swung to be a bonus, not an essential component of his game. With his career at one of its periodic low points, he drove a plumber's van for a mate, and his mate soon chirped up, suggesting that Troy Cooley, Australia's bowling coach, had wrecked him. Cooley chose not to retaliate by slagging off his mate's boiler units.

England, no longer wary of the ball dipping back, religiously left anything wide of off stump at the Gabba. Johnson did not take a single wicket and his method looked simplistic. In Western Australia they privately indicated that they could solve the problem in an hour, that his balance was wrong at the crease, his arm was too low, and so the swing failed to materialise. His arm was not exactly high yesterday, but perhaps it was a touch higher. Perhaps there is a tipping point.

When he was dropped for the second Test in Adelaide, and any number of former Australia fast bowlers insisted that he should recover form playing for his state, he was consigned to the nets, where presumably Cooley taught him to swing the ball again. There is no news on whether Cooley has received a new gas boiler in exchange.

Third day

The morning session

BY ANDY BULL

Preamble: Morning, everyone. Anyone feeling like this is one too many mornings and we're a thousand miles behind? I scraped four hours' sleep yesterday afternoon. I draped a heavy blanket over the thin curtains to black out the sun reflecting in off the blankets of fresh snow outside and lay there, listening to *Test Match Special*'s highlights on the radio. At the moment I have no life outside of the cricket and these four office walls. Strange times.

34th over: Australia 119–3 (Watson 61, Hussey 24) Tremlett takes the first over, with Hussey on strike. Straight off his length is a little fuller than he seemed to be bowling yesterday, which is a good sign. The first five balls all skip by the off stump, Hussey leaving most of them well alone.

35th over: Australia 120–3 (Watson 62, Hussey 24) And at the other end it is Jimmy Anderson. Watson pats his first ball to mid-off. He leaves the next few alone. There's just a hint of shape on the ball, you couldn't quite call it swing. The sixth delivery is squeezed away square for a single.

36th over: Australia 121–3 (Watson 63, Hussey 24) 'Is this the turning point we all expected?' writes Duncan Smith, as Watson knocks a single away to the leg side. 'Where the Aussies realise they don't lose to us at home and crush the hopes that they let us foolishly build almost to the point of triumphalism?' No, no, no. England should have earned more of our faith than that – they are a tough team.

37th over: Australia 124–3 (Watson 66, Hussey 24) Prior spreads his arms and screams out an appeal for a catch behind, but no one else goes up with him. Watson was trying to leave the ball on length, but it broke back in and just skimmed his forearm on its way through.

38th over: Australia 127–3 (Watson 67, Hussey 25) Tremlett is bowling so straight that the two batsmen are able milk him for singles this way and that either side of the wicket.

39th over: Australia 134–3 (Watson 72, Hussey 25) Again Anderson gets it wrong, and Watson whips two away square. The next ball is spot on though, and catches the outside edge before shooting off towards gully.

40th over: Australia 137–3 (Watson 76, Hussey 26) This opening combination is not working for Strauss. Watson pats another single away to the leg side. Tremlett switches around the wicket to bowl at Hussey, but again the upshot is only another single. 'This', mutters Smyth, 'could turn into a very long day if these two get in.'

41st over: Australia 138–3 (Watson 77, Hussey 26) Here's Paul Billington: 'Normally when I tune into the OBO in the summer I'm at work (q.v. the morning after roof-of-the-takeaway debacle) [Andy's note: eh?] and I watch with eagerness a regular Test series without the threat of dumpage and/or sackings. Today though finds me having ushered the missus off to bed post-pub with the forlorn hope that (1) Australia are skittled for less than a 250 lead, (2) the missus doesn't leave me before the 5th Test, and (3) my hangover doesn't render me too cantankerous should things go awry today. Never mind, eh.'

42nd over: Australia 138–3 (Watson 77, Hussey 26) The first change of the day brings Steve Finn into the attack to replace Tremlett, whose opening four-over spell cost just seven runs. Watson picks out the fielders at mid-on and mid-off with a couple of crisp drives.

43rd over: Australia 139–3 (Watson 77, Hussey 27) Hussey sneaks a single after chopping Anderson's latest delivery out to gully. There's nothing doing for England out there, and Jimmy knows it. He's got a disgruntled scowl on his face.

44th over: Australia 145–3 (Watson 78, Hussey 28) Finn, like Tremlett, comes around the wicket to Hussey. But he is pitching the ball up near the batsman's toes, trying to trap him with a yorker. When he does pitch a little shorter, the ball flicks off the thigh pad and trickles away for four leg byes.

45th over: Australia 147–3 (Watson 80, Hussey 28) Watson cuts a couple out to deep cover. This is drifting. We may need to think of something else to talk about if we're going to get through this session awake.

46th over: Australia 147–3 (Watson 80, Hussey 28) A maiden from Finn, largely because Hussey seems to have developed an unfortunate habit of hitting all his shots straight to the fielders.

47th over: Australia 152–3 (Watson 80, Hussey 32) 60 minutes, 30 runs, no chances so far today – Australia's approach is pretty clear. Hussey pushes four away past point. Under his breath Smyth mutters a couple of words I can't print.

48th over: Australia 165–3 (Watson 90, Hussey 36) And now I'm muttering a few myself as well. That's a lovely stroke by Watson, a drive through extra cover for four. Finn may be the leading wicket-taker, but he is going for so many runs that the selectors are going to have a bad headache deciding what to do about him ahead of the next Test. That's 13 from the over. Mercy me, I thought I was doing well to stay awake till I read this email from James Roscoe: 'Sitting in a drab UN conference room in NY in our 15th consecutive hour of negotiating UN budgets. Can't say news from Perth is cheering up the UK delegation. We're trying to maintain focus by slipping in cricketing metaphors: good innings, straight bat and sticky wicket deployed so far. We'd be grateful if fellow OBOers could suggest others.'

49th over: Australia 174–3 (Watson 93, Hussey 42) Tremlett comes back into the attack after a drinks break. 'He's quickly become Strauss's go-to bowler,' says Nasser, a split second before Watson wallops his first ball to long-off for three. Moments later, the sightscreen breaks down and the entire game comes to a halt for five minutes while the ground staff try to fix it. This is the biggest talking point of the morning yet. 'If they can't fix the sightscreen do we get a draw?' asks Gregory Wilkinson. 'Please say yes.'

50th over: Australia 177–3 (Watson 94, Hussey 43) 'If Roscoe at the UN can work in "queering the pitch" that ought to bring the translators to a grinding halt,' suggests a man known only as Longmemory. The lead, by the way, is now up to 256. The Barmy Army's trumpeter is playing a doleful rendition of 'Waltzing Matilda'.

WICKET! 51st over: Watson lbw b Tremlett 95 (Australia 180–4) The scream of an lbw appeal snaps me out of my torpor. It's Watson, struck just in front of middle by an in-dipper from Tremlett. Watson refers it, but it's out. That's the fourth time he has been dismissed in the 90s.

REFERRAL! 52nd over: Smith c Strauss b Finn 1 (Australia 182–4) Smith is in. And out again! England appeal for a catch at slip off the inside edge, and umpire Doctrove raises his finger in agreement. But Smith refers it. This could be out caught or it could be out lbw. But in fact it's neither. The ball missed the bat and flew to slip off the pad. And if it hadn't hit the pad it would have missed the stumps. So the decision is overturned and Smith bats on.

53rd over: Australia 190–4 (Hussey 50, Smith 5) Hussey raises his fifty – his sixth in successive Ashes innings, which is a new record – with a streaky slice through the gully. Bah. Smith and Hussey almost contrive a run-out here, hopping back and forth as Smith was a third of the way down the wicket. Smithy survives, beating Tremlett's throw home, but it still feels like Australia have, astonishingly, managed to find an even worse No. 6 than the one they had in the last match.

54th over: Australia 197–4 (Hussey 55, Smith 8) My word, what a shot that is from Hussey. He plays a murderous pull through midwicket for four, swinging at the ball as though it had just said something awful about the provenance of his parents. 'Just a word of caution for any English fans hoping for a manageable fourth-innings target,' says Ian Rubinstein. 'The Australians are almost at the end of the nightwatchmen, and the specialist bats are due to come in soon.'

55th over: Australia 204–4 (Hussey 55, Smith 14) Smith is getting peppered here, Tremlett bombing him with a trio of short balls. He limbos right over onto his back to avoid the third of them, but leaves his bat poking up like a periscope. To be fair to the man, he smashes the next ball away for a superb four through long leg.

56th over: Australia 208–4 (Hussey 58, Smith 14) A bowling change, though it's not Graeme Swann who is coming on but Jimmy Anderson. Hussey thrashes his first ball back in the attack for three to midwicket.

57th over: Australia 211–4 (Hussey 60, Smith 15) Anyone

who can remember Chris Schofield bat during his brief Test career will have a fair idea of how Smith is playing now. Schofield was certainly the last man I can remember seeing play the inadvertent periscope shot to long stop.

REFERRAL! 57th over: Hussey lbw b Tremlett 60 (Australia 211–4) Have they got him? Yes! – or at least umpire Erasmus thinks so, but Virtual Eye doesn't. The decision is overturned and Hussey plays on. And that's the end of the session, and you'd have to say that from England's point of view it is the end of the match too. Australia lead by 292.

Australia 268 and 211–4; England 187

The afternoon session

BY ROB SMYTH

Preamble: England aren't dead yet, and were arguably in a worse position at this stage of the Brisbane Test, but the circumstances aren't really comparable: the pitch was much flatter and it's generally a lot easier to save a game when you are batting in the third innings rather than the fourth. It looks like it will be 1–1 and that we will all receive the best possible Christmas present: a live Ashes going into the Boxing Day Test for the first time since 1994–5.

58th over: Australia 218–4 (Hussey 61, Smith 22) Steven Finn's first ball – stop me if you think you've heard this one before – is too short and forced through the covers for three by Smith.

59th over: Australia 224–4 (Hussey 61, Smith 28) And still no Swann. That is very odd. I assumed he would start at this end, but it's Jimmy Anderson. Smith is looking much more comfortable against the quicks now, as he shows with a storming thrash through the covers for four.

60th over: Australia 230–4 (Hussey 67, Smith 28) Hussey pulls Finn disdainfully for four. England look pretty flat at the moment. 'Were many people calling England a great team?' sniffs Gary Naylor. 'It's a very handy batting line-up backed up by a well-balanced attack comprising an outstanding spinner and decent quicks, albeit with less experience than is ideal. Either England's or Australia's 2005 line-up would beat either of these sides 3–0, I feel.'

REVIEW! 61st over: Smith lbw b Anderson 28 (Australia 230–4) England appeal for caught behind when Prior takes a spectacular catch down the leg side off Smith. Anderson seemed quite keen on a review, but Strauss decided against it, and rightly so because it was pad only. Anderson has another biggish shout for lbw against the same man later in the over, but that was sliding down past leg stump. And now there's another lbw appeal turned down – and this one looks close. England decide to review it, but Virtual Eye shows it was only hitting the outside of leg stump. Smith survives.

61st over: Australia 230–4 (Hussey 67, Smith 28) They have just shown the Anderson decision again, and at least half of the ball was hitting leg stump. It was clattering it! I don't know that it's right to go with the umpire's call when that much of the ball is hitting the stumps. Anyway, them's the rules, and the breaks. 'Watching Steve Smith is like watching the chancer who strolls up to the crease in village cricket and bashes you for a fifty,' says Dave Forrest. 'You're left shaking our head as you say, "That's the worst fifty I have ever seen."' And he scores quickly and perkily, which compounds the frustration.

62nd over: Australia 232–4 (Hussey 68, Smith 29)

Graeme Swann finally comes on for his first over of the day, and only his fifth of the innings. Hussey tries to dominate from the start in his usual fleet-footed style. Two from the over, and this will be a good contest.

63rd over: Australia 237–4 (Hussey 72, Smith 30) Anderson overpitches, and Hussey drives him gloriously through extra cover for four. He is playing marvellously. 'Spare a thought for all of us roasting at the Waca and watching this carnage,' says Riley Stevens. 'The bloody Aussies have put all us Poms in the sun, while they all sit comfortably in the shade. Sympathy, anyone?' As I am only just starting to feel my feet again, having arrived at work four hours ago, I suppose I don't have that much sympathy. Or, like, any.

64th over: Australia 241–4 (Hussey 73, Smith 33) Smith sweeps Swann for a couple in an over that brings four. England have problems here. The lead is 322 and we are not even at the halfway point of the game.

65th over: Australia 242–4 (Hussey 74, Smith 33) One from Anderson's over, in which he gets some noticeable reverse swing. As this partnership develops, so thought turns to when Australia might declare. They would a few overs tonight, but I doubt they'll have enough runs to do that. An hour into tomorrow with a lead of about 550?

66th over: Australia 248–4 (Hussey 79, Smith 34) Hussey dances down the track and rifles Swann through extra cover for four. That's just an outstanding shot. 'I really can't see Swann going two consecutive innings without taking a wicket,' says Ryan O'Hare. Nor can I, but as he took two in the first innings . . . (Unless you meant consecutive innings without bowling a maiden, which really would be a surprise, and a first in his Test career.)

67th over: Australia 249–4 (Hussey 79, Smith 35) As

Anderson toils through another over, Sir Ian Botham suggests that England should 'use their nonce' with regard to field placings. Where's Chris Morris when you need him?

68th over: Australia 251–4 (Hussey 80, Smith 36) Swann isn't having much fun out there. Nor are England. The lead ticks up to 332.

WICKET! 69th over: Smith c Prior b Tremlett 36 (Australia 252–5) Steven Smith walks. England brought on Tremlett to rough him up from around the wicket, and it took just two balls. It was banged in on middle stump and Smith, moving across to the off side, gloved it down the leg side to Prior. It was a big deflection and Smith didn't wait for the decision. That's a happy by-product of the UDRS, and we should see more and more walking as a result. It's almost a lie-detector test.

69th over: Australia 253–5 (Hussey 81, Haddin 0) So that's six wickets in the match for Tremlett, and he has been comfortably the pick of the England bowlers. He carries on the same line and length to Haddin, digging it in from around the wicket. 'Warne is absolutely ripping into Strauss's captaincy here on Australian TV,' says Ryan O'Hare. 'Everything from field placings – his personal favourite – the overuse of Anderson, to the lack of Swann, to Finn being first up after lunch. He's got more than a point.' What was it Aristotle said? People who are the subject of grainy photos involving comedy inflatables shouldn't throw stones?

70th over: Australia 264–5 (Hussey 86, Haddin 6) Swann's first ball is a fraction too short and Hussey rocks back to smash a pull for four. His foot movement against the spinners is majestic. As is Haddin's stroke play. He gets off the mark with the most magnificent shot, a slog sweep high over midwicket for six.

71st over: Australia 269–5 (Hussey 90, Haddin 7) Tremlett has switched to over the wicket to Haddin. No idea why, and

Haddin gets off strike with a comfortable steer to third man. Hussey then belabours a pull towards the fence at midwicket, and the diving Finn does superbly to turn four into two. That's drinks, and that means we are halfway through the series.

72nd over: Australia 270–5 (Hussey 91, Haddin 7) Paul Collingwood comes on to replace Graeme Swann and bowl some filler before the second new ball. That was a chastening little spell for Swann, whose figures are now 9–0–51–0. I had a £10 bet before the series that he would average over 40. I felt an idiot after Adelaide, but that series average has crept up to 38.63. One from Collingwood's over.

WICKET! 73rd over: Haddin b Tremlett 7 (Australia 271–6) That's seven in the match for Tremlett. Haddin pushes defensively at a good delivery that cuts back off the seam, and the ball cannons off the inside edge, onto the pad and back onto the stumps. The lead is 352.

73rd over: Australia 276–6 (Hussey 96, Johnson 1) Hussey hooks Tremlett brilliantly for four to move to 96. Haddin has been fortunate to survive the previous delivery. Hussey took a dodgy single into the covers and Haddin was not even in the frame when Collingwood swooped to throw just wide of the stumps.

WICKET! 74th over: Johnson c Bell b Collingwood 1 (Australia 276–7) England persist with Collingwood, a surprising decision that is immediately justified when the dangerous Johnson drives to short extra cover. Bell takes an unobtrusive low catch, and that's a vital breakthrough, because an hour of Johnson swinging like Joe DiMaggio and England were done.

74th over: Australia 277–7 (Hussey 96, Harris 0) Collingwood, of all people, is wided for a bouncer. 'He's turned into Bob Willis . . .' chuckles Bumble.

75th over: Australia 284–7 (Hussey 102, Harris 1) Hussey hooks Tremlett for four more to bring up a century on his home ground, before setting off down the pitch and leaping to punch the air. This has been an awesome innings, absolutely awesome, and it's staggering to think his Test career was on its deathbed at the start of the series. He has 501 runs at 125.25!

76th over: Australia 284–7 (Hussey 102, Harris 1) Hussey is a dangerous man with the tail, because he can slip into one-day mode pretty easily. 'Given how Anderson has fared so far, will England now issue a conception embargo nine months prior to an Ashes series?' says Shankar Kalyanaraman. 'Not saying that he hasn't bowled well, but there's no knowing if he would have been much sharper had he stayed on.'

WICKET! 77th over: Harris c Bell b Finn 1 (Australia 284–8) What a moronic piece of cricket from Ryan Harris. He just needed to hang around with Michael Hussey; instead he pulled Steven Finn straight to deep midwicket. There were three men out there for the shot! That's preposterous. Not even Homer Simpson would have played that shot. The lead is now 365.

77th over: Australia 284–8 (Hussey 102, Siddle 0) Finn had come on to replace Tremlett, who will have a short breather before the second new ball. The batsmen crossed while that dunderheaded garbage from Harris was in the air, and Hussey plays out the rest of the over.

78th over: Australia 284–8 (Hussey 102, Siddle 0) Graeme Swann's day gets worse with a dropped catch. Siddle drove Collingwood to Swann at extra cover, but he couldn't hang on two-handed as he dived to his right. In the 2010s, and for this England team, that was a relatively straightforward chance.

79th over: Australia 289–8 (Hussey 107, Siddle 0) Hussey starts Finn's over with a storming extra-cover drive for four. The placement and timing were almost perfect. Before that, he had given Siddle a minor rollocking over that shot in the previous over. 'He's sick of tail-enders coming in and trying to bat like Don Bradman,' spits Nasser Hussain with regal contempt.

80th over: Australia 290–8 (Hussey 107, Siddle 0) Collingwood gets through another tight over. He's done a brilliant job (5–2–3–1), and now it's time for the new ball.

81st over: Australia 292–8 (Hussey 109, Siddle 1) Finn carries on with the old ball, and Siddle pushes a short one just to the left of Cook at short leg. 'I watched a lot of the Aus v. SA Test two years ago at the Waca (alas only on telly), and SA would have chased 800 never mind 414,' says Gary Naylor. 'This is on all right.' And the thing about that game is that as in the first innings here, Johnson was unplayable. He took eight for 61 in the first innings but then just three for 98 in the second.

82nd over: Australia 292–8 (Hussey 109, Siddle 1) Collingwood is still bowling. That's a very surprising decision. I suppose there are only five minutes to tea, so maybe Strauss wants to give Anderson and Tremlett a longer rest and just choke an end until then. Collingwood does just that with a maiden. Siddle, trying to bat like Robin Smith now, misses an attempted cut stroke from the third delivery. 'England to skittle the Aussies out in the next ten overs and then make 444–4 in reply,' says John Macnamara. 'Not only securing the Ashes, but rubbing the Aussie noses in it with the highest-ever fourth-innings run chase.'

83rd over: Australia 297–8 (Hussey 111, Siddle 3) England do take the new ball for the last over before tea, which is bowled by James Anderson. Not much happens, and that's the end of a pretty decent session for England, who took four for 86, and an extremely good one for Michael Hussey, who made a fantastic century and is still there. Australia lead by 378.

Australia 268 and 297–8; England 187

The evening session

BY ANDY BULL

Preamble: Evening, everyone. No, that's not right. Morning, everyone. I'm through the wall now. I was almost catatonic at times during that morning session, but there's nothing like a few wickets for a pick-me-up. Well, there are. But I can't get my hands on any of them in the office. All we have to keep us going is the vending machine's No. 3 coffee-flavoured beverage.

84th over: Australia 308–8 (Hussey 116, Siddle 8) Tremlett opens the session with a wide. A single puts Siddle on strike, and he wafts four runs away to fine leg. He clips the next away for a single between short leg's spread legs. Poor over this, capped off by a four from Hussey, cut through extra cover.

WICKET! 85th over: Siddle c Collingwood b Anderson 8 (Australia 308–9) Siddle pokes a catch straight to third slip. That's Anderson's 200th Test wicket, in his 54th Test. He's had to wait on 199 a little longer than he would have liked. Still, that makes him the ninth-fastest Englishman to the mark, one match behind both Steve Harmison and Matthew Hoggard. He's the second youngest to do it though, after old Iron Bottom. What odds that he could be the man to go on and break Botham's all-time record for Test wickets for England?

85th over: Australia: 309–9 (Hussey 116, Hilfenhaus 0) Every ball that swings only makes me worry more about what it will be like when England bat, but still. Hussey has shown them how to do it. Back to that last over, he may be the man of the series at the moment, but will he still be by Monday? There are a couple of English batsmen riding close on his shoulders.

WICKET! 86th over: Hussey c Swann b Tremlett 116

(Australia 309 all out) Well, I'll be. They've got him, at last. Tremlett finished with figures of 24–4–87–5. But the important statistic is this one: England need 391 to retain the Ashes.

England second innings

Preamble: Whatever happens next, if nothing else hopefully it will make Jamie Kirkaldy's day a little better: 'My feet are freezing, I've got baby sick on my shoulder, England seem to have time-warped back to 1993 and all I've got to look forward to is a lukewarm shower because our boiler is broken. Did I mention that it's my birthday?'

1st over: England 0–0 (Strauss 0, Cook 0) England need 391 to win. Hilfenhaus takes the first over. He has three slips. Smyth is full of confidence: 'Nine of England's top 14 chases to win have been since 1997,' he chirrups, suggesting that expectations for what is possible in the fourth innings have changed out of all recognition. This is a zippy first over from Hilfenhaus, mixing stock balls outside off with a vicious bouncer and a wicked yorker. Strauss ducked the first of those and blocked the second.

2nd over: England 6–0 (Strauss 0, Cook 6) And at the other end it's Ryan Harris. He serves up a tasty-looking leg-side delivery which Cook pats away for two. The next ball is in a similar place, and this time Cook glances it fine for four.

3rd over: England 8–0 (Strauss 2, Cook 6) Strauss pats two runs past mid-on. 'Forget all the doom and gloom, this is a real match at last,' beams Mark Hooper. 'Aussies favourites to win, but with England still in with an outside chance of retaining the Ashes after the THIRD Test. On top of that, the Aussie crowd have come alive too. Verbals, bouncers, Haddin baiting the Barmy Army: this is the stuff.'

4th over: England 13–0 (Strauss 6, Cook 7) Ponting, a thin white veil of sun cream smeared across his chops, shouts and points directions to his field. Strauss drives four down through long-off, a lovely shot. 'I got approached by a girl in Starbucks here in Beijing to "help her with her final assignment", whatever that means,' says James Galloway. 'I turned her down because I was too busy reading the OBO report. I kind of regret it now, as it was only Smyth. Oh the shame!'

5th over: England 13–0 (Strauss 6, Cook 8) An edge! But it falls short of Ponting at second slip. Australia are bowling a much fuller length to Cook than they did in the first two Tests. He clips a single away square.

6th over: England 23–0 (Strauss 6, Cook 8) Well, here we go. Hilfenhaus has bowled very well, but Ponting can't wait to get the pawns out of the way and bring his queen into play. On comes Johnson. This is the match right here. And immediately he almost runs out Cook by booting the ball towards the wicket. Cook takes two from the next ball, and three from the one after that. Then Strauss chops a four down to third man. England are going hard after everything loose that Johnson offers.

WICKET! 7th over: Cook lbw b Harris 13 (England 23–1) Oh no. Cook's gone. And he hasn't even paused to review it. The ball looked to have hit him high up on the pads from here, but Cook had a quick chat with his captain and they decided not to refer it. He trudges off. Trott is in, laboriously marking his guard. Harris's first delivery to him is full and swinging in, and Trott glances it away for four to third man. A good start that. Nervous times.

8th over: England 29–1 (Strauss 11, Trott 5) That's a gem from Johnson, hurtling an away-swinger past Strauss's outside edge.

9th over: England 33–1 (Strauss 11, Trott 9) Already things are feeling just a little steadier, simply because Trott is at the crease. He dead-bats a couple of deliveries from Harris, and then steers a four away past point.

10th over: England 37–1 (Strauss 15, Trott 9) Johnson's line drifts out wide again, and Strauss's eyes open wide in anticipation. He gleefully cuts the ball away for four through backward point.

WICKET! 10th over: Strauss c Ponting b Johnson 15 (England 39–2) Captain, the ship is sinking. How are all you optimists feeling now? Johnson has his first wicket. Strauss got forced back in the crease and dangled his bat at a ball that broke away from him. The ball popped up off the edge and guess who was there to catch it? Punter, of course. Here's KP, on a pair. Oh, that's an ominous ball. It was full and swung back in towards KP's middle stump, beating the inside edge and ricocheting away for a leg bye. England are up to their necks in it here.

11th over: England 41–2 (Trott 11, Pietersen 0) Hilfenhaus has changed ends. Both openers gone. This could hardly have worked out any better for Australia. 'I'm still optimistic,' insists Gary Naylor. 'England need two tons from five remaining batsmen – the ability to get tons is why they were selected and they all have plenty.' If only 'two tons' was as easy to score as it is to type, eh, Gary? Trott steps across the stumps and pushes two runs out to leg. A risky shot, that.

12th over: England 44–2 (Trott 13, Pietersen 1) Johnson bangs in a short ball, but Pietersen seems to be in the same sort of aggressive frame of mind as Cook and Strauss, and he swats it away off his nose for a single.

13th over: England 44–2 (Trott 13, Pietersen 1) The game pauses for a beat as Pietersen plays out a maiden from Hilfenhaus.

14th over: England 51–2 (Trott 18, Pietersen 3) Trott

gloves a looping catch down the leg side, but there is no one there to take it. 'Desperately disappointing as it will be if we lose this, in a way it's the best thing that could have happened for the series,' says Phil White. 'Boxing Day will now be an incredible occasion and surely England's biggest Test match since the Oval 2005.' A good shot from Trott, stepping out to drive three runs to extra cover. Then Pietersen picks off Johnson's inswinger and pats it away to long-on.

15th over: England 51–2 (Trott 18, Pietersen 3) Hilfenhaus pins Trott down in his crease with a series of balls that hug off stump. He flings down a filthy bouncer by way of variation, but it sails well over the batsman's head.

16th over: England 51–2 (Trott 18, Pietersen 3) Here's Siddle. Since his 6–54 in the first innings of the series he has taken one for 236. Those figures will stay just as they are because he has managed a maiden to Pietersen here.

17th over: England 51–2 (Trott 18, Pietersen 3) Ponting is laughing and grinning at Hilfenhaus. As well he might do. One more wicket tonight and his team will be sitting pretty. That's his second straight maiden.

18th over: England 55–2 (Trott 20, Pietersen 3) My second wind must be spent because we just had a five-minute delay while a streaker ran around the pitch, but the entire episode passed me by. Didn't even register. A beautiful ball from Siddle, whistling past Pietersen's outside edge. Sadly for him he overstepped, so he only added an extra to the score.

WICKET! 19th over: Pietersen c Watson b Hilfenhaus 3 (England 57–3) Pietersen pauses the game to get a new bat from the 12th man, and after spending a good while picking one out he slaps a catch straight to second slip. 'That', thunders Nasser, 'was a terrible shot.' And Pietersen knows it too. He trails off, staring at the turf and hardly picking up his feet. That's

Hilfenhaus's first wicket since the very first over of the series. And it took one of his worst balls to get it – it was short, wide and utterly innocuous.

20th over: England 59–3 (Trott 20, Collingwood 1) If Ponting was laughing and grinning a couple of overs ago, he is absolutely beaming now. And this time it's not just because some clown from the crowd has invaded the pitch.

21st over: England 60–3 (Trott 20, Collingwood 2) 'Oh yeah,' says Doug Green. 'That's what it feels like to be English again. I remember.'

22nd over: England 64–3 (Trott 20, Collingwood 6) Collingwood pops out of his shell just enough to loft a four up and over the slips, though it wasn't exactly what you would call an intentional stroke. 'Is the word for KP's turnaround "complacent" or "karmic"?' asks Gary Naylor. 'The game has made fools of better players than KP.' I'd say he did a fairly good job of making a fool of himself with that last dismissal. Not sure he needed any help from 'the game'.

23rd over: England 70–3 (Trott 29, Collingwood 6) 'You lot still have Trott, Colly and Bell,' says Ian Rubentein. 'So we are preparing to be sleepwalked to death.' Well, Trott slashes four down to backward point here, and then hops across his stumps to pat two more out to midwicket.

24th over: England 73–3 (Trott 31, Collingwood 7) Mitchell Johnson is back into the attack for one last burst before the close. 'Have you missed the beer-glass anaconda being displayed between overs by a clearly bored and pissed Barmy Army?' asks Haward Soper. Surprisingly enough I have missed it. It doesn't seem to have made Sky's highlights reel. 'At least it stops them chanting "You all live in a convict colony" to an audience experiencing a huge economic boom and low unemployment and great public services, but Poms are not strong on irony.'

25th over: England 74–3 (Trott 31, Collingwood 8) Ten minutes left to play then. Still, it could be worse. South Africa are 490–3 following India's first innings 136. Kallis is 138 not our and A. B. de Villiers has crashed 63 from 54 balls. Good luck dragging that one back, lads.

WICKET! 26th over: Trott c Haddin b Johnson 31 (England 81–4) There goes another one. But it has come at a cost. Trott edged the ball hard and fast to Ponting at second slip, but it caught awkwardly on his fingers and ricocheted up into the air. Haddin ran across and took the rebound, so Trott is out, but Ponting is down on the floor in a lot of pain. Looks like he may have broken something. He follows the batsman off the field in search of a little medical aid.

WICKET! 27th over: Collingwood c Smith b Harris 11 (England 81–5) And the very last ball of the day puts a full stop on any hope England had left. Paul Collingwood edges a catch to slip. And that, ladies and gents, is that. I'm reeling, and so are England. Excuse me if I scarper but I've a bed to get to. We'll be back here tomorrow for the sorry denouement. I wouldn't stay awake expecting any twists.

England 187 and 81–5; Australia 268 and 309

Fourth day

The morning session

BY ANDY BULL

Preamble: Morning, everyone. What happens today matters, and England know that from personal experience. If they fold inside the first hour, then there are going to be very few positives to pluck from the wreckage. Bat on into the afternoon and at least they will have ended the match on a sweet note. Australia are out on the pitch, but Ricky Ponting is not with them. Michael Clarke is in charge.

28th over: England 85–5 (Anderson 3, Bell 0) Three slips, two gullies, and Johnson opens with a pair of bouncers that whizz past Jimmy Anderson's head. He's between a rock and the proverbial is Jimmy, because he is not going to get much sympathy from the English press after his batting last night. He turned down a single off the penultimate ball of the day, sending Paul Collingwood back to the striker's end. Of course, Colly got out next ball.

29th over: England 89–5 (Anderson 3, Bell 4) And at the other end it's Ryan Harris. Bell beautifully drives his third ball away for four to extra cover.

30th over: England 89–5 (Anderson 3, Bell 4) Anderson flashes a cut shot at a wide ball from Johnson but doesn't connect. Otherwise he leaves and blocks the rest. It's a maiden. 'Should I go to bed?' asks Matthew Tom. 'I'm flying to Australia in the morning.' Turned turncoat have you? Well, you've nothing to lose by staying up then, I'd suggest.

31st over: England 94–5 (Anderson 3, Bell 9) That's a good-looking shout for an lbw, but Australia opt not to refer it. Bell was trying to flick the ball to leg, but it swung back inside the bat and hit him high on the pad in front of leg stump. And that is a sweet shot, the kind that makes the connoisseurs purr, a late cut for four past backward point. The next isn't so good – it squirts away off the inside edge for a single.

WICKET! 31st over: Anderson b Harris 3 (England 94–6) Well, there's one of them. Anderson is undone by an in-swinger from Harris. He offered a rather abject defensive prod to a ball that slanted across towards the off stump after pitching on leg. It splattered his stumps all across the turf. That's Harris's sixth wicket in the match, for just 90 runs.

32nd over: England 94–6 (Bell 9, Prior 0) Bell is beaten by a ball that slides across him, passing perilously close to his outside edge. In the first Test they were able to leave deliveries like that one from Johnson well alone, secure in the knowledge that they could do no harm. But now he has started to move the ball back in the batsmen have to play at them to try and cover the swing, which means they are far more likely to nick it off to the slips.

33rd over: England 104–6 (Bell 9, Prior 10) After what we've seen this week I imagine the curators at Melbourne and Sydney will be wondering whether it is too late to scatter some more grass seed on their wickets. Prior launches a six up and over Haddin's head. He was aiming through square leg but made a mess of the shot.

34th over: England 111–6 (Bell 16, Prior 10) Bell eases a drive away to extra cover. He stops to admire what seems set to be a certain four, before it dawns on him that Peter Siddle will chase the ball down before it crosses the rope. There's still time to sprint two. He doesn't need to run for the next one though – it races away to wide third man for four. A single from the sixth ball, driven uppishly to point, means he will keep the strike.

WICKET! 35th over: Bell lbw b Harris 16 (England 114–7) Bell's done by an in-dipper. He's toast. Kicked the bucket. Bought the farm. The referral is just a formality. And hardly one worth bothering with – the ball would have hit the middle of middle stump. Harris is bowling well here. He has 4–41, the best figures of his brief Test career. Swann is in and the end is nigh. He whips his first ball away to midwicket for three.

WICKET! 35th over: Prior c Hussey b Harris 10 (England 114–8) That's a stinker of a shot, but a beauty of a catch by Hussey in the gully. It was a short ball, again, and Prior flailed at it. Harris has his first-ever five-for, and he celebrates by raising the ball into the air. England have capitulated in truly sorry fashion here.

36th over: England 120–8 (Swann 9, Tremlett 0) Swann top-edges a four away to third man. He may as well enjoy himself while it lasts. Not that it lasts long.

WICKET! 36th over: Swann b Johnson 9 (England 120–9) Swann throws a drive at a full ball and only edges into his own stumps. D'oh. Johnson needs one more for ten wickets in the match.

36th over: England 123–9 (Tremlett 1, Finn 2) I should warn you, readers, that I've had eight hours' sleep in the last 48 hours and so I'm on a short fuse. And there is something about this email from Lee James that sticks in my craw: 'Are you still confident of this newfound toughness? We still have serious deficiencies in our batting that were hidden by the wicket and top order in Adelaide.' Yes. That's right. Never mind that this team won the Ashes in 2009. And drew a series in South Africa, twice holding on for draws when they were nine wickets down. On the evidence of this one match we should revise our entire opinion of their achievements and write them off as feeble and deficient.

WICKET! 37th over: Finn c Smith b Harris 2 (England 123 all out) This shambles is all over. Finn slices a catch to third slip. Australia have won the third Test by 267 runs and the Ashes are level, 1–1 with two games to play. England lasted just ten overs today. Harris leads Australia off, waving a stump above his head as he goes. He finishes with Test-best figures of 6–47, meaning that he and Johnson have taken 18 wickets between them in the match. Looks like Australia have finally figured out what their best bowling attack is. Happy birthday, Ricky. On to Melbourne. See you back here in a week or so. Cheerio and Merry Christmas.

Australia 268 and 309; England 187 and 123.
Australia win by 267 runs

It's all in their heads. Cup-final mentality is England's downfall

BY DUNCAN FLETCHER

MONDAY 20 DECEMBER 2010

When I was England's coach, one of the biggest difficulties I had was making sure the team kept their foot on the pedal. Strange as it seems, the occasions when I used to get most nervous about how well England would perform followed on from their best wins. So often, in my early years in charge, they would veer from highs to lows in the space of a match or two. One good result and then, bang, the team would crash. This England side have the same problem. We saw it at Headingley in 2009, at Johannesburg in 2010, and now we have seen it at Perth.

Australia played well, and Mike Hussey in particular deserves huge credit. His was a display of true Aussie grit. But which team made the bigger turnaround in that match? Was it Australia? They only made 268 and 309. You are not going to win too many Tests with that kind of score in the first innings. Or was it England? They collapsed twice in the space of under 100 overs. For me the answer is obvious. They lost because they were not able to repeat the ruthlessness they showed in the first two Tests. We have known for a long time that England can capsize when they are batting. And not just on faster, bouncier pitches like the ones we saw at Perth and Johannesburg.

The key period of the match was the hour before lunch on the second day, when Mitchell Johnson took four wickets for seven runs in four overs. Johnson's work with Troy Cooley has obviously paid off. He started to swing the ball back into the right-handed batsmen. But England's middle order should have had the technique to be able to cope. They face swing bowling all the time in England, and it is often said that one of the reasons their batting averages tend to be lower than those of other Test nations is that they play their home games in conditions that offer bowlers seam and swing.

During his spell late on the first day Johnson was moving the ball away from the two left-handers, Andrew Strauss and Alastair Cook. As soon as England spotted that, word should have gone around the dressing room: 'Hold on, boys, this is what he is doing with the ball.' The team should have immediately started thinking about how to adjust. But they did not seem to be able to switch to plan B. Instead they got stuck like rabbits in head-lights.

This was a mental failure more than a technical one. It was a complacency issue. Which is not to say that they were so naive that they took victory for granted. But after winning so well in the second Test they were not able to stay sharp for the third. They needed to keep their finger on the pulse for every single moment of this match. They did it in Adelaide but not in Perth.

As I say, this is a familiar problem. I used to wonder if England suffered from a 'cup-final' mentality. They were under such pressure from the media that players would celebrate victories as though they were cup-final wins. Do that and it becomes very difficult to isolate the next match from what has come before it. You have to make sure you are entirely focused on replicating the approach that won you that game in the first place.

A great example of a team who did this well were the All Blacks under Sean Fitzpatrick in the 1990s. If they were playing a top team and they won a penalty in the first 15 minutes, they would put it through the posts. If they won three penalties in the first 15 minutes, they would put them all through the posts. If they were playing a weaker team the next week, they would do ex-actly the same thing.

Other sides would take those three points in a match against New Zealand, but if they found themselves in the same scenario against a weaker team they would suddenly decide to kick for the corner or try to run the ball. That inconsistency meant they might win one week, but they would only scrape home the next.

For two years, between early 2004 and late 2005, the England team got it right. They were almost unbeatable. Michael Vaughan made sure that the team's mindset stayed the same no matter who we played. But we had a lot of self-driven characters in that side. It is not an easy thing to instil in a team. There is only so much the management can do. They can help provide the glue, but they still need to have the right parts in place.

Fourth Test

Melbourne Cricket Ground
26–29 December 2010

First day

The morning session

BY SEAN INGLE

Preamble: And so this is Christmas. And what, England must be asking themselves, have we done? A fortnight ago, before their batting collapsed like skittles under a wrecking ball, they were 1–0 up and dominant – and retaining the Ashes looked a matter of five days and twenty wickets away. Then came Perth. Suddenly Andrew Strauss's men arrive at the MCG with the series all square, the team as underdogs, and with 90,000 (mostly) Australian fans crowing, braying and smelling blood. But just as most people overreacted to Adelaide, have we all overreacted to Perth? We'll soon find out.

The toss: Ponting flicks, Strauss calls heads – correctly – and England will bowl. That's a huge call. They line up: Australia: Watson, Hughes, Ponting, Clarke, Hussey, Smith, Haddin, Johnson, Harris, Siddle, Hilfenhaus. England: Strauss, Cook, Trott, Pietersen, Collingwood, Bell, Prior, Bresnan, Swann, Tremlett, Anderson.

1st over: Australia 0–0 (Watson 0, Hughes 0) Anderson opens to Watson, and immediately there's a hint of swing. And from his fifth delivery, Watson nervously paws it towards Collingwood . . . who drops it at third slip! 'Would it be fair to say that Ricky Ponting now thinks that there isn't a spinner in Australia worth picking?' says Chris Langmead.

2nd over: Australia 10–0 (Watson 0, Hughes 10) Runs for Hughes! First he rocks back before chopping Tremlett through the covers, then he picks up another couple off his legs, then he drives another to the boundary.

3rd over: Australia 15–0 (Watson 5, Hughes 10) Oh dear, oh dear, oh dear. Watson chases after a wide one and swings at the ball like a man trying to chop down a great elm with one hefty blow. It flies to Pietersen at gully, at a nice height, only to pop out of his hands. Andy Niven isn't happy with the selection of Bresnan. 'The day we bottled it and blew the Ashes,' he says. 'It better swing. Never has so much been trusted in so few bowlers.' Er, aren't England playing four bowlers . . . like they have been all series?

WICKET! 4th over: Watson c Pietersen b Tremlett 5 (Australia 15–1) England strike! Watson is surprised by the unexpected bounce Tremlett is able to generate, and his top edge loops from bat to helmet to Pietersen's grateful hands. England immediately implement one of their familiar plans for Ponting, and a delivery deliberately down leg side is nearly brushed to Prior. Wicket maiden. 'Here I am in Sydney and unable to watch the Boxing Day Test because my kids are watching *Scooby Doo*,' says a cheery Ben Pobjie. 'So thanks for picking up the slack there. Also, can any fellow readers explain to me why on earth people have kids?'

5th over: Australia 16–1 (Hughes 11, Ponting 0) Just a single off the over from Hughes, who, so far at least, isn't looking as flimsy as he did in Perth.

6th over: Australia 18–1 (Hughes 12, Ponting 1) So close to a run-out! Ponting chops one around the corner, and Hughes would have been run out by two metres if Cook had hit. Impressive, muscular bowling from Tremlett, this. Meanwhile, more Bresnan debate. 'The problem with the four-bowlers option is that there's no margin for error,' says John Starbuck. 'Injury or loss of form mean we're stuffed.'

7th over: Australia 18–1 (Hughes 12, Ponting 1) More good bowling, this time from Anderson (4–1–7–0), who nearly had Hughes edging behind there.

8th over: Australia 19–1 (Hughes 12, Ponting 2) Ponting is often a twitchy starter, but he's looking particularly nervous out there right now. There are lots of unconvincing stabs and clunks off the side of the bat.

9th over: Australia 26–1 (Hughes 13, Ponting 2) This continues to be a difficult opening session for Australia – Anderson has got it to swing and Tremlett is getting extra bounce – and both batsmen are looking as uncomfortable as a Business Secretary in front of a pack of News International journalists. 'In response to the "Why do we have kids?" question – surely the answer is on the off chance you get to see them open the batting or bowling for England at the MCG or Lord's?' suggests Lizzy Ammon, not unreasonably.

10th over: Australia 26–1 (Hughes 13, Ponting 2) Ponting is scratching around horribly here, and there's a heart-in-mouth moment when he's late to another Tremlett lifter: the ball pinballs from bat to thigh pad to leg and dribbles past the Australian captain's leg stump.

11th over: Australia 26–1 (Hughes 13, Ponting 2) Huge appeal from Anderson and Prior, who think they have Hughes caught behind. The umpire isn't buying it. England refer it . . . and the umpire is right: the ball only flicked Hughes's shirt and he is not out. Anderson has bowled very well here, to little reward. 'Could you tell Ben Pobjie (4th over) that he should have planned Christmas better,' sighs Sara Torvalds. 'The thing with combining children with the Boxing Day Test is to make sure they get something for Christmas that will keep them occupied away from the TV.'

12th over: Australia 26–1 (Hughes 13, Ponting 2) A change in the bowling as Bresnan comes on for Tremlett. 'I'm a junior doctor halfway through my week of nights, and I wondered if you could give a shout out to all my glum patients stuck in hospital on orthopaedic wards 26 and 27,' says Dave Hogg. 'Each time we take a wicket I shout "Howzat!" and they give a little cheer, albeit somewhat diminished as we get into the early hours. They appreciate my providing top-class entertainment whilst meeting their medical needs, I'm sure.'

13th over: Australia 37–1 (Hughes 16, Ponting 10) After Hughes takes three from a clip off his legs, Ponting finally finds his mojo – twice pulling for four.

WICKET! 14th over: Hughes c Pietersen b Bresnan 16 (Australia 37–2) Horrible shot from Hughes, who drives a fullish delivery straight at Pietersen at gully. He'd batted reasonably well for an hour in tricky conditions, then he just threw his wicket away. Clarke is watchful as he sees off the rest of Bresnan's over.

WICKET! 15th over: Ponting c Swann b Tremlett 10 (Australia 37–3) Ponting goes! Tremlett replaces Anderson, and the switch immediately pays off. There was a little extra lift, a little extra back in the delivery, and the Australian captain flicked one behind as he tried to draw his bat inside. It looked to be going straight to Strauss at first slip, but Swann – at second – went across and took a decent catch. So, here we go again. Mike Hussey v. England – round seven.

16th over: Australia 39–3 (Clarke 1, Hussey 1) Bresnan has bowled well so far, and Hussey has to be pretty smart to get some bat on one that nips back sharply. 'I'm following the OBO from the Cayman Islands,' says Annemarie Elson, who seems to be having it tough. 'It's been a fairly normal Christmas . . . turkey, stuffing, roast potatoes, lots of wine and the odd glass of rum punch in the 30-degree sunshine by the sea. The best bit, though, is that I am able to show my *Daily Mail*-reading dad the benefits of switching to the *Guardian*. Not only does it have THE BEST over-by-over Ashes coverage but it is also infused with topical political humour. *Guardian* 1–0 *Daily Mail*.'

17th over: Australia 43–3 (Clarke 1, Hussey 5) Shot of the day from Hussey, who steers an overpitched Tremlett delivery straight down the ground for four in an otherwise uneventful over. 'I'm also a junior doctor, and I'm also sober after a long day in neonatal intensive care,' says Rossa Brugha. 'Have to be back tomorrow at 8 a.m. How late is it safe to stay up? We keep taking wickets, and I can't help myself.' As someone whose daughter spent Christmas 2008 in a neonatal ward, I'm full of admiration for all you types.

18th over: Australia 46–3 (Clarke 4, Hussey 5) Bresnan continues to hassle and harry.

19th over: Australia 49–3 (Clarke 4, Hussey 7) Hussey continues to provide a masterclass in defensive batting: ignoring deliveries that others would poke at, offering meaty resistance to anything on stumps, and choosing his moments to score. That said, it was a decent over from Tremlett (8–3–23–2), who is still offering plenty of spite, even though he's barely had a rest this session.

20th over: Australia 53–3 (Clarke 8, Hussey 7) A boundary off Bresnan's final delivery takes Australia past 50. But they have crawled to it, almost as uncertainly as an eight-month-old scratching around on the living-room carpet. 'What's with the rampant bottom tapping in the England team?' asks Alex in London. 'Even a half-decent stop in the field leads to five sets of players rushing over to pat the player on the cheeks. Is this motivational?'

21st over: Australia 53–3 (Clarke 8, Hussey 7) Another excellent maiden from Tremlett (9–4–23–2), and it was nearly even better: Hussey played and missed at his final delivery. 'At the beach in Brazil and internet connection is too slow for dubious p2p feeds so following you on the Blackberry,' sighs Martin Perrie. Sorry, Martin. 'Wife and baby in bed, so confined to the free bar for the rest of the evening, or at least till lunch. Hard life, eh? Saw Santa arrive on water skis this morning, preceded by a reindeer on an inflatable – hadn't even had any caipirinhas by that stage so am pretty sure it happened.'

22nd over: Australia 57–3 (Clarke 12, Hussey 7) Clarke crashes an on-drive down the ground for four. Still, Bresnan has bowled well so far today. Meanwhile, I am starting to worry that a legion of junior doctors across the UK are stabbing away on their BlackBerrys while all sorts of frantic beeps are being sounded from their patients' machines. Speaking of which . . . 'Another junior doctor weighing in,' says Rebecca Heller. 'I stayed up till at least two for the nights of the second Test, having to be in at 8 a.m. to work 12-hour days on a gastro-intestinal ward. So I'd say you've got another hour in you at least. Don't forget, though, to factor in how long it will take you to get to sleep when you're taut with excitement about how well we're doing.'

23rd over: Australia 58–3 (Clarke 12, Hussey 8) Twenty minutes before lunch, Strauss opts for Swann, who finds himself up against Hussey again. It's a feeling-out sort of over, with just a single from the final ball. This partnership is now 21 from 52 deliveries.

24th over: Australia 58–3 (Clarke 12, Hussey 8) Another thrifty over from Bresnan (7–3–13–1) and another maiden. 'Not sure on the analogy about the uncertainty of eight-month-old babies on carpet,' says Dave Adams. 'My son is just past that age, and whenever placed on the floor, crawls off with great determination directly towards the nearest available source of danger. Like Phil Hughes batting, I guess.'

25th over: Australia 58–3 (Clarke 12, Hussey 8) Not much turn for Swann so far, not that you'd expect any on the opening morning. Clarke is using his feet plenty here, repeatedly stepping forward to get to the pitch of the ball. Maiden.

WICKET! 26th over: Hussey c Prior b Anderson 8 (Australia 58–4) Australia's Berlin wall finally comes down! Anderson returns to the attack and strikes with a slanting delivery that moved a fraction and got the slightest brush of Hussey's bat; the sort of faint, did-I-did-he brush you might get passing a stranger down the Tube escalator. Hussey goes – and for single figures! Lunch.

Australia 58–4

The afternoon session

BY ROB SMYTH

Preamble: Postman! Tell the neighbourhood! Michael Hussey has failed! He made just eight, and his dismissal on the stroke of lunch turned a promising morning for England into an exceptional one. To get Mr Cricket – or Sir Cricket, as we should really call him after his performance in this series – was, as a cricket commentator once said, massive. It was also a deserved reward for the brilliant James Anderson. His first, wicketless spell this morning was almost as good as his wicketless spell on the third morning at Brisbane, but he switched ends and got Hussey with a beauty. England definitely made the right decision in bowling first – and it was a brave one too, given what happened at Perth. They knew they had to bowl well, and they did: the three seamers had combined figures of 23.3–9–55–4.

26th over: Australia 63–4 (Clarke 14, Smith 3) Anderson has three balls left of his eighth over, which he started before lunch. Smith punches the second confidently through the covers for three to get off the mark. Tea has been pushed back to 4.40 a.m. English time – just under two hours from now – with the close of play some time in 2011.

27th over: Australia 66–4 (Clarke 14, Smith 6) Tim Bresnan replaces Graeme Swann from the other end. He's a fascinating case, Bresnan. No matter how many boxes he ticks – and he ticked a few more during a good spell this morning – he will always be Bressie lad, or the big lad, or not bad for a stout lad. 'Pitch might be tickled but the damp outfield might hinder reverse,' says Lord Selvey.

28th over: Australia 66–4 (Clarke 14, Smith 6) Smith plays all around Anderson's first delivery, which jags back to rap him on the pad. Too high. Then he leaves a delivery that swerves back and just goes over the top. 'Has that gone through the stumps?' says Bumble. Extraordinary. Smith really is kinda funny lookin' at the crease. An excellent maiden from Anderson.

29th over: Australia 66–4 (Clarke 14, Smith 6) A maiden from Bresnan to Clarke. England are 'bowling dry', to use the vogue phrase, building pressure through maidens. Am I the only person who had never heard the phrase 'bowling dry' until Perth, and now keep hearing it every 12 seconds? Also, am I the only one who finds the phrase a little uncomfortable? What next: bowling moist? 'I too have an eight-month-old, and I agree with Dave Adams – he is a far quicker crawler than this run rate at the moment,' says Andy Wilson.

WICKET! 30th over: Smith c Prior b Anderson 6 (Australia 66–5) Bowling dry brings its reward. Anderson has a huge shout for lbw against Smith rightly turned down by Aleem Dar, but he gets his man two balls later with a fine delivery: pretty full and moving away off the seam as Smith pushes unconvincingly away from his body. The ball took a thin edge and went straight through to Matt Prior.

30th over: Australia 71–5 (Clarke 14, Haddin 5) Haddin is turned round by his first ball and edges it low and through the cordon for four. This is a huge partnership in the context of the match, the series and indeed the entire known universe.

31st over: Australia 71–5 (Clarke 14, Haddin 5) Bresnan curves a cracker past the groping Haddin. Haddin is beaten again next ball, this time after the windiest of woofs well wide of off stump. Another maiden from Bresnan, whose figures are exceptional: 10–5–16–1. 'I seem to recall a wager between two denizens of GU Towers as to whether Bresnan would take 50 Test-match wickets in his England career,' says Marie Meyer. 'I think you were the one backing him. Any of this ringing any bells?' None whatsoever.

32nd over: Australia 72–5 (Clarke 15, Haddin 5) Anderson tries a surprise yorker, and Clarke works it off his toe for a single. That's the only run of the over, and Australia are going nowhere fast.

33rd over: Australia 77–5 (Clarke 20, Haddin 5) That was nearly another wicket. Clarke drove very loosely at an away-swinger from Bresnan and the ball just cleared the substitute, Morgan, leaping spectacularly to his left at point. 'I'm actually in favour of having Bressie in the team, due to the frankly despicable sight of teams filled with metrosexual man-bag modellers trying to sledge each other,' says Gareth Fitzgerald.

WICKET! 34th over: Clarke c Prior b Anderson 20 (Aus-

tralia 77–6) Postman! Tell the neighbourhood! Australia are 77 for six! Clarke lunges desperately at another good delivery from Anderson that moves just enough to take the edge on its way through to Prior. Very similar to the Smith dismissal – Clarke didn't need to play – and England are in a stunning position. They have denied the Aussies the oxygen of runs, and that has made their batsmen do silly things.

WICKET! 35th over: Haddin c Strauss b Bresnan 5 (Australia 77–7) Now this is what I call a Christmas present. England are running riot! Bresnan draws Haddin into a huge drive – another very loose stroke, it has to be said – and it flies off the edge to Strauss at first slip. England have bowled extremely well, but Australia's batting has been shocking. Disgraceful, in fact. That's back-to-back wicket maidens, and Bresnan's figures are quite outstanding: 12–6–21–2.

WICKET! 36th over: Johnson c Prior b Anderson 0 (Australia 77–8) And to think some people say familiarity breeds contempt! It's yet another catch behind the wicket, with Johnson thin-edging a fine leg-cutter angled across him from over the wicket. Unlike so many before, Johnson was fairly blameless, but Australia are 77 for eight. Postman!

37th over: Australia 82–8 (Harris 0, Siddle 5) Siddle edges Bresnan towards third slip, where Swann dives forward to grab the ball and then signals that he's not sure whether it carried. 'Breserotica,' phrase-coins Gareth Fitzgerald. 'Who can doubt this man now? The wimminfolk of Ilkley Moor Bah Tat will have to dance round their handbags for a while to attract this man-god's attention. He'll be skittling batting line-ups, biffing an agricultural century, working on t'coalface, drinking his own (considerable) body weight in stout and lathering the effing ess out of Mike Tyson with his other hand. Malt whisky and cricket? Marvellous.'

38th over: Australia 86–8 (Harris 4, Siddle 5) Harris top-edges an attempted pull off Anderson over the slips for four.

39th over: Australia 89–8 (Harris 4, Siddle 8) Tremlett replaces Bresnan, and his first ball is pinged through the covers for three by Siddle. Harris then fresh-airs a windy woof. The lower order might as well play their shots here. It's the best approach, as we saw at Perth, but it also means they'll have more time to bowl at England today. Ryan Harris in particular could be a real threat in these conditions.

40th over: Australia 92–8 (Harris 4, Siddle 11) OK, joke's over: I made it all up. Australia are 172 for none and Phil Hughes is on 169, having been dropped 17 times. Merry Christmas!

WICKET! 41st over: Siddle c Prior b Tremlett 11 (Australia 92–9) Is it still déjà vu if it happens again and again and again? This is like so many other dismissals today: in the slot, loose drive, thin edge to Prior. That's Prior's fifth catch of the innings.

42nd over: Australia 98–9 (Harris 10, Hilfenhaus 0) Harris back-cuts Anderson for four to take Australia closer to 100. The last time they were bowled out for double figures against England was in 1968.

WICKET! 43rd over: Hilfenhaus c Prior b Tremlett 0 (Australia 98 all out) You might want to sit down before you hear this: England have bowled Australia out for double figures. Hilfenhaus edges Tremlett through to – yep – Matt Prior, who takes his sixth catch, and I honestly don't know what to say. 98 all out. Four for Tremlett, four for Anderson and two for Bresnan. Tea.

Australia 98

The evening session

BY ROB SMYTH

Preamble: The sun has come out for the start of this marathon evening session – 47 overs remain – and that is good news for England. Australia are in so much trouble here that their heads will hurt just thinking about it. If they don't take at least four wickets tonight they will be right on the brink.

1st over: England 1–0 (Strauss 1, Cook 0) Ben Hilfenhaus's first over contains some promising swing, and Strauss gets off the mark with a quick single into the covers.

2nd over: England 1–0 (Strauss 1, Cook 0) Harris angles a good one across Strauss, who pulls his bat inside the line at the last minute. A maiden. England will just bat time against the new ball, as they should in these conditions.

3rd over: England 4–0 (Strauss 3, Cook 1) Cook gets off the mark with a work to leg, and then Strauss pulls a couple into the wide-open spaces on the leg side. 'Clutching at straws department – 1977 Centenary Test,' says Andrew Pinkerton. 'We were all out for 138 and still won the Test. But then, in those days, we had a guy called Dennis Keith Lillee . . .' Ah, but now you've got the man D. K. Lillee called a 'once-in-a-generation bowler'.

4th over: England 12–0 (Strauss 4, Cook 8) Cook pushes Harris through extra cover for a couple and then, later in the over, edges a push along the ground to third man for four. The MCG is silent. You could hear a tinnie drop. 'Would love to be basking in the sunshine of the great Boycott's smiles right now,' says Martin Cunning, who at least has the next best thing, 'but sitting in a hotel room in South Beach, Miami, sipping Napa Valley's finest whilst glued to the OBO will do for now.'

5th over: England 14–0 (Strauss 6, Cook 8) Strauss clunks a full delivery from Hilfenhaus through the covers for two. 'The advantage about following today's OBO in the US is that today's play is an extra, long-lasting Christmas present,' says Stefan Llewellyn Smith. 'My sister-in-law has asked to be taken to a cricket game. Not sure where we'll find one in Boulder or in San Diego.'

6th over: England 25–0 (Strauss 11, Cook 13) Johnson replaces Harris. His first over is a hodgepodge of line and length. 11 from the over. 'Well, I'm sure you're enjoying this!' says Terry Baucher. 'Here in beautiful sunny Auckland it's been extremely entertaining hearing the Channel 9 commentators slide steadily from confidence to clutching at any straw available. There is nothing sweeter to these ears than Australians trying to talk up a fiasco. (And believe me they are trying.)'

8th over: England 31–0 (Strauss 17, Cook 13) England look extremely comfortable and are already almost a third of the way towards a first-innings lead.

9th over: England 33–0 (Strauss 18, Cook 14) The sun is out, the ball is not moving sideways in the air or off the pitch, and even hardened English cricket vets are struggling to see how this can go wrong. 'Drop-in pitch, they say,' says Alistair. 'Looks like it was dropped in straight from Headingley.' England could hardly have chosen a more perfect wicket. But thank goodness they won the toss, or we could all be sat here weeping furiously right now.

10th over: England 42–0 (Strauss 22, Cook 15) Johnson gets one to lift from a length at Strauss, who softens the hands just enough to edge it short of the slips and through for four.

11th over: England 44–0 (Strauss 22, Cook 17) This series is daft. 517 for one. 623 for five. 98 all out. And it's still only 1–1.

12th over: England 46–0 (Strauss 24, Cook 17) Peter Siddle replaces Mitchell Johnson (3–0–17–0). That gets the crowd going a wee bit, with him being the only Victorian in the side. England are cruising.

13th over: England 46–0 (Strauss 24, Cook 17) A maiden from Harris to Cook. England have left the ball well so far. Apart from Michael Hussey, Australia had no idea – or did not care – where their off stump was. The more their innings marinates, the more it stinks. There were some appalling strokes. 'I've now sort of got sober and checked the scores on your scorecard, the BBC and Cricinfo, and so unless someone is playing a monumental joke on me, we do seem to be in the box seat,' says Clare Davies.

14th over: England 52–0 (Strauss 30, Cook 17) Strauss pings Siddle wide of mid-on for four to bring up the fifty partnership. They are now just 46 runs behind. I'm still not convinced this is actually happening.

15th over: England 52–0 (Strauss 30, Cook 17) Hilfenhaus replaces Harris, and it's a maiden to Cook. Australia look very flat in the field. 'What a huge crowd,' says David Thomas. 'Yet another world record for Australian sport! Makes one wonder just how many red-blooded, macho Aussies will be able to tell their grandchildren in years to come, "Yep, I was part of it – I was there Boxing Day 2010!"'

16th over: England 52–0 (Strauss 30, Cook 17) This has been a very methodical partnership. England are much better when they play cold, disciplined, almost emotionless cricket. They got sucked in a little during that hot-blooded affair at Perth, but today they have returned to their best.

17th over: England 57–0 (Strauss 34, Cook 18) Strauss

tucks two more off his pads. Sky show an excellent Hawk-Eye graphic of the ten dismissals today: only one was anywhere near hitting the stumps.

18th over: England 57–0 (Strauss 34, Cook 18) A maiden from Siddle. So how do Australia get out of this? Realistically, the best they can hope for is a deficit of around 200 and hope that England panic in the fourth innings.

19th over: England 57–0 (Strauss 34, Cook 18) Australia are bowling wide of off stump, trying to bore the batsmen out, but you'll do well to do that with Strauss and Cook. Strauss ignores everything he doesn't have to play at, so it's another maiden. You have to feel for the Australian bowlers: their batting teammates have given them a sow's ear and said, 'Silk purse please!'

20th over: England 58–0 (Strauss 34, Cook 19) Siddle has a huge shout for lbw against Cook turned down by Aleem Dar. Cook planted his front leg and was in big trouble when the ball straightened, but it looked too high and replays confirmed it. Excellent umpiring from Aleem Dar – and from Brad Haddin, who advised his captain not to review the decision.

21st over: England 58–0 (Strauss 34, Cook 19) 'I think you're absolutely right about emotionless cricket,' says Gavin Phillipson. 'Watching England batting this innings, they're palpably relaxed, feeling no need to force the scoring, happy to leave, leave, leave, then tuck the slightly straighter one away; watch the bowlers tire gradually; expand the range of shots slowly.' I think people have been too harsh on momentum recently. Poor old momentum; it only meant well. It didn't want to hurt nobody. And I still think it is a very relevant sporting concept.

22nd over: England 58–0 (Strauss 34, Cook 19) Having tried to bore Strauss out, Siddle now decides to try to beat him up. One very good bouncer whistles past his nose in the course of a very good maiden.

23rd over: England 66–0 (Strauss 34, Cook 27) After just one run in five overs, Cook releases what pressure there was with two boundaries in three balls off Hilfenhaus: a push down the ground and a withering cut stroke. 'Rob, CMJ has just welcomed any listeners joining *TMS* at 6.00 with the line: "It's been a very good day for England,"' says Tim Woollias. 'Exactly what would have to have happened for it to be "magnificent" or "extraordinary"?'

24th over: England 70–0 (Strauss 34, Cook 27) Ryan Harris replaces Peter Siddle, and his first ball swings down the leg side for four byes. Cook has an lbw decision overturned on review.

Sorry about this, folks. All sorts of technical tomfoolery going on. England have gone into the lead.

32nd over: England 109–0 (Strauss 44, Cook 54) Johnson back on. His second ball is short, wide and slapped for four by Cook. That brings up a very good half-century, from 93 balls with eight fours.

33rd over: England 109–0 (Strauss 44, Cook 54) A maiden from Watson, most of which I missed when the computer crashed again. Is provocation a legitimate defence if you assault a computer?

34th over: England 112–0 (Strauss 46, Cook 55) Strauss works Johnson off the pads for two, which takes him past 6,000 Test runs. Not bad for a bloke who made his debut at 27.

35th over: England 115–0 (Strauss 47, Cook 57) Australia must be dying to get off the field and start again tomorrow. 'On the second day of Christmas, my true love gave to me: an Australian batting collapse and an unbroken England opening stand,' says Emma John, dispensing with niceties such as rhyme in order to make a pretty undeniable point.

36th over: England 124–0 (Strauss 48, Cook 64) This is a rout. On Sky, Shane Warne says that Australia have to bring on a spinner, either Steve Smith or Michael Clarke. They could bring on Warne and Clarrie Grimmett – it doesn't matter.

37th over: England 128–0 (Strauss 50, Cook 66) Steven Smith comes on to bowl for the first time in the series, and Strauss takes a quick single to mid-on to reach his 23rd Test fifty. 'OK, we've had our fun, but enough is enough,' says Chris Pearce. 'Time to tell Clare Davies that yes, it really is just a big joke on her. Did Ponting reach 150 yet?'

38th over: England 135–0 (Strauss 54, Cook 69) Strauss flashes a cut behind square for four off Johnson. He's going at a run a ball. This is preposterous. England are 134 for nought in reply to Australia's 98. In Australia. At the MCG. On Boxing Day. In front of 90,000 Australian fans. Poor old Mo Mentum. After this series, nobody will ever trust a word he says again.

39th over: England 138–0 (Strauss 55, Cook 71) 'Dare I try to improve on Emma John's ditty?' says David Toze. 'On the second day of Christmas, my true love gave to me/ Eleven wilting Aussies and Strauss 'n' Cook each with fifty . . .'

40th over: England 138–0 (Strauss 55, Cook 71) Siddle replaces Johnson (7–0–42–0). He's been Australia's best bowler today. A maiden. 'Chris Pearce (37th over), I don't think Punter has 150 runs in total in this series,' says Sara Torvalds. 'Which, frankly, is stunning.' Before today he had the highest strike-rate on either side in the series, which is a wee bit odd.

41st over: England 147–0 (Strauss 56, Cook 79) Cook pulls consecutive boundaries – the first wide of mid-on and the second high over midwicket.

42nd over: England 148–0 (Strauss 57, Cook 79) One from Siddle's over. How the hell do Australia get out of this? If the pitch dies, as drop-in pitches often do, maybe they could bat for two and a bit days to save it, but I don't fancy theirs much. It's staggering that they are in such a mess before the end of the first day.

43rd over: England 151–0 (Strauss 60, Cook 79) Strauss, driving at Smith, edges wide of slip for a couple to bring up the 150 partnership. It's been clinical stuff. 'Not that I'm a sucker for hyperbole, but quite possibly the best day in the history of English cricket, if not the universe?' says Andy Seaman. 'Discuss!' I still have a soft spot for the first day at Lord's in 1993.

44th over: England 153–0 (Strauss 62, Cook 79) Strauss pulls Siddle for two. I don't know about you, but I am very tired, and very happy.

45th over: England 156–0 (Strauss 64, Cook 80) Strauss edges Smith again, and this time it falls a fraction short of Clarke at slip. Strauss played for turn that wasn't there.

47th over: England 157–0 (Strauss 64, Cook 80) That's the end of one of England's greatest-ever days in Test cricket, a day we'll be talking about for as long as we can flap our gums. They are 59 runs ahead with ten first-innings wickets remaining; they have four whole days to seal the deal and retain the Ashes. Sleep on it; it might make more sense then.

England 157–0; Australia 98

England pick up wolf-pack mentality and leave the Australians howling

BY MIKE SELVEY IN MELBOURNE

MONDAY 27 DECEMBER 2010

'The strength of the pack is the wolf, and the strength of the wolf is the pack.' Rudyard Kipling, *The Jungle Book*.

The tortuous corkscrew nature of this series continued as England shrugged aside the humiliation of Perth to enjoy a day of domination of a kind rarely seen or experienced by Australia, and from which they would need a dramatic change in the conditions and a search deep into untapped areas of their souls if they were to come back strongly.

By the close of a dramatic first day Andrew Strauss and Alastair Cook had added 157 together in a partnership of great certainty and common sense that made a mockery of Australia's 98 all out, their lowest score against England in this country for 122 years (excluding their 80 all out in 1936, which involved a withdrawal due to injury).

Cook, moving into his strokes with a fluency unmatched even by his exalted standards in this series, had made 80, while the England captain had 64, on the way passing 6,000 runs in Tests. With no swing for them, as the sun came out in the afternoon, Australia's four-man pace attack was devoid of a cutting edge, Mitchell Johnson reverting to his early-series extravagance.

The day had been set up for England by the seamers, with Jimmy Anderson, simply brilliant, finally getting some reward to take four for 44, Chris Tremlett following his Waca wickets with four for 26, including the Australia captain, Ricky Ponting, for 10, and

Tim Bresnan, the quickest of the England men to the surprise of many, taking two for 25. All ten wickets fell to catches in the slip cordon, with Matt Prior's six catches equalling the England record against Australia held jointly by Jack Russell, Chris Read and Alec Stewart.

Bowling is about partnerships. An attack competes individually but achieves as a collective. It is a chain as strong as its weakest link. A week ago in Perth, England's bowling wilted, drawn into distracting confrontation, their discipline vanishing when most they needed it. One bowler, Steven Finn, in a magnanimous gesture of pre-Christmas charity, haemorrhaged runs at a rate of one every delivery, a rate for which, in the conditions, and with only two other seamers, wickets taken could not compensate. England's entire bowling strategy in this series has been founded on the twin rocks of success with the new ball and attrition with the old, and, on the back of his performance at the Waca, Finn lost his place to Bresnan, parsimonious in spirit and intention, underestimated and utterly steadfast.

The attack was transformed back into a unit. For the 42 overs and five balls that England required to dismiss Australia, save only for the second over of the match, from which Phil Hughes took Tremlett for more than 10 per cent of the final total, Anderson, Tremlett and Bresnan were in complete control. They bowled to a plan, did not deviate from it (nor had they to) and generally kept their own counsel and emotions in check. Actions, they were saying, speak louder than words. And just as England had no answer to Johnson, Ryan Harris and the Perth bounce, so Australia, try as they might (and by no means did they all simply throw away their wickets), could find no solution to the subtle swing and nibbly seam, frustrated by the tattoo beaten out on a nagging length and a challenging line that strangled the life from their shot-making.

Eventually, almost with inevitability, each successive batsman was drawn into a stroke, occasionally rash, sometimes hypnotically, that resulted in an edge to the vultures perched behind the wicket. There was simply no freedom to play shots: a big acreage the MCG may be and the outfield is sluggish, but Australia managed only seven boundaries, not all of them voluntary.

The pitch was a help, and so was the toss, which once more fell the way of Strauss, for here, in the first two sessions, were conditions that far from assisting Australia might have been made with the express purpose of making the England bowlers feel at home: not so much Headingley supplanted on the banks of the Yarra (for England bowlers have come a cropper too often in Leeds) but the sort of thing that old county pros might recognise at Derby or Chesterfield, with Mike Hendrick coming at them and ghosting past the bat. There was cloud cover too and a temperature that demanded a sweater rather than sweatband.

From it, all three seamers found movement, nothing extravagant mark you, but just sufficient to challenge the edge of the bat. Sometimes it was in the air; sometimes it was off the seam; sometimes it was the smallest amount of the first lending the appearance of the latter. Relentless probing. Shane Watson, having been allowed two escapes before he had scored (fiendish both, one to slip and the other to gully), found Tremlett's height too much and spliced to gully, while in the space of two overs Hughes had flung the bat wildly at Bresnan (how Australia need Katich to return) and Ponting had edged another lifter to second slip, departing with a rueful look at the surface that had betrayed him.

When shortly before lunch Anderson finally exposed Mike Hussey to be merely mortal, and on the resumption, after a rain delay, Steve Smith was shown to be so far out of his depth at six that he should be batting in a lifebelt, Australia were 66 for five.

At this stage England, on a roll certainly, needed to take stock. In successive Tests Australia in their first innings have been variously 143 for five in Brisbane, 156 for five in Adelaide and 69 for five in Perth, gaining a first-innings lead on two of the three occasions. They needed to finish the job, while mindful that the intelligence suggested that the pitch habitually eases after a couple of sessions.

And finish it they did, Anderson bowling wonderfully, with absolute control, and Tremlett steaming in to collect the perks at the end, so that Australia lost six for 40 in the afternoon. No respite, no salvation, just processional. Michael Clarke top-scored with 20. Each bowler fed from the efforts of the others. Their individual skills had melded into a team. The pack were hungry and they had their fill.

Second day

The morning session

BY ROB SMYTH

Preamble: Preamble? Australia 98 all out. England 157 for nought. There's your preamble! 'Come on, Rob,' says Vicki Prout. 'Have frozen my proverbials off wandering round a French mountain village in the vain hunt for anywhere showing "*le creekette*" but to no avail, so, OBO, over to you, come on, I want to get excited!' 'It is effing horrible here today,' says Lord Selvey. 'I am dressed in T-shirt, shirt, weatherproof jacket and woolly hat. And I'm in the press box. Blowing warp factor 9 on the Beaufort, pewter sky and flurries of rain. Just like Derby again.'

48th over: England 158–0 (Strauss 64, Cook 81) It'll be Peter Siddle to begin. He was Australia's best bowler yesterday but surely you'd want the fuller bowlers, Harris and Hilfenhaus, in these conditions? That said, he's not as stupid as he looks – that's biologically impossible – and he finds a full length from the start.

49th over: England 158–0 (Strauss 64, Cook 81) A maiden from Harris. Cook is 19 away from becoming the eighth Englishman to make three hundreds in an Ashes series.

50th over: England 158–0 (Strauss 64, Cook 81) The sun is starting to creep out, which is good news for England. 'Given

Mike Selvey's comments on wind and *TMS* speculating about the force needed for a stray sombrero to tack against, how powerful is it?' says John Starbuck. 'Enough to affect the bowling? Maybe, if not a full Fremantle Doctor, at least a paramedic?'

51st over: England 159–0 (Strauss 64, Cook 82) Cook works another one off middle stump for a single, this time off Harris. Miss those and you are dead, but he hasn't missed much in this series. 'Fab insight from Lord Vaughan on *TMS* where he "assures" us Punter's form is compromised by other concerns, including his future career,' says Richard Read. 'Vaughan draws comparisons with his last few knocks as captain where "the game is telling you something". Any ideas on what the game is saying to Ricky right now? I'd like to think the game is saying, "Bowl Johnson all morning."'

WICKET! 52nd over: Cook c Watson b Siddle 82 (England 159–1) Alastair Cook misses out on his third century, but there's no shame in falling to a fine delivery from Peter Siddle. It was angled across and the ball flew low to first slip, where Shane Watson just held on with both hands. That was an excellent piece of bowling. I told you it was a mistake to open the bowling with Siddle!

52nd over: England 161–1 (Strauss 64, Trott 2) Trott drives a couple through the covers to get off the mark.

53rd over: England 163–1 (Strauss 66, Trott 2) Harris has a strangled shout for lbw against Strauss. If they can bowl England out for, what, 350, we'd have a pretty interesting last three days.

54th over: England 163–1 (Strauss 66, Trott 2) Australia have a number of theories as to how to get Trott early, chiefly the short ball and then lbw whipping around a full, straight delivery. Anyway, that's a maiden from Siddle. Australia's discipline has been excellent this morning: seven overs have produced six runs. Bowling dry is the new bowling wet.

55th over: England 169–1 (Strauss 69, Trott 5) There's that full, straight delivery to Trott, but – as with the same delivery to Ponting in his pomp (remember the first innings at Edgbaston 2005) – it's a gamble because you know that he will nail the shot 19 times out of 20. And Trott does so here, easing a couple through midwicket.

WICKET! 56th over: Strauss c Hussey b Siddle 69 (England 170–2) This is a bit of a snorter from Peter Siddle. Strauss is turned round by a nasty lifter on leg and middle, and the ball flies off the shoulder of the bat towards backward point, where Mike Hussey leaps and extends his telescopic arm to take an outstanding one-handed catch. I told you Siddle shouldn't have been on this morning!

56th over: England 170–2 (Trott 6, Pietersen 0) Siddle's figures are now 15–6–17–2. He has been superb.

57th over: England 171–2 (Trott 7, Pietersen 0) Hilfenhaus replaces Harris. It's a good over, in that Trott is forced to play at all but the first delivery. 'Patriotically (despite being Scottish), I've been avoiding using any Australian hair products for the duration of the Ashes,' says Ryan Dunne. 'But I could really do with breaking out the Fudge hair varnish to lift some Boxing Day frizz. Safe to chance it after Australia's collapse yesterday?'

58th over: England 172–2 (Trott 8, Pietersen 0) It seems strange to say this about a man who whapped a career-best score two Tests ago, but Kevin Pietersen still has plenty to prove. He fails far too often these days, and he's lucky not to get a duck there when he fences needlessly at Siddle.

59th over: England 175–2 (Trott 9, Pietersen 2) Hilfenhaus beats Trott with one that shapes back in, but it was too high and his lbw appeal was caught in the throat. Pietersen then gets off the mark from his 11th delivery, working two off the pads.

60th over: England 188–2 (Trott 13, Pietersen 11) That's the shot of the morning from Pietersen, who times Siddle down the ground for four. The next ball goes to the boundary as well, but it was flicked in the air and only just wide of the diving Clarke at midwicket. Trott completes an expensive over – 13 from it – by pinging three more through midwicket. That might have been one over too many for Siddle; it was his seventh of the morning. 'Tell Vicky that she should head to the hotel Lion d'Or and ask the bar staff there to put the cricket on,' says Andrew Levitt. 'I used to work there a few years back, and we showed not only the cricket, but also some very tense Vauxhall Conference matches involving Forest Green and other international footballing mega-brands. The staff training was as follows: if you answer the phone and someone is speaking French – ask them if they speak English. If they keep speaking French – hang up. The English were loved in that town. Oh yes.'

61st over: England 188–2 (Trott 13, Pietersen 11) A maiden from Hilfenhaus to Trott. Time for drinks.

62nd over: England 193–2 (Trott 17, Pietersen 12) It's time for Mitchell Johnson. Five from the over in all, so Johnson (8–0–47–0) is now going at less than a run a ball.

63rd over: England 193–2 (Trott 17, Pietersen 12) Hilfenhaus is bowling dry – I can't get that phrase out of my head now, despite (or probably because of) it being a bit uncomfortable.

64th over: England 193–2 (Trott 17, Pietersen 12) There is some light rain in the air, although not enough to bring the players off yet. Johnson bowls a much-needed (for him, not the team) maiden to Trott. 'Although you weren't on when I emailed yesterday, you'll be pleased to hear that *Daily-Mail*-Reading Dad ran to the computer here in the Cayman Islands for today's

Guardian online OBO,' says Annemarie Elson. 'I think we've won him over . . . the tides are turning!'

65th over: England 196–2 (Trott 17, Pietersen 15) It's fairly attritional cricket, with Australia ~~bowling dr~~ keeping it tight and England's batsmen playing respectfully in view of the quality of the bowling.

66th over: England 200–2 (Trott 18, Pietersen 18) Trott hooks Johnson for a single to bring up the 200. After a difficult start, England are comfortable now.

67th over: England 204–2 (Trott 21, Pietersen 18) That's a very nice shot from Trott, a flick through midwicket for two when Hilfenhaus drops short.

68th over: England 206–2 (Trott 22, Pietersen 19) Pietersen pulls a short one for a single. It's not happening for Johnson. He isn't spraying it round like he did yesterday, but there's no discernible wicket-taking threat. 'Opposites of "bowling dry",' begins John Starbuck. 'Atmospheric, damp, moist, wet, soggy, sodden, drowned.' That bloody word again. Moist.

69th over: England 206–2 (Trott 22, Pietersen 19) Maiden from Hilfenhaus, featuring good defence from Pietersen.

70th over: England 210–2 (Trott 25, Pietersen 20) There's not much noise at the MCG. England are getting 'em in ones and twos – those consecutive boundaries from Pietersen are the only ones in this hour-long partnership – and that has made for a quiet spell.

71st over: England 210–2 (Trott 25, Pietersen 20) Hilfenhaus bowls some marathon spells. This is his eighth over, but those huge shoulders are showing no signs of wilting and it's another accurate maiden.

72nd over: England 219–2 (Trott 26, Pietersen 28) I like this move from Ricky Ponting. With 15 minutes to lunch, he decides to investigate whether Kevin Pietersen can resist going after the leg-spinner Steve Smith. What do you think? Pietersen charges down the track and drags him in the air between mid-wicket and deep mid-on for four. Two balls later he walks down the track and smokes Smith back over his head imperiously for another boundary. Next!

73rd over: England 219–2 (Trott 26, Pietersen 28) An off-cutter from the indefatigable Hilfenhaus keeps a touch low and Trott just drags his bat down in time. It's another maiden from Hilfenhaus. He's bowling desert. 'Vaughan is/was a better captain,' says John Harrison. 'But I think I'd take Andy Flower over Big Dunc as a better coach.' That's a tough one. Fletcher is certainly a better technical and tactical coach – a genius – but then Flower is such an impressive man in so many different ways. What the hell, let's have them both.

74th over: England 219–2 (Trott 26, Pietersen 28) There are only a few minutes to lunch, but Pietersen is not going to rein himself in against Smith. He comes down the track and is almost stumped down the leg side.

75th over: England 222–2 (Trott 27, Pietersen 30) A run off Hilfenhaus! Postman! Actually it's not a run, it's a leg bye, and it brings up the fifty partnership from 115 balls.

76th over: England 226–2 (Trott 31, Pietersen 30) Smith bowls the last over before lunch, and Trott works an all-run four through midwicket. That was a decent recovery from England after the early loss of Strauss and Cook, because Australia bowled very well. England have a lead of 128 and 11 sessions in which to retain the Ashes. Lunch.

England 226–2

The afternoon session

BY ROB SMYTH

Preamble: The players are coming out onto the field. We have four overs before the second new ball, which is probably Australia's last chance to keep the series alive.

77th over: England 235–2 (Trott 35, Pietersen 35) That was an appalling over from Watson, full of leg-stump garbage. The first ball was clipped crisply through midwicket for four by Pietersen, and the fifth flicked to fine leg for another boundary by Trott.

78th over: England 236–2 (Trott 35, Pietersen 36) Steve Smith continues, which is a good move for the couple of overs before the new ball. Pietersen drives his first ball for a single, and Trott blocks the rest.

79th over: England 237–2 (Trott 35, Pietersen 37) A harmless over from Watson.

80th over: England 240–2 (Trott 36, Pietersen 39) Three singles from Smith's over, and now the contest can resume, with Australia taking the second new ball.

81st over: England 246–2 (Trott 36, Pietersen 45) Ben Hilfenhaus bowled ten overs in a row this morning. He bowls one loosener that Pietersen drives down the ground for four and then takes the second new ball. This is the Ashes, right here. Pietersen leaves a number of non-swinging deliveries outside off stump. England's batsmen have left the ball so much better than Australia in this match. Mind you, a tank could have left the ball better than Australia in this match. Pietersen then squirts one through backward point for a couple. 'Further to John Starbuck's list, "humid" would be a nice addition,' says Phil Withall. 'And on the subject of "moist", I once used the word in an email to my sister and she refused to speak to me for two months.'

82nd over: England 251–2 (Trott 41, Pietersen 45) Ryan Harris galumphs in and almost snares Trott with his first delivery, which flies off the inside edge and wide of leg stump for four. I can't see England declaring tonight. The game is so far advanced that this feels like the third day rather than the second. I think they'll bat for at least another day, if they aren't bowled out. If Australia then bat seven sessions to save the game, good luck to them.

83rd over: England 254–2 (Trott 44, Pietersen 45) The Sky commentators, Bumble and Warne, are surprised that Siddle hasn't taken the new ball. Darn tootin'. He's been the best bowler for Australia on both days, and when Hilfenhaus bowled that marathon spell before lunch I assumed it would be Harris and Siddle with the new ball. Anyway, it's Hilfenhaus to continue, but with the ball not swinging England are comfortable. 'Your remark to the effect that this team is greater than the sum of its parts seems apt,' says Jeff Hunter. 'Their sense of unity is in stark contrast to that of our team, most of whom are now plagued by head noises.'

84th over: England 259–2 (Trott 45, Pietersen 49) It's all going off. Pietersen pushes forward defensively at Harris, who doesn't appeal at all for the caught behind. Haddin does, however, and when Aleem Dar says not out Australia go for the review. The replays are not conclusive – although I reckon he might have hit that – and so the original decision stands: Pietersen is not out. That's absolutely correct in accordance with the UDRS. But Australia are furious and a group of them, led by Ricky Ponting, moan at Aleem Dar for at least a minute, wagging their fingers and demanding an explanation. This is bang out of order. Now Ponting is moaning at Tony Hill. He'll not be taking a match fee home after this game, or at least he shouldn't.

85th over: England 261–2 (Trott 46, Pietersen 50) Pietersen works Hilfenhaus to leg to bring up a very good fifty, one that is dismally greeted with a few boos.

86th over: England 262–2 (Trott 46, Pietersen 51) Snicko suggests that Pietersen definitely did not inside-edge that ball. So Australia's complaints were not only excessive, but also ill-founded.

WICKET! 87th over: Pietersen lbw b Siddle 51 (England 262–3) Peter Siddle strikes with the third ball of his new spell. Pietersen jumped back in his crease and missed an attempted whip at a straight one that kept a touch low and would have hit leg stump halfway up. That was plumb. Pietersen started to walk off, turned around for a second to contemplate the review and then walked off again after Trott advised him that he was stone dead. A bit of a soft end to an excellent innings, but well done Peter Siddle: he has figures of three for 31 and, crucially, Australia now have Paul Collingwood in against the new ball.

87th over: England 263–3 (Trott 46, Collingwood 1) Collingwood gets off the mark in unconvincing style, pushing a good delivery not far wide of leg stump.

88th over: England 267–3 (Trott 46, Collingwood 5) Harris has a confident shout for lbw against Collingwood, but it was too high. Collingwood then snicks a drive in the air through gully for four. He is all over the place, but there's something perversely reassuring about that. No Collingwood match- or career-saving epic is complete without a disgraceful first 20 balls.

89th over: England 270–3 (Trott 49, Collingwood 5) Trott survives a spandex-tight run-out referral. It was a split-frame affair. On the first he was out of his ground but the bails had not been broken; on the second the bails were dancing but Trott was home.

90th over: England 277–3 (Trott 53, Collingwood 8) Trott works Harris to leg for a single that brings up another unobtrusive fifty, this one with just two fours. His Test average is inching back towards 60. Collingwood's is inching below 40. 'What was Ponting thinking?' says Steve Anthony. 'Sheer desperation, I fear. Actually it was genuinely quite depressing to watch, for one horrible minute I thought he was gonna thump Aleem Dar (the best umpire in the world today, in my view).'

91st over: England 281–3 (Trott 57, Collingwood 8) A good over from Siddle ends with a shortish delivery that is whapped through midwicket for four by Trott. England's lead is 183. 'The best thing Ponting could do now is go on TV after the day's play, say he was wrong to act like that towards the umpires, apologise, and say that he will donate to charity whatever portion of his match fee he is left with after any pending punishment,' says Jon Allison.

WICKET! 92nd over: Collingwood c Siddle b Johnson 8 (England 281–4) Another bowling change brings an instant wicket. Mitchell Johnson returns and strikes with his third ball, which Collingwood pulls right down the throat of Siddle at fine leg. That's a dreadful shot in truth. Australia celebrate in a way that suggests they still feel they are in this Test. Collingwood's appalling run continues, and if he doesn't get runs at Sydney it will surely be his last Test.

92nd over: England 283–4 (Trott 58, Bell 1) Ian Bell has all the time in the world to play a proper innings now, with Trott for company and a beefed-up lower order to come.

93rd over: England 283–4 (Trott 58, Bell 1) Siddle is steaming in and beats Bell with a fine delivery. A maiden. 'Agree that Ponting's display was abhorrent, but can you people just let it go?!' says Sarah Bacon. 'FFS, it was AWFUL, and I am disappointed and disgusted in equal measure, but most of all, I was very sad watching him reduced to such desperate measures.'

94th over: England 284–4 (Trott 59, Bell 1) A tidy over from Johnson brings just a single. 'I find about half a dozen double entendres in the Shane Warne poker ad,' says Marie Meyer. 'Anyone else?'

95th over: England 286–4 (Trott 61, Bell 1) In isolation, Australia have had a really good day, restricting England to 129 for four from 48 overs on a flat deck. Trouble is, of course, they have a lot more catch-up cricket to do after they were lapped on the first day. Twice. 'Bad news and good news simultaneously,' says Steve Anthony. 'I think this series is the end of Colly as a Test player, but the good news is that he can be quietly eased from the side at the end of what will (hopefully!) be a triumphant series for England, and we'll have those brilliant catches to remember and never mind about his poor form with the bat. Hope he carries on for a year or two in the one-day and Twenty20 sides though . . .'

WICKET! 96th over: Bell c Siddle b Johnson 1 (England 286–5) Oh, Belly. He tried to hook a good short ball from Johnson that was too high and too wide for him to control the stroke, and Siddle at fine leg charged in to take a brilliant low catch as he tumbled forward. It was a daft stroke from Bell, really, but what a day Siddle is having. Three wickets and two catches. I bet he doesn't drink Carling Black Label.

96th over: England 286–5 (Trott 61, Prior 0) England's lead is 188. If Australia can keep that lead to 250, or 300 at most, and then get 450 themselves, ~~I may pull a sickie on the last day and immerse myself in a bottle of Laphroaig,~~ we will have quite the denouement. 'Two junior doctors from Leeds sat at the MCG!' write Shiba Sinha and Sarah Stevens. 'As voted for by the fourth umpire, we support KP for beard of the year, especially after that fifty! The Barmy Army have just also trounced the Aussies in a sing-off!' I am not jealous I am not jealous I am not jealous I am not jealWHY MEous.

97th over: England 289–5 (Trott 63, Prior 1) Hilfenhaus replaces Siddle and bowls his last delivery almost before Trott is ready.

98th over: England 294–5 (Trott 63, Prior 5) Johnson tries that very high bouncer to Prior, but this is far too high and called wide. Prior then pokes nervously outside off and edges low to third man for four. 'View from over here in Oz is that Haddin made the P sign, Ponting did not confirm, but Dar referred up anyway – when confirmed not out, Dar told Ponting he had lost a referral,' says Chris Gottlieb. 'Complaints were about losing the referral when Ponting had not asked for one. Still not appropriate though.' That's interesting. I'm almost certain I saw Ponting make a referral sign. Aleem Dar also clearly demonstrated the movement of Pietersen's bat, which suggests that Ponting's complaints were about the decision rather than a referral.

99th over: England 294–5 (Trott 63, Prior 5) A maiden from Hilfenhaus to Prior.

100th over: England 301–5 (Trott 64, Prior 10) You could not make this up. Matt Prior edges a fine delivery through to Brad Haddin and walks off – but Aleem Dar tells him to hang on because he wants to check with the third umpire whether it is a no-ball. And it is! Johnson had overstepped! 'Count to ten, Ricky . . .' chuckles Bumble, before adding that it's 'brave umpiring'. Too right it is.

101st over: England 304–5 (Trott 65, Prior 12) Prior cuts Hilfenhaus through the covers for a couple from the last ball before tea. He will play positively, and if he gets in he could take the game away from Australia. For now they are still in it, just about, with England leading by 206. Tea.

England 304–5; Australia 98

The evening session

BY ROB SMYTH

102nd over: England 311–5 (Trott 70, Prior 14) Mitchell Johnson resumes after tea, and Trott works each of the first three deliveries through midwicket: the first two for two and the third for one. Trott has hit only three boundaries in his innings, and he will not give a solitary one about that. His concentration is eerie.

103rd over: England 312–5 (Trott 71, Prior 14) Just the one from Hilfenhaus's over.

104th over: England 313–5 (Trott 72, Prior 14) Johnson is in a nice groove and is using the bouncer sparingly and effectively. 'Greetings from A&E at Trafford General in Manchester, where I sit with a five-year-old Oliver who hasn't eaten in eight days,' says Chris Leigh. 'Since many doctors seem to enjoy OBO, could I perhaps plead that if any are in said A&E and could see him, that would be lovely. Or maybe a simple "get well" would be nice.' Man, that's awful. Good luck getting treatment for him.

105th over: England 317–5 (Trott 76, Prior 14) Trott inside-edges Hilfenhaus right onto the knee bone and collapses to the floor. He is in a lot of pain. He really is struggling, but after a couple of minutes' treatment he gets to his feet, swallows a couple of painkillers and resumes his innings.

106th over: England 321–5 (Trott 79, Prior 15) Trott pings Johnson through the covers and limps through for three runs. Australia have gone a little flat. Time to unleash Siddle on his old chum Prior, surely.

107th over: England 328–5 (Trott 80, Prior 21) Hilfenhaus, whose series average of 136.50 is more than a little unjust, continues to plug away on and around off stump. 'It's kind of like an orgasm getting a nod on OBO,' says Harry Jervis. 'You have a wand there, Rob. Use it.' I'll swap the wand for one snifter of what you're drinking, Jervis.

108th over: England 337–5 (Trott 85, Prior 25) Ryan Harris is on for Mitchell Johnson. His fourth ball is too straight, and Trott's handsome on-drive races to the boundary. His career average is back above 60, and very few players with 1,000 Test runs can match that. It's slipping away from Australia.

109th over: England 340–5 (Trott 87, Prior 26) Hilfenhaus labours on. Three runs from the over.

110th over: England 340–5 (Trott 87, Prior 26) Harris bowls a maiden over. Trott calm and careful.

111th over: England 347–5 (Trott 91, Prior 29) Michael Clarke comes on to bowl his left-arm spin for the first time in the series.

112th over: England 347–5 (Trott 91, Prior 29) On Sky, Nasser and Bumble are wondering why Siddle hasn't bowled for an hour and a half. It's a pretty reasonable point, not least because Prior is at the crease. Prior, who has been skittish in the extreme, is beaten by consecutive deliveries from Harris during another maiden.

113th over: England 348–5 (Trott 92, Prior 29) I have no idea why Clarke is bowling. These are just free runs. Buy one, get one free.

114th over: England 348–5 (Trott 92, Prior 29) Trott is drawn into a drive well wide of off stump by Harris, and squirts it on the bounce to Hussey at gully. He reaches for an even wider delivery later in the over and is beaten. Australia have obviously decided to try to bore Trott out. Good luck with that.

115th over: England 352–5 (Trott 94, Prior 31) Four

singles from Clarke's over. This is utterly pointless from Australia, like the middle overs of a one-day game.

116th over: England 354–5 (Trott 95, Prior 32) Prior has a fiddle at a good one from Harris and is beaten. He's in hopeless nick.

117th over: England 354–5 (Trott 95, Prior 32) Michael Clarke is replaced by Steve Smith. He bowls a decent first over to Prior, a maiden.

118th over: England 365–5 (Trott 106, Prior 32) Trott reaches an excellent century with his favourite shot, a flip through midwicket for four off Harris. It's his third hundred against Australia in only five Tests, and his fifth overall. What a find he has been. Geoff Miller and the other selectors deserve so much credit for picking him at a time when some idiots were calling for Key, Ramprakash, Key and more Key, vicar.

119th over: England 367–5 (Trott 107, Prior 33) A quiet over from Smith. Sky have just shown Trott's wagon wheel, and 85 of his 107 runs have come on the leg side.

120th over: England 371–5 (Trott 107, Prior 37) Siddle returns after an absence of almost two hours. After five good deliveries, the sixth is a touch wide and Prior flails it behind point for four.

121st over: England 378–5 (Trott 109, Prior 42) Smith goes around the wicket to Trott. It's important that England don't let the game drift and allow Smith to bowl some cheap overs. Says Jon Allison: 'If we were all to follow Mike Hussey's lead and give players nicknames which double as Mr Men, Trott would be Mr Invisible, because he just accumulates without anybody really noticing he is there.'

122nd over: England 384–5 (Trott 115, Prior 42) Four more to Trott, played down through the cordon off Siddle. They must be completely sick of him. If you employ a not unreasonable qualification of 500 runs, nobody in the history of the game has a higher Test average against Australia.

123rd over: England 388–5 (Trott 117, Prior 44) That's the hundred partnership, a relatively breezy effort from 162 balls. England are closing in on a first-innings lead of 300 – for the second time in the series. Incredible. Smith is wheeling away from around the wicket. Every now and then you forget where you are and see a blond leggie going at England from around the wicket and you think it's 1994–5 and the ball's going to rip violently from the rough and you think DOOM. But then you realise that it's OK. Everything's OK.

124th over: England 388–5 (Trott 117, Prior 44) There are two big factors: Swann and scoreboard pressure. We've seen some pretty improbable draws on dying pitches in recent times, but this game is so far advanced. Australia will need to bat for at least six sessions. If they do that, well played, lads, and see you in Sydney.

125th over: England 393–5 (Trott 121, Prior 45) A full toss from Smith is put away expertly by Trott, who splits the men at midwicket and mid-on. England's lead is 295, which is more than the largest first-innings deficit that has been overturned to win a Test match: 291 in that wonderful game in Colombo in 1992. 'Do you remember Beckham deliberately getting a yellow card so he would be banned for the next (meaningless) match?' says Phil Keegan. 'I think Punter is onto the same scam here . . . he is trying to get himself banned before he is sacked . . . and it is kind of annoying because the Aussies will have to pick someone who might actually score some runs . . . damn annoying really but pretty crafty on Punter's part.'

126th over: England 400–5 (Trott 125, Prior 48) Trott drives Siddle through the covers for four to bring up the 400. Runs are coming easily against a tiring attack. 'Just had to get this off my chest,' says Arvind Ramanan, before doing precisely that. 'Jonathan Trott is a modern-day Javed Miandad. Fairly competent, hangs around always and is an absolute irritant of a batsman.'

127th over: England 404–5 (Trott 125, Prior 52) Prior pulls some utter filth from Smith over midwicket to reach his first fifty of the series.

128th over: England 405–5 (Trott 126, Prior 52) A sharp bouncer from the returning Johnson forces Trott to abort his planned hook stroke. He then squirts the last delivery for a single.

129th over: England 415–5 (Trott 131, Prior 57) Prior gets down on one knee and swipes Smith over midwicket for a handsome one-bounce four, the third run of which is his 2,000th Test run. 'So Arvind Ramanan thinks Miandad as fairly competent,' says Mike Down. '8,832 runs at 5.57. I suppose on that basis Bradman was half-decent!' You've got to love typos.

130th over: England 425–5 (Trott 132, Prior 66) Oh my. What a day Australia have had. They'll be bringing Frank Spencer on to bowl in a minute. It's been a long day. Prior steers four more to third man. He is playing well now.

131st over: England 427–5 (Trott 134, Prior 66) Trott pulls the new bowler Watson for two, and that makes this England's highest sixth-wicket partnership at Melbourne: 141 not out. Blimey, on Sky Bumble says that some respected judges are calling for Ponting to be sacked for wagging his finger at Aleem Dar. That would be over the top, surely. One thing's for sure: he probably shouldn't have any barmaids in his hotel room tonight.

132nd over: England 432–5 (Trott 138, Prior 66) Trott flicks a short one from Johnson along the ground for four, right through a tired attempt from Hilfenhaus at fine leg.

133rd over: England 437–5 (Trott 138, Prior 71) That's a superb stroke from Prior, a trademark smack through the covers for four off Watson. It brings up the 150 partnership. 'Question for you: has any Test cricketer ever wielded a cricket bat like it's a light sabre more than Matt Prior?' wrote Dan Barker just before Prior played that stroke.

134th over: England 439–5 (Trott 138, Prior 73) Five minutes' play remaining. 'Now that everyone has latched onto the "fairly competent" and forgotten the point about Trott, you have to publish my defence as well,' says Arvind Ramanan. 'Miandad had great numbers, just like Trott. Miandad was an absolute pain to watch, just like Trott. Trust me, the numbers aren't everything. I have had the misfortune of watching him play.' I do see what you mean, in terms of unobtrusive accumulation. But Miandad is one of the all-time greats.

135th over: England 442–5 (Trott 139, Prior 75) Time for one more over.

136th over: England 444–5 (Trott 141, Prior 75) That's the end of another superb day for England, who lead by 346 and are so close to retaining the Ashes. Congratulations to Jonathan Trott, who again demonstrated his immense mental strength and ability. Yet today will be remembered for Ricky Ponting's contretemps with Aleem Dar. It was a long way from Mike Gatting and Shakoor Rana, but it was still unacceptable, and he will be assuming the position in front of the match referee Ranjan Madugalle at some stage over the next few hours.

England 444–5; Australia 98

Third day

The morning session

BY ANDY BULL

Preamble: As well as a stock of turkey sandwiches, I have a bottle of rather good whisky to crack into just in case – and I know this is wishful thinking – England can pull this off tonight. In other news, Ricky Ponting has just said 'sorry' for acting like a complete tool (I paraphrase) yesterday. He's been fined 40 per cent of his match fee for his histrionics. My personal highlight today will be Ponting given out caught behind off a no-ball that touched his shirt and was taken on the bounce by Prior, but he can't refer it as they've already used up their referrals. Here he comes, leading his team out onto the field.

137th over: England 444–5 (Trott 141, Prior 75) Harris takes the ball. But the Australian team feels so flat, and Prior's defensive shots are so resolute, that it feels as though it's the 50th over of the day, not the first. It's a maiden. 'I have the Laphraoig on ice' – good choice, Dave Bell – 'and I am verging on being moist with excitement (© Smyth).'

138th over: England 447–5 (Trott 144, Prior 75) As for my own whisky, and there seem to be plenty of you out there (i.e. three) who want to know, it's an 18-year-old Glenmorangie. Anyway, at the other end it's Peter Siddle. Out? No. Siddle delivers a fine away-nipper that slips off the edge of Trott's bat but lands just short of the slips.

139th over: England 447–5 (Trott 144, Prior 75) A good diving stop by Mike Hussey in the gully cuts off a squint drive from Prior.

140th over: England 452–5 (Trott 146, Prior 78) 'It's heart-breaking to see one of the great players of the last decade end up resembling an ageing lothario getting into pub brawls as the ladies turn their backs on him so he takes his frustration out on the bouncers,' says Phil Withal. 'But just maybe it's how the Tasmanian "street fighter" would want to be remembered, punching till the end.'

141st over: England 459–5 (Trott 146, Prior 85) Prior's had enough of playing himself in. He throws a vicious drive at a wide ball from Harris, and slashes four past backward point.

WICKET! 142nd over: Prior c Ponting b Siddle 85 (England 463–6) Ah, what shame. Prior falls fifteen runs shy of his century, patting a catch to Ponting at mid-on.

143rd over: England 465–6 (Trott 148, Bresnan 3) 'Oh no,' shouts Warne as he sees Harris pull up in the middle of his run-up. This doesn't look good. He's twisted his ankle, and now he's sitting down on the turf, his teammates gathered around him. Now he's limping off the field with the team physio. I wager it will be a while before we see him bowl again. He's not the only one feeling morose, here's Malcolm Parks: 'Why are you still eating turkey sandwiches? I've already moved on to turkey curry, turkey stir-fry and turkey cheesecake.'

144th over: England 465–6 (Trott 148, Bresnan 4) Bresnan plays out a maiden from Siddle.

145th over: England 465–6 (Trott 148, Bresnan 4) Hilfenhaus replaces Harris. Steve Smith throws down the stumps with a dead-eye throw from cover. So that's why he is in the team. Bresnan's bat was grounded, anyway.

WICKET! 146th over: Bresnan c Haddin b Siddle 4 (England 465–7) Siddle has his fifth wicket. Lovely bowling by him, swinging the ball back in waspishly towards off stump. Along with his two catches, that means he has had a hand in all seven dismissals so far. It was a straightforward snick behind that did for Bresnan, easily collected by Haddin. That might not be a bad thing for England. At least the game is moving on. Oh, and Harris, we're told, will not bowl again in this match.

147th over: England 466–7 (Trott 148, Swann 0) Swann sways away from a startling bouncer by Hilfenhaus. That's the best bit of a maiden over. 'I was keeping this,' writes Mike Selvey. 'But as Warne appears to be talking about it, I can tell you that KP told the Australians he hit it yesterday but actually did not. It was a great wind-up.'

148th over: England 473–7 (Trott 151, Swann 4) Johnson is on, but this over is all about Trott. He nods his bat briskly at the crowd and then strides down the wicket to shake Swann's hand. It's a very business-like way to go about celebrating your 150, but that's the nature of the man. As Lord Selvey neatly put it in his match report yesterday, Trott 'is the batting equivalent of the fellow at a party who no one recognises, who stays in the kitchen on his own but is last to leave'.

149th over: England 473–7 (Trott 151, Swann 4) 'Why the jings are England still batting?' pleads Alan Greenwood, and he's not the only man asking that question. 'On the off chance that Australia get more than 400 surely we should be backing our top order to knock off the required runs.' Bull's tenth rule of cricket, old boy: the players are always a lot slower to declare than the fans would have them be. PS Don't ask what the other nine rules are. I haven't made them up yet.

150th over: England 483–7 (Trott 154, Swann 11) Johnson gives Swann just a little too much room and suffers the predictable consequences. He doesn't learn his lesson though, because the next ball is in the same place, even if it was delivered from around the wicket. This time Swann doesn't quite catch it cleanly, so it gets him three rather than four. Trott then wafts a pull away for three more. Just the ten runs from the over then.

151st over: England 489–7 (Trott 160, Swann 11) That's the shot of the day so far from Trott, a plumb straight drive for four back past the bowler.

152nd over: England 499–7 (Trott 163, Swann 18) Swann cuffs a rumbustious bunt back past Johnson's head and away for three to long-on. Later in the over, when Trott has returned the strike, Swann carts a four away through deep square leg. This is, Smyth points out, the first time in history that Australia have conceded a first innings lead of over 400 at home. 'Australia were 12–0 when my wife went into labour,' writes Tom Nicholls. 'We were admitted to the labour ward at 289–5 but sent home at 444–5. If OBO readers could suggest what the England lead will be at the time of birth I'm sure it would put her mind at rest!'

153rd over: England 499–7 (Trott 163, Swann 18) Trott plays out a maiden from Hilfenhaus, which is a nice cameo of his overall approach. England are 400 up, he has over 150, they have just plundered 20 runs from two overs of Mitchell Johnson, and yet he still has the patience and presence of mind to play out six dot balls.

154th over: England 503–7 (Trott 165, Swann 19) Up comes the 500. StatsSmythGuru says that this is only the second time that any team have had three scores over 500 against Australia in a series. All these stats are different ways of saying the same thing – Australia have rarely been so bad. Here's John Starbuck: 'One of the Bull Rules should relate to the time taken to sack a captain. Very few get it right, except maybe for Cowdrey Junior some years back.'

155th over: England 503–7 (Trott 165, Swann 19) The man just can't get out. Trott makes an utter mess of a pull shot, looping the ball up in the air. It lands safely between the bowler, mid-off and mid-on. Hilfenhaus laughs ruefully to himself.

156th over: England 506–7 (Trott 168, Swann 20) Siddle is back into the attack now. He almost gets Trott with a fine yorker. Almost. 'Following on from Selvey's description of Trott,' says Alan White, 'does that make Phil Hughes the annoying guy who always pops in while you're trying to get the flat ready, sees off a couple of free drinks and then slips off to a dinner party before anyone else has even arrived?'

WICKET! 157th over: Swann c Haddin b Hilfenhaus 22 (England 509–8) Swann swung his bat in an approximation of a hook shot and sliced the ball behind to Haddin. He had to leap high into the air to take the catch, both hands extended above his head. Nasser, who I never had pegged as a *Guardian* reader, has also just singled out Mike Selvey for his description of Trott as the last man to leave the party in yesterday's paper.

158th over: England 512–8 (Trott 168, Tremlett 4) Tremlett guides three runs away past the slips to third man.

WICKET! 159th over: Tremlett b Hilfenhaus 4 (England 512–9) Not long to go now before we get into the meat of this match. The last man is in, Tremlett having been clean bowled by an inswinging delivery from Hilfenhaus, who has doubled his wicket tally for the entire series in the last five balls. 'At this cricket dinner party, are you and Smyth the two gatecrashers who watch the invited guests from a safe distance, continuously commenting on their flaws?' asks Mac Millings. No, we're the two urchins with our noses pressed up against the window trying to sneak a peak through the crack in the curtains.

WICKET! 160th over: Anderson b Siddle 1 (England 513) That's six for Siddle. It was a lovely ball, far too good for Jimmy, but given the state of the scoreline he doesn't bother to celebrate too much. The man walking off to all the applause is Jon Trott, who has just finished one of the great Ashes innings. He is 168 not out. England lead by 415 and are ten wickets away from retaining the Ashes.

England 513; Australia 98

The afternoon session

BY ROB SMYTH

Preamble: The last two series have been so full of daft plot twists, improbable turnarounds that have made a monkey of momentum and an idiot of impetus, that it's dangerous to assume anything. Yet surely England are going to win this match and retain the Ashes. For flip's sake, they lead by 415 and the match is not even at the halfway point!

1st over: Australia 6–0 (Watson 1, Hughes 5) It's Jimmy Anderson to open the bowling. Watson takes a single, and then Hughes shows how he intends to play by carving his first ball behind point for four.

2nd over: Australia 18–0 (Watson 8, Hughes 10) Watson drives Tremlett's second ball right through the man at mid-on for four. That was poor fielding. The next ball is driven handsomely through mid-off for three more. It looks like Australia are going to go for their shots. Hughes completes an expensive over with a very streaky boundary, sliced through the vacant fifth-slip area with a horizontal bat.

3rd over: Australia 20–0 (Watson 9, Hughes 11) A couple of singles in that Anderson over. No real swing as yet. This should and probably will be hard yakka for England. Australia 452 all out is my prediction.

4th over: Australia 20–0 (Watson 9, Hughes 11) Hughes misses a cut stroke at a ball from Tremlett that goes underneath the bat. His feet are skidding all over the place in the crease.

5th over: Australia 24–0 (Watson 13, Hughes 11) Watson has started well, as he usually does, and in that over from Anderson he leans into a good-looking cover drive towards the long boundary. They come back for an all-run four.

6th over: Australia 30–0 (Watson 16, Hughes 14) 'As this game could be the swansong for Punter and Colly, let's hope they'll be both involved in the former's wicket,' says John Starbuck. 'A daring run-out is what we could do with, something to remember both of them by.' I really hope Ponting gets a century. If Australia lose this, I suppose there's a chance that he will be dumped for the final Test. As Allan Border, Mark Waugh, Ian Healy and others will tell you, Australian selectors don't really do sentiment.

7th over: Australia 39–0 (Watson 23, Hughes 16) Watson slaps a cut behind square for four off Anderson and drives the next ball through the covers for three. This has been an outstanding start from him, full of controlled aggression. In the Sky box, Nasser Hussain and Shane Warne reckon Graeme Swann should be on first change. Hard to argue with that.

8th over: Australia 43–0 (Watson 25, Hughes 17) Shane Warne is back on one of his favourite hobby horses: Andrew Strauss's cautious captaincy. 'Two slips, Nass. Two slips! Staggering to me. Tactically he can improve, a lot.' At the end of the over,

Bumble proudly plays his ring tone: Bill Lawry shouting 'God-dim!' Oh, that's priceless.

9th over: Australia 49–0 (Watson 26, Hughes 22) Hughes backs away and forces Anderson square on the off side for three. Runs are flowing at nearly six an over. Time for Swann, definitely.

10th over: Australia 52–0 (Watson 29, Hughes 22) Here is Swann. 'There was a lot of confident talk earlier about the match finishing tonight,' says Mofaha. 'Does that still seem likely? The reason I'm asking is, I'm on Eastern Standard Time here, and fun though it was last night I got a right ponting off of my wife this morning for staying up all night.' No chance.

11th over: Australia 52–0 (Watson 29, Hughes 22) Bresnan replaces Anderson (5–0–27–0). Warne has tagged in Sir Beefy to moan about the fields. Strauss is definitely a bit too defensive, but some of the complaints about his field settings are stuck in the twentieth century. A good maiden. I might set up a catchily titled Facebook page for Tim Bresnan To Be Formally Recognised As A Worthy Test Cricketer Of Some Substance. He is so underrated.

WICKET! 12th over: Hughes run out 23 (Australia 53–1) Madness. Having started so well, Australia have thrown their first wicket away with a suicidal single. Watson pushes Swann into the off side and sets off; Trott swoops and fizzes a low throw towards the stumps, which Matt Prior demolishes with Hughes just short of his ground. Aleem Dar checked with the third umpire, but it looked out live and replays confirmed it. Watson puts his hand to his head, rubbing at his eyebrows, trying to work away the regret. The regret will always be there, son.

12th over: Australia 53–1 (Watson 29, Ponting 0) Here comes the great man, for what might just be his last Test innings. What must be going through his mind right now? This next half-hour is going to be electric.

13th over: Australia 53–1 (Watson 29, Ponting 0) Bresnan is bowling dry already. That's another maiden to Watson, full of deliveries designed to tempt him into the corridor. Watson doesn't bite.

14th over: Australia 54–1 (Watson 29, Ponting 0) James Anderson is back ahead of schedule, specifically to bowl at Ricky Ponting. I really want England to win, but I think I want Ponting to make a score just as much. He was totally out of order yesterday, but he has had to bear an almost unique burden over the last few years, so we shouldn't be too down on him.

15th over: Australia 58–1 (Watson 33, Ponting 0) Bresnan isn't swinging it. The lack of swing means that Watson, after a good sighter at Bresnan, can lean into an on-the-up cover drive that goes all the way for four. Those are the first runs off Bresnan, from his 17th delivery. 'Australia's odds to win this Test have gone from 80–1 to 25–1 in the last five overs,' wrote my colleague Tom Lutz, just before the wicket.

16th over: Australia 60–1 (Watson 33, Ponting 2) Ostensibly this is tedious cricket – Anderson bowling wide of off stump, Ponting leaving – but then ostensibly De Niro and Pacino were just having a cup of coffee in *Heat*. On Sky, Mikey Holding tells us that Ryan Harris has a stress fracture and is out of the rest of the series.

17th over: Australia 60–1 (Watson 33, Ponting 2) A maiden from Bresnan to Watson, and it's drinks.

18th over: Australia 60–1 (Watson 33, Ponting 2) England have two huge shouts for lbw against Ponting turned down in that Anderson over. For the first, the ball came back really sharply, and Ponting couldn't get his bat down in time. Tony Hill said not out, and after a fair amount of deliberation England decided not to review it. The second wasn't such a good shout: he was probably just outside the line and it was going over the top.

A maiden, and Ponting has 2 from 21 balls. He is hanging on for dear life.

19th over: Australia 60–1 (Watson 33, Ponting 2) The lack of singles in recent overs means that we have two distinct contests: Watson v. Bresnan and Ponting v. Anderson. The former is a compelling battle of wills; with Bresnan very accurate and Watson loath to take any risks outside off stump, it's another maiden. 'Two nights ago I dreamed that James Anderson had to take me aside and quietly drop me from the one-day team because I was too slow a run-scorer,' says Emma John. 'I remember feeling utterly aggrieved because I knew for a fact that no one else had turned up for nets the day before. I don't dare ask what this says about me.' I think you do.

20th over: Australia 62–1 (Watson 33, Ponting 4) Ponting is right on the edge here, because Anderson is bowling masterfully. His first ball is a fuller, straighter delivery that Ponting just manages to inside-edge to fine leg for a couple. Ponting defends for the remainder of the over. He now has 4 from 27 balls, and never has an innings with a strike-rate of 14.81 been so interesting. 'I just woke up and checked the OBO,' says John Bowker. '"Oh look, Trott made 168 not out," I say to my sleeping, non-cricket-loving girlfriend. "That's a shame, I wanted him to make 200," she unexpectedly replies. Encouraged, I continue. "Oh look, Australia just had a run-out – that's the last thing they need." She: "It's 6 a.m. I don't give a flying eff." The battle continues.'

21st over: Australia 63–1 (Watson 34, Ponting 4) Bresnan gets one to snarl back off the seam towards Watson.

22nd over: Australia 71–1 (Watson 41, Ponting 5) Watson is heading towards yet another fifty, his fourth of the series. It might be time for a bowling change, maybe two. 'Surely', says Prahalad Bhat, 'one would have thought that the average Englishwoman's dream involving James Anderson would result in her being picked up rather than dropped?'

23rd over: Australia 71–1 (Watson 41, Ponting 5) Ponting is all over the place here. He's having a shocking time. In that over he's squared up by Bresnan and then survives another huge lbw appeal. Another maiden, and Bresnan's figures are 7–5–5–0.

24th over: Australia 71–1 (Watson 41, Ponting 5) After a fine second spell of 5–1–13–0, Anderson is replaced by Tremlett. His fourth ball brings yet another big lbw shout, this time against Watson. Tony Hill says not out. England decided not to review it. I reckon that's the right decision, and replays again show that the ball was just hitting the bails and therefore the original decision would have stood.

25th over: Australia 74–1 (Watson 43, Ponting 5) Swann replaces Bresnan, and Ponting's struggles continue. He comes dancing down the track to the third ball but is barely halfway through his stroke when the ball hits him on the bottom of the toe and loops wide of slip. He now has 5 from 39 balls. If he makes a century, it'll be even more epic after this hideous start.

26th over: Australia 79–1 (Watson 43, Ponting 10) Tremlett draws an outside edge from Watson with a fine delivery, but the ball just dies a fraction in front of Prior, who immediately signalled that he was not sure whether it carried. The umpires went upstairs, just to make sure, and replays confirmed that it was not out. Prior is then booed by the crowd, which is pathetic. 'Usually a knowledgeable crowd in this part of the world,' spits Nasser Hussain on Sky.

27th over: Australia 81–1 (Watson 44, Ponting 11) Ponting works Swann all along the floor to mid-on. That was his 44th delivery; incredibly, this is therefore his longest innings of the series.

28th over: Australia 90–1 (Watson 49, Ponting 15) This

is a supreme spell from Tremlett, who so nearly dismisses Watson with consecutive deliveries. Nine from the over, but it was a bloody good one.

29th over: Australia 90–1 (Watson 49, Ponting 15) Swann beats the groping Watson with a glorious slider. At least I think it was a slider. Either way, that's an excellent maiden from Swann. In other news, here's Keith, whose email begins with that usual, familiar, tedious opening sentence that we all read each and every day. 'I've got a party of five Aussies staying at my guest house in Thailand undergoing dental work. To ease their pain upon return from hours in the chair I have taken to pinning up a copy of the OBO on the front gate. Don't think they'll be staying long.'

30th over: Australia 95–1 (Watson 50, Ponting 19) Watson plays tip-and-run off the next delivery and the single gives him another excellent half-century. There's no logical reason why he has such a diabolical conversion rate (two hundreds and 15 fifties now); he just looks like a very good Test opener. Ponting then leans into one and pushes it pleasantly down the ground for three. He is definitely over the worst. Tea.

Australia 95–1; England 513

The evening session

BY ANDY BULL

Preamble: Australia trailed by 415 after the first innings. Graeme Swann will start the final session, with a solitary slip and a short leg in place.

31st over: Australia 95–1 (Watson 50, Ponting 19) Ponting hops out to meet the ball, crouching low over his bat and trying to smother any spin that Swann does get. It's a maiden.

WICKET! 32nd over: Watson lbw b Bresnan 54 (Australia 99–2) That's out, surely? Umpire Hill thinks so. Watson disagrees and, after a chat with Ponting, decides to refer it. But Hill has been vindicated. Watson walks. Watson made a hash of that: he came across his stumps but then tried to leave a straight ball, tucking his bat behind his pad. The ball hit him flush in front of off and would have just trimmed the top of the bail. Watson takes the long slow walk off the field.

33rd over: Australia 99–2 (Ponting 19, Clarke 0) The once and future captains come together in the middle then, Michael Clarke joining Ricky Ponting. This is the partnership that will define the match, I think.

34th over: Australia 101–2 (Ponting 19, Clarke 2) Bresnan to Clarke, striking first his stomach and then his pad.

REVIEW! 35th over: Ponting st Prior b Swann 19 (Australia 102–2) How's that? England appeal after Prior gathers a ball that dribbled off Ponting's pads. He whipped it up off the ground and knocked over the stumps, but Ponting had slid his foot back over the line just in time to save himself. Not out then, and Punter bats on. It was umpire Hill who asked for that review, by the way, not Andrew Strauss. And that's a missed stumping! Prior got the first right but he fluffed the second chance of the over. Clarke, on strike after Ponting took a single, was pulled forward out of his crease but he was beaten on the outside edge by Swann. Prior missed a simple take.

WICKET! 36th over: Ponting b Bresnan 20 (Australia 102–3) He's gone. That could be the ball that costs Ricky Ponting his job. And what a sorry way to go. The ball was straight and simple, the kind he would have played – left even – with ease in his pomp. This time though it slipped off his inside edge and cannoned into his stumps. Bresnan spreads his arms out wide and sprints down the wicket to jump into the arms of his jubilant teammates. As he passes Ponting the camera closes in on the Australian captain's creased face, his mouth turning down into a frown. He tucks his bat under his arm and walks off. Bresnan has figures of 10–6–11–2. He is the man who is winning it for England.

37th over: Australia 104–3 (Clarke 4, Hussey 0) Just two runs from Swann's over. I'd say more but I'm already running late . . .

WICKET! 38th over: Hussey c Bell b Bresnan 0 (Australia 108–4) Can you hear my expletives in Australia? I was just asking Rob to look up some statistics about Australia's scores when Hussey has come to the crease in this series. We won't be needing them now. Hussey is out, well caught at short extra cover by Ian Bell. Tim Bresnan is bowling one of the best spells of his life here, and I'm lost for words as I watch it. Did I say well caught? Because I meant brilliantly caught. Hussey strode forward and thumped the ball towards the boundary, but Bell leant over to his right and plucked the ball from the air as it passed him.

39th over: Australia 108–4 (Clarke 4, Smith 4) England have only applied a little light pressure since tea, but Australia have crumpled under it. Swann races through a maiden. He's doing a very good job of containing the batsmen at his end, while Bresnan – yes really, Bresnan – tears Australia apart at the other.

40th over: Australia 108–4 (Clarke 4, Smith 4) Another maiden from Bresnan, as England pull this tourniquet tight. Bresnan has bowled 12 overs with six maidens and taken three wickets for 15. His pitch map shows all of two deliveries pitching inside off stump. 'Still backing my previous assertion that this can be done tonight,' says David Adams. 'Must confess though that I was against Bresnan being picked on the grounds that he was a fat pie-chucker, not up to Test class. Perhaps a little hasty.'

41st over: Australia 108–4 (Clarke 4, Smith 4) What can Australia do now? Not much other than stand tall on the deck as the ship disappears beneath the waves?

42nd over: Australia 112–4 (Clarke 4, Smith 8) There's no doubt that at some future point Smith may well turn into a very good player, but this series his come too soon for him and his selection has been just another manifestation of the catastrophically chaotic thinking of the Australian management.

43rd over: Australia 117–4 (Clarke 9, Smith 8) Beautiful bowling from Swann, who ghosts a straight ball past Smith's outside edge. 'My son has only ever known total England domination of the Ashes,' says Paul Thompson. 'He's only one week old, but long may it continue.'

44th over: Australia 120–4 (Clarke 12, Smith 8) It's hard to appreciate just how much pressure there is going to be for serious changes to be made to the Australia team and their management after this series.

45th over: Australia 120–4 (Clarke 12, Smith 8) 'Blimey,' gushes Billy Mowbray. 'This is seriously impressive. With our fifth-choice seam bowler running through Australia's top order like a man possessed, I think it's time to start relaxing into the glorious knowledge that finally, finally we've got a squad that could become proper class, with depth, will, balls, technique, smarts, fielding genius, serious ambition, camaraderie and match-winning chutzpah.'

46th over: Australia 120–4 (Clarke 12, Smith 8) Tremlett comes into the attack. I'd have been tempted to give Anderson a spell myself. Still. It seems tough to quibble with a captain who is about to go 2–1 up in an Ashes series Down Under.

47th over: Australia 120–4 (Clarke 12, Smith 8) All the while I've been harping on about Bresnan, Swann's figures have rather passed me by. Another maiden here means he has got through 14 overs for 16 runs so far. 'Punter would have been put out to pasture but for the fact that his alleged understudy Mr Clarke has been every bit as pathetic as he has,' gripes a man known only as Longmemory.

48th over: Australia 122–4 (Clarke 12, Smith 9) Old Iron Bottom has got a furious cob on about the fact that Strauss has only had two slips in place for most of the afternoon.

49th over: Australia 122–4 (Clarke 12, Smith 9) Atherton has the temerity to suggest that Botham might be being a little over the top, and is rewarded with a beetroot-faced up-close-and-personal encounter in the commentary box.

50th over: Australia 125–4 (Clarke 13, Smith 12) 'I am sailing on a ship with eight Aussies who are all claiming that they have no interest in cricket,' says Bentley. 'Never mind moist, here I am awash with joy and no one wants to play with me.'

51st over: Australia 128–4 (Clarke 13, Smith 15) Smith slashes three runs out square, ending a run of 23 consecutive dot balls from Swann. It's beginning to feel very much like Australia will limp into a fourth day rather than fall over flat face first on the third.

52nd over: Australia 134–4 (Clarke 13, Smith 21) That's a jaffa from Tremlett, moving the ball off the pitch away from Smith's outside edge. He throws drives at Tremlett's next two deliveries, pushing two runs through cover and then slicing four more through point.

WICKET! 53rd over: Clarke c Strauss b Swann 13 (Australia 134–5) Just as I was starting to drift into sleep, my eyelids sagging down as I stared at the partnership stats (30 off 90 balls), the snap of the ball hitting the outside edge and the roar of a celebration startled me out of it. Clarke has gone, caught at slip. Swann switched around the wicket and produced a lovely ball, drifting away towards the slips and then straightening up after pitching. Clarke groped at it, and the ball popped up to Strauss. With Harris injured, probably unable to bat, England have four wickets left to take.

54th over: Australia 138–5 (Smith 25, Haddin 0) Tremlett rips an away-swinger past Smith's outside edge. Later in the over, though, Smith smears him for four past point.

55th over: Australia 139–5 (Smith 25, Haddin 1) 'If England claim an extra half-hour, Andy, does that mean we can all claim it and be late for work? Please.' Clare Davies, I don't see why not. You can tell your boss I gave you permission.

56th over: Australia 144–5 (Smith 25, Haddin 6) Swann's 19th over is yet another maiden. He really has bowled well in this session. He's done exactly the job the team needed him to do, tying one end up in knots while the seamers worry away at the other.

57th over: Australia 144–5 (Smith 29, Haddin 6) Smith has played very well since I slated him earlier in the session. He steers four runs through third man here.

58th over: Australia 150–5 (Smith 30, Haddin 7) A desultory chorus of applause rings around the MCG in acknowledgement of Australia's 150. And they say Australians have no sense of irony.

59th over: Australia 154–5 (Smith 34, Haddin 7) Smith pats a neat on-drive away for four.

60th over: Australia 154–5 (Smith 34, Haddin 7) 'Yet another maiden' has become something of a catchphrase for Mikey Holding this afternoon, much as it seems to have become the mantra for the England team. And that's just what this is, yet another maiden.

WICKET! 61st over: Smith b Anderson 38 (Australia 158–6) Delete, delete, delete. I was just about to rebuke Jimmy for serving up some short and wide filth which Smith walloped away for four when he took the wicket with his very next ball. He didn't deign to celebrate though, as it was batsman's error rather than bowler's skill that did it. Smith threw his bat at another wide delivery, and chopped it straight onto his stumps. Jimmy doesn't think he needs the cheap ones any more. Mitch Johnson is in, and with Ryan Harris out crocked ('Apparently Harris heard something snap as he ran in to bowl,' says Botham) England are three wickets away from retaining the Ashes. Anyone else feeling a little giddy?

63rd over: Australia 160–6 (Haddin 7, Johnson 1) Just four overs to go now, and Warne and Botham both think that unless England take one more wicket they will struggle to convince the umpires to let them have that extra 30 minutes.

64th over: Australia 162–6 (Haddin 7, Johnson 3) 'I don't know what was more exciting about that over,' says Ellie Rofe as Johnson glances two runs out to square leg. 'Smith's wicket, or Gower, re. Anderson's shoddy ball beforehand, purring, "He gave the cherry a good spanking . . . it was a bad ball and it got what bad balls deserve."'

65th over: Australia 162–6 (Haddin 7, Johnson 3) I did have an entry here. Then my computer crashed and now there is only one ball left in the day. Moving swiftly on then . . .

66th over: Australia 162–6 (Haddin 7, Johnson 3) And that's that. Stumps. England have a lead of 246 and need four more wickets.

Australia 98 and 162–6; England 513

Ponting strides into an uncertain future

Hoodwinked by Pietersen, a series average of just 16, but can Australia afford to drop him?

BY KEVIN MITCHELL IN MELBOURNE

WEDNESDAY 29 DECEMBER 2010

Ricky Ponting is riding out of town wearing a black hat and a bruised ego, victim of his own stretched impatience and a devilish piece of gamesmanship by Kevin Pietersen. While he looks to have survived this week's passing ignominy, his latest tangle with authority is sorely mistimed, bookending a career that started in a rage and is winding down amid echoes of past misdemeanours.

A player of his standing would not expect to be remembered for the pop-eyed and ill-considered rant he unleashed on the umpire Aleem Dar on day two, or even for the skittish innings that brought his participation in the fourth Test to an ugly end not long after tea on day three. Still, it would be a brave man to gamble on Ponting not responding with something heroic in the fifth Test in Sydney. And Punter is a brave man.

It emerged last night, meanwhile, that it was Pietersen who tricked the Australian captain into his high-octane monologue with Dar, after kidding him he had nicked the ball from Ryan Harris – when he knew he hadn't – which set off the Decision Referral System row on Monday. Whether it was a nod or a wink, KP put one over on Ponting.

Then, further and falsely emboldened to believe that the white Hotspot mark on Pietersen's bat was evidence of a genuine dismissal – when, clearly, it was nowhere near where the ball had innocently passed the bat – Ponting argued so vehemently with Dar and his colleague Tony Hill that it subsequently cost him a $5,400 (£3,500) fine and a caution for Level I dissent.

More damagingly, it inspired almost universal criticism from former colleagues and fans across Australia; in five minutes of televised rage, Ponting went from keeper of the national cricket team's honour to TV villain *du jour*.

Ian Chappell, no stranger to curt words when captain of a team now fondly remembered as the first of the ugly Australians, wanted him suspended. Other greats, from Bill Lawry to Andrew Flintoff, poured on various degrees of scorn. A poll of fans on the Australian Broadcasting Commission's website was running 3–1 yesterday in favour of him being stood down.

Ponting, still nursing a cracked little finger on his left hand, thus went into bat on day three trying against all odds to rescue more than a cricket match. He was fighting for his standing as one of the finest batsmen of the modern game, and perhaps claw back some of his lost dignity.

As the determined Tasmanian crossed that 70-yard expanse of green to the wicket, it seemed he might more appropriately have made the journey in a tumbril. Yet, as fickle sporting crowds are inclined to do, the 68,733 voyeurs who had come to see the kill rose to greet him with a mixture of affectionate boos from the Barmy Army and weirdly emotional cheering from his own supporters. The full, uncertain chorus filled a ground on which he averages 62 in Tests and where he had hopes of one last major contribution. But he did not look at ease.

He fidgeted and was turned square by the moving ball, a pale imitation of the player who has graced Test cricket for 15 years with more than 12,000 runs and 39 centuries. The last of that extraordinary collection of players – Warne, McGrath, Gilchrist, the Waughs, Gillespie, Langer et al. – he suddenly looked all of his 36 years, and the tattered green cap was not so much an emblem of defiance now as a remnant of past glory.

Ponting's personal involvement ended with an inside edge onto his stumps after tea that barely nudged his series average above the mid-teens (take out his 51 in the dead second innings in Brisbane, and his average is 9) and left his team at the mercy of a rampant Tim Bresnan and rejuvenated Graeme Swann.

But the selectors, surely, cannot drop him; Michael Clarke, his prematurely anointed understudy, is as woefully out of form, and Pup's one-day captaincy, as well as his celebrity lifestyle choices, have been inept. Besides, there is nobody else.

Ponting will survive this Ashes campaign, then hope that memories fade. He has made it known to friends he is desperate for one last trip to England, even if just as a player. They indulged the more politically astute Steve Waugh with a farewell home tour. Will they do the same for Ponting? That will be a serious test of their loyalty to a man who is on his way to losing his third Ashes series.

Even if Ponting is coming towards the end of a career garlanded in gold but tinged with a few regrets, it needs at least some perspective to dilute the vitriol that his intemperate behaviour has inspired this week.

He once was, indeed, a larrikin, and there will always be some of that indefinable quality in him. But he is a fighter for his corner, too. They go hand in hand. He has been simultaneously encouraged and indulged by his cricketing culture, on the one hand lauded for his toughness, yet knocked down for his indiscretions. That is not an excuse, just an explanation.

And what of the wily Pietersen? What an unexpected wheeze it was. Justified? In the context of the modern game, it fits a pattern. You would not find many of his opponents complaining loudly. The etiquette has changed, and not so dramatically as some moralists would have you think.

Because of its carefully embroidered history and a dearth of probity elsewhere in the sporting universe, cricket has long had the reputation as the last outpost of fair play, a tenuous notion that has been stress-tested to breaking point in this Test and many others in recent years.

These are the rules by which Ponting plays, and Pietersen too. To pretend otherwise is to ignore the evidence before our eyes every time the poor umpire is implored to 'go upstairs'.

Fourth day

The morning session

BY ROB SMYTH

Preamble: Evening. How d'ya sleep? Me neither. For the last 16 hours I've been thinking about the last 24 years, and what England are about to achieve. It might take three balls; it might take three hours. Either way, fix yourself a big dumb grin and a big gin and cherish every second.

67th over: Australia 169–6 (Haddin 11, Johnson 6) The ground is barely a quarter full – it's a Poms' party, basically – as Tim Bresnan prepares to bowl the opening over of the day. Technically England need four wickets, but in reality it's just three as the injured Ryan Harris will not bat. Bresnan's second ball is a beauty that comes back between Johnson's bat and pad and just misses off stump. His fourth ball brings a pretty big shout for lbw, but it pitched outside leg and might have been too high.

WICKET! 68th over: Johnson b Tremlett 6 (Australia 172–7) That's the first one. Tremlett gets Johnson with a very good delivery that comes back a fair way to take the inside edge before deflecting onto the body and back onto the stumps. Two more wickets to go.

69th over: Australia 174–7 (Haddin 15, Siddle 1) These last two wickets could come at any moment, and there were four near-misses in that Bresnan over. Siddle would have been run out by a direct hit from Pietersen at point; then Haddin survived a gentle appeal for caught behind; then Siddle drove just past short extra cover; and finally Haddin was beaten. England's discipline with the ball has been so impressive in this series.

70th over: Australia 178–7 (Haddin 15, Siddle 5) Siddle tickles Tremlett fine for four. As Walter Sobchak didn't quite say in *The Big Lebowski*, 'You're exiting a world of pain, OBO fraternity.'

71st over: Australia 185–7 (Haddin 18, Siddle 5) Haddin drives Bresnan through the covers for three, and Siddle touches a reverse inswinger to fine leg for four more. Actually it was just off the pad. Australia have avoided a record home defeat. 'My wife wants to watch the *Sex and the City 2* DVD that she got for Christmas,' says Ant Pease, 'but I'm angling to watch the cricket based on telling her that our seven-week-old daughter finds the sound of Nasser Hussain relaxing. Who will win?' Nose fetishists?

72nd over: Australia 188–7 (Haddin 21, Siddle 5) Haddin laces three more through extra cover off Tremlett. 'I am disconcertingly excited,' says Richard O'Hagan. 'The last time England won the Ashes in Australia I was sitting in a study bedroom in a North Midlands University Who Shall Remain Nameless, following events over crackly long wave. I never thought it would take so long for this moment to come around again. And why can I not celebrate with a skiff of Copperhead and chips and curry from the chip van?'

73rd over: Australia 196–7 (Haddin 27, Siddle 6) Haddin is hitting it pretty sweetly, especially through the covers.

74th over: Australia 202–7 (Haddin 34, Siddle 10) A couple of edges from Haddin off Tremlett, the first for four and the second a fraction short of Prior, diving to his right.

75th over: Australia 210–7 (Haddin 33, Siddle 14) The runs continue to flow. Haddin clunks Bresnan over mid-off for three, and then Siddle slices four behind point. 'Help, Rob and Andy, I think I am going mental,' says Suzanne Hall. 'A traditional family Christmas complete with low-level hostility and subtle recriminations, too much celebratory whisky on the return to London and now the anticipation of retaining the Ashes . . . Isn't it brilliant? I have a pork pie and a bottle of Talisker to help me through. Do you think that's enough? I can't help thinking beta blockers would be useful.' When I was a kid I thought beta blockers were used to stop computer viruses. Seriously. I wasn't in the top class.

76th over: Australia 214–7 (Haddin 37, Siddle 14) Jimmy Anderson replaces Chris Tremlett, and Brad Haddin drives superbly back over his head for four.

77th over: Australia 218–7 (Haddin 37, Siddle 18) Graeme Swann comes on for Tim Bresnan. As Mike Atherton says on Sky, Swann gave a stunning display of drift bowling yesterday, culminating in the wicket of Michael Clarke when he switched to around the wicket. It was incredibly good in view of the fact that the ball was barely spinning. It's not spinning this morning either, and Siddle carts a short ball to third man for four.

78th over: Australia 220–7 (Haddin 39, Siddle 18) 'You've got to stay up, I insist!' says Bumble. 'No excuse, get the coffee on.' Then he asks Mike Atherton whether he has a dog. He's on one now; this is great stuff. He's telling us how he keeps his dad's ashes on the mantelpiece alongside the ashes of his two dead dogs. Now he's onto Michael Vaughan's check shirt. 'Is it *Brokeback Mountain* . . .?' Two from Haddin's over.

79th over: Australia 234–7 (Haddin 46, Siddle 25) Siddle swipes Swann over midwicket for four to bring up a proud and admirable fifty partnership. Haddin completes an expensive over with a gloriously pure straight drive for six. 'Suzanne Hall, I think

I love you,' says John Starbuck. 'Cricket, Talisker and pork pies! It would only work if the pie was a Pork Farms or otherwise Melton Mowbray, though. None of that rubbish you get down south, but I suppose you can't help living there.'

80th over: Australia 235–7 (Haddin 47, Siddle 25) Haddin wears a very good short ball from Anderson on the right breast. The second new ball is due, but Swann might have another over, I reckon. 'WE CAN STILL WIN THIS!!!' says Henry Scowcroft. Yes, Henry is English.

81st over: Australia 237–7 (Haddin 48, Siddle 26) Swann beats Haddin with consecutive deliveries. The lack of spin has brought out all his variations of flight, pace, drift, line, gurn, and he has used them brilliantly.

82nd over: Australia 239–7 (Haddin 49, Siddle 27) Anderson continues with the old ball, which is reversing appreciably. He almost traps Siddle with an excellent full-length delivery that just takes the inside edge at the last minute. That was a masterful over.

83rd over: Australia 254–7 (Haddin 54, Siddle 38) Haddin edges Swann just under the crouching Collingwood at slip, and that takes him to another classy half-century. Siddle slog-sweeps the next ball over mid-on for six and carts the next for three. You have to admire this pair's defiance. It takes some stones to be up in front of a firing squad and loudly share observations about the snipers' mothers that even Goldie Lookin' Chain would baulk at. 15 from the over.

84th over: Australia 257–7 (Haddin 55, Siddle 40) Bresnan is back on, so I presume the new ball is imminent. Siddle misses a violent swing outside off stump, the sort that Leatherface would have enjoyed were he a cricket connoisseur rather than a clinical murderer of zesty teenagers.

WICKET! 85th over: Siddle c Pietersen b Swann 40

(Australia 258–8) Swann has struck. Strauss kept him on and was rewarded when Siddle swiped the second ball high towards long-on, where Pietersen took a well-judged catch just inside the rope. One more wicket.

85th over: Australia 258–8 (Haddin 55, Hilfenhaus 0) Graeme Swann has taken the last wicket in each of England's last three Ashes victories – at Lord's, the Oval and Adelaide. He has four balls at Haddin (the batsmen crossed), who defends comfortably.

WICKET! 86th over: Hilfenhaus c Prior b Bresnan 0 (Australia 258 all out). ENGLAND WIN BY AN INNINGS AND 157 RUNS. OR, TO PUT IT ANOTHER WAY, ENGLAND RETAIN THE ASHES! That's it! The team charge straight into a big dumb sloppy group hug, jumping deliriously up and down on the spot. Matt Prior, having picked himself up from the floor after that catch, can't penetrate the huddle. He decides not to ruin the moment by punching someone smack in the face and instead just jumps up and down like a madman on the back of one of his teammates. You could watch scenes like this for the rest of your days. England have retained the Ashes, and they have done so with their biggest win over Australia since 1956!

There's much to do for the paper, and you'll be wanting a glass or two of Revelry Enhancer, so I'll not hang around. Congratulations to England. We all want to support a winning team, but so often winning teams aren't actually very likeable. That's the game. But this lot are. This is a team we can all be so proud of: a resourceful group of likeable, humble, good-humoured fellas who wring every last drop from their talent, and who have an equilibrium that allows them to meet with innings victories and thumping defeats and treat those two imposters just the same. They also have a great backroom team, led by the incredibly impressive Andy Flower, and watching him hug Andrew Strauss a moment ago almost brought a tear to the eye. Two finer men you'll not meet. (I've not met either, admittedly, but you know what I mean.) Even that famous scrutiniser of modern masculinity Tony Soprano would look at both of them and say, '*Ah salute.*'

Ah salute, indeed, to Strauss and to Flower and to England and – what the hell – to everyone in the whole wide world.

Australia 98 and 258; England 513. England win by an innings and 157 runs

England take the high ground but the summit has still to be conquered

BY MIKE SELVEY IN MELBOURNE

THURSDAY 30 DECEMBER 2010

This is not yet done. The scenes at the Melbourne Cricket Ground half an hour before lunch were unforgettable: a joyful celebration of victors and their supporters, vociferous and otherwise, and 'We Are the Champions' on the public address as the team did their lap of honour. England's massive win was the result of a team performance as compelling as that which brought an innings defeat to Australia in Adelaide. Thus far, though, in retaining the Ashes the team have reached the Hillary Steps of their ambition. The summit, actually to win the series, remains elusive until the final Test in Sydney is done and dusted. So there is still work. England were caught napping in Perth through overconfidence, and it taught them the lesson of level-headedness. The Andys, Flower and Strauss, will not let it happen again.

Australia were not beaten by a record margin as might have been anticipated at the start of play, but the defeat by an innings and 157 runs, after Brad Haddin (55 not out) and Peter Siddle (40) had managed to add 86 annoying runs for the eighth wicket, was still their heaviest home reverse in 98 years, and the first time they have been beaten by an innings twice in a home series.

Ricky Ponting may have his moments on the field, but he is an honourable and generous man in defeat. Inside he must be bereft. He is not yet the first Australian captain since Billy Murdoch more than a century ago to lose an Ashes series three times, but he is mighty close. When his career does come to an end, he deserves to be remembered as one of the game's finest batsmen, not as an Ashes failure.

To win this match represented yet another triumph for Flower, Strauss and the management team who recognised in the Perth defeat not a gathering of momentum by Australia that would translate inevitably to Melbourne, but an intolerable failure of elements within their own side to stay in the moment, as the management-speak has it.

England defeats and near-defeats in the past four years have almost invariably resulted in a resurgence in the following match. Quite how they manage it remains their secret, but there is too consistent a pattern now for there not to have been a strategical input. Turning disaster into triumph in the manner they do is every bit as impressive as achieving the heights in the first place.

This match was won by a return to the values that England had laid out even before they left for Australia. Bat deep was part of it. Create scoreboard pressure and the bowlers can do their work. In three of the four matches to date, England, in the second innings in Brisbane and their only innings in Adelaide and Melbourne, scored 517 for one, 620 for five and 513. They are not going to lose matches with scores such as these and, if they come first time around, they have every chance of winning.

Leading on from that came a bowling strategy that relied on three pace bowlers attempting to take new-ball wickets and then bowling restrictively, and Graeme Swann filling a dual role of stock bowler and, later in a match as a pitch began to wear, the most testing wicket-taking spinner in the game.

Crucially, Flower recognised that placing such demands on his pacemen would inevitably result in collateral damage, and a squad was chosen accordingly, both with seamless replacements in place if necessary through injury and tactically according to conditions.

The choice of Tim Bresnan for Melbourne – at the recommend-ation of David Saker, the England bowling coach, without a shad-ow of doubt – has been a masterpiece of judgement and a surprise to many who did not realise his capabilities beyond be-ing a worthy one-day containment specialist.

Last summer, though, Australians themselves were commenting on the weight of ball he delivered and the surprising pace he gen-erated. The speed gun suggested that, give or take, he was as fast as anyone in this match.

England had lost their control in Perth, egged into indiscretion by the sledging war. That the batsmen were unable to cope in particular with the bounce and the excellent way the Australians used it was a concern, for it happened against South Africa at the Wanderers too: this is an area that will require much diligent work so that never again are they surprised or lacking in tech-nique. But the bowling failed to pull them back into that match, with runs squandered they could ill afford.

By Melbourne, on a pitch that played precisely as predicted by those who know the ground, England won an important toss, kept their cool and, after the first day already with a lead of 59 and all ten wickets in hand, were in the driving seat. Not for a second thereafter did they lose control.

The team can now decamp to Sydney tomorrow secure in the knowledge it is Australia not they who have selection issues. The home team are in a mess, with among other things an injured captain unsure of his future or whether he will ever score runs again; a vice-captain who cannot buy a run and, as heir apparent to Ponting, is, it is said, neither universally liked nor respected within the side; an injured pace bowler; no spinner worth his salt except one whom Ponting will not countenance; a technically deficient opener; and a new-ball bowler who has managed only four wickets in three games.

In his post-match interviews Ponting conceded there was a great deal his players, and Australian cricket in general, could learn from the manner in which England prepared for the series and then played it. Whatever the outcome of the final match, Australia should gear themselves for a root-and-branch restructuring.

The England and Wales Cricket Board has poured resources into its endeavour to turn the England team into the world's best. Flower wants for nothing, respects that and uses it wisely. That they are not top dog yet is indisputable, although the gap is closing rapidly. Strong challenges lie ahead, but then they always did. First Sydney.

If humility follows humiliation, we may be ready to win again

Australians must accept they can learn a lot from how England play the game

BY MALCOLM KNOX

THURSDAY 30 DECEMBER 2010

The King's Speech opened in Australian cinemas this week, ironically when its central message, to our ears at least, was being denied on the cricket field.

That every Englishman, no matter how high, has something to learn from any Australian, no matter how low, has become part of the recent dialogue between our cultures. The corollary – that no Australian can learn anything useful from an Englishman, least of all in sport – is held equally close to Australian hearts.

In cricket, since 1989, our cocky creed has been: 'You invented it, but we perfected it.' For 16 years that was backed by talent and self-belief. But just as the emperor took a little time before he realised he was naked, there has been a lag between the moment English cricketers realised Australians were trying to bluff them, and when Australia realised it.

Test cricket is now divided into two tiers, and to an objective eye it was apparent a year ago that England were playing in division one, Australia in division two. Having defeated Australia at home in 2009, England put up a splendid fight in South Africa, putting themselves in the top league along with India and Sri Lanka. Australia, meanwhile, played poorly enough to make close contests against the West Indies and Pakistan. It was obvious then that the gap between the fourth- and fifth-ranked teams in world cricket was one of quality, not just degree.

In September I interviewed Michael Clarke, the Australia vice-captain, and asked him what he had learnt from watching England play South Africa.

'I didn't watch it at all,' he said. 'We're thinking about what we do, not what they do.'

The only explanation for such an approach is that this is how Australia did things in the era of Warne, McGrath and the Waughs, when their self-belief could reliably kid England into submission. But in 2009 England showed they would not be psyched out any more. That they had further improved since 2009 eluded the self-absorbed Australians.

In casting an eye forward, Australian cricket will be asking two questions: Who? And how?

The first question is simpler. Australia is currently producing better short-form than long-form players. If Steve Smith and Phil Hughes have looked like T20 boys maladjusted to Test cricket, that's essentially what they are. The limited-overs pool brims with talent such as Cameron White, David Warner, Shaun Tait, David Hussey and Shaun Marsh, none of whom has a record promising consistency in Test cricket. We are not producing Jonathan Trotts or Alastair Cooks, batsmen with the composure to measure their innings in days, not minutes.

The worst news for Australians is that our 'rabble', as Michael Vaughan calls them, is the best we have. If any young batsmen were demanding selection, they would have been picked. The presence of Hughes and Smith shows how thin the talent base is. At present, New South Wales's Usman Khawaja, South Australia's Callum Ferguson, Tasmania's George Bailey and Western Australia's Marsh brothers, Shaun and Mitchell, are still figures of hope. Some promising fast bowlers are in the pipeline, namely

Josh Hazlewood and Trent Copeland of NSW and James Pattinson of Victoria, but time will tell if they are the real thing or, like the present Test bowling crew, somewhere between first-class and Test-class. And there is no spin bowler in sight.

We may dream that a Shane Warne will waddle out of the suburbs, but we might also forget that Warne entered a Test team of Border, Taylor, Healy, Boon, Hughes, McDermott and the Waughs.

Satisfyingly for England, this summer they have wrecked not only Australia's present but its immediate future. Clarke, who averages 47 in Test cricket, is no longer heir apparent to the captaincy but a man battling for survival. Shane Watson has batted courageously, but forceful two-hour innings are the job of a No. 6, not an opener. Mitchell Johnson's bowling is a roulette wheel, occasional big wins diverting attention from a regularity of dross. These three were meant to be the nucleus of the future. Instead the team have been held together by Mike Hussey and Brad Haddin, who are near retirement age.

As to how Australia move forward, Greg Chappell's appointment as selection and high-performance supremo is a start. His ideas are sometimes wacky, but he stimulates others and has a record, from the late 1980s, of being able to identify durable material to work with.

His first task will be to find smart cricketers. Of all the differences this summer, the clearest is intelligence. It's hard to remember an Australia team so repetitiously dumb. Stupid run-outs, lazy preparation and poor decision-making have characterised this team for a few years now. In Clarke, Watson and Johnson, Australians do not recognise the instinctive cricket smarts that were so obvious in the late-1980s rebuilding generation of Mark Taylor, Ian Healy and the Waugh twins.

Stupidity manifests itself in arrogance. When England defeated

Australia through the exploitation of reverse swing in 2005, Australia credited one of its own. So we got Troy Cooley back. Lo and behold, one man was not the magician. If Australians think David Saker, a Victorian, is behind the bowling of James Anderson, Tim Bresnan, Chris Tremlett and company, then we have not outgrown our self-delusion.

Without vast reserves of talent, Australia will have to do better with what they have. They must study English cricket and cricketers, and learn how to swing the ball and how to bat against it. They must go back to basics at all levels.

At the moment, like our second-division rivals Pakistan, we are selecting Test cricketers who are still learning how to run between the wickets. English batsmen this series have been diving to just avoid being run out, while Australians merely reached and were caught short.

Bob Simpson, coaching the underpowered Australia teams of the mid-1980s, taught that better application to out-cricket may not make poor players great, but it could at least make them better.

Humility is the most necessary and difficult attitude adjustment. Australia did not make it after 2009, but they might now.

England have won three of the last four Ashes series and, having been the only local pundit treasonous enough to have predicted a 3–1 England win this summer, I feel equally confident that the next Australian Ashes win is at least four years away. The public has welcomed and applauded Andrew Strauss's team, but beneath our good grace lies a sense that the locals have got their comeuppance.

In their pomp, Australian teams were more respected than loved. This year, they are neither. We always suspected this team to be made of chocolate, sweet at first taste but suspect under high heat. There is little public sympathy for them.

But soon we will stop taking defeat so well. As Allan Border and Steve Waugh showed, hardness of character often arises from bitter memories of defeat. When our leading cricketers fully accept that – gulp – England are better than us, we might look to English methods for guidance. We might develop our own Barmy Army to live in hope and cheer for lost causes. We might lose our innate sense of superiority. Then we might be ready to win again.

Ricky Ponting finds himself compared with Billy Murdoch, still the only Australian captain to lose three series to England (though Ponting's fate is not yet sealed). In September 1882 Murdoch, whose team had just won their first series in England, concluded his tour-ending speech at London's Crichton hotel with the words: 'If we have attained any position as cricketers, you in England have yourselves to thank for it, for you have been our instructors.'

It will take a giant leap for Australian cricketing minds to get from *The King's Speech* to Billy Murdoch's speech. Let's see how much humiliation is needed to engender a bit of humility.

It's an A-star for Anderson

Five years after making his debut in 2003 he was on the periphery of the Test squad, but his performance in Australia has been exemplified by self-belief, discipline and patience – and Jimmy Anderson is now undisputed leader of the England pace attack

BY VIC MARKS IN SYDNEY

SUNDAY 2 JANUARY 2011

For England to win in Australia they generally need a fast bowler to be at the top of his game. Think Frank Tyson in 1954–5 or John Snow in 1970–1.

Jimmy Anderson's haul of wickets and his impact on this series do not yet equal the deeds of those giants of Ashes history, but he has achieved something that neither Tyson nor Snow could possibly match: he popped back home between the second and third Tests to be present at the birth of his daughter.

The old-timers may regard that 21,000-mile flit across the globe as a self-indulgence, but one measure of Anderson's increasing self-discipline is that while in England during that period he kept himself on Australian time. As a consequence he hardly seemed the worse for wear when he returned to Perth.

Discipline has been the hallmark of the England pace attack on this Ashes expedition, as exemplified by their efforts in Adelaide and Melbourne, and Anderson is now the undisputed leader of that attack.

Sometimes it is necessary to pinch oneself before recognising his new standing. Anderson is only 28 and looks younger; he still speaks in a Burnley whisper, yet it is eight years since he made his Test debut; he is the only bowler in this series, on either side, who has played Ashes cricket in Australia before; he has 205 Test wickets to his name and his coaches are queuing up to say that he is just about the best fast bowler in the world.

Peter Moores, once his England coach, who now sees Anderson – very infrequently – at Lancashire, thinks he can be the best. David Saker, England's bowling coach, only just remembered the claims of South Africa's Dale Steyn in time. 'He [Anderson] has improved his game so much he's either No. 1 or No. 2,' Saker said a couple of days ago. 'Obviously Steyn is a class bowler. It's neck and neck for those two as the best fast bowlers in the world.'

Anderson has certainly been the leading fast bowler in Australia this winter, despite the late intervention of Chris Tremlett. Yet it seldom looks as if it comes naturally for him to lead – or to sledge, for that matter. He has been doing a bit of both in this series.

In explaining how his career was rejuvenated a couple of years ago Anderson mentions Moores, whose name keeps cropping up in relation to the retention of the Ashes this winter. Moores, in his spell as England coach, appointed some of the key men currently behind the scenes: Andy Flower and Richard Halsall have rightly been lauded for their coaching. The England and Wales Cricket Board should be grateful for that. Meanwhile, Kevin Pietersen invites our gratitude for helping to get rid of Moores back in January 2009.

But Anderson takes a far more generous view of Flower's predecessor. 'A key moment for me', he says, 'was in 2008 in New Zealand when Moores told me that he wanted me to lead the attack. Matthew Hoggard and Steve Harmison were both dropped [after the first Test in Hamilton], and he put a lot of faith in me. That boosted my confidence a lot.'

Since then Anderson has kept on improving. For five years he had been a peripheral member of the Test squad after his debut season in 2003. But now he has not missed a Test match for England since the Wellington game of 2008, except when he was rested for the tour of Bangladesh last winter – a sure sign of his growing importance to the side. In that time he has taken 143 wickets in 36 matches. In the list of England wicket-takers he will be cruising past the men he replaced before too long. Hoggard took 248, Harmison 226.

The sledging is a bit of a mystery. He always looks much more like Brian Statham than Freddie Trueman in his approach to batsmen, and he is so soft-spoken that it seems unlikely his voice would carry far enough down the pitch to be audible. But he has obviously been indulging in this series.

He was pressed on the topic last week. 'The verbals get me fired up,' he said. 'But I pick my players.' He did not sledge Ricky Ponting, he explained, because that might be counter-productive, serving only to get the Australia captain going (whereupon he missed the opportunity to add that Ponting has not stayed around long enough to feel the force of his tongue). 'In the past it [sledging] has been an emotional thing. The last couple of years I've been more controlled.'

Anderson's improvement has practically nothing to do with what he does with his tongue, though. It stems from what he does with the ball once he has glided effortlessly up to the crease at a canter, always with something in reserve. He has swung the Kookaburra conventionally when it is new. Sometimes he has found reverse swing when it is older. In the second innings at Melbourne the pitch was so abrasive that there was some reverse swing as early as the 11th over. Just occasionally he pops down the bouncer but by and large he has grown more conservative with experience. He has bought into Saker's 'bowl dry' philosophy.

Anderson is quick to praise Saker for developing his ability to swing the ball by either method. He says he has also learnt how to hit the seam more often from watching Mohammad Asif, and he has studied how Zaheer Khan goes about his swing bowling. He is now confident in his technique but also in his general attitude to the task in hand. He no longer feels naked and despondent when the ball is not hooping around corners, which is a critical advance for a swing bowler.

'Body language is a huge thing,' he says. 'I try to keep my shoulders back now and to be positive. In the past I've been pretty average at that.' On occasions he has looked like a city trader who has lost his iPhone as he sulked back to his mark in the middle of a barren spell. He seems a little more cheerful now.

Alongside the skills has been a new discipline, relentlessly encouraged by an England bowling coach who does not try to overcomplicate matters. In Brisbane Anderson bowled one of the best wicketless spells imaginable on the third morning against Brad Haddin and Mike Hussey. There was only exasperation as the two Australians played and missed and survived. Perhaps the old Anderson would have been disheartened. At the time one wondered whether he could cope with the injustice of it all.

'It was pretty much one of the best spells I've ever seen,' Saker says. 'Every ball he bowled was challenging the top of off stump. As many plans as you can have in world cricket, the best is to hit the top of off stump.'

This was not the same Anderson who had traipsed around Australia four years ago with five wickets at an average of 82 to show for his troubles. At the Gabba he was not too discouraged that such a brilliant spell would go unrewarded.

'What he's taught the rest of the fast-bowling group is to be patient and to bowl in good areas because you'll get the results in the end,' says Saker. So far this means 17 wickets for Anderson in the first four Tests at 29 apiece. More importantly his first-innings bowling in Adelaide and Melbourne gave England the impetus for their two wins.

It was not necessary to be an incurable optimist to envisage success for Anderson in this series. However, the progress of the young or inexperienced pace bowlers, in the absence of Stuart Broad, has exceeded expectations. This is why it now seems conceivable that England might eventually overhaul the three sides above them in the ICC Test rankings table. They now sense that they have genuine depth and variety in their bowling attack.

It is no longer straightforward to pick what might constitute their best attack. The wiseacres pontificated that it was impossible to take 20 wickets in Australia with a four-man bowling attack. Yet England have managed to do that with time to spare in three of the Tests, and their bowlers' haul of 67 wickets in the series is 21 better than the efforts of their Australian counterparts.

Suddenly Steve Finn is a forgotten man, even though he took 14 wickets in the first three Tests – more than any of the Australians has managed so far. 'These have been intense Test matches, and this has been his first Ashes series,' says Flower. 'And it is harder in Australia, especially for a 21-year-old. He has done very, very well.'

Flower may be delighted by Finn's development but he has been taken aback by the progress of Chris Tremlett. 'He has been outstanding on this tour. He was not even a certain pick for the squad. I was actually surprised by the skill he showed in Hobart [against Australia's A team before the first Test].' With Tim Bresnan nervelessly displaying his ability to reverse-swing the ball in Melbourne, England now have real options, especially when Broad is fit and if Graham Onions ever recovers properly from his back operation.

But for the moment Anderson rightly joins the chorus from within the England camp emphasising that they should not look beyond Sydney.

'2–2 is no good to us,' he says. 'It is important to go out on a high.' But there is a jaunty confidence as well as he anticipates the final Test. He adds with a fresh glint in his eye, which was never in evidence on the Ashes tour of four years ago: 'David Saker thinks it will swing in Sydney. And there may be some reverse swing as well.'

Fifth Test

Sydney Cricket Ground
3–7 January 2011

First day

The morning session

BY ANDY BULL

Preamble: Evening, everyone, and a happy new year to you. So here we are at last, the end of the road and the last Test of a long cold winter. So far as I can tell, the prospect of this match has split England supporters into two camps. The first could not give a fig about whether it is won, lost or drawn, and are content with the fact that the Ashes have been secured for another two years. The second thinks that this is the most crucial match of the series, and that given they have not actually won anything yet, England's celebrations have have had more than a touch of hubris about them. They have been making all the right noises, of course, though I did hear Graeme Swann let it slip that he would have settled for 2–2 at the start of the series. But are they all just empty words? England do not tend to deal well with being favourites for anything much, so in a curious way they are as vulnerable right now as they have been at any point since Perth.

The toss: The news from the middle is that Michael Clarke has won his first toss as a Test captain and chosen to bat first. He looks nervous and fidgety as he talks to Sky's Mark Nicholas in the middle. His team is exactly as his coach Tim Nielsen said it would be on Twitter a couple of days back: Hughes, Watson, Khawaja, Clarke, Hussey, Haddin, Smith, Beer,

Johnson, Siddle, Hilfenhaus. And England, of course, are un-changed: Strauss, Cook, Trott, Pietersen, Collingwood, Bell, Pri-or, Bresnan, Swann, Anderson, Tremlett.

1st over: Australia 1–0 (Watson 1, Hughes 0) James Anderson's first delivery swings right onto the meat of Watson's bat. It is pushed to mid-off. A truly dismal piece of fielding from KP gifts Australia the first run of the innings. He was only throw-ing the ball back to Prior after fielding it in the gully, but he man-aged to buzz away an overthrow. 'I've read a lot in the press about how Australia are struggling because they are losing ath-letic young potential cricketers to their nation's most popular sport, Aussie Rules football,' says Tom v. d. Gucht. 'Well, England has suffered the similar problem of youngsters turning their back on cricket for a more glamorous and rewarding sport for years without moaning. The amount of quality would-be sportsmen who have been lost to the UK's number-one pastime, spending all weekend drinking in Wetherspoons, is criminal. I'm sure that some of the bloated burping yahoos I see on a Sunday afternoon in Leeds would have had it in them to make it as an interna-tional cricketer – hell, they seem little use for anything else, and Botham had nearly 20 years at the top.' Not to mention all those who have ended up manning the night desk at the *Guardian*, Tom.

2nd over: Australia 4–0 (Watson 3, Hughes 0) Tremlett will take the second over. His first ball fizzes over the top of middle stump, Watson sucking in his stomach as he plays an ex-aggerated leave. Watson throws a cover drive at the next one but makes an awful mess of it, chopping the ball away to short leg off the inside edge. He connects cleanly with the next deliv-ery though, and gets two runs to extra cover.

3rd over: Australia 5–0 (Watson 3, Hughes 1) Hughes cuffs a single down the leg side.

4th over: Australia 9–0 (Watson 3, Hughes 5) It's an odd feeling to look at an Australian scorecard and not see the name

Ponting at No. 3. It makes the side look fresher but also a lot less intimidating, without any connection at all to the great Australian teams we have seen in the last 15 years. Punter had played as captain in 73 consecutive Tests before this one, a streak second only to Allan Border, who managed 93 in a row. Anyway. That's a lovely shot from Hughes to a rather ropey ball from Tremlett, an emphatic on-drive for four through long-on.

5th over: Australia 10–0 (Watson 4, Hughes 5) Hughes has the sickly pallor of a consumptive taking a stroll by the sea on a cold day at Southwold. 'I wonder,' says Tom Miles, who I suspect may be a glass of wine or two to the wind. 'You may have been asked this before, but who would win in a fight between Chris Tremlett and a shark?' That depends on two things: the type of shark, and which side of bed Tremlett got out of on the day in question.

6th over: Australia 12–0 (Watson 5, Hughes 6) Judging by this delivery, which snorts and shoots past Watson's stumps after pitching, Tremlett got out the right side today. Watson taps the next away square for a single. Then it is Hughes's turn to be beaten all ends up.

7th over: Australia 13–0 (Watson 5, Hughes 7) The camera cuts away to a box in the stands that contains both Giles Clarke and Michael Parkinson. Astonishingly, several other people have actually managed to find a little space between their two egos and squeeze into the seats around them. A brace of lbw appeals from England against Watson, as Anderson twice hits him on the pads. The first was too high and the second was swinging down leg.

8th over: Australia 13–0 (Watson 5, Hughes 7) 'I think the England team may be a little downbeat due to earlier events in Ambridge,' says our resident Marxist beard-fancier Keith Flett. 'The future of the village cricket team may be in doubt if the crisis of the Ambridge ruling class is not resolved, particularly as the counter-hegemonic Grundys appear to be banned from the side.'

9th over: Australia 14–0 (Watson 6, Hughes 7) Watson glances a single away to fine leg. He falls over as he finishes the run. Like Anderson, he seems to be finding it tough to keep his footing on this surface, which has conspicuous green patches dotted across it.

10th over: Australia 14–0 (Watson 6, Hughes 7) Earlier today, by the way, Mr Flett revealed that Matt Prior has been named the hirsute cricketer of the year by the Beard Liberation Front, narrowly beating off competition from Hashim Amla and that regular contender Mohammad Yousuf. Tremlett jags a delivery back in towards Watson, who loses control of his back-foot defensive. The ball pops up towards short leg. Cook dives for it, but the ball lands just outside his grasp.

11th over: Australia 16–0 (Watson 7, Hughes 8) Tim Bresnan is into the attack now, taking over from Anderson. He could be a real threat in these conditions. 'I note that Ponting is sitting in the Aussie dressing room,' points out Vernon. 'I think that is a mistake. Clarke will be judged by this result and should have the opportunity to do it his way. Typical of the mismanagement around the team.'

12th over: Australia 17–0 (Watson 7, Hughes 8) Another good, tight over from Tremlett, with only a solitary leg bye coming from it. Tom Wells says he is 'Snatching the opportunity to be distracted from the nagging feeling this match is all going to go wrong. Re: Tom Miles's shark v. Tremlett query (5th over), surely the greater variable would be if the fight is held on land or at sea? Perhaps, to ensure a level playing field, it should take place in space, with suitable breathing apparatus?'

13th over: Australia 28–0 (Watson 10, Hughes 16) Hughes prods at a length delivery from Tremlett, shovelling it away to point. Moments later Strauss is swearing to himself under his breath as Bresnan fizzes another delivery past the bat. England have had no luck this morning, and their captain is obviously feeling a little disgruntled with his lot.

14th over: Australia 31–0 (Watson 13, Hughes 16) Strauss moves to take Tremlett off, but the bowler asks his captain for one more over before taking a spell. Watson pushes three down the ground, and then Tremlett almost gets the breakthrough. Almost. Hughes edged the ball just short of third slip. 'As I sit here polishing off the last of the leftover New Year champagne, I surmise that this has "Century Opening Stand" written all over it.' What, the champagne? I suggest you need to switch to a better brand, Andrew.

15th over: Australia 33–0 (Watson 13, Hughes 16) It's a sorry reflection of how the Australians have tended to play so far in this series that their batting this morning has felt so impressive. Really all they are doing is fulfilling the most basic requirements of the job – hitting the loose balls, leaving alone everything threatening and blocking anything on target.

16th over: Australia 37–0 (Watson 15, Hughes 20) Four more for Hughes, who slots a full ball from Anderson through long-off for four.

17th over: Australia 43–0 (Watson 15, Hughes 25) Hughes drives two through cover, and then clumps three more down to long-off. This is now his highest score of the series. If he bats into the afternoon this could turn into an ugly day for England.

18th over: Australia 43–0 (Watson 15, Hughes 25) Anderson bowls a maiden to Hughes, but it's a rather flat over, all six balls either sailing by off stump or being blocked by the middle of the bat.

19th over: Australia 45–0 (Watson 15, Hughes 25) 'Polishing off the leftover New Year champagne (14th over)?' gasps Phil Sawyer. 'Andrew's a bit swish. I'm drinking the last of the leftover New Year Old Spice.' Austerity Christmas was it, Phil?

20th over: Australia 46–0 (Watson 17, Hughes 25) Australia have only managed to bat through an entire session once in this series, points out Rob Smyth. What an astonishing statistic. Apart from that stand between Mike Hussey and Brad Haddin in the first Test, Australia's longest partnership has occupied just 33 overs. 'My Mexican girlfriend is asking me to choose between her and the cricket,' says John Holman. 'Currently letting her down gently.'

21st over: Australia 50–0 (Watson 17, Hughes 29) Strauss has cottoned on to the fact that the quicks aren't quite getting it done and has decided to bring Graeme Swann on a little earlier than he typically might on the first day of a match. Mmm. His second ball is short, wide and walloped away for four. 'Who has *leftover* champagne?' scoffs Kat Petersen. 'Slackers. Invite me next time.'

22nd over: Australia 51–0 (Watson 18, Hughes 29) Anderson has a proper scowl on his face now, and is pawing at the bowling crease in dissatisfaction. Here's Steve Kennett: 'Please warn John Holman that the phrase "letting her down gently" could imply an inflatable "girlfriend".'

23rd over: Australia 53–0 (Watson 19, Hughes 30) Bumble is revealing how he spent his new year: 'Hotel room, room service, darts on TV.' It's enough to make you shed a little tear on his behalf. Two singles from Swann's second over.

24th over: Australia 53–0 (Watson 19, Hughes 31) Hughes contents himself with another single. He's played watchfully and well so far today.

25th over: Australia 54–0 (Watson 19, Hughes 31) Swann continues to bowl from around the wicket to Hughes, pinning him back in the crease with a series of faster, flatter deliveries. It's another maiden. 'Being a sad, geeky sort, I was wondering if anyone has ever bowled at first-class or international level using both spin and pace – mixing it up mid-over?' asks Anil Haji. 'It would be interesting to see the bowler coming in from a short run-up and the batsman having no idea whether the delivery would be an 80 mph seamer or an off-break.'

26th over: Australia 54–0 (Watson 19, Hughes 31) Tremlett is back into the attack as Strauss tries to conjure a wicket before the break. It's an excellent maiden over. Back to that last over: curiously enough, Anil, someone else was asking that exact question earlier on in the innings. The answer is that no one has mixed spin and real pace on a ball-by-ball basis. Plenty of quicks have bowled cutters, but otherwise the difference in action and approach would just be too easy to pick. There have been plenty of people who have been able to mix medium-pace and spin bowling though. Colin Miller is one who comes to mind, and Bomber Wells would be another.

27th over: Australia 54–0 (Watson 19, Hughes 31) A third maiden in a row, so here is David Adams: 'Good to see the Aussies make a fight of it. Reading Kevin Mitchell in the *Observer* today, I was almost feeling guilty about us kicking them while they're down. Then I remembered that Test cricket in England has survived despite: (1) The national team being awful for about 15 years, (2) The incompetence and venality of its administrators, (3) Football-obsessed media, (4) Having had Ray Illingworth as coach, and (5) Having John Major publicly declare his support for the game while still in office. All the Aussies have to worry about is competition from various forms of egg chasing. I'm sure they'll be fine.'

28th over: Australia 55–0 (Watson 19, Hughes 31) A solitary leg bye. Australia seem to have had an extensive lesson in the art of 'proper creekit' between the fourth and fifth Tests.

Maybe they hired that walking continent of common sense Geoff Boycott as a batting consultant.

29th over: Australia 55–0 (Watson 19, Hughes 31) Bresnan is back on with lunch looming.

WICKET! 30th over: Hughes c Collingwood b Tremlett 31 (Australia 55–1) England have managed to squeeze in one last over, and oh what a waste! After all that hard work, Hughes falls to the third ball of the final over of the session. He didn't have to play at that delivery from Tremlett. It was short and wide, but he lost concentration and flapped at it. The ball shot off the edge and went straight to slip. What a fillip for England.

Australia 55–1

The afternoon session

BY ROB SMYTH

Preamble: Hello. That was a peculiar little session. It was pretty high-class stuff – and the phrases 'proper Test cricket' and 'old-fashioned Test cricket' have been used approximately 974,123,913 times in the last two hours – but it was so low-key that it could have been soundtracked by Brian Eno. The series is alive, but the Ashes aren't, and that showed this morning. This isn't a dead rubber but nor is it quite a live one. So we need a name for this rubber (as the actress didn't say to the bishop, honk). And as I can't think of one, you lot had better come to the party, step up to the plate, etc.

30th over: Australia 61–1 (Watson 19, Khawaja 6) There are three balls remaining of the over that Tremlett started before lunch, and they will be faced by the first Muslim to play Test cricket for Australia, Usman Khawaja. He has a first-class average of 51.70, so clearly he's no Usman Afzaal. He tucks his first ball off the pads for two, prompting the loudest cheer of the day, and then pulls his second ball handsomely through midwicket for four. Shot! What a lovely moment that was. 'Would the term a limp rubber just go too far beyond the smut levels of even the OBO?' says Lizzy Ammon.

31st over: Australia 67–1 (Watson 24, Khawaja 7) Watson was boundary-less before lunch, but he pings Anderson off the pads for four to continue Australia's good start to the session. 'Given that this rubber is something that you find after the ashes,' says Gary Naylor, 'is it a damp squib?'

32nd over: Australia 75–1 (Watson 24, Khawaja 15) Tremlett spears in a filthy leg-stump half-volley that Khawaja pings through square leg for four. The next ball is too close for the cut, but Khawaja plays it anyway and the ball flies into the ground and then over the slips. That takes him to 15 from eight balls. 'Not dead, not alive – a zombie, surely,' says Kat Petersen. 'Or a vampire. Or some sort of undead creature. (Not really my area of expertise.)'

33rd over: Australia 79–1 (Watson 28, Khawaja 15) Watson uppercuts Anderson over the slips for four more and then rifles a drive to mid-on. He did the hard work this morning, and now he is going to have his fun.

34th over: Australia 79–1 (Watson 28, Khawaja 15) Khawaja has shown us a few attacking strokes; now we see some defensive ones in a maiden from Tremlett. He has looked really good so far. 'If it's not quite alive nor quite dead, does this make this Test Schrödinger's rubber?' says James Galloway. 'Probably not.'

35th over: Australia 83–1 (Watson 32, Khawaja 15)

Anderson's first ball is short, and Watson dumps it disdainfully over midwicket for four. He had 19 from 85 balls this morning, and that makes it 13 from 12 since lunch.

36th over: Australia 84–1 (Watson 32, Khawaja 16) Khawaja looks the goods, as they say, and defends solidly before flicking a single off the pads.

37th over: Australia 84–1 (Watson 32, Khawaja 16) A maiden from Anderson to Khawaja.

38th over: Australia 89–1 (Watson 33, Khawaja 20) Tremlett has a strangled lbw shout against Khawaja, who then cuts wristily for four. It was in the air but he picked the gap carefully. 'As it's neither alive nor dead, is this Lembit Opik's Career Rubber?' says Ant Pease.

BAD LIGHT STOPS PLAY 39th over: Australia 92–1 (Watson 34, Khawaja 22) 'Nasty band of rain creeping up on the radar,' writes Mike Selvey at the SCG. 'Here by tea at latest, I reckon.' And now the players are coming off anyway, because of bad light. Bah.

2.56 a.m.: I have no idea what's going on. So what's new, etc. The artificial lights are now on, and the umpires – who didn't leave the field – are signalling for somebody to come onto the field. It could be the players, or they might just want to inspect David Lloyd's socks.

2.59 a.m.: The players are back on, for the time being.

40th over: Australia 96–1 (Watson 38, Khawaja 22) Tremlett (14–6–32–1) continues after that short break. He has been formidably good in this series, and just as I type that he drifts onto the pads and is flipped through midwicket for four with a wristy flourish by Watson. Beautiful stroke. 'The answer you are looking for, Rob, is GHOST Rubber,' says Ben Hendy. 'In terms of the prize at stake, it's dead, but it's lingering around to pass on a message to those that have survived it – either (a) England are all that and Australia have a lot of work to do, or (b) England aren't quite there yet and there's life in the old Australia yet.'

41st over: Australia 98–1 (Watson 38, Khawaja 24)
Khawaja cuts Bresnan for a couple. 'Shall I compare three to an IKEA sofa?' was not one of Shakespeare's great lines, but watching Khawaja thus far makes me think of that Ed Norton line in *Fight Club*: 'Whatever else happens, I've got that sofa problem solved.' Australia might think the same about their No. 3 problem in a couple of hours' time.

42nd over: Australia 101–1 (Watson 41, Khawaja 24) It seemed likely that Andrew Strauss would soon challenge Usman Khawaja with a change of pace – but it's Paul Collingwood rather than Graeme Swann who is coming into the attack. He might get it to do a bit in these sweaty conditions, and indeed Watson drives an outswinger just short of the man at short extra. The next ball is too short and cut for three. This is Watson's 14th Test innings against England; 11 of them have been between 34 and 62. 'That rain break was surely something akin to when an amateur sports club's tour bus gets to 40 minutes after the first toilet stop,' says Lee Calvert, 'with Strauss as the club sec pleading with driver Aleem Dar: "I know you're not meant to stop here, mate, and I know we should have gone back there, most of us did, but we've all broken our seal and it's either let us off or your floor is in danger. We'll only be two minutes, honest."'

43rd over: Australia 101–1 (Watson 41, Khawaja 24)
Bresnan goes up confidently for lbw when Watson plays no stroke, but it looked too high and Billy Bowden didn't engage the crooked finger. Replays showed it was going miles over the stumps.

44th over: Australia 101–1 (Watson 41, Khawaja 24)
Collingwood sneaks one past Khawaja's outside edge. 'The wobbler!' says Nasser Hussain, with the glee of a wrestling comment-

ator describing a signature move. Another maiden. Australia look like a side who know a break is coming and who, as a result, don't want to take any risks. Is it cowardly to play for rain? 'If this is not a "dead" rubber, then as any fan of US presidential politics (aka "nerd") will tell you, this must be a "lame duck" rubber,' says Ian Rubinstein. 'It is still officially in power, but everyone knows that nothing real can come of it.'

WICKET! 45th over: Watson c Strauss b Bresnan 45 (Australia 105–2) Shane Watson's bizarre run of scores against England continues, and he punches his bat in frustration. He has more hard-luck stories than a Steve Buscemi character propping up a dimly lit bar. Watson pushed with hard hands outside off stump at Bresnan, it flew off the edge, and Strauss at first slip took a good low catch.

45th over: Australia 108–2 (Khawaja 24, Clarke 3) Clarke waves his first ball as Australian Test captain through the covers for three. The stump cam, meanwhile, picked up a desperate cry of 'Awww no!' from Watson even before the ball had reached Strauss. 'Not sure you would have used the same words, Nass,' deadpans Beefy.

46th over: Australia 108–2 (Khawaja 24, Clarke 3) A maiden from Anderson to Clarke. 'Could someone get a clip of that "oh no" from Watson and tart it up a bit?' says Marie Meyer. 'I want it for my ring tone.'

47th over: Australia 111–2 (Khawaja 26, Clarke 4) Clarke is having words with Billy Bowden, and I don't think he's asking him what facial moisturiser he uses. There is nothing to gain for Australia in this little spell, so he'll want to get off the field as soon as possible. 'What's your view on estate-bottled rum?' says John Starbuck, somehow knowing that this is the one question I've spent my entire life waiting to be asked. 'It doesn't have quite the cachet of single malts or named chateaux, but Appleton's is the only one our local supermarket stocks. I've never been able to compare it to its peers. I'm drinking it now as we've finally got round to the (Captain Morgan rum-fed) Xmas cake and have the taste. Can any OBO reader advise?' I've steered clear of rum after a once-in-a-generation hangover in Jamaica a few years back, so it's over to our twos of readers.

RAIN STOPS PLAY 48th over: Australia 111–2 (Khawaja 26, Clarke 4) Anderson gets one to pop from a length, and Khawaja does well to soften his hands and drop the ball down in front of him. He then nods his head towards Anderson, but in a way that an experienced batsman might nod his head at a young bowler, rather than the other way round. Keep bowling like that, Jimmy, and you might go far. We've only seen 59 balls, but this kid has been really impressive. And that'll be our lot for the time being. After five balls of that over, with rain starting to fall, the umpires call for the covers to come on.

3.45 a.m.: They have taken an early tea.

Australia 111–2

The evening session

BY ANDY BULL

4.05 a.m.: Teatime is over, folks, but the rain is still falling. Sky have settled for the long haul and are showing a documentary on the 2005 Ashes.

4.50 a.m.: The covers are coming off and the ground staff are mopping up. There are still a few clouds overhead though. Play will start in 15 minutes, at 5.05 a.m. That's a satisfyingly swift restart.

49th over: Australia 111–2 (Khawaja 26, Clarke 4) Bresnan starts at the other end, on a pitch that has been sweating under a plastic sheet for the last 90 minutes or so. His first few deliveries all hug off stump, and Clarke comes forward to meet them all. The final two deliveries are wider, and Clarke leaves them well alone.

50th over: Australia 112–2 (Khawaja 27, Clarke 4) Anderson continues. Khawaja taps away a single to square leg and Australia are off Nelson, so we can all put both feet back on the floor.

51st over: Australia 113–2 (Khawaja 28, Clarke 4) Khawaja taps another single off his hips. 'Lovely comment from Gower there,' says Ben Hendy. '"[Khawaja's] a qualified pilot so obviously I admire him . . ." He looks to be a pretty decent cricketer too, David.'

WICKET! 51st over: Clarke c Anderson b Bresnan 4 (Australia 113–3) Clarke cuts a catch straight to Jimmy Anderson at gully. That's a sorry way to get out, and he walks off with his head hanging down, dragging his bat behind him. On some other, happier day the ball would have shot away for four. Bizarrely, as Bresnan ran over to his teammates to celebrate the wicket he clattered into KP, and the two of them tumbled over onto the turf like a pair of Keystone cricketers.

52nd over: Australia 116–3 (Khawaja 29, Hussey 2) Hussey is in then, and Anderson is on. He snicks his first ball just short of slip, as he has done so often in this series. He averages over 100 in his five Tests on this ground, so England can't afford to let him get away.

53rd over: Australia 120–3 (Khawaja 33, Hussey 2) The kid Khawaja has *cojones*, and no word of a lie. He unfurls his whippy pull shot, fetching a length ball from outside off and depositing it over towards backward square leg for four. 'Trying to fathom the score (111), Nelson and feet on the floor,' says Andrew Goulden. 'Two fat ladies and legs eleven I get but I'm a little lost on that one.' If it's any consolation, Andrew, the feeling is mutual because your email makes half sense at best.

54th over: Australia 123–3 (Khawaja 33, Hussey 5) Hussey slices three runs past gully. A rather creaky-limbed Andrew Strauss hurries after it, pulling the ball back just inside the boundary rope.

55th over: Australia 128–3 (Khawaja 37, Hussey 6) The Barmy Army's trumpeter bursts into a chirpy rendition of 'John Brown's Body' as Khawaja slots a drive away past gully. The ball was in the air as it passed by the fielder, so England indulge in a few eye-rolls and heavenwards glances. Khawaja is in behind the next delivery. This has been a very impressive debut so far.

56th over: Australia 130–3 (Khawaja 37, Hussey 8) Is that out? England think so. 'Good leave, great leave!' shouts Nasser. 'But is it out?' The answer, fortunately for Nass, is no. The ball spat like fat from the pan after pitching, trimming Hussey's shirt on its way through. Strauss figured as much, and talked his teammates out of asking for a referral.

57th over: Australia 130–3 (Khawaja 37, Hussey 8) Bresnan tears through a maiden over to Khawaja.

58th over: Australia 134–3 (Khawaja 37, Hussey 12) Chris Tremlett is back into the attack. The light is closing in again at the SCG, and Bumble suggests that there is more rain on the way. I confess I'm just about ready to drift off – my eyelids are weighing awful heavy – so I wouldn't mind another rain break too much. Hussey chops four past slip. He's looking in ominously good touch. Here's Adam Levine: 'With Botham constantly banging on about Strauss's conservative captaincy and how he should have a third slip, this seems like an opportune moment to remind everybody of Sir Ian Terence Botham's record as England captain: 12 matches, 0 wins, 4 losses, 8 draws.'

59th over: Australia 134–3 (Khawaja 37, Hussey 12) Strauss decides to see whether Khawaja can play spin as well as he does pace. Swann comes on for a bowl from around the wicket, with a slip, a forward short leg and a silly point in place.

WICKET! 59th over: Khawaja c Trott b Swann 37 (Australia 134–4) After poking and prodding nervously at Swann's first five balls, Khawaja snaps and tries to launch a slog sweep for four. He doesn't catch it correctly and the ball floats up to Jonathan Trott, whom Swann and Strauss had cannily placed at short fine leg. Khawaja's accomplished debut innings comes to a rather abrupt and disappointing end. He's been outfoxed by the savvy Swann. In the stands, Khawaja's mother looks glum but eventually joins the applause as her son strolls off.

RAIN STOPS PLAY By the time Sky have cut back from their ad break, the rain has returned at the SCG and the players have gone off the field. Bah. That was an excellent little spell for England. They took two wickets for 23 runs in ten overs.

6.30 a.m.: There are only a few stragglers left in the stands. I've already fallen asleep in my chair, rousing myself with a loud inadvertent snort as my head snapped down onto my chest. Assuming there isn't any more play, the match will have lost 31 overs today. They can make up some of that by starting 30 minutes early tomorrow. The good news is that the forecast is just fine for the next four days.

Right, that's it folks. Stumps have been pulled and play is over for the day. I'll see you back here tomorrow.

Australia 134–4

Second day

The morning session

BY ANDY BULL

Preamble: Evening, everyone, how do? I'm looking forward to today's play, after a rather sluggish start to the match yesterday. You'll be pleased to hear that the weather forecast is set fair, for what it is worth. There are 98 overs to play today, so sit back and enjoy.

60th over: Australia 134–4 (Hussey 12, Haddin 0) Chris Tremlett, outstanding yesterday, will start the attack for the day. Mike Hussey is on strike, and he has three slips lining up over his shoulder. I was reading about Tremlett's grandfather today, the great Somerset batsman Maurice. He started out as a fast bowler, and earned rave reviews from Jim Swanton after taking five wickets in five overs against Middlesex on his first-class debut in 1947. But he developed the yips after England took him on tour to the West Indies, and his bowling slipped away to the point where he could hardly get through an over at all in the middle, though he was always excellent in the nets. He was terrified of the barracking he would get from the crowds if he messed up. His grandson has started with a maiden.

61st over: Australia 137–4 (Hussey 14, Haddin 1) Haddin snicks an inside edge down to fine leg, his first runs of the day.

62nd over: Australia 141–4 (Hussey 14, Haddin 3) Haddin whips two more down to fine leg. 'At a risk of sounding like a whinging Pom, I just want to share the awful regulations on drinking,' says Jerome Harris. 'The SCG limits customers to mid-strength beer and cider only, small glasses and no pass-outs so people can't nip across the road to have some proper drinks at lunch or tea. This means that the atmosphere is totally subdued and the crowd never gets properly pumped.' Let's be straight, Jerome, by 'properly pumped' you really mean 'utterly hammered', don't you?

WICKET! 63rd over: Haddin c Prior b Anderson 3 (Australia 141–5) Oh mercy, what a terrible shot that is. Haddin swings a loose and lazy cut shot at a wide ball from Anderson, snicking it straight into Matt Prior's mitts. Strange player, Haddin. He can seem so capable and committed a batsman, but is also so prone to playing truly awful shots outside off stump.

64th over: Australia 146–5 (Hussey 17, Smith 0) This Australian line-up is so flimsy, it almost feels as though England only have to dry up the runs for a ten-minute stretch and they'll be sure to take a wicket. 'Please pass on my commiserations to Jerome Harris for the tribulations he had to endure yesterday,' deadpans Ant Pease. 'Here I was sat in Essex watching the cricket on a faltering Sky Player connection with my inconsolable eight-week-old daughter screaming in my ears for the whole of the morning session. But I did have full-strength beer to hand. He's a trooper.'

65th over: Australia 146–5 (Hussey 17, Smith 0) Another maiden over for England, despite Smith's best efforts to hit the ball out of the ground before he has got off zero.

66th over: Australia 151–5 (Hussey 20, Smith 2) That's a wonderful ball from Anderson, sliding across the face of Hussey's bat and slipping past the outside edge. 'There's nothing you can do about those ones,' says Athers sagely. 'You just have to hope you miss them.'

67th over: Australia 155–5 (Hussey 24, Smith 2) Tim Bresnan is on. Hussey leaves his first five balls well alone, and then slots the sixth down the ground for four. Marvellous batting from Mr Bloody Cricket, as our esteemed correspondent Mike Selvey called him earlier in the series.

68th over: Australia 155–5 (Hussey 24, Smith 2) A double change. Strauss is giving his two strike bowlers a break before the new ball, which is available in 12 overs. So Swann is on.

69th over: Australia 157–5 (Hussey 26, Smith 2) 'A word of advice for Jerome Harris on his future trip to the SCG,' says Damian Hocking. 'Take a half-bottle or hip flask of whisky/vodka/rum tucked in the back of your shorts and just top up bottles of coke or lemonade. That removes the boredom of the half rat-power beers.'

70th over: Australia 158–5 (Hussey 26, Smith 3) Swann hustles through another over to the jittery Smith, who manages to toe-end a single down to fine leg.

71st over: Australia 159–5 (Hussey 26, Smith 4) Another tight over from Bresnan.

73rd over: Australia 163–5 (Hussey 29, Smith 5) What a lovely duel this series has seen between Hussey and Swann. And again you'd say that Hussey is just getting the better of it. He flicks three away to leg.

74th over: Australia 163–5 (Hussey 29, Smith 5) Another maiden from Bresnan. It's drier than Prohibition America out there.

75th over: Australia 165–5 (Hussey 29, Smith 6) Just a single from Swann's latest over.

76th over: Australia 165–5 (Hussey 29, Smith 7) Another over, another solitary run. Tick tock, tick tock, who is going to break first?

77th over: Australia 167–5 (Hussey 30, Smith 8) Swann finally serves up a loose delivery, but Smith isn't able to do much with it. He and Hussey trade singles later in the over.

78th over: Australia 167–5 (Hussey 30, Smith 8) Strauss applies a little Collyfilla to the innings, giving Collingwood a couple before the new ball. And he is almost repaid with a brilliant wicket: the ball snicks off the inside edge, hits Hussey's pad and loops up into the air. Collingwood runs forward in his follow-through and dives forward, arms outstretched. His fingertips can't quite reach the ball though.

79th over: Australia 167–5 (Hussey 31, Smith 9) Either Swann is speeding up or I'm slowing down, because I can hardly keep up with him. Two singles from his latest.

WICKET! 80th over: Hussey b Collingwood 33 (Australia 171–6) Well, I'll be . . . Collingwood has bowled Mike Hussey! That's preposterous. It was the final ball of the 80th over as well, so the tail will have to face the new ball. Collingwood is jubilant, leaping up into the air and shouting out loud till he is red in the face. You just cannot keep this man out of the game. He had fed Hussey five balls wide of off, and then slipped in a slightly tighter, straighter delivery. Hussey tried to drive it, but the ball ricocheted off the inside edge, into his pads and on into off stump. 'That's it!' bellows Gary Naylor. 'Colly should retire right now and bathe in the glory!'

81st over: Australia 173–6 (Smith 10, Johnson 1) Anderson has taken the new ball and is making it hoop around, but to be honest everyone is still talking about that last over. 'People need to kick Paul Collingwood whilst he's down more often,' suggests Dan Lucas. 'As a Colly Apologist (Colipologist?) of six years, I take great pleasure in seeing him get crucified in the media as it always seems to bring out (yet another) great performance from him. Hopefully this wicket is the start of a match-winning performance.'

WICKET! 85th over: Smith c Collingwood b Anderson 18 (Australia 187–7) Smith goes in the most predictably soft fashion, caught flailing a drive at a delivery outside off stump. It was a very wide ball, and he flashed at it, turning his head just in time to see Collingwood – who else? – take the catch at third slip. I've had some bad technical Gremlins since England took the new ball – sorry about that. You missed a couple of good overs from Tremlett and Anderson.

WICKET! Siddle c Strauss b Anderson 2 (Australia 189–8) That's far too good for Siddle, who edges an away-swinger from Anderson straight to first slip. Australia are collapsing fast here.

86th over: Australia 190–8 (Johnson 6, Hilfenhaus 0) That's a brute of a ball from Tremlett, spitting up at Hilfenhaus's throat from a full length. Earlier in the over he had the ball swinging both ways in the air after pitching, which caused Prior all sorts of problems. He's bowled wonderfully well.

87th over: Australia 199–8 (Johnson 13, Hilfenhaus 2) Mitchell Johnson smears four runs down through long-off as Anderson tries a full inswinger. He repeats the dose later in the over, but doesn't catch it quite so cleanly. So he gets three. Hilfenhaus adds two to that, making it nine from the over. England want to be just a little careful here. Johnson could easily add 40 quick runs that could make a lot of difference to the match.

88th over: Australia 202–8 (Johnson 16, Hilfenhaus 2) And now Johnson is turning down singles to try and protect Hilfenhaus from the strike. He does it twice, and is booed and jeered by the crowd on both occasions. By the end of the over they are giving him a full slow handclap. It's idiotic behaviour. Johnson is just trying to do his job properly.

89th over: Australia 207–8 (Johnson 16, Hilfenhaus 6)
Johnson swings wildly at a length ball from Anderson, missing it altogether. He's fortunate that his stumps haven't been scattered across the ground. Again he leaves it till late in the over to take a run, this time off the fourth ball.

90th over: Australia 208–8 (Johnson 17, Hilfenhaus 6)
Tim Bresnan is into the attack now, and all of a sudden Johnson decides to take a single off the first ball of the over. Bresnan bowls well at Hilfenhaus, targeting his off stump. But the batsman's defensive technique is equal to it.

91st over: Australia 213–8 (Johnson 18, Hilfenhaus 10)
What a frustrating little stand this is turning into. Hilfenhaus bunts a boundary away to square leg, and that takes him into double figures. 'Just had a look at Michael Beer,' says James Andrews. 'He's 26. 26! I had hoped that if the Australians were calling up a new cap with just seven first-class appearances to his name he'd at least be young. Tim Bresnan is younger. Stuart Broad is younger. Steve Finn is five years younger. Alastair Cook is younger – and has a lower first-class bowling average.'

92nd over: Australia 219–8 (Johnson 24, Hilfenhaus 10)
Johnson heaves a pull over mid-on, and then drags the next ball around the corner for four. Bresnan walks away muttering darkly to himself.

93rd over: Australia 221–8 (Johnson 25, Hilfenhaus 11)
Hilfenhaus windmills his bat through an optimistic hoick at a length ball from Tremlett, who has now replaced Anderson. He gets nowhere near it. 'Don't begrudge the Aussies a tail that wags,' says Cheri Powers. 'Didn't Panesar once do a great job in batting against Australia? [I guess you are thinking of Cardiff

2009?] I can't remember, but especially when they are probably going to lose the match anyway, let them enjoy the tail.'

94th over: Australia 224–8 (Johnson 25, Hilfenhaus 13) These two have put on 33 together now. That becomes 35 as Hilfenhaus toe-ends a lofted cut down to backward point. Bresnan is bowling some lovely deliveries now, breaking the ball towards the slips off the pitch. The shame of it is that Hilfenhaus can't get anywhere near the ball.

95th over: Australia 230–8 (Johnson 31, Hilfenhaus 14) This should be the last over of the session, and Johnson starts it with a flick for four down to fine leg. By the end of the over he and Hilfenhaus have taken their stand on to 41. So that's lunch. What an entertaining session.

Australia 230–8

The afternoon session

BY ROB SMYTH

Preamble: Hello. So, what'll it be, folks: a repeat of Adelaide and Melbourne, or of Perth? England piling up a monstrous lead, or a run-fuelled Mitchell Johnson swinging Australia back into the game? The latter might be marginal favourite, you know, because the ball was doing a fair bit this morning, and Johnson and Ben Hilfenhaus have added 41 priceless runs for the ninth wicket in a manner that evoked the third Test. England would want a first-innings lead of at least 100 to feel comfortable.

96th over: Australia 238–8 (Johnson 33, Hilfenhaus 15) Tim Bresnan starts after lunch, and his first ball is sliced in the

air but wide of gully by Hilfenhaus. Johnson then plays a storming straight drive for two. Later in the over Bresnan spears some
total nonsense down the leg side for four byes. 'What do you do
in the lunch break, Rob?' asks Clare Davies. I tend to just leer
at the screen, same as during play. There isn't much else to do
in King's Cross at 2 a.m. on a weeknight. Well, there is, but ~~we
don't get paid for a couple of weeks~~ it's probably best not to
think about that.

97th over: Australia 239–8 (Johnson 34, Hilfenhaus 15)
Andrew Strauss turns to Graeme Swann, and Mitchell Johnson
drives a single to bring up a superb fifty partnership, from only 68
balls. 'You're a cricket expert,' says Mac Millings, 'paid to watch,
report on and give your opinion about the game. You have an
absurdly detailed memory for the history of the game, allied
to an unquenchable thirst for Statsguru-based research. So, tell
us: how's your Ashes fantasy team doing?' Some of us, Millings,
aren't so sad that we need to validate our existence through
Fantasy Cricket. Some of us can validate our existence by naming
all of England's 29 players from the 1989 Ashes series. So there.

98th over: Australia 250–8 (Johnson 39, Hilfenhaus 21)
England are a wee bit sloppy at the moment. 11 from that
Bresnan over, including a magnificent six off the last ball from Hilfenhaus, driven mightily over midwicket on the walk. The partnership is up to 61 from 78 balls.

99th over: Australia 261–8 (Johnson 50, Hilfenhaus 21)
This is wonderful stuff from Johnson. He DiMaggios Swann's first
two deliveries over midwicket for four and then six. A single two
balls later brings him to a superb fifty, his sixth in Tests, from only
63 balls. England are right in a game here.

100th over: Australia 263–8 (Johnson 53, Hilfenhaus 21)
Johnson hardly stopped to celebrate that fifty, confining himself
to a brisk, business-like wave of his bat. He wants more. And he
gets them. He carves two out to deep point, then pushes a single

to the on side. A misfield at slip allows the batsmen to sneak another single and then . . .

WICKET! 100th over: Johnson b Bresnan 53 (Australia 265–9) That's one big shot too many from Johnson, who plays around a straight ball that goes on to knock over his off stump. He walks off to an ovation from a grateful Australian crowd, who have been starved of much worth clapping in recent days.

101st over: Australia 266–9 (Hilfenhaus 22, Beer 0) Thanks to Andy for describing that wicket while I took the briefest cat-nap in history. Swann skids an arm ball past the outside edge of Beer, who defends solidly for the remainder of the over.

102nd over: Australia 267–9 (Hilfenhaus 24, Beer 0) Hilfenhaus misses a monstrous mow at Bresnan, digs out a yorker and then gets a single off the penultimate ball to keep the strike. That ball from Bresnan was the fastest of the match: 91.0 mph. It's 27 years since Australia failed to make 300 in four consecutive first innings on home soil.

103rd over: Australia 270–9 (Hilfenhaus 25, Beer 2) Beer, contrary to reports, is not a total clown with the bat. He defends pretty solidly and then tucks Swann to fine leg for his first runs in Test cricket.

104th over: Australia 274–9 (Hilfenhaus 28, Beer 2) Hilfenhaus has another swipe at Bresnan, and the ball flies over the slips for a couple. Pietersen shakes his head and cusses. Bresnan's next ball is a bouncer that Aleem Dar calls wide, and the next, to compound his frustration, boings past another almighty heave from Hilfenhaus.

105th over: Australia 279–9 (Hilfenhaus 33, Beer 2) Hilfenhaus is seeing it like a cricket ball, which isn't always the case. Australia loves a cool Beer, and he's defending calmly just now. Gotta love those Beer puns.

106th over: Australia 280–9 (Hilfenhaus 34, Beer 2) Hilfenhaus drags Bresnan's fourth ball for a single, and the next two deliveries won't be in the 'What Happened Next?' section of *A Question of Sport* any time soon.

WICKET! 107th over: Hilfenhaus c Prior b Anderson 34 (Australia 280 all out) Just as I was marking out my run-up for the great window jump – it's two whole floors, not counting the mezzanine – a wicket falls. Jimmy Anderson was brought back to end the nonsense, and did so with his first ball. Hilfenhaus tried to tennis-smash a short ball that flew off the edge, and Prior took a fine leaping catch. Anderson ends with the splendid figures of 30.1–7–66–4, but that's a superb comeback from Australia, who slapped 91 runs for the last two wickets.

England first innings

1st over: England 3–0 (Strauss 2, Cook 1) Ben Hilfenhaus will take the new ball. It's what he does for a living. His first ball swings nicely back into Strauss, who tucks it off the pads for a single. The second ball is a carbon copy, with Cook getting off the mark.

2nd over: England 10–0 (Strauss 3, Cook 7) This is an interesting and admirably positive move from Michael Clarke, who has given the new ball to Mitchell Johnson. This is only the fourth Test in which he has opened the bowling since that illusion-shattering tour of England in 2009. It's worth the gamble. His first ball is very encouraging, full and swinging away from Strauss.

3rd over: England 20–0 (Strauss 13, Cook 7) Strauss punishes some unusually brainless bowling from Hilfenhaus, pulling consecutive short balls for four. 'Have there been any English wrist-spinners in recent times?' asks Michael Gascoigne. 'Since

1989 I can remember watching Hemmings, Such, Croft, Udal, Swann and Pietersen. Have there been any leggies?' In Test cricket I can think of three: Mike Atherton, Ian Salisbury and Chris Schofield. Their combined Test bowling average? 88.59.

4th over: England 21–0 (Strauss 13, Cook 8) Johnson is working up a fair pace – everything over 90 mph in that over – and beats Cook with a decent delivery that swings away at the last minute. 'Evening, Rob, evening, Andy,' says John Foster. 'I'm currently reading *Beyond a Boundary* and loving it. Can you or my fellow night-owl OBOists recommend any other cricket books suitable for the relative novice?' Buy everything Gideon Haigh has ever written. Then buy them again, in case the dog eats one.

5th over: England 21–0 (Strauss 13, Cook 8) A maiden from Hilfenhaus to Cook.

6th over: England 26–0 (Strauss 18, Cook 8) Johnson's first ball is tripe, short, wide and slapped for four by Strauss. Cook tries to repeat the shot later in the over but is beaten for pace, and then he clips one into the left arm of Hughes at short leg. Technically that's a dropped catch but, well, you try catching those.

7th over: England 30–0 (Strauss 21, Cook 9) This has been an impressive and positive start from Strauss, who drives Hilfenhaus through mid-off for three more. 'I am at Vancouver Airport, waiting for a flight home to London,' says Tara Taylor. 'Though Vancouver is a sensational place for a holiday, it's not so good for news on cricket. I used up my phone's data-roaming allowance reading the OBO during the Boxing Day Test – my lifeline of sanity in these historic times! Thanks, guys!'

8th over: England 36–0 (Strauss 26, Cook 10) Siddle replaces Johnson, who bowled a reasonably encouraging spell of 3–0–13–0. Strauss takes five from three deliveries – two, two and one – and now has 26 from 20 deliveries. It's like watching a left-handed Trevor Ward.

9th over: England 46–0 (Strauss 36, Cook 9) Hilfenhaus is only a fraction short that time but it's enough for Strauss to swivel-pull a stunning six, one leg sticking out with a dainty elegance of which even Craig Revel Horwood would approve.

10th over: England 50–0 (Strauss 36, Cook 13) Siddle swerves some barely forgivable nonsense down the leg side to Cook, and Haddin does extremely well to save four byes. They can't stem the flow of runs, however, and later in the over Cook creams a pull in front of square to bring up an authoritative, initiative-seizing fifty partnership in only ten overs.

11th over: England 54–0 (Strauss 38, Cook 13) Shane Watson replaces Ben Hilfenhaus (5–1–27–0) and swings some more filth down the leg side, and again Haddin saves four byes with a full-length dive. The wagon wheel of the fifty partnership shows how poor Australia's bowling has been, with just three runs in the 'V'. They have bowled far too many short balls, and England have nailed them. 'I'm in Buenos Aires – can any OBOers offer advice on where I can catch coverage of the Test?' asks Tom Aldred. 'In return I can offer the nugget that a good friend of mine was in a barber-shop quartet with Alastair Cook. There goes his reputation as a goodie two-shoes.'

12th over: England 55–0 (Strauss 38, Cook 13) David Hasselhoff is at the SCG, talking to Glenn McGrath. 'Give over,' says Bumble. 'Give over! I'm not having it! The Hoff!' Haddin lets a straight one go through for a bye. 'Reading the OBO here in Tokyo,' says Steve King. 'Why don't you celebrate sixes more in the OBOs? They're pretty rare – rarer than Aussie wickets even – and that Strauss effort sounded sumptuous. You could at least put them in bold or something.' We have a strict no-chevron-abuse policy at the *Guardian*.

13th over: England 58–0 (Strauss 40, Cook 14) This game is all about David Hasselhoff at the moment. The camera only has eyes for him between deliveries.

14th over: England 65–0 (Strauss 45, Cook 15) Strauss drives Siddle gun-barrel straight for four. This has been a delightful innings; he has 45 from 41 balls now. It's like watching a left-handed David Fulton!

15th over: England 69–0 (Strauss 45, Cook 19) Cook flicks Watson right off middle stump for a couple, prompting Watson to put his hands to his head. The camera cuts to the tunnel, where Shane Warne is bowling to David Hasselhoff. Dear me. Imagine those two on the pull. Lock up your comedy inflatables. Cook flicks two more through square leg.

16th over: England 73–0 (Strauss 49, Cook 19) That's another storming stroke from Strauss, this time an extra-cover drive for four off Siddle. As Bumble points out on Sky, Australia's run rate was 2.63 per over, whereas England's is 4.56. They have batted so well in that hour, and that's tea.

England 73–0; Australia 280

The evening session

BY ANDY BULL

Preamble: Morning, everyone, welcome to the late, late hours, when eyelids start to weigh heavy and mouths stretch wide in infectious yawns. 'Aren't you missing the point?' gasps Ian Johnston. 'The Hoff's majestic presence can only mean one thing: he is going to star in a movie as Beefy.'

17th over: England 78–0 (Strauss 49, Cook 23) The five overs Hilfenhaus has bowled so far have cost all of 27 runs, but Clarke has opted to start with him after the break all the same. Bizarre to think that he has only taken four wickets in the series.

18th over: England 82–0 (Strauss 53, Cook 23) And at the other end it's the fragile little flower, Mitchell Johnson. He duly serves up a ball that stinks worse than that stilton hanging around the back of your fridge, a wide half-tracker. Strauss crashes it past point for four. That brings up his fifty from just 49 balls, tying for his second fastest in Test cricket.

19th over: England 85–0 (Strauss 53, Cook 26) This Australian attack is falling apart in front of us. Hilfenhaus is bowling some real filth.

20th over: England 91–0 (Strauss 57, Cook 27) Strauss eases a half-tracker on leg stump away fine for four. Johnson runs his fingers through his immaculately coiffured hair and fires out a volley of abuse at his own fine leg, calling him out for being in the wrong place.

21st over: England 91–0 (Strauss 57, Cook 27) Many hearty congratulations to James Dart, a redoubtable colleague of ours who does an awful lot of the hard work behind the scenes that makes this site what it is. He has just emailed in to say: 'Cheers for keeping us (well, me) amused here in the maternity ward, where my wife and I have just become parents.' I'm a little surprised that Mrs Dart wasn't reading too, JD. Anyone would think she had other things on her mind. This one was a maiden from Hilfenhaus, by the way.

22nd over: England 98–0 (Strauss 60, Cook 31) We're in serious danger of exhausting all the rude words we can feasibly use to describe Mitchell Johnson's bowling here. I don't think we've deployed 'dross' yet, have we? He bungs a full toss down the leg side. He actually looks embarrassed by that, and desperately tries to avoid making eye contact with any of his teammates as he turns back to his mark.

WICKET! 23rd over: Strauss b Hilfenhaus 60 (England 98–1) Hubris? Meet my friend Mr Nemesis. Strauss plays all around a rather fine delivery from Hilfenhaus and is clean bowled. He missed it by a mile.

24th over: England 99–1 (Cook 31, Trott 0) Johnson will continue, Clarke keen for him to have a crack at the right-handed Trott.

WICKET! 24th over: Trott b Johnson 0 (England 98–2) Hubris and Nemesis seem to be getting pretty forward with each other. I'm starting to feel like a spare wheel. Trott is cleaned up, bowled off the inside edge. It was an ugly dismissal. All of a sudden England are wobbling.

25th over: England 105–2 (Cook 33, Pietersen 5) 'Your colleague appears to be having better luck than us,' says James Smith. 'I persuaded my wife to allow me to get the TV put on in the birthing suite during the Perth Test, which meant she not only had to endure a long and painful labour but also had me sighing as England's batting collapsed. That we now live in Australia and have named our daughter Matilda suggests we were asking for it, however.' Pietersen calls for a quick single, and grounds his bat at the non-striker's end just in time to beat Peter Siddle's direct hit on the stumps.

26th over: England 106–2 (Cook 33, Pietersen 6) Johnson swings a delivery back in towards the top of off stump. KP left it, and was left sweating as the ball came back at him and clipped his pads. Australia appealed, but it was a touch too high to convince. 'Judging from the quick wickets, David Hasselhoff IS a motivational guru,' points out Liam Rooney.

27th over: England 108–2 (Cook 33, Pietersen 6) Hilfenhaus is bowling better now as well; his length is fuller and he is getting a little swing away from the bat. It's extraordinary what a difference a couple of wickets can make to a team.

28th over: England 113–2 (Cook 36, Pietersen 10) Cook cuts the ball in the air, perilously close to the man at gully. Johnson is into the sixth over of his spell now, and he is bowling considerably better than he was just ten minutes ago. What a strange man he is. Mercurial doesn't do him justice.

29th over: England 118–2 (Cook 36, Pietersen 14) What a shot that is from KP. He threads four through long-off. I feel like there is something to be said about boundaries, camels, rich men and needles here, but my brain can't quite make it work at this hour of the morning.

30th over: England 124–2 (Cook 43, Pietersen 14) Peter Siddle is on now, and Cook has flicked his third ball away fine for four.

31st over: England 129–2 (Cook 44, Pietersen 19) A double change. Here's Beer, about to bowl his first over in Test cricket. Let's see how Pietersen plays this. Ouch. Beer trots up and floats his first ball up outside off. Pietersen strides forward and thumps four through long-off. 'Just had a chat with a chap from our warehouse,' says Paul Tooby. 'He's the good side of the "craggy old Aussie larrikin" stereotype if ever I saw it. He was a teammate of Michael Beer when he made his club debut for Malvern aged 13. Apparently he was knee high to a koala back then, before an impressive late growth spurt. He'll become a forgotten footnote in Test cricket, but I guess he's at least making a community proud today.'

32nd over: England 134–2 (Cook 45, Pietersen 22) 'G'day, Andy,' says Sean Boiling. 'Were Strauss and Trott bowled on Hoff stump?' Boom boom. 'Where does David field when he plays cricket? Mid-Hoff.' A glorious shot from Pietersen, sashaying his hips over to the leg side and leaning forward to fetch a ball from off stump and whip it away for three runs to long leg.

33rd over: England 137–2 (Cook 46, Pietersen 24) First impressions of Beer's bowling are distinctly underwhelming. He is floating the ball up and being picked off by Pietersen, who wallops one out to cover, slots another down the ground and flicks a third out to square leg.

34th over: England 139–2 (Cook 46, Pietersen 24) Look, everyone! A *Daily Mail* reader has blundered onto the site by mistake! 'I'd love to be able to feel pleased that England has finally produced a side capable of beating Australia, but the reality is, of course, that England hasn't produced such a team at all,' thunders Tom Hayes from Ramsgate. 'It is Combined England/Africa which (just) won the Ashes a couple of years ago (at home) and has now retained them away. The pathetically cosy appellation "KP" you use for Pietersen says it all: the man should be representing his own country, as those Australians do, and England should stand on its own, as it once did.' On its own? What a lot of bilge and bunkum you are talking. Ranjitsinhji, Duleepsinhji, Basil D'Oliveira, Tony Greig . . . I would go on old boy, but . . .

REVIEW! 35th over: Cook c Hilfenhaus b Beer 46 (England 145–2) Cook has gone! Beer has got his first wicket in Test cricket, and what a good one it is. Cook lofts a catch to mid-on, and he is out. Or is he? Umpire Bowden has asked for a review because he thinks it's a no-ball! And he's right. It is. Beer's foot was over the line, and Cook can bat on. What a farce. I don't know whether to laugh or cry on Beer's behalf.

37th over: England 145–2 (Cook 47, Pietersen 29) Siddle bowls a good maiden to Pietersen, pinning him down with six sharp deliveries on off stump.

38th over: England 146–2 (Cook 48, Pietersen 29) What a strange start to Beer's Test career. 'Beer getting plenty of hops off the pitch,' smirks Jack G. 'I feel a comeback brewing. I'm sure he'll be drunk with emotion if he takes a wicket. It's bound to come schooner or later.'

39th over: England 148–2 (Cook 50, Pietersen 29) Cook passes fifty for the fifth time in the series by pushing a single out to midwicket. I knew I should never have printed those awful beer puns in the last over. It was asking for trouble. As Sean Boiling says, 'Jack G was scraping the barrel.'

40th over: England 152–2 (Cook 54, Pietersen 29) Ben Hilfenhaus replaces Siddle, and Cook swats four down to fine leg. 'Can you confirm that the celebrity guest and the Aussie spinner are sharing accommodations at the Hofbrauhaus in Sydney?' asks Jeffrey Feim, to which I can only reply, has it really come to this?

41st over: England 158–2 (Cook 54, Pietersen 35) Pietersen lashes Beer for four through point, and then pushes two out to leg.

42nd over: England 162–2 (Cook 58, Pietersen 35) Cook clips four fine down the leg side. Let's have a few emails please, and please can they be about something other than Beer puns.

43rd over: England 164–2 (Cook 59, Pietersen 36) Beer plods through another pedestrian over, notable chiefly for Cook reaching 5,000 runs in Test cricket. He is the second-youngest man to get there, after Sachin Tendulkar.

WICKET! 44th over: Pietersen c Beer b Johnson 36 (England 165–3) There goes KP, caught on the hook. It was a good, sharp bouncer from Johnson, back in the attack for a final spell before the close. Pietersen threw a hook at it but was a little late on the shot. England have sent Anderson in as a night-watchman, and he survives the rest of the over.

45th over: England 166–3 (Cook 60, Anderson 0) Cook

plays a couple of tentative strokes at Beer, who is now bowling over the wicket.

46th over: England 166–3 (Cook 60, Anderson 0) Cook plays out a maiden from Johnson. 'You guys, you're too much,' sighs Joe Johnston. 'A bowler bowls a tidy first spell of his Test career, and after eight overs he's the worst spinner in world cricket. The only thing funnier than reading the English pontificate on cricket while their side is winning is reading when it's losing. Which we've had a lot of.'

47th over: England 167–3 (Cook 61, Anderson 1) Clarke crowds the bat, leaving Cook to face the fifth and sixth balls of the over. There's an ugly moment when Cook pokes a catch down near the feet of leg slip.

48th over: England 167–3 (Cook 61, Anderson 1) The last over of the day then, from Johnson to Anderson. I presume he won't be so rash as to take a single from one of these six. Not least because he can hardly get the bat on the ball. Johnson is bombing him with bouncers. Anderson blocks the first, and sways away from the second. And that is stumps. I've a bed to get to. Cheerio.

England 167–3; Australia 280

Third day

The morning session

BY ROB SMYTH

Preamble: Evening, folks. Not since the last days of university has the prospect of a 2:2 been so unnerving. England have been so manifestly superior in this series that even though they have retained the Ashes, a drawn series will gnaw at their belly button until it smarts. For 95 per cent of this game they have again looked a class above Australia, yet a couple of very dodgy spells and an important toss mean the contest is precariously poised. England will resume on 167 for three in reply to Australia's 280, but on a pitch that should break up they'll want a three-figure lead. We have quite a day in prospect.

49th over: England 168–3 (Cook 62, Anderson 1) There are 98 overs to be bowled today, the first by Ben Hilfenhaus, who was unusually expensive yesterday. There's some encouraging early swing, and only a late inside edge stops Cook from being plumb to the second ball. Hilfenhaus has a big shout for lbw against Anderson turned down off the last ball. It looked like it was sliding down leg, so Clarke doesn't refer. The camera cuts to the Sky box, where Michael Holding is sporting a pink bandana. And, of course, he looks like the coolest pink-bandana-wearing motherflipper that ever there was. One from the over.

50th over: England 170–3 (Cook 64, Anderson 1) David Brent said, 'Always start with a joke,' but Michael Clarke has given the ball to Peter Siddle rather than Mitchell Johnson. I jest.

51st over: England 170–3 (Cook 64, Anderson 1) Hilfenhaus slowly increases his length as the over progresses, and Anderson defends a maiden. A slow start to the day. England need to be careful that they don't dig a trench with Anderson at the crease.

52nd over: England 176–3 (Cook 69, Anderson 2) Cook touches a straight delivery from Siddle off the pads for four. 'Surely Silvio Dante would wear the pink bandana better than Mikey,' says Phil Rhodes. 'Now thats a site id like to see Michael Holding bowling at Silvio Dante.' Clearly. After a flawless first sentence you got so overexcited at the thought that you missed two apostrophes and a colon, capitalised one letter that should have been lower case, and had another lower case that should have been upper. Imagine if you'd been thinking about Michael Holding bowling to Tina Fey!

53rd over: England 181–3 (Cook 69, Anderson 7) Maybe that's why Hilfenhaus was loath to pitch the ball up to Anderson, because when he does he is lashed through the covers for four. Shot, Jimmy!

WICKET! 54th over: Anderson b Siddle 7 (England 181–4) Maybe that's why you should pitch the ball up to Anderson, because he has just missed a straight one. Full, straight and ramming into off stump with feeling as Anderson played down the wrong line.

54th over: England 183–4 (Cook 69, Collingwood 2) Here's Paul Collingwood. He was not supposed to play even one Test innings; this is his 115th and, just maybe, his last. I suspect I might shed a tear were he to get a hundred today. He gets off the mark with an assertive square drive for two off the second ball.

55th over: England 186–4 (Cook 72, Collingwood 2) Cook works yet another one off middle stump, this time through midwicket for three off the bowling of Hilfenhaus. He looks very comfortable thus far.

56th over: England 186–4 (Cook 72, Collingwood 2) Siddle tries a slower ball – get him – and Cook defends. It's a maiden, so that's 19 runs from eight overs. A pretty sedate start, then.

57th over: England 189–4 (Cook 72, Collingwood 5) Hilfenhaus jags one back into Collingwood, who inside-edges onto his pads at the 11th hour. The next ball curves late and beats Collingwood, but he responds nicely with a cut through the covers for three.

58th over: England 195–4 (Cook 77, Collingwood 6) Michael Clarke has brought on Mitchell Johnson. This will be a really tricky half-hour for Collingwood. Life looks much more comfortable for Cook, who uppercuts some sickening filth for four. 'Warne seems to be making a statement with his suit today – that being that he can't pick a tie,' says James Andrews of Shane Warne's bright pink blazer. 'Sadly, Atherton got the "all mouth no trousers" comment in before me.'

59th over: England 197–4 (Cook 79, Collingwood 6) Cook is playing really well, in his usual unobtrusive way. We take him for granted, but yesterday he became the second-youngest player after Sachin Tendulkar to reach 5,000 Test runs. What an achievement that is.

60th over: England 205–4 (Cook 86, Collingwood 7) I don't think Collingwood fancies Johnson, so he does the sensible thing and gets a single. Cook squirts Johnson to third man for four to take England past 200.

61st over: England 207–4 (Cook 87, Collingwood 8) Shane Watson is coming on to replace Ben Hilfenhaus. I would have let Siddle off the leash for another quick burst before Collingwood gets his eye in. And I am an idiot, because Watson so nearly struck with his last delivery. Cook, pushing with hard hands, edged *this far* short of Clarke, diving to his left at second slip.

62nd over: England 209–4 (Cook 87, Collingwood 10) Collingwood works Johnson into the leg side to move into double figures.

63rd over: England 212–4 (Cook 90, Collingwood 10) Despicable filth from Watson, short, wide and slapped through the covers for three by Cook. That moves him into the 90s. Cook has fallen twice in the 90s in Tests, but never on a Wednesday to a man called Shane.

64th over: England 217–4 (Cook 95, Collingwood 10) Cook pings Johnson through midwicket for two, and then crunches a cut through extra cover for three more. Only three touring players have ever scored more runs in a series in Australia: Wally Hammond, Herbert Sutcliffe and Aubrey Faulkner. It's astonishing stuff, even before you factor in his Ashes struggles in 2006–7 and 2009.

REVIEW! 65th over: Cook c Hughes b Beer 99 (England 221–4) Cook is standing his ground. He worked the new bowler Michael Beer low to Hughes at short leg, and although Australia celebrated straight away Cook went nowhere. It isn't a review, just a check as to whether it carried. And it didn't. It bounced into his hands, so Cook is not out. Ian Botham is absolutely furious about Hughes's behaviour, and quite right too. But imagine how Michael Beer feels.

65th over: England 221–4 (Cook 99, Collingwood 10) 'Cheating!' thunders Beefy. And he's right. Looking at the replays, Hughes's performance was pathetic. As he claimed the ball he let out a big 'ooh' – as in 'ooh, that was close' – but then, when he saw a few of his teammates celebrating, tossed the ball up in triumph. Oh, man, that was a mighty loss of dignity.

66th over: England 221–4 (Cook 99, Collingwood 10) A maiden from Watson to Collingwood.

67th over: England 225–4 (Cook 100, Collingwood 13) Alastair Cook has done it again! He reaches his 16th Test hundred, and his third of the series, with a work to leg off Beer. He has had the series of his life: 677 runs at 135.40. Amazing. Apparently some of the Australian fielders pointedly declined to clap Cook because of his two entirely legitimate escapes against Beer. If that's the case, it's utterly pathetic.

68th over: England 225–4 (Cook 100, Collingwood 13) Another maiden from Watson to Collingwood, who has looked fairly comfortable since Johnson went off. Although he did have one daft mow at Beer that I forgot to describe. It flew off the bottom edge and between Haddin's getaway sticks for three runs.

WICKET! 69th over: Collingwood c Hilfenhaus b Beer 13 (England 226–5) Michael Beer has his first Test wicket at last! Collingwood came down the track and tried to loft him over mid-on, but the ball was a bit too wide for the shot and he toe-ended it up in the air. Hilfenhaus ran back from mid-on to take a well-judged catch. Beer looks around for a few seconds, wondering what the catch is this time – 12 fielders on the pitch, a little-known law of the game that says a man called Michael is not allowed to dismiss a man called Paul – before finally running to embrace Hilfenhaus. Well done to him.

69th over: England 227–5 (Cook 101, Bell 0) So here's Ian Bell, at No. 7 again.

70th over: England 227–5 (Cook 101, Bell 0) A brilliant over from Watson. He almost nailed Cook with consecutive yorkers, and then wobbled and seamed a beauty past the outside edge. Wonderful bowling. 'Predicting events in the game is one thing, but I'm going to try to predict an OBO reaction to them, too,' says Josh Robinson. 'Namely: Bell b Beer 36, allowing you to recycle the "he played for turn" gag. Again.' You know the saying: if it's broke, don't fix it. Beer looks good, actually. He clearly has healthy levels of mental strength, which is a good start.

71st over: England 232–5 (Cook 104, Bell 3) Bell gets off the mark confidently, cutting Beer through the covers for three.

72nd over: England 232–5 (Cook 104, Bell 3) Watson is bowling really well now, and that's a tight, wicket-to-wicket maiden to Bell. 'The Aussie commentators were claiming good sportsmanship by Hughes on that catch that wasn't,' says Jesse Linklater. 'They seem to think he knew it was close, but wasn't sure one way or the other and didn't really go for the appeal all that much.' Hmm, maybe.

73rd over: England 234–5 (Cook 105, Bell 4) Beer v. Bell should be a fascinating contest. Bell is wonderfully light-footed against slow bowlers but he is staying in his crease for now, getting a good look at Beer.

74th over: England 239–5 (Cook 108, Bell 5) Cook squirts Watson to third man for three. In other news, Glenn McGrath has slipped into the Sky commentary box. He always comes across as such a good guy; just a gentle, shy soul. 'I'm breaking out into a cold sweat just at the sight of him,' chuckles Mike Atherton.

75th over: England 243–5 (Cook 112, Bell 5) Beer over-pitches and Cook spanks a cover drive for four. The number of four-balls that Beer bowls would be the main concern from a nonetheless encouraging start.

76th over: England 243–5 (Cook 112, Bell 5) Siddle is back, after that fine little spell from Watson. It's a maiden to Bell, who has started in a very circumspect fashion. Nobody has ever scored more Test fifties against one country without reaching a hundred – Bell has 11 – and he looks determined to sort that statistic out.

77th over: England 251–5 (Cook 120, Bell 5) Cook rifles another boundary through the covers off Beer. These are good runs ahead of the second new ball, and England are only 29 behind now.

78th over: England 254–5 (Cook 120, Bell 8) Siddle cuts Bell in half with a good delivery that jags back and keeps a touch low. England won't want to chase much more than 150 in the fourth innings on this. Bell responds with a good square drive that is pulled up just short of the rope. Talking of which . . . 'What's going on with the outfield here, eh?' says Niall Harden. Talking of which . . . 'I've not seen a single four, they seem to chase every ball down with ease. It's making me SO ANGRY.'

79th over: England 254–5 (Cook 120, Bell 8) A maiden from Beer, played respectfully by Bell. He still hasn't really left his crease, which reflects well on Beer. No duff Beer this! I said, no duff Beer this!

80th over: England 259–5 (Cook 121, Bell 12) Siddle bangs in a short one wide of off stump and Bell uppercuts for four. That's his first boundary from his 32nd delivery.

81st over: England 267–5 (Cook 129, Bell 12) Australia take the new ball immediately. Cook squeezes the first ball from Hilfenhaus past point for two, and that brings him to 700 runs in the series. Seven. Hundred. Runs. That's a mind-blowing performance.

82nd over: England 274–5 (Cook 129, Bell 19) The risk with the new ball, of course, is that it will often go to the boundary even on Niall Harden's outfield, and Bell plays a sumptuous off-drive for four off the bowling of Siddle. He repeats the stroke two balls later, but Niall Harden's outfield wins and there are only three runs.

83rd over: England 277–5 (Cook 130, Bell 20) Michael Clarke ends with a joke, bringing Mitchell Johnson on for the final over of this extended session. His first ball is a farcical off-side wide, and then Bell works a single to bring up a very calm fifty partnership. That's the end of the morning session. It's been an excellent one for England, who scored 110 for two relatively expendable wickets: the nightwatchman Jimmy Anderson and the out-of-form Paul Collingwood.

England 277–5; Australia 280

The afternoon session

BY SIMON BURNTON

Preamble: Ready for a bit more action, and I've spent the lunch break trying to decide which out of Sky and 5 Live Sports Extra was broadcasting more interesting random padding. Have listened to both, alternately, for about five minutes at a time, and am thus fairly bewildered and have little idea what was happening on either of them. Anyway, shall we play some cricket?

84th over: England 277–5 (Cook 130, Bell 20) Siddle slings six balls across Cook, the first four of which are left alone, the remainder prodded not very far for not a sniff of a run.

85th over: England 283–5 (Cook 130, Bell 26) Bell flicks one off his pads for four to put England into the lead.

86th over: England 292–5 (Cook 132, Bell 33) Ten runs off

Siddle's over: a four, one two, the rest singles – including Cook's first two runs since lunch.

87th over: England 295–5 (Cook 135, Bell 33) Cook nurdles three runs with last-moment prods into little holes in the close field. Hilfenhaus is the other bowler, incidentally.

88th over: England 296–5 (Cook 136, Bell 33) Johnson comes on, to the considerable delight of the travelling England fans. His first delivery is miserably wide, begging to be dispatched to the boundary, but is unaccountably ignored by the charitable Cook. 'Anyone else think Michael Slater's had a heavy liquid lunch?' asks *TMS*-listener Jack Savidge. 'He's been banging on about pigeons and doing shite Mark Nicholas-as-Austin Powers impressions. Poor bland old Simon Mann is trying to bring him back to banal observations about how everyone's wearing hats.'

89th over: England 296–5 (Cook 136, Bell 33) Watson replaces Hilfenhaus, and it's a maiden; though Cook gets decent contact on a few occasions, his strokes zip straight to fielders. We remain eagerly in wait of the first wicket-taking opportunity, or otherwise particularly interesting moment, of the session.

90th over: England 303–5 (Cook 142, Bell 34) Johnson continues to be considerably less parsimonious, and Cook cuts him away for an insouciant four to bring up 300 for England.

91st over: England 303–5 (Cook 142, Bell 34) The *Guardian*'s swish King's Cross bachelor pad has canny motion-sensitive lighting. I just made half of the entire floor's lights come back on simply by taking off my shoes. In other news, it's another maiden for the trundling Watson.

92nd over: England 311–5 (Cook 150, Bell 34) Johnson starts his over with the traditional hopeless loosener, and Cook watches it drift down the leg side, licks his lips and smacks the next three balls for eight to bring up his 150. '"Parsimonious" and "insouciant" in one OBO entry? Bloody hell, it's nearly 3 a.m. Have a heart, man,' writes Alex Wilson.

93rd over: England 315–5 (Cook 153, Bell 35) Watson having done his thing to little reward, from either team's perspective, Beer's having a go. It looked like they were going deliberately easy on Watson, preserving their energy for the most effective humiliation of Johnson.

94th over: England 318–5 (Cook 156, Bell 35) Watson was only changing ends, it turns out. Cook hits his second ball for three, allowing Bell to resume the deliberate defensive posturing with which he dealt with Watson's two previous overs. 'Boycs has lumbered into the commentary box and announced his arrival with "Michael Slater's messed up our commentary and now he's gone. He's very naughty. Very naughty,"' reports Richard Read.

95th over: England 323–5 (Cook 157, Bell 39) 'I think he's a good player,' says Geoff Boycott of Cook on *TMS*. I think that's already been established, no? Beer finds Bell's edge, but the ball flies past the solitary slip and away for four.

96th over: England 327–5 (Cook 161, Bell 39) Unlike Bell, Cook is apparently happy to actually hit the occasional Watson delivery, and despite Khawaja's desperate diving effort the resulting boundary brings up the hundred partnership. 'Parsimonious is nice, yes,' concedes Steve Banjo. 'But abstemious is even better in the same circumstances. With the added bonus that it's one of only two words in the English language that have all the vowels, and in the correct order (a, e, i, o, u). I'm not telling you the other. How's that for a 3 a.m. teaser?' That does not please me.

97th over: England 329–5 (Cook 163, Bell 39) There is now just one Englishman in the whole of history who has scored more runs in a single Ashes series than Cook in this one. England's lead is 49, heading into a drinks break. And the other word with all the vowels in alphabetical order is 'facetious'. Thanks to Simon Lacey and Paul Tooby for that one.

98th over: England 334–5 (Cook 164, Bell 41) Siddle's first ball, a bouncer, is called a wide. About a million other people also got 'facetious' fractionally too late to get a name check. Samuel Riding gets a special mention for knowing many others, including 'fracedinous', 'arsenious', 'heriously' and 'Phragelliorynchus', but I'm pretty sure he made them all up.

99th over: England 338–5 (Cook 165, Bell 45) You know that rising sense of excitement you get when the batsmen are under such sustained pressure that you can almost feel a wicket coming? I have never been further from it.

100th over: England 339–5 (Cook 166, Bell 45) There was a run off that Siddle over. If it wasn't for that, I'd have missed it entirely. It just passed. One minute it hadn't happened, the next it had. 'Do the lights go back out if you put your shoes back on?' wonders Sean Boiling. The lights are already off, it seems. Figuratively, at least.

101st over: England 344–5 (Cook 171, Bell 45) Beer's first ball is loose and dispatched for four by Cook to send yet more statisticians into a state of frenzied excitement. That's 1,000 first-class runs for him on this tour, I'm told.

102nd over: England 347–5 (Cook 173, Bell 46) Smith gets a rousing reception from fans who were surely starting to question his existence. 'I believe Smith said when he was initially selected that his brief was to have fun and make sure the team were enjoying themselves,' wrote Scott Wilkinson, about two minutes before the ball was thrown to the young leg-spinner. 'One can't help but wonder when he will emerge from the dressing room sporting floppy shoes and a red nose.'

103rd over: England 348–5 (Cook 174, Bell 46) Beer and

Smith are now ready to exert a stranglehold of deadly spin on England's mighty batsmen. Or something. The main difference as far as I'm concerned is that overs pass considerably more quickly, forcing me to do some high-speed nearly-4 a.m.-typing.

104th over: England 353–5 (Cook 175, Bell 50) Bell reaches his fifty with a lovely boff down the ground for four, and Australia seem entirely clueless as to how to stop England's relentless, chanceless accumulation of runs. 'I'm following the OBO in my office in Hong Kong,' writes Robert Russell. 'Can anyone advise me what to do during the uneventful minutes to stop myself staring at my young, beautiful colleague Shirley Smith [name changed to protect the innocent] (aside from actually getting down to some work)?'

105th over: England 354–5 (Cook 176, Bell 50) Another over passes with nothing but a single run and a faintly pleasant whooshing noise to show for itself.

106th over: England 355–5 (Cook 177, Bell 50) 'Have the minister for education visiting the school tomorrow to view the PE at the school,' says John Woodberry, head of PE at Shanghai United International School. 'Not sure looking at OBO is the best preparation for this?' Never fear, he'll have been reading it too.

107th over: England 358–5 (Cook 180, Bell 50) 'Using the monkeys-banging-on-typewriters principle, if Johnson was made to bowl from the Randwick End until the end of time, would he collect the remaining five wickets by 2014?' wonders Ranajit S. Dam. Really, Australia might as well just ask England to name the score they'd declare at and save us all a bit of time.

108th over: England 362–5 (Cook 183, Bell 51) Smith's four overs have passed without incident. Literally, none. Hilfenhaus is coming back now. 'I am also working at a school here in Hong Kong,' writes Robert Russell. 'I would advise John Woodberry, rather than following the OBO, to stare at a young, beautiful colleague. It's far more uplifting.'

109th over: England 366–5 (Cook 183, Bell 55) Four runs off the over, a terrifically straightforward four from Bell. 'You've got to bowl to your field,' rages Nasser Hussain. 'Two men on the drive and you're bowling cut balls to a batsman who likes the cut.'

110th over: England 371–5 (Cook 184, Bell 59) Bell, whose innings thus far has been pretty much faultless under the very flimsiest examination, thwacks Smith's full toss for four.

111th over: England 374–5 (Cook 186, Bell 60) Sky cut to a camera situated high above the ground. 'You can just about see Sydney, those tall buildings in the distance,' Michael Holding helpfully informs Sky's viewers, who might otherwise have been straining to identify the enormous metropolis just yards from the SCG. Thanks, Mike.

112th over: England 376–5 (Cook 187, Bell 61) Mike Hussey gets a bowl, to the absolute delight of many in the crowd, the vast majority of them presumably English. Two singles off it bring up the 150-run partnership. One over before tea. 'The Channel 9 signal has failed here in Perth but the "No Signal" sign on the TV is only slightly more boring than the Aussie attack, so I'm not sure it's worth complaining,' notes Neil.

113th over: England 378–5 (Cook 188, Bell 62) England lead by 98 runs And that's the end of a fabulous session for England, bringing as it did 101 runs, though it was almost entirely bereft of dramatic incident. This game was on a knife-edge a few hours ago. No longer. Now it's on the edge of a very thick thing. It's on a land-mass edge.

England 378–5; Australia 280

The evening session

BY ROB SMYTH

Preamble: Hello again. Given the pair's ubiquity, it's surprising how few Cook-and-Bell stories have been written for England over the last five years. This is only their second century partnership in Tests, and they are closing in on the 170 they added at Perth in 2006–7 (also the highest Test partnership by two men who still get asked for ID). The afternoon session was cherubic torture for Australia, and there might be more to come.

114th over: England 380–5 (Cook 189, Bell 63) Shane Watson winces his way to the crease for the first ball after tea. It's short, wide and cut to the cover sweeper for one by Cook. Bell then rolls the wrists for another single, and that brings England's lead up to 100.

115th over: England 380–5 (Cook 189, Bell 63) A maiden from the willing but unable Hilfenhaus. Here's a statistic: Australia have never conceded 500 four times in one series. In fact, it's only happened three times in Tests, and West Indies were on the receiving end each time.

WICKET! 116th over: Cook c Hussey b Watson 189 (England 380–6) Bah! That's a frustrating end for Alastair Cook, who reaches for a very wide delivery from Watson and edges it low to Hussey at gully. So Cook has missed out on a second double century, but it's been another epic innings. Simply immense. He has scored 766 runs in this series, and the Cook grandchildren are going to hear about each and every one in years to come. Cook walks off to a standing ovation from the crowd, although there is little applause from the Australian players. Hard to know whether that's just because the camera cut to them late, after they had applauded him, or whether they still have a sense of injustice over those Beer incidents. If it's the latter, they need to grow up.

116th over: England 380–6 (Bell 63, Prior 0) If they get in, the likes of Prior and Swann could flog this tired Australian attack. But if Australia can pick up the last four wickets for no more than 50, they won't be out of this game.

117th over: England 384–6 (Bell 67, Prior 0) Nearly another one. Bell, driving at a delivery angled across him from around the wicket by Hilfenhaus, edges just short of Watson at around fifth slip. The ball scuttles away for four.

REVIEW! 118th over: Bell c Haddin b Watson 67 (England 385–6) This looks like a waste of a review. Or is it? Bell felt for a ball from Watson that cut back and apparently went off the inside edge through to Brad Haddin. He was given out and decided to review – but only after a chat with Matt Prior, which is very odd for a caught-behind decision. Either you know you hit it or you know you didn't. This is a really interesting decision . . . and Bell is given not out. Is Hotspot 100 per cent reliable? I don't think it is, and I wouldn't be at all surprised if, in a couple of overs' time, Snicko showed an inside edge. Anyway, Bell survives.

118th over: England 385–6 (Bell 67, Prior 1) Another replay of that incident includes a big sound – and with Bell's bat away from his body, that could only have been an edge. And now Snicko does show an edge. That's a major failing – not of the UDRS, but of its implementation. The third umpire ~~Daryl Harper~~, the usually excellent Tony Hill, has buggered up really badly there. Australia's grievances are following the pattern of an OBOers friendship: first imaginary, and now real.

119th over: England 393–6 (Bell 67, Prior 9) I wonder what Bell was thinking with that review. Was he reviewing for a no-ball? Anyway, Prior takes two boundaries off three deliveries from Hilfenhaus, a cover drive and then an edge to third man. 'Middle of the night, Smyth, middle of the night, everybody,' says Josh Robinson. 'I can't quite help wondering why they didn't stay with the decision of the on-field umpire for that one. And if Snicko shows that Bell edged it, what does that say about (a) Bell, and (b) the review system?'

120th over: England 397–6 (Bell 70, Prior 10) Poor old Belly. He's finally going to score a century against Australia at the 98th time of asking, and it will forever have an asterisk against it.

121st over: England 400–6 (Bell 70, Prior 13) Prior has started aggressively, and pulls the new bowler Johnson for three.

122nd over: England 408–6 (Bell 77, Prior 14) Bell cover-drives Watson beautifully for four. 'So just to be clear, if Hughes appeals for a catch he knew he didn't take, he's a villain, but when Bell appeals an edge he knew he hit, it's the system at fault?' says Matt Starr. This is the contradiction we mentioned earlier – that some things in cricket are seen as cheating (claiming catches that bounced) and others aren't (not walking) – but you can't pin a culture (of not walking) that has existed for 40 years on the gentle, beautiful shoulders of Ian Bell. That would be utterly ridiculous.

123rd over: England 409–6 (Bell 78, Prior 14) Johnson appears to have pulled something in his backside. Plenty of emails calling me an eff and a cee for defending Bell. All I would say is this: if Bell was reviewing in the hope of a no-ball – which I would not rule out – it would be a perfectly legitimate tactic in view of the fact that Australia's bowlers have been about as adept at keeping their front foot behind the line as John F. Kennedy was at keeping it in his trousers.

124th over: England 417–6 (Bell 84, Prior 14) Bell takes a dodgy two into the leg side and would have been in the trouble had the throw from the deep not been well wide of the stumps.

125th over: England 421–6 (Bell 86, Prior 16) Steve Smith drops Ian Bell off his own bowling. It was the second ball of Smith's second spell, and Bell scorched a half-volley back whence it came. Smith is usually superb off his own bowling, but that was a piping-hot chance and he couldn't quite hang on. 'Why on earth', says Duncan Groves, 'would JFK keep his foot in his trousers?'

126th over: England 425–6 (Bell 88, Prior 18) Johnson is back into the attack, which is peculiar in view of his apparent buttock strain. England's lead inches closer to 150.

127th over: England 433–6 (Bell 89, Prior 25) Prior comes down the track and drives Smith right back over his head for six. That's a cracking shot, and it brings up a rapid fifty partnership.

128th over: England 433–6 (Bell 89, Prior 25) Johnson gets one to pop from a length, and Bell does well to get on top of the ball so that it only goes to gully on the bounce. A maiden. 'Obvious answer is to only allow Hotspot to be used to give someone out (i.e. if umpire misses the snick) – it can't be used to save a batsman,' says Ciaran Murphy. I thought that was the case anyway. If not, it surely will be after this.

129th over: England 437–6 (Bell 90, Prior 28) England continue to milk Smith with no problems, and Bell moves into the 90s for the first time against Australia.

130th over: England 441–6 (Bell 94, Prior 28) Bell drives the new bowler Siddle gloriously through extra cover for four. He was briefly rattled after that fortunate escape, but it is coming right off the middle again now.

131st over: England 447–6 (Bell 98, Prior 30) Bell premeditates a lap at Smith – he can do what he wants against him, basically – and gets it very fine for three.

132nd over: England 455–6 (Bell 99, Prior 37) Bell cuts

Siddle for a single to move to 99. Which, coincidentally, is the square root of his heart rate as he contemplates a first century against Australia. Prior then checks a drive and the ball spoons *just* over Siddle and away for four.

133rd over: England 460–6 (Bell 102, Prior 39) Ian Bell has just removed King Kong from his back. After 11 half-centuries and over five years of being told he couldn't do it, he has made a Test hundred against Australia. He cuts Smith for two and then jumps to punch the air. 'He's graduated from the Shermanator to the Terminator,' says Shane Warne. 'Ian Terminator Bell!' He should have been given out on 67, but otherwise he has played another wonderful innings.

134th over: England 467–6 (Bell 109, Prior 39) Bell plays another gorgeous cover drive for four, this time off Siddle. The lead is 191. We can very nearly utter the words 'England have won the Ashes'. But not yet. Don't you DARE MOVE THOSE LIPS.

135th over: England 469–6 (Bell 109, Prior 41) Michael Beer (25–1–80–1) replaces Steve Smith (10–0–48–0). Two from the over.

136th over: England 478–6 (Bell 114, Prior 45) A wonderful stroke from Bell, who waits for Siddle's bouncer and then guides it high over the cordon for four. Later in the over Prior plays a not dissimilar stroke wide of the only slip for another boundary. These are free runs.

137th over: England 478–6 (Bell 114, Prior 45) 'Mitchell Johnson's spells have been 3, 6, 3, 4, 1, 3 and 2 overs,' says Peter Hanes. 'It's like yanking the cord on a rusty lawnmower in the hope that it will sputter into life.'

138th over: England 484–6 (Bell 114, Prior 51) Michael Clarke has had another yank, because here comes Johnson again. Prior drives his second ball through the covers for four to bring up the hundred partnership and the 200 lead. Later in the over he squeezes two behind square on the off side to reach a trade-mark Prior fifty, selfless and aggressive, from only 54 balls.

139th over: England 485–6 (Bell 115, Prior 52) Beer again.

WICKET! 140th over: Bell c Clarke b Johnson 115 (England 487–7) Ian Bell has gone, edging Johnson low to Clarke in a wide slip position. Bell should have reviewed it, just for a laugh. He should have reviewed it with the most extravagant review signal there has ever been. Instead he walks off to a mixture of cheers and boos (about 70/30 I reckon).

140th over: England 487–7 (Prior 53, Bresnan 0) That was good bowling from Johnson, who switched to around the wicket and found Bell's edge with the change of angle and just a little late movement.

BAD LIGHT STOPS PLAY England 488–7 (Prior 53, Bresnan 0) In fact, that's the end of the day's play because we are past the 5.30 p.m. cut-off point. So England lead by 208 after a long, exhausting day. The 1989 England side would do well from here. The 2010–11 England side are *this* close to a series victory in Australia. Night.

England 488–7; Australia 280

Fourth day

The morning session

BY SIMON BURNTON

Preamble: Evening, world. Well, here it is. Just 24 hours ago, before the third day got under way, this match was ever so delicately poised, like a princess sipping tea from a Fabergé teacup while balanced on a pinhead. Then England scored 321 runs for the loss of four wickets, to take a 208-run first-innings lead with three further wickets in hand, and delicacy and poise fled the building. Australia need to have a good day, a very good day, for the match to return to any semblance of competitiveness. On the other hand, today could be the day when England's muscle-bound trolls finally and decisively flay their piteous prey like so many highly armed Sarah Palins on a weekend wolf hunt.

Apparently Paul Collingwood has retired. Just a rumour at present. More to come, for sure.

Paul Collingwood has indeed retired. Ideally he won't get a chance to have one last glorious Test knock, but it would be kinda nice if he did.

141st over: England 489–7 (Prior 55, Bresnan 0) Johnson with the first over, just missing Bresnan's outside edge with his final ball. But Collingwood's retirement, announced just moments before the start of play today, is still dominating debate.

142nd over: England 493–7 (Prior 57, Bresnan 1) Hilfen-haus from the other end. 'Shouldn't there be a mention for Jacques Kallis in here, who has just hit twin hundreds against India to move on to an incredible 40 Test tons?' demands Dan Lucas. 'The guy's stats with both bat and ball are quite remarkable.' Yeah, s'pose so.

143rd over: England 493–7 (Prior 57, Bresnan 1) Johnson's first ball finds Bresnan's outside edge, but it lands two feet short of Haddin. Good, positive bowling from Johnson.

144th over: England 496–7 (Prior 58, Bresnan 2) 'Great player,' says Dennis Johns, 'for the catches, the 206, but mainly the 74 off 245 at Cardiff.'

145th over: England 502–7 (Prior 59, Bresnan 7) Another edge from Bresnan flies well wide of second slip away for four and brings up England's 500. This is the first England team ever to pass that mark four times in a series, and this is the first time any team from anywhere has done it against Australia.

146th over: England 504–7 (Prior 59, Bresnan 9) 'Former England coach David Lloyd described Collingwood as "a yeoman, a stalwart and a grand lad" and lauded his decision to leave the side on his own terms,' says the Press Association report. 'Lloyd, commentating on Sky Sports 1, said: "He's still as fit as a fiddle but he said he needed runs in this series and it hasn't happened. He'll continue to play one-day cricket I'd assume and lead the Twenty20 side as well. I think it's an outstanding decision. He's a yeoman, a stalwart and a grand lad."' More Collingwood news as we get it.

147th over: England 511–7 (Prior 66, Bresnan 9) Johnson's first ball is chipped, safely, over extra cover by Prior for two, and his second is edged low, well short of first slip. The third is deliberately steered through third man. England are getting away with a few loose shots this morning.

148th over: England 514–7 (Prior 69, Bresnan 9) Hilfen-haus's last ball snarls up off the pitch and into Bresnan's glove. No danger, but a promising hint of fun to come for England's bowlers. 'I'm thinking of buying a hat so I can take it off to Paul Collingwood,' writes John Johnston. 'In the not-too-distant dark days of English cricket seeing his name on the team sheet reassured me that at least somebody was going to walk to the middle with a bat in his hands and give his all for the team. He's the kind of player I adore, not blessed with divine skills but a grafter and a battler, and I wish him well.'

149th over: England 523–7 (Prior 78, Bresnan 9) Johnson's first ball is swatted through extra cover by Prior. The third, shockingly loose and wide by Johnson, is similarly tucked away. 'This is just carnage,' says Botham. He finishes the over going round the wicket, on his captain's instructions. Botham, emboldened by the fact that Australian news broadcasts have been leading with his calling Phillip Hughes a cheat, calls Phillip Hughes a cheat again.

150th over: England 524–7 (Prior 79, Bresnan 9) Beer comes on, but there doesn't seem to be great encouragement for him.

151st over: England 524–7 (Prior 79, Bresnan 9) Johnson continues round the wicket to Prior, occasionally causing him some discomfort, and the result is his fifth maiden of the innings.

152nd over: England 524–7 (Prior 79, Bresnan 9) 'I'd like to suggest retiring the word "gritty" when used in connection with cricket as a tribute to Colly,' suggests Steve Churnin. 'Even if it's just a stereotype, it has been a much-loved one.'

153rd over: England 525–7 (Prior 80, Bresnan 9) Peter Siddle has a bowl, to no great effect.

154th over: England 528–7 (Prior 82, Bresnan 10) Beer meanders through another over.

155th over: England 529–7 (Prior 83, Bresnan 10) One ball to Prior, who gets a single, and five to Bresnan, who gets nowt. Bresnan's faced 66 deliveries for his 10 runs, with one four. Thrilling stuff.

156th over: England 530–7 (Prior 84, Bresnan 11) The highlight of Beer's over is a rare run for Bresnan off the last ball, his first for a few overs.

157th over: England 539–7 (Prior 85, Bresnan 18) Emboldened by that run off Beer, Bresnan smacks Siddle for a splendid four through point. And here's some poetry, from Danny Clayton:

> So. Farewell Then,
> Paul Collingwood,
> English cricketer,
> Taker of miracle catches.
> Collywobbles they called you,
> But you will wobble for us,
> No more.

158th over: England 542–7 (Prior 87, Bresnan 19) Beer's success is such that Smith's coming on from the other end. There'll be a new ball due at the end of this next over.

159th over: England 547–7 (Prior 90, Bresnan 21) Since the first couple of overs this morning, the level of comfort enjoyed by England's batsmen has been astonishing. They'll be coming out in slippers next.

160th over: England 551–7 (Prior 94, Bresnan 21) Australia don't take the new ball, sticking with Beer for now. Off the penultimate ball Prior has a go at paddling the ball down to fine leg. It works well, so he does it again, bringing up England's 550 in the process.

161st over: England 561–7 (Prior 95, Bresnan 31) Bresnan boshes Smith's second ball straight down the ground for a one-bounce boundary, then does it again off the last. This could be turning into the most embarrassing session of the series for Australia. There's nothing there at the moment. No passion, spirit or apparent ability.

162nd over: England 567–7 (Prior 101, Bresnan 31) Prior duly trundles to his century from 109 balls with a simple four off a loose Beer ball. 'It doesn't get any more demoralising than an innings defeat in two consecutive matches,' says Hayden Kendall. 'We'll never really know the true extent with which we've been comprehensively smashed. Still, watching Colly and co. is far less drab and irritating than watching say, Jonny Wilkinson.'

163rd over: England 571–7 (Prior 104, Bresnan 31) 'Michael Clarke was still saying Australia could win this match last night,' reports Matt Reilly. 'About as convincing as a Phil Hughes appeal.'

164th over: England 573–7 (Prior 105, Bresnan 32) These two could just bat out the remaining five and a bit sessions at this rate.

165th over: England 584–7 (Prior 111, Bresnan 35) Australia take the new ball, and hand it to Mitchell Johnson, whose lazy half-volley is smashed away by a rapidly emboldening (is that a word?) Bresnan. Prior also scoops a boundary down past third man. 'He's going to flash hard,' warns David Lloyd.

166th over: England 584–7 (Prior 111, Bresnan 35) A maiden from Hilfenhaus, who on one occasion tempts Bresnan to flash hard, but there's no contact. 'Looking at Steve Smith's face reminds me of a small boy constantly on the verge of bursting into tears,' writes Phil Withall. 'He seems to be struggling to comprehend what's going on.'

167th over: England 589–7 (Prior 116, Swann 0) 'Why no

declaration?' asks Sara Williams. 'We've double their score and Prior's got his century. Why are we still batting?'

WICKET! 168th over: Bresnan c Clarke b Johnson 35 (England 589–8) Finally, a breakthrough. Given how unlikely it's looked for so long, Clarke does excellently well to take a diving catch at second slip.

168th over: England 589–8 (Prior 116, Swann 0) Johnson bowls wide outside off stump, and a delighted Prior flashes hard for another boundary. That, presumably, was not the plan, though Bresnan's wicket improves matters slightly. 'Why no declaration?' asks Sara Williams. 'This is just gifting critics who say Strauss has no tactical nous.' But what have England to gain from turning down the chance to accumulate extra runs with the best part of two days to go?

169th over: England 595–8 (Prior 117, Swann 1) Four leg byes off a loose first ball from Hilfenhaus. This is, apparently, the first time any Test team – anyone's, ever – has seen their sixth-, seventh- and eighth-wicket partnerships each garner over 100 runs.

170th over: England 608–8 (Prior 118, Swann 13) Swann flashes hard, gets a thick edge, and the ball flies through the slip cordon for four, taking England past 600. Australia have never before conceded 600 twice in a series at home. Swann's not messing about here. Another four and a ludicrously boshed shot over the covers that stopped a couple of yards short of the boundary.

WICKET! 171st over: Prior's gone! No, hang on – it's a no-ball! Again! Umpires reviewing this. It's very close . . . He's out after all! **Prior c Haddin b Hilfenhaus 118 (England 609–9)** A slight edge chasing after a very poor ball from Hilfenhaus, the heel of whose foot turned out after several replays to have landed maybe two millimetres behind the line.

171st over: England 609–9 (Swann 14, Tremlett 0) And

that's the last ball of the over. Prior probably doesn't care, but that was a poor delivery to lose your wicket to.

172nd over: England 629–9 (Swann 31, Tremlett 3) Swann's going to go down fighting. 20 runs off Johnson's over, including an attempted hook top-edged by Swann for six. It's humiliation piled on humiliation, with some embarrassment on top.

173rd over: England 629–9 (Swann 31, Tremlett 3) Tremlett fairly easily survives Hilfenhaus's over, only actually having to hit one ball. England lead by 349.

174th over: England 630–9 (Swann 32, Tremlett 3) Tremlett doesn't look likely to stick around long, though someone should probably try aiming at his stumps, something that Siddle didn't seem very keen on.

175th over: England 633–9 (Swann 34, Tremlett 4) Hilfenhaus sticks another 50p in the comedy generator by letting the ball slip out of his hand just as he's about to bowl to Tremlett, near enough hitting his own foot. A dead ball, but a clown attempting to do a comedy hilarious calamity delivery couldn't improve on that one. Snickometer has since revealed that the ball flicked Swann's collar.

176th over: England 636–9 (Swann 33, Tremlett 7) That's lunch, 148 runs in the session at four-ish an over and England aren't done yet. 'Are we not witnessing the death – or something like it – of Australian cricket?' ponders Dan Jeffreys. 'The stumps from this humiliating innings should be burnt and placed in a tiny urn for future generations of cricketers to battle – and weep – over whenever the phrase "600+" is uttered. Oh wait, hasn't something like this been done before?'

England 636–9; Australia 280

The afternoon session

BY ROB SMYTH

Preamble: Hello, folks. That's how to close out a series, eh? In the morning session England achieved the ostensibly impossible task of putting the foot on the Australian throat while simultaneously rubbing their nose in the dirt. And all this while giving them a wedgie of surgery-necessitating proportions.

Some other business. There is tentative talk of an OBO book for this series. I know, fools. The title *Is It Cowardly to Pray for Rain?*, nicked/homaged from a reader email, was inspired in 2005. Any suggestions for this one?

177th over: England 643–9 (Swann 35, Tremlett 12) Michael Beer bowls the first ball after lunch, and Graeme Swann works it to leg. This is England's highest-ever score in a Test in Australia. Dear me, what kind of world are we living in where the England cricket team are doing this? And they only need 260 for the highest score in any Ashes Test. Tremlett clatters four of them through the covers.

WICKET! 178th over: Tremlett c Haddin b Hilfenhaus 12 (England 644 all out) Tremlett tickles Hilfenhaus through to the 'keeper, and that's the end of a monstrous innings from England: 644 all out. *Six* hundred and forty-four all out. Six *hundred* and forty-four all out. Six hundred *and* forty-four all out, etc. and so forth. And 418 of those for the last five wickets. Who needs flowery prose when you have numbers like that? England lead by 364.

Australia second innings

Preamble: So here we are. One way or the other, whether England win or Australia survive, this will probably be the last innings of the 'Can bat, can bowl, can field' tour. England should savour every moment because they might never experience anything as good as this again in their careers.

1st over: Australia 7–0 (Watson 7, Hughes 0) Have some of that! Shane Watson starts the innings with seven runs off the first two balls: a disdainful pull over midwicket for four and a nice cover drive for three. Anderson and Watson are having words already. It'll be forgotten over the post-series beer. Either that or they'll have a massive punch-up over who should have the last VB stubby.

2nd over: Australia 7–0 (Watson 7, Hughes 0) Chris Tremlett, who some folk thought shouldn't even be on this tour, will share the new ball. He's been the revelation of the series. Watson rifles a couple of drives straight to the fielder at extra cover. As Carly Simon didn't say, nobody pings them straight at the fielders better. It's a maiden. '*Assaulting Matilda*,' says Mac Millings. I don't know whether this is a status update or a suggested book title, but it has something going for it.

3rd over: Australia 10–0 (Watson 8, Hughes 2) Anderson strays onto the pads and Hughes tucks a single to fine leg to get off the mark. 'Zooey Deschanel did *500 Days of Summer*,' says Paul Neilan. 'She'd never declare.' Didn't she declare at 350-odd, only for that sorry goon to keep playing for another 150 days even though everybody else had gone home?

4th over: Australia 13–0 (Watson 8, Hughes 5) England have Cook in an interesting leg-gully position for Hughes, who works Tremlett off his pads for a couple. Hughes never really looks comfortable against Tremlett, and gets a leading edge into the off side later in the over.

5th over: Australia 18–0 (Watson 12, Hughes 6) If Hughes is trying to build an innings, Watson is hitting out, and plays another withering and flamboyant pull stroke for four. '*Punter's Last Stand*?' offers Paul Tooby. 'Actually, I prefer *Gladstone Small's Last Interview*.'

6th over: Australia 18–0 (Watson 12, Hughes 6) Two excellent deliveries from Tremlett ricochet off the inside edge of Hughes's crooked bat and back into his body. A very good maiden. Tremlett is working Hughes over, again. 'Can we just call the OBO book for this series *517–1*?' says Jamie Jermain.

7th over: Australia 25–0 (Watson 19, Hughes 6) That's another boundary for Watson, this time a back cut off Anderson. The next ball is a nasty, lifting off-cutter that Watson desperately inside-edges onto his rump. 'It has to be *Fetch That, Jim Maxwell!* in honour of the OBO–ABC sledging war,' says Peter Hanes. Cripes, I'd forgotten all about that.

8th over: Australia 34–0 (Watson 28, Hughes 6) Watson is playing almost a shot a ball, and he slices a booming drive behind point for four off Tremlett. Two balls later he plays a wonderful drive through mid-off for four more. He has 28 from 24 deliveries. 'Book title: *Beijing*,' says Rossa Brugha. 'As far as I can tell, every day for the entire series has included the phrase, "Does anyone know where I can watch the cricket in Beijing?" So I think that's apt.'

9th over: Australia 34–0 (Watson 28, Hughes 6) Graeme Swann is into the attack after eight overs, which is surely a good move. A maiden.

10th over: Australia 43–0 (Watson 36, Hughes 7) Hughes calls Watson through for a tight single. Watching Watson wince his way through quick singles is a thing of comic beauty. He approaches them with the same *joie de vivre* of Basil Fawlty being called into the office for a chat with Sybil. But Watson sure knows how to hit boundaries, and he laces another delicious extra-cover drive for four.

11th over: Australia 43–0 (Watson 36, Hughes 7) Swann gets his first bowl at Hughes, who inside-edges an arm ball onto his pads. He is struggling here. Another maiden for Swann. 'Yeah,' says Chris Matthews, 'what ever came of the ABC v. OBO row?' They bottled it.

12th over: Australia 45–0 (Watson 36, Hughes 7) Bresnan replaces Tremlett. Two from a tight over. 'Given the Bring Back Warne campaign, surely the title should be *Is It Cowardly to Pray for Shane?*' That suggestion comes from Rick Foot, but maybe, in honour of the champagne moment of the series, it should simply be called *David Gower's Foot.*

WICKET! 13th over: Watson run out 36 (Australia 46–1) What a shemozzle. What a total, abject farce. Hughes turns Swann through midwicket and sets off; they take one and then Watson trots leisurely back for a second, completely oblivious to the fact that Hughes has not moved. Pietersen and Prior do the rest. Both of them were ball-watching. England are happy as Larry; Watson is as happy as Larry David.

13th over: Australia 46–1 (Hughes 8, Khawaja 0) Watson has played 15 Test innings against England, and 12 of them have been between 34 and 62. I've started so I won't finish.

14th over: Australia 50–1 (Hughes 12, Khawaja 0) Hughes uppercuts Bresnan for four to bring up the fifty. Australia trail by 314.

15th over: Australia 51–1 (Hughes 12, Khawaja 1) It's a different challenge for Khawaja, coming in against the spinner. He works a single off the pads to get off the mark. 'Book title?' says Anthony Boge. '*About Effing Time.*' He didn't say effing.

16th over: Australia 51–1 (Hughes 12, Khawaja 1) There's a man just off the cut strip on the leg side for Khawaja, who is beaten by a delivery slanted across him by Bresnan. Encouragingly, Bresnan's fourth delivery reverse-swung. Somewhere in Sydney Michael Vaughan is doing the reverse-swing hand signal. I miss that. 'Chronic sleep deprivation has been the theme of the series,' says Dave Adams, 'so I suggest something like *Just One More Over*.'

17th over: Australia 52–1 (Hughes 13, Khawaja 1) Swann is toying with Hughes. He clearly feels there's a relatively cheap top-order wicket to be had and is working him over with all his variations. There's a biggish lbw shout when Hughes pads up, but it didn't straighten enough and would probably have bounced over as well. Still, these are really tough times for Hughes. '*They Shoot Aussies, Don't They?*' offers Lev Parikian.

18th over: Australia 52–1 (Hughes 13, Khawaja 1) This is good stuff from Bresnan, very accurate and with just enough movement to challenge the batsmen. It's a maiden to Hughes, who has 13 from 56 balls now. After 30 years of hunting high and low, Australia may just have found their own Chris Tavare.

19th over: Australia 52–1 (Hughes 13, Khawaja 1) Swann is loving this. Two left-handers to play with; a lead of nine million; a wearing pitch. He's in his element, and at the moment the batsmen have no aims beyond survival. The fifth ball was a beauty to Khawaja that drifted in and then spat past the outside edge. It's another maiden, so Swann's figures are 6–3–3–0.

WICKET! 20th over: Hughes c Prior b Bresnan 13 (Australia 52–2) Phil Hughes's excruciating innings comes to an end, although it took a very nice delivery from Bresnan to get rid of him. It bounced from a length and left him a touch as well. Hughes had to play in his danger area outside off stump and edged it to Prior, who just held onto the catch as he dived in front of first slip.

20th over: Australia 52–2 (Khawaja 1, Clarke 0) Michael Clarke is booed to the crease for the second time in the match, a total nonsense. He's beaten on the inside by his second delivery, which doesn't miss off stump by much. He then survives a big shout for lbw. No review from England. It was going down leg, I think. '*644 Flew Over the Cuckoo's Nest,*' offers Neil.

21st over: Australia 54–2 (Khawaja 3, Clarke 0) Khawaja cuts Swann behind point for a couple. '*Cook & Bell: Cock & Bull by Smyth and Bull,*' says Paul Tooby. If I change my name by deed poll to Rob Cock that title will look even better.

22nd over: Australia 63–2 (Khawaja 3, Clarke 6) Clarke reaches outside off stump to time Bresnan nicely through the covers for four. 'If Australia loses this Test by an innings (or Cook fails to score in the last innings), there can't be much competition for *766 and All That?*' says Jacco Schalkwijk. It's just dawned on me that this discussion of what the book should be called will be in the book itself. It's like a bloody Chris Nolan movie!

23rd over: Australia 69–2 (Khawaja 4, Clarke 11) Khawaja has played Swann well thus far, with a clear head, and has been beaten only by that snorter a couple of overs back. He gets a single and then Clarke blasts Swann over the covers for four. Good shot.

24th over: Australia 69–2 (Khawaja 4, Clarke 11) Bresnan is definitely reversing it, and that's a maiden to Khawaja. 'Given the reversal in fortunes seen in this Ashes, how about taking a title from the cracking OBO line: *Hubris? Meet My Friend Mr Nemesis,*' suggests Jon Watts.

25th over: Australia 70–2 (Khawaja 4, Clarke 12) Swann gets one to bounce nastily on Khawaja, who does extremely well to get on top of the ball and drop it short of the close fielders. He's getting an invaluable examination here, and he's handling it pretty well. 'Sorry,' says Oliver Benson, 'but can you please just print this so I can have my name in a book?' Have you not heard of the phone book?

26th over: Australia 77–2 (Khawaja 4, Clarke 19) Tremlett replaces Bresnan, who bowled an excellent spell of 7–4–12–1. Clarke cuts his second ball up and over backward point – though not by that much – for four. In this innings the experienced right-handers have 57 from 62 balls and the young left-handers have 17 from 94 balls. It's an ageist, leftist scorecard.

27th over: Australia 77–2 (Khawaja 4, Clarke 19) Swann has gone around the wicket to Clarke, with both a slip and a gully. He did Clarke like this at Melbourne, caught at slip from one that ran straight across him. 'You haven't included any of my emails,' says Jack from Sydney. 'And the ones you have included are mostly shit. Can you hurry up and get this book published, I'm running low on toilet paper.' It's a maiden, and that's tea.

Australia 282 and 77–2; England 644

The evening session

BY ROB SMYTH

28th over: Australia 79–2 (Khawaja 6, Clarke 19) Ready? Good. There are 32 overs remaining, the first of which will be bowled by Chris Tremlett. 'Book title: *Adelaide!*' says Dave Pople. 'With the exclamation mark, I think.' It's a deal-breaker.

29th over: Australia 87–2 (Khawaja 7, Clarke 26) Swann continues around the wicket to Clarke. A contest between these two is always fascinating because Clarke is such an excellent, fleet-footed player of spin. He comes down the track to the second ball, chipping it splendidly over mid-on for four, and then pings the next delivery through midwicket for three. 'I'm not going to read this book,' says Richard Sparks, 'because I already know the cook did it.'

30th over: Australia 88–2 (Khawaja 7, Clarke 26) Tremlett beats Clarke with a laughably unplayable monster that roars and growls and seams past the outside edge.

31st over: Australia 95–2 (Khawaja 11, Clarke 29) Swann drops short and is cut through the covers for three by Clarke. I'd be quite tempted to try seam from both ends for half an hour, as Clarke is looking really good against Swann at the moment. 'Surely the point of releasing a book is to sell loads of copies and makes lots of money,' says Stuart Wilson. 'As such can I suggest a title that will appeal to the masses: *Lesbian Bath Time*? The dual bonus is that if you print my suggestion, the hits on OBO will suddenly rocket via the disappointed Google searches of thousands of teenage boys.'

32nd over: Australia 96–2 (Khawaja 12, Clarke 29) Khawaja completely misses an attempt hook at a ball from Tremlett that was fairly wide of off stump. I think he was too early on the shot. Then he flicks a single to leg. He has 12 from 53 balls, and Australia trail by 268. I reckon that's the first time in history that that exact sentence has been used. 'Book title?' says Tom Savage. '*Pride and Prejudice*.'

33rd over: Australia 96–2 (Khawaja 12, Clarke 29) When Khawaja defends against Swann, England tentatively appeal for a catch at silly point via the boot. Aleem Dar says not out, and nobody looks too fussed – but that was very close.

34th over: Australia 100–2 (Khawaja 12, Clarke 33) Clarke slaps an urgent cut for four off Tremlett.

35th over: Australia 104–2 (Khawaja 16, Clarke 33) I was going to say that Khawaja only looked comfortable attacking Swann when he dropped short, but that was a classy extra-cover drive for four to bring up the fifty partnership. '*16.44: The Emasculation of Richard Ponting*,' suggests Mark Reed.

36th over: Australia 104–2 (Khawaja 16, Clarke 33) Jimmy Anderson is going to replace Chris Tremlett. His first over is a maiden to Clarke. 'Can I reserve *Khawaja Like Them Apples?* for the 2013 series book title?' says Joe Meredith. 'Just in case like.' That is so bad it's gone past good, back to bad and then back to good again.

37th over: Australia 113–2 (Khawaja 17, Clarke 37) That's a ludicrous delivery from Swann. It was a touch wider and turned viciously to beat the outside edge of Khawaja's bat and fly past the left hand of Prior for four byes. There are four more runs later in the over, strong-armed through midwicket by Clarke. That sets Warne off on an incredulous one about the 4–5 field for Swann.

WICKET! 38th over: Khawaja c Prior b Anderson 21 (Australia 117–3) That's wicket No. 22 of the series for Jimmy Anderson, although it was a pretty tame dismissal. The ball after dumping a pull for four, Khawaja feels for a very wide, reverse-swinging delivery and gets the thinnest of edges through to Matt Prior. Smart bowling, but a needless shot.

38th over: Australia 117–3 (Clarke 37, Hussey 0) '*@theashes: I Am Not a Freakin' Book!!!!*' suggests Harry Parker.

39th over: Australia 118–3 (Clarke 38, Hussey 0) Swann has gone back over the wicket to Clarke. I had a bet before the series that he would average over 40. His average is currently 39.92. '*To Not Sleep, Perchance to Dream*,' says Dan MacDonald.

40th over: Australia 118–3 (Clarke 38, Hussey 0) Clarke chases a wide one from Anderson, but his bat gets intimate with nothing but fresh air. A maiden, and Anderson is bowling beautifully with the ageing ball.

41st over: Australia 118–3 (Clarke 38, Hussey 0) A maiden from Swann to Hussey. That's the kind of plasticine-sharp insight you expect from the OBO.

42nd over: Australia 118–3 (Clarke 38, Hussey 0) Another excellent maiden from Anderson. His first spell was 4–0–22–0; in this spell he has 4–3–4–1. '*Bollinger Opened, Johnson Out, Hussey Bowled Over,*' suggests Jack in Sydney. You can see where this is going, can't you? 'Not an Ashes report . . . it's Shane War–' [That'll do – imaginary ed.]

43rd over: Australia 124–3 (Clarke 41, Hussey 3) Six from Swann's over, including a leading edge after Hussey was done in the flight. '*Good Mitchell, Bad Mitchell, and Superbad Jimmy,*' suggests Marie Meyer.

WICKET! 44th over: Clarke c Prior b Anderson 41 (Australia 124–4) This is absolutely magnificent bowling from Jimmy Anderson. Quite stunning. He has been working Clarke over with the reverse-swinging ball, and he gets him with a lovely delivery that invites the drive and moves late to take the edge on its way to Prior. Clarke is furious with himself, but Anderson was just too good there.

44th over: Australia 124–4 (Hussey 3, Haddin 0) Anderson's spell is now 5–4–4–2. How will he cope with the old Kookaburra?!

45th over: Australia 126–4 (Hussey 5, Haddin 0) I missed that Swann over because I was pawing gently, lovingly, at a poster of Jimmy Anderson.

46th over: Australia 130–4 (Hussey 5, Haddin 4) Anderson beats Haddin with an away-swinger, but then he goes for the magic ball and instead drifts onto the pads. Haddin chips it over midwicket for four. 'What about this quote from *1984* as the title,' begins Neil Gouldson, '*The Past Was Dead, The Future Was Unimaginable?* Might be taken a bit out of context, but with a positive spin it kind of sums up my feelings at the end of this glorious series.'

47th over: Australia 132–4 (Hussey 7, Haddin 4) Hussey has been typically positive in his foot movement against Swann, and he comes down the track to crunch a couple through midwicket. There are 12 overs remaining.

48th over: Australia 135–4 (Hussey 7, Haddin 7) England have a huge shout for caught behind turned down when Hussey chases a wide one from Anderson. His bat definitely hit the ground, but it's hard to be sure either way whether he edged it. England were thinking about a review, but then – and this is good to see – both umpires signalled that their 20 seconds (or however long it is) were up.

49th over: Australia 139–4 (Hussey 7, Haddin 11) Two very close shaves for Haddin. First he chipped Swann *just* over Bresnan at mid-on, and then he was dropped by Bell at short extra cover. It was an extremely tough chance for Bell, diving forward and trying to scoop his fingers under the ball. Still, it was technically a dropped catch. I can't remember when Ian Bell last dropped a catch.

50th over: Australia 142–4 (Hussey 8, Haddin 13) Bresnan replaces Anderson, who bowled an exceptional spell of 7–4–11–2. Haddin is duped by a good inswinger, but it was swinging down leg. 'If James taught us anything, it's that if we hadn't seen such riches, we could live with being poor' says Tom Savage. 'How typical of the English cricket fan in me that the joy of watching the Aussies being beaten like lads in a 1930s borstal is tinged with sadness that it will probably not only never be this good again, but will probably be worse for having tasted this success.'

51st over: Australia 146–4 (Hussey 12, Haddin 13) Swann drops short and Hussey rocks back to pull behind square for four.

52nd over: Australia 149–4 (Hussey 12, Haddin 16) Haddin drives Bresnan through mid-off for three. Hussey is then beaten by a superb leg-cutter. Seven overs to go. These updates may get shorter and shorter, because I think I might actually be asleep.

53rd over: Australia 152–4 (Hussey 12, Haddin 19) Haddin cuts Swann for three. On the Australian balcony, Steve Smith is gnawing zestily at his fingernails. Any body-language experts out there who can tell us what that means?

WICKET! 54th over: Hussey c Pietersen b Bresnan 12 (Australia 161–5) What a gift just before the close. Hussey has cut Bresnan straight to backward point. He didn't get on top of the ball and it flew past Pietersen, who took a sharp two-handed catch above his head. England are five wickets away from the crushing victory they deserve.

54th over: Australia 161–5 (Haddin 27, Smith 0) 'On the topic of sleep,' says Amirali Abdullah, 'any chance you might wake to find Australia 3–1 up, and England following on 200 behind?' Yes, this is the cricket version of *Inception*. It's called *Insertion*. We're all about to wake up on 7 November 2002; there's a coin landing at the feet of Nasser Hussain and Steve Waugh . . .

55th over: Australia 165–5 (Haddin 29, Smith 1) Tremlett returns in place of Swann, and his first ball is a preposterous jaffa that beats Haddin outside off stump. Later in the over Smith is sent back and is barely in the frame when Anderson's throw whizzes just past the stumps. Anderson is an awesome fielder by any standards, never mind those of a fast bowler.

56th over: Australia 171–5 (Haddin 30, Smith 5) Smith plays a cracking cover drive for four off Bresnan. Australia will hope that, one glorious day, he looks back on this series as Steve Waugh does the 1986–7 Ashes.

WICKET! 57th over: Haddin c Prior b Tremlett 30 (Australia 171–6) This is a *snorter* from Chris Tremlett. He rams in a superb straight short ball, the line so good that Brad Haddin can't get out of the way, and the ball loops up in the air off the splice for Matt Prior to take a simple catch. There are 15 balls left today, but England might well take the extra half-hour.

WICKET! 57th over: Johnson b Tremlett 0 (Australia 171–7) Tremlett is on a hat-trick! This is another jaffa: full, straight and ramming into Johnson's off stump. 'What a nut!' screams Nasser Hussain. Wonderful stuff, and England are going to claim the extra half-hour here.

57th over: Australia 171–7 (Smith 5, Siddle 0) The hat-trick ball is a majestic inswinging yorker, and Siddle does extremely well to jam the ball into his boot. What a storming over from Tremlett, a double-wicket maiden. There are two overs remaining, plus the extra half-hour, which the umpires have agreed to give England.

58th over: Australia 172–7 (Smith 5, Siddle 0) Bresnan bowls a relatively anodyne maiden to Smith. Mind you, Michael Holding's over to Geoff Boycott was relatively anodyne in contrast to that last one from Tremlett. 'I am in Gurgaon Delhi interning at this hole,' says a nameless email. 'I just realised tomorrow is our last date. I miss you so much already. Bye.' Marry me, nameless one?

59th over: Australia 176–7 (Smith 5, Siddle 4) Tremlett's making the old ball sing. It's doing a bloody falsetto. I've definitely woken up now. Who needs Class B drugs when you've got a double-wicket maiden from Chris Tremlett? 'You need a title which will appeal to the target market, carry a little bit of whimsical humour, a whiff of nostalgia and a soupçon of wordplay, and which will entice the impulse buyer on the shelf of WH Smith,' begins Paul Griffin. 'On that basis, how about: *This Lot Are Effing Shit*. My agent will be in touch re. royalties.'

60th over: Australia 176–7 (Smith 5, Siddle 4) Smith defends diligently against Bresnan, who will surely give way to Anderson now.

61st over: Australia 181–7 (Smith 7, Siddle 7) Great shot from Siddle, who blasts a reverse-swinger from Tremlett through the covers for three. Six overs to go.

62nd over: Australia 181–7 (Smith 7, Siddle 7) Bresnan continues, and Siddle, pushing around his front pad, chips one a fraction short of Bell, diving forward at short midwicket. A maiden, and there are five overs remaining.

63rd over: Australia 191–7 (Smith 12, Siddle 7) Smith gets down on one knee and slices a cut to third man for four. Tremlett responds by swinging a couple past the edge, the second of which goes through Prior for four byes. Four overs, three wickets; I don't think it's going to happen tonight.

64th over: Australia 198–7 (Smith 19, Siddle 7) Now Anderson does replace Bresnan, and Smith slices a booming drive through the vacant fourth-slip area for four. Bah! Eighteen balls to go.

65th over: Australia 198–7 (Smith 19, Siddle 7) Swann replaces Tremlett. Smith has done well to monopolise the strike, but that's a maiden so now Anderson will have a go at Siddle.

66th over: Australia 208–7 (Smith 19, Siddle 17) Siddle edges Anderson's last delivery just over the slip cordon for four. That was hilarious: they all leapt in unison, even those who were nowhere near it. Even the crowd all jumped up instinctively.

67th over: Australia 213–7 (Smith 23, Siddle 17) That's it. Credit to Smith and Siddle for a proud and defiant partnership that ensures the match will go into a fifth day, but credit mainly to England for another cold, clinical defenestration of Australia. On a flat pitch their bowlers were superb, and they will return tomorrow needing three wickets to complete an emphatic 3–1 victory.

Australia 280 and 213–7; England 644

Fifth day

The morning session

BY ANDY BULL

Preamble: Well, for one final time this winter, good evening, ladies and gents. And welcome to the victory parade. First, a confession. The last time England did what they are about to do, I was four years old. The reissue of Jackie Wilson's 'Reet Petite' was Christmas No. 1, Margaret Thatcher was plotting how to win her third term as prime minister, everybody was going crazy for Paul Hogan, star of the hit new comedy *Crocodile Dundee*, Steve Finn was not even a devilish twinkle in his mother's eye, Liverpool had just won the double, nobody knew what the internet was yet, Mike Selvey, David Hopps and Vic Marks *all* had *full* heads of hair. Actually, *full* may be stretching a point. No matter, it was only a convoluted way of saying that moments like this do not come around very often. So savour it.

Paul Collingwood leads England out onto the field, pausing only to doff his cap to the Barmy Army. Jimmy Anderson marks out his run. Andrew Strauss stands at slip, rubs his hands together and allows a smile to flicker across his face.

68th over: Australia 213–7 (Smith 24, Siddle 17) The Barmy Army are having a good old sing-song. They follow 'Jerusalem' with a chorus of the Jimmy Anderson song. He has started the day with a maiden over. Michael Holding is holding up a copy of today's *SMH* to the camera. The back-page headline? 'Our Worst XI'.

69th over: Australia 216–7 (Smith 26, Siddle 18) And at the other end it's Chris Tremlett. He starts with a snorter, but Smith and Siddle take a handful of runs from the remainder of the over. 'This may not have been as good a series as 2005, but for me it still ranks above 2009,' says Dan Lucas. 'The quality of cricket on show has been far, far superior to 18 months ago, from one side at least. Having wept from a small dark computer room in a small dark German town four years ago, I'm wondering if even 2005 gave me as much pleasure as this series has; I've broken up with my girlfriend recently, it was my grandfather's funeral today, Colly has failed to get the runs I've so desperately wanted to see from him, and yet tomorrow I will wake up happier than I have in a long time.'

70th over: Australia 217–7 (Smith 26, Siddle 19) Another run for Siddle. Amazing as this may sound, I'm being sledged by a Frenchman – Raphael Vigneau. As Camilla said after she was poked by a stick last month, there's a first time for everything, I suppose. 'I am very disappointed not to see England's usual humiliation,' says Raphael. 'England's form has galled my Gallic nerves. So I have decided to give a cold shower to your egos by suggesting a title for your book – *2010: How South Africa won the Ashes*. If France was interested in cricket, we would thrash you.'

71st over: Australia 223–7 (Smith 26, Siddle 24) Lovely stuff from Tremlett, seaming the ball past Siddle's outside edge. He gets just enough bat on the next delivery, a no-ball, to squeeze it past slip. The sixth ball is punched down the ground to long-off for three more.

72nd over: Australia 227–7 (Smith 26, Siddle 25) Just a solitary single for Siddle. Perhaps no Aussie quip was more misguided this series than Tim Nielsen's tweet in response to the criticism of his team after the first Test: 'We're going terribly, we're going awfully, I can't believe they said that, and I'm not sure we're going to turn up on Friday.' The sarcasm got a little lost when, come Friday, Australia fell to 0–2.

73rd over: Australia 227–7 (Smith 26, Siddle 28) Siddle hoicks three more back over Tremlett's head with an ugly swish. Ahh, humbug. It has started to rain. The umpires are calling the players off.

RAIN STOPS PLAY. But don't worry, the rain radar is quite reassuring.

Sky are showing some highlights of the series while they wait for the rain to clear. 'Man of the series?' asks Graham Sherriff. 'Aleem Dar. He got all the big decisions right and stood toe to toe with Ricky Ponting in full rant. Excellent umpiring at a time when the umps are under greater scrutiny than ever.' Good point. I think I'll give my own version of that particular prize to Andrew Strauss though, for his leadership more than his batting.

Having seen their team conquer Australia, the English fans have got their dander up. 'Has Raphael Vigneau never heard of French cricket?' scoffs Adam Hirst. 'I'd like to see him trying to guard his legs on the beach as Tremlett steams in from behind him with a red cherry to bowl from about five yards away. England would hammer France.'

There are a lot of happy people out there. Charles Mawer is just one of them: 'It's very hard to look past Tim Bresnan's virtuoso version of the Sprinkler dance. If anything could underline both the unity and mental courage of the current England side, it was a man from Castleford prepared to express himself on film via the medium of dance.'

This one will take some beating: 'As well as being a tad solipsistic, my moment of the series involves some shameless name dropping,' says Seth Levine. 'I was walking through the media section when I encountered Shane Warne bowling dollies to none other than David Hasselhoff. As the erstwhile *Knight Rider* star flat-batted one to roughly mid-on, I stuck out a hand before nonchalantly throwing it back to Warney. In the scorecard in my head, it read The Hoff 0 b Warne c Levine.'

Sometimes I just *love* the OBO. Where else, after all, would you be able to read a comeback like this one: 'Désolé Raph, I used to open the bowling for France and am now the Under 17 and U19 coach,' says Christopher Bartlett. 'In 1998 a Middlesex 2nd XI, possibly with a young A. Strauss in it, spanked us for about 360 in 40 overs (only 40-odd of which came off my eight overs in return for four wickets), so I doubt very much that we would beat England at present. I do have high hopes for my U19s at the European Championships this summer, but hosts Isle of Man and Italy will be the teams to beat.'

73rd over: Australia 230–7 (Smith 27, Siddle 30) All right, the worrywarts among you can mop your brows. England are coming back out onto the field. They need three wickets. Australia need a miracle. Tremlett swings his first two deliveries onto Siddle's leg stump. The second of them is swatted away for two runs. Here is Dan Smith: 'The 2010–11 Ashes OBO, a review: Unreliable narrators "Smyth" and "Bull", sleep-deprived and fuelled by the local BP garage's snack-food range, essay a series of ever more preposterous England cricketing "triumphs", in the vein of Baron Munchausen, Hunter S. Thompson or Tony Blair. In this unique take, "Australia", a scarcely imaginable collection of clowns, caper their way through a series of slapstick mishaps, culminating in an absurd finale in which we are led to believe that Paul Collingwood, engaged on "one last job", has splayed the stumps of Mr Cricket. I laughed till I cried till I laughed till I had to go to bed because some of us have to work tomorrow morning you know.'

74th over: Australia 236–7 (Smith 32, Siddle 33) Bresnan is into the attack now, trying to fiddle one of these tail-end wickets. Collingwood runs over to field the ball, and is treated to a rousing ovation in return for his troubles.

75th over: Australia 244–7 (Smith 32, Siddle 38) Swann is on, welcomed to the crease with a creaky-sounding chorus of Joy Division. Smyth has a bet on that Swann will finish the series with a bowling average above 40 (it is currently 41) and is a little anxious about the possibility that he may clean up the tail. Then he lets out a hearty chuckle as Smith wallops three out to cover. By the time Siddle has carted four more through point he is positively guffawing.

76th over: Australia 248–7 (Smith 37, Siddle 38) Sorry, I'm lost for words. Keith Flett, founding member (sole member?) of the Beard Liberation Front, has announced that he is shaving off his beard. Truly this is a momentous day.

77th over: Australia 252–7 (Smith 37, Siddle 42) 'Can I start a list of players for a naff pun-related French cricket team?' pleads Steve Pye. 'Bruce French, Paul Eiffel, Graham Onions.' I've thought about this for a minute Steve, and the answer is no, you can't. Sorry. This irritating little stand continues, Siddle pushing two past point and two more past slip. This is now his top Test score. Well played him.

78th over: Australia 257–7 (Smith 40, Siddle 43) The Barmy Army haven't stopped singing since the start of play. I guess they had Special Brew for breakfast. Bresnan continues. 'Ever since getting to Oz in 1998 I have planned a Shakespearian theme to my "when England win the Ashes here" gloating,' says Nick Leeding, who must have been planning this email for a very long time indeed. 'And as I am in Sydney today (albeit not at the game) I think I can finally use it. From Henry V's speech before Agincourt: "And gentlemen in England now a-bed shall think themselves accursed they were not here." Unfortunately a bit long for a T-shirt.'

WICKET! 79th over: Siddle c Anderson b Swann 43 (Australia 257–8) That's one. Siddle plays one big shot too many. He tries to slog-sweep Swann for four over square leg, but only picks out Jimmy Anderson on the boundary rope. Better yet, Smyth is furious. That wicket has brought Swann's average for the series down to 39.something. 'Can anyone offer any suggestions on how us Aussies should best go about life after this shellacking?' asks Robert Cartmill. 'I'm concerned that henceforth all Test-match cricket from now on will be watched with a feeling that everything is "about to go horribly wrong". Surely you lot can sympathise with this?' Indeed we do, Robert. Can I suggest you ~~give Ray Illingworth complete control over team selection and management, appoint David Lloyd as head coach~~, umm, look, we'll get back to you on this one.

80th over: Australia 261–8 (Smith 41, Hilfenhaus 3) One more over from Bresnan, and as nothing much happens in it I'm going to move swiftly on because England are about to take the new ball, and the curtain is about to fall.

81st over: Australia 266–8 (Smith 43, Hilfenhaus 7) Tremlett takes the first over with the new ball. Somewhere not so far off you should be able to hear the fat lady warming up her vocal chords.

WICKET! 82nd over: Hilfenhaus c Prior b Anderson 7 (Australia 267–9) Hilfenhaus strops off with an ugly frown on his face, grimacing at the ignominy of it all. He's gone, caught behind by Matt Prior after edging a neat away-swinger from Jimmy. Just one more wicket to go then, and Strauss has three slips and two gullies in place to take it. 'Rule Britannia' rings out around the SCG. 'As the *Guardian* OBO is obviously the fount of all late-night knowledge,' says Nigel Wheatley, 'does anyone know where I can buy kangaroo steaks at one in the morning in Barcelona, so as to celebrate this historic occasion in an appropriate manner?'

83rd over: Australia 275–9 (Smith 48, Beer 2) Smith slaps two runs away square. For English fans, this is quite an extraordinary feeling. I think I even have a few hairs standing up on the back of my neck. There's no such satisfaction for Neil McGwyre though. 'I'm old school. I've already accepted that we'll be batting again, just wondering how many they'll set us.' Smith taps three out to midwicket leaving Beer to face three deliveries. Somehow he survives them.

84th over: Australia 280–9 (Smith 53, Beer 2) You're not going to believe this, but Bumble reckons there is a 'shed-load' of rain coming in over the SCG. Back on the field, Smith has just raised his fifty. Well played. Amazing how easy it is to say 'well played' to the opposition when your team is about to go 3–1 up and has an innings in hand, isn't it? 'I reckon it's hard to top Bumble playing Bill Lawry's "GOTTIM!!!" over and over on his phone when he was third man during the Melbourne Test,' says Peter Flanagan. 'And then playing it at random for the rest of the day. What a legend.'

85th over: Australia 281–9 (Smith 53, Beer 2) Smith is swinging like a lumberjack at every single delivery but is hardly getting the ball off the square because he can't make clean contact. 'My name is Ben and my DOB is 070171. I've just turned 40, approx. 30 minutes ago.' Well, congratulations, old stick. 'I'm sat at home with a single malt. Never have I felt quite such a feeling of calm and happiness.'

WICKET! 85th over: Beer b Tremlett 2 (Australia 281 all out) I don't think I'll ever enjoy typing one little line more than I will this one – England have won the Ashes, in Australia, 3–1. Michael Beer drags a full ball onto his own stumps, and England's players have gone ballistic, supercalifragilistic. It's all over, folks.

So England have won the fifth Test by an innings and 83 runs, following on from their victories by an innings and 71 runs and an innings and 157 runs at Adelaide and Melbourne. 'That's an ab-so-lute drubbing that is,' chortles Bumble.

Phew. Atherton is trapping a few of the England players down on the pitch. Jimmy Anderson and Chris Tremlett offer up a few quick platitudes, but now Paul Collingwood has some lovely words on his retirement. 'There must be a little regret that you'll never get to wear that cap again,' suggests Atherton. 'Well . . .' replies Colly, 'I can still keep it and then take it out and look at it sometimes.'

Open the bottle, pour yourself a glass, swing up your feet, fold your hands behind your head, light a cigar, let that long, slow smile of self-satisfaction creep across your face and enjoy that one little thought bouncing around your brain: England have won. England have won. England have won. England have won. England have won. England have won.

The players are back out on the field, walking through a tunnel of security guards blocking off a throng of rapturous fans. 'Is it wrong,' frets Ben Hendy, 'at this time of indefinable joy, is it wrong to be thinking, "God, I hope it's not another 24 years before I get to see this again"? I was ten the last time we won the Ashes in Aus, I don't want to be 58 the next time it happens.'

'I have just done a tour of our Melbourne office with my replica urn wearing a pink sparkly pointy party hat,' grins Jamie, a man who knows how to win friends Down Under.

Man of the Match, and also Man of the Series, is, you guessed it, Alastair Cook. He nominates his 200 at Brisbane as his favourite innings of the series. He wins a plastic Vodafone bat (thanks, no really, thanks), $5,000 and the rather fine Compton-Miller trophy. Michael Clarke refers to himself, quite conspicuously, as 'still the vice-captain', and then waffles on about how there is really a lot of talent in the team but they just need to execute blah skill sets blah blah credit to England blah blah blah.

We should find room for an email from an Australian reader: 'Oh to be back in the first over of the series when the earth was still flat, the sun rotated around it and we continued to dominate you feckless Poms. Well done, England, too good, may your reign be short and sweet.'

'Just wondering how Strauss is going to approach the eternal conundrum this time round: how *do* you celebrate with the world's smallest trophy without looking like a bit of a nit?' asks Paul Harrison. The answer is that he lifts it up above his head in both hands and screams like a little boy on Christmas morning, as his team jump up and down around him and the air fills with ticker tape.

And that, readers, is that. The players are still walking around the ground, clapping back at the fans. We can all sleep the good sleep tonight. I'd like to doff my cap to the man sat to my right, Rob Smyth, before I sign off. I've been a bit of a dilettante these last few weeks, flickering in and out of the Tests. But Rob has only taken one day off in the entire series. Anyway. Thanks too to all of you for keeping us company through the night. It was worth it in the end, wasn't it?

Australia 280 and 281; England 644. England win by an innings and 83 runs, and win the series 3–1

Heroic masters of the Ashes

Tremlett claims the final Australian wicket to seal the glory for England

BY MIKE SELVEY IN SYDNEY

FRIDAY 7 JANUARY 2011

They came in their thousands to form an English corner of a foreign field for the climax, a day of days in the history of the England team and another one of abject misery for a once-proud Australian team fallen on hard times. Not even the snap showers washing in to interrupt play, and a flatness to the team on the field, could deny them a third overwhelming victory, which came, by an innings and 83 runs, at 11.56, four minutes before the shipping forecast, and just as Billy the Barmy Trumpeter was playing a poignant 'Last Post' for the demise of Australian cricket.

To Chris Tremlett went the honour, the debutant tail-ender Michael Beer chopping onto his stumps to spark the celebrations that would go on long into the night. But it took the second new ball to finish the job, as Steve Smith, who remained unbeaten on 54, and Peter Siddle, who had denied England when they had hoped to finish things on the fourth evening, took their eighth-wicket stand to 86 before Siddle (43) hit Graeme Swann precisely to Jimmy Anderson at deep midwicket.

Anderson then found the edge of Ben Hilfenhaus's bat for Matt Prior to take his 23rd catch, an England record for a five-match Ashes series. It took Anderson – the fellow too soft to bowl to Australians, remember, according to Justin Langer – to 24 wickets for the series, more than any England pace bowler in Australia since Frank Tyson terrorised them in 1954–5. Australia have now been beaten by an innings three times in the series, unprecedented for them.

It was set up on the fourth day by Anderson, not just Good but Brilliant Jimmy, indisputably the bowler of the series, with daylight second. Anderson plunged the knife into what life was left in the twitching carcass of the Australian cricket team. The old ball reversed, as it always seems to do for England – the same England, said the sages here in the pre-series propaganda war, who would not know how to use a second-hand Kookaburra – and not for Australia.

But Anderson did not just use it, he had it talking, gabbling away, a ball with verbal diarrhoea. With it, he produced one of the best cameo spells of the series and knocked the heart out of the middle of the Australian innings: the left-hander Usman Khawaja, tyro and promising but given a strong lesson in this match that there is a giant step up to the top level, seduced outside off stump as the ball wafted away from him; the right-handed skipper Michael Clarke, destined perhaps to try to pick this side from the basement and with not a great player in sight, put through the wringer, utter torture, before he found no answer to an away-swinger and mercifully also edged to Prior.

This was an Australian side in distress. The first innings in Brisbane and the third Test in Perth were their peaks in a series of otherwise total England domination. The stuffing had long been knocked out of them by the England batsmen, but there was a sorry capitulation where fight was needed. Shane Watson flamed briefly but ran himself out for once rather than his partner, and Tim Bresnan took advantage of Phil Hughes's laboured endeavours to become an opening batsman of substance by sliding one across him and watching as the bat nibbled out like a fish taking the bait. It was all too easy.

Throughout the bulk of the series, Australia have been offered little respite by the England attack. Wave of attack had followed wave. Key to this has been reverse swing, and England are masters at it, their ability to get a ball into a condition to go after no more than 20 overs a skill that in part involves bowling it with a cross seam so that it first scuffs on the surface (such a delivery accounted for Hughes) and is then polished on one side only. But then comes the further skill in using it, for anyone might have a lock pick but not everyone can pick a lock.

Each of the three seamers is a practitioner and each benefited. When Anderson gave way to Bresnan after his mesmeric spell, the Yorkshireman responded by getting Mike Hussey caught in the gully, just as Hussey had opened the series by catching Andrew Strauss there with the third ball. And when, at the Randwick end, Graeme Swann conceded the crease to Chris Tremlett, the giant thundered in to rip out Brad Haddin and Mitchell Johnson with successive deliveries, a brutal bouncer followed by a wicked inswinger. When he had the bit between his teeth and the crowd roaring behind him, he looked a very serious proposition.

The thing that truly disheartened Australia though, from which there was no response, was another monumental innings from England. In the second innings at Brisbane they made 517 for one to give notice of their potential; in Adelaide it was 620 for five; and Melbourne 513. Killer innings all. But here they made 644 before the final wicket fell, by which time Australia had taken a third new ball and sent down almost 178 overs.

To place it in context, it is the seventh-highest total England have ever made and their highest in Australia. It meant that England's runs per wicket for the series stood at 51.14. There were more records, for surely this has been a record series for records. The century that Prior scored, the fourth and most robust of his Test career, came from 109 balls, the fastest for England since Ian Botham's flogathon at Old Trafford in 1981, with nine fours, a six and a lot of scampering. Having added 107 for the seventh wicket with Ian Bell, Prior then helped Bresnan put on 102 for the eighth, before Swann added insult to Johnson's bowling injury. No side in the history of Test cricket has managed century stands for the sixth, seventh and eighth wickets in the same innings.